CONSTITUENT ASSEMBLIES

Comparative constitutional law has a long pedigree, but the comparative study of constitution making has emerged and taken form only in the last quarter-century. While much of the initial impetus came from the study of the American and French constituent assemblies in the late eighteenth century, this volume exemplifies the large comparative scope of current research. The contributors discuss constituent assemblies in South Asia, North Africa and the Middle East, Latin America, and in Nordic countries. Among the new insights they provide is a better understanding of how constituent assemblies may fail, either by not producing a document at all or by adopting a constitution that fails to serve as a neutral framework for ordinary politics. In a theoretical afterword, Jon Elster, one of the inspirators of current interest in the topic, offers an analysis of the microfoundations of constitution making, with special emphasis on the role of crisis-generated passions.

Jon Elster is Robert K. Merton Professor of Social Science, Department of Political Science at Columbia University. He has authored more than twenty monographs, translated into eighteen languages, and edited or coedited more than twenty other books. He has received nine honorary doctorates from universities on three continents, has been elected member of five scientific academies, and is the 2016 recipient of the Skytte Prize, generally viewed as the most prestigious award in Political Science.

Roberto Gargarella has written and edited more than twenty books, including *Latin American Constitutionalism* (2013) and *The Legal Foundations of Inequality* (Cambridge University Press, 2010). He has been awarded a John Guggenheim Foundation grant, a Harry Frank Guggenheim grant, and a Fulbright grant. He has been a visiting professor with universities in Latin America, Europe, and the United States.

Vatsal Naresh is a PhD student in Political Science at Yale University. His research interests lie in democratic theory, political violence, and constitution making.

Bjørn Erik Rasch is Professor of Political Science at the University of Oslo. He has written or edited thirteen books, most recently *Parliaments and Government Formation: Unpacking Investiture Rules* (2015), and numerous journal articles in comparative politics and political economy.

COMPARATIVE CONSTITUTIONAL LAW AND POLICY

Series Editors

Tom Ginsburg
University of Chicago

Zachary Elkins
University of Texas at Austin

Ran Hirschl
University of Toronto

Comparative constitutional law is an intellectually vibrant field that encompasses an increasingly broad array of approaches and methodologies. This series collects analytically innovative and empirically grounded work from scholars of comparative constitutionalism across academic disciplines. Books in the series include theoretically informed studies of single constitutional jurisdictions, comparative studies of constitutional law and institutions, and edited collections of original essays that respond to challenging theoretical and empirical questions in the field.

Books in the Series

Judicial Review in Norway
Anine Kierulf

The DNA of Constitutional Justice in Latin America: Politics, Governance, and Judicial Design
Daniel M. Brinks and Abby Blass

Engaging with Social Rights: Procedure, Participation and Democracy in South Africa's Second Wave
Brian Ray

Constitutions, Religion and Politics in Asia: Indonesia, Malaysia and Sri Lanka
Dian A. H. Shah

Proportionality: New Frontiers, New Challenges
edited by Vicki Jackson and Mark Tushnet

Constituents Before Assembly: Participation, Deliberation, and Representation in the Crafting of New Constitutions
Todd A. Eisenstadt, A. Carl LeVan, and Tofigh Maboudi

Assessing Constitutional Performance
Tom Ginsburg and Aziz Huq

Buddhism, Politics and the Limits of Law: The Pyrrhic Constitutionalism of Sri Lanka
Benjamin Schonthal

(continued after Index)

Constituent Assemblies

Edited by

JON ELSTER
Columbia University

ROBERTO GARGARELLA
CONICET (Argentina)/CMI (Norway)

VATSAL NARESH
Yale University

BJØRN ERIK RASCH
University of Oslo

CAMBRIDGE
UNIVERSITY PRESS

CAMBRIDGE
UNIVERSITY PRESS

University Printing House, Cambridge CB2 8BS, United Kingdom

One Liberty Plaza, 20th Floor, New York, NY 10006, USA

477 Williamstown Road, Port Melbourne, VIC 3207, Australia

314–321, 3rd Floor, Plot 3, Splendor Forum, Jasola District Centre, New Delhi – 110025, India

79 Anson Road, #06-04/06, Singapore 079906

Cambridge University Press is part of the University of Cambridge.

It furthers the University's mission by disseminating knowledge in the pursuit of education, learning, and research at the highest international levels of excellence.

www.cambridge.org
Information on this title: www.cambridge.org/9781108427524
DOI: 10.1017/9781316998748

First published 2018

Printed in the United States of America by Sheridan Books, Inc.

A catalogue record for this publication is available from the British Library.

ISBN 978-1-108-42752-4 Hardback

Contents

Contributors

Udit Bhatia is Lecturer in Political Theory at Lady Margaret Hall, University of Oxford. He is a doctoral candidate in the Department of Politics and International Relations at Oxford, and his research interests lie at the intersections of democratic theory, political representation, and social epistemology. He is the editor of *The Indian Constituent Assembly: Deliberations on Democracy* (2018).

Cristina Bucur is Lecturer/Assistant Professor in the School of Politics and International Relations at University College Dublin. Her research interests focus on executive–legislative relations and party politics in parliamentary and semi-presidential democracies. Her recent work has been published in journals such as *Party Politics*, *Political Research Quarterly*, *Comparative European Politics*, and *French Politics*.

José Antonio Cheibub is the Mary Thomas Marshall Professor in Liberal Arts at Texas A&M University. He has most recently coedited *Parliaments and Government Formation: Unpacking Investiture Rules* (2015) and is working on a manuscript titled *Constitutional Parliamentarism: Executive–Legislative Relations in Early and Contemporary Parliamentary Regimes*. Among his other books are *Presidentialism, Parliamentarism, and Democracy* (2007) and *Democracy and Development: Political Institutions and Well-Being in the World, 1950–1990* (co-author, 2000).

Jon Elster is Robert K. Merton Professor of Social Science, Department of Political Science at Columbia University. He has authored more than twenty monographs, translated into eighteen languages, and edited or coedited more than twenty other books. He has received nine honorary doctorates from universities on three continents, has been elected member of five scientific academies, and is the 2016 recipient of the Skytte Prize, generally viewed as the most prestigious award in Political Science.

Roberto Gargarella has written and edited more than twenty books, including *Latin American Constitutionalism* (2013) and *The Legal Foundations of Inequality* (Cambridge University Press, 2010). He has been awarded a John Guggenheim Foundation grant, a Harry Frank Guggenheim grant, and a Fulbright grant. He has been a visiting professor with universities in Latin America, Europe, and the United States.

Thorvaldur Gylfason is Professor of Economics at the University of Iceland. He was one of twenty-five representatives in Iceland's Constitutional Council in session from April 1 to July 29, 2011, elected by the nation and appointed by the parliament to revise Iceland's constitution.

Hanna Lerner is Senior Lecturer in the School of Political Science, Government and International Affairs at Tel Aviv University. She is the author of *Making Constitutions in Deeply Divided Societies* (Cambridge University Press, 2011) and coeditor of *Global Justice and International Labour Rights* (with Yossi Dahan and Faina Milman-Sivan, Cambridge University Press, 2016) and of *Constitution Writing, Religion and Democracy* (with Aslı Ü. Bâli, Cambridge University Press, 2017).

Mara Malagodi is Senior Lecturer at the City Law School, University of London. She is the author of the monograph *Constitutional Nationalism and Legal Exclusion in Nepal* (2013) and various articles on constitutional law and history in South Asia. She obtained her doctorate and MA in South Asian Studies and BA in Nepali & Politics from the School of Oriental and African Studies, University of London. She is a nonpracticing barrister and a scholar of the Honourable Society of the Middle Temple.

Shane Martin is Reader in Comparative Politics at the University of Essex. His research focuses on how electoral incentives shape representatives' preferences, legislative organization, and executive oversight. Recent research by him has appeared in the *British Journal of Political Science, Comparative Political Studies, Electoral Studies, Irish Political Studies, Legislative Studies Quarterly, and Political Research Quarterly*. He is coeditor of the *Oxford Handbook of Legislative Studies* (2014) and *Parliaments and Government Formation: Unpacking Investiture Rules* (2015).

Vatsal Naresh is a PhD student in Political Science at Yale University. His research interests lie in democratic theory, political violence, and constitution making.

Gabriel L. Negretto is Professor of Political Science at the Center for Research and Teaching in Economics (CIDE) in Mexico City. His research focuses on comparative constitutional politics, institutional design, and electoral reform. He has published numerous academic articles and book chapters on these topics in the United States, Europe, and Latin America. His most recent book is *Making*

Constitutions: Presidents, Parties, and Institutional Choice in Latin America (Cambridge University Press, 2013). Professor Negretto has been a consultant to the UN, IDEA International, UN Development Programme, and various national public institutions on constitutional design and political reform.

Bjørn Erik Rasch is Professor of Political Science at the University of Oslo. He has written or edited thirteen books, most recently *Parliaments and Government Formation: Unpacking Investiture Rules* (2015), and numerous journal articles in comparative politics and political economy.

Introduction

Jon Elster, Roberto Gargarella, Vatsal Naresh, and Bjørn Erik Rasch

I. INTRODUCING CONSTITUENT ASSEMBLIES

The contributors to this volume examine constituent assemblies in a number of countries and historical periods, from different comparative and theoretical perspectives. In doing so, they join a wave of studies of constitution making that has gathered momentum over the last decades (see Choudhry and Ginsburg 2016; Miller and Aucoin 2010; and Voigt 2013 for some previous edited volumes). The present book supplements these studies in several respects. In this Introduction, we discuss some salient themes and place them in context; we also refer to constitutional episodes not discussed in this volume.

The chapters have a large geographical breadth and historical depth. Going beyond the much discussed (and still fertile) questions posed by constitution making in Europe and North America, five of the nine chapters in the volume discuss constituent assemblies in Latin America, Africa, and Asia. Concerning Latin America, the chapters by Gargarella and Negretto range from the early nineteenth to the early twenty-first century, and cover constitution making in Argentina, Bolivia, Colombia, Chile, Ecuador, and Venezuela. Concerning North Africa and West Asia, Lerner's chapter includes case studies of constitution making in Egypt, Tunisia, and Israel. Concerning South and Southeast Asia, the chapters by Bhatia and Malagodi address constitution making in India, Pakistan, and Nepal, while Lerner, in her chapter, includes case studies of Sri Lanka and Indonesia, as well as of India. Elster's chapter on the making of the Norwegian 1814 constitution and Gylfason's chapter on the process of constitutional reform in Iceland that began in 2010 offer case studies of these two small Nordic countries. In their chapter, Bucur and coauthors cite France, Ireland, and Romania as the main cases

Karen Barkey and Jessica Lilien's invaluable guidance and generosity made possible the conference where the chapters in the volume were first presented. The Department of Political Science at the University of Oslo and the Institute for Religion, Culture, and Public Life at Columbia University provided financial and logistical support. Finally, we thank Mads Motrøen for preparing the index.

illustrating their general thesis. At the subnational level, the American state constitutional conventions that Negretto discusses in his chapter constitute an invaluable resource for comparative analysis.

The word "assembly" needs some context. First, and most obviously, a constitution made by an assembly differs from that handed down by a single individual. In Plutarch's *Parallel Lives* we find stories about how Solon and (more uncertainly) Lycurgus wrote the constitutions for Athens and Sparta respectively. Descartes (1637, § 2) argued that this procedure has the advantage of enhancing the coherence of the document: "If Sparta was in earlier times very prosperous, that was not on account of the goodness of each of its laws in particular, seeing that several were very strange and even contrary to good morals, but on account of the fact that they were *devised by only a single man* and thus they contributed towards the same end" (italics added). In recent times, the 1958 constitution of the Fifth French Republic comes closest to this model. In his speech in Bayeux in 1946, de Gaulle had already laid out all the basic principles of the 1958 constitution, except for the procedure of referendum (Maus 1992, 262). All institutions were to serve the overarching goal of creating a strong executive. While de Gaulle did work with a constitutional assembly in preparing the document, its role was merely consultative. Although the upstream instructions from the parliament of the Fourth Republic prevented him from adopting an American-style presidency, this was not his preference in any case (Peyrefitte 1994, 446). There is no indication that the downstream constraint on ratification by referendum interfered with his freedom of choice, in the way ratification by state electoral assemblies constrained the choices open to the Federal Convention (Amar 2005, 279–80).

Second, we need to distinguish genuine constituent assemblies from sham assemblies. Consider the following statement, sometimes imputed to Napoleon: "Il faut qu'une constitution soit courte et obscure. Elle doit être faite de manière à ne pas gêner l'action du gouvernement." ("A constitution should be short and obscure. It should be written so as not to interfere with the action of the government.") It is understandable that an autocrat would want to be unhampered by rules and restrictions, but the criterion for a constitution being genuine is that it does impose limits on the government; otherwise it is a mere pretense. In other words, either the upstream actors or some of the framers must be motivated to write a genuine constitution for the assembly to be considered genuine.[1] Hence the bodies that adopted Soviet-style communist constitutions, for instance, should not count as constituent assemblies.

[1] Upstream constraints are imposed by those setting up the assembly, whereas downstream constraints result from those involved at later stages (Elster 1995, 373).

II. INTERNAL RULES AND PROCEDURES

Except for the 1958 French case, all modern (nonsham) constitutions have been *made* by elected assemblies. Often, however, they have been *prepared* by unelected bodies or informal groupings. In her chapter, Lerner argues that the study of the constitution-making process in divided societies "should pay close attention to the politics that preceded the formal stage of drafting," and shows that in her six case studies the success or failure of the formal process correlated highly with the presence or absence of informal talks and negotiations. Beyond her case studies, the 1989 Round Table Talks in Poland and Hungary also shaped constitution making in crucial ways, and may have been necessary conditions for the peaceful transitions that took place (Elster 1996). These cases should be distinguished from those in which informal bargaining *substitutes for*, rather than *prepares the ground for*, the formal process. In her chapter, Malagodi discusses the making of the 2015 Nepal constitution as a case in which the assembly was largely bypassed.

In modern constitution making, it can be misleading to assert that constitutions are *made by assemblies*, if by that expression one intends to say that they emerge solely and organically from plenary debates among independent delegates. Although this characterization partly fits the two Nordic assemblies discussed in the chapters by Elster and Gylfason, it is less adequate for the other cases in this volume. For one thing, many crucial decisions are elaborated in committees rather than in the full assembly. For another, delegates are often not independent, but subject to party discipline. Since committees as well as political parties tend to be black boxes, in the sense that we usually know little about their internal decision-making processes (see Martin and Rasch 2013 for the opacity of parties in constitutional change), our understanding of the causal chains that lead up to the adoption of the final document may be incomplete.

The *size* and *duration* of constituent assemblies vary, and can matter. The smallest constituent assembly on record is the Icelandic one, which Gylfason describes in his chapter. Its twenty-five members could engage in even more focused deliberation than the fifty-five members of the Federal Convention (not all of whom were present at all times). The debates among the 112 members of the Norwegian assembly that Elster considers in his chapter on 1814 also seem to have been orderly. At the other end of the spectrum, the 1789 French assembly counted around 1,200 members. As most debates took place in plenum, chaos reigned. Gouverneur Morris (1939: 382), one of the most active members at the Federal Convention who was in Paris during the sitting of the *Constituante*, describes the proceedings as follows:

> One large half of the time is spent in hollowing and bawling-their manner of speaking. Those who intend to speak write their names on a tablet, and are heard

> in the order that their names are written down, if the others will hear them, which often they refuse to do, keeping up a continual uproar till the orator leaves the pulpit. Each man permitted to speak delivers the result of his lucubrations, so that the opposing parties fire off their cartridges, and it is a million to one if their missile arguments happen to meet. The arguments are usually printed; therefore there is as much attention paid to making them sound and look well, as to convey instruction or produce conviction.

Another foreign observer, the British agronomist Arthur Young (1794, p. 283), was equally shocked:

> The want of order, and every kind of confusion, prevails now almost as much as when the Assembly sat at Versailles. The interruptions given are frequent and long; and speakers, who have no right by the rules to speak, will attempt it ... There is a gallery at each end of the saloon, which is open to all the world; and side ones for admission of the friends of the members by tickets: the audience in these galleries are very noisy: they clap, when anything pleases them, and they have been known to hiss; an indecorum which is utterly destructive of freedom of debate.

In the large modern assemblies discussed in this volume, chaos was probably avoided by delegating much of the work to committees.

The size and duration of constituent assemblies are, at least roughly, correlated. The small Icelandic assembly debated for four months, the *Constituante* for more than two years. Since the size of the assembly is also roughly correlated with the size of the country, the latter variable may in fact be decisive: the Indian assembly, with fluctuating membership between 200 and 300 members, took more than three years to complete its task. A large country may have to address more issues than a smaller one, and require a larger number of delegates to ensure knowledge about local conditions. Other variables, too, can affect the duration of the process. In particular, as Elster argues in his chapter on 1814, a tense international situation may lead to a speeding up of the process. In France in 1958, the urgent need to solve the Algerian problem had the same effect. More mundanely, at the Federal Convention many delegates were in a hurry to get home to their families and businesses. In India, external and internal threats had the opposite effect – delaying the assembly's progress by more than two years past a self-imposed deadline.

In a tradition initiated by Sieyes (2014, 126–7), the hallmark of a constituent assembly is often said to lie in its unrestricted power. A constituent power cannot be bound (he argued), since the organ binding it would have to be one of the constituted powers that the constitution is to regulate. To allow it do so would be to have it act as judge in its own case. If, for instance, the organ convoking a constituent assembly tries to impose procedural or substantive constraints on its work, it is free to ignore them. A famous example is the decision by the Federal Convention in

Philadelphia to ignore the instructions from the Continental Congress with regard both to substance (the Convention took it upon itself to create a wholly new constitution rather than simply revise the Articles of Confederation) and to process (the proposed document would be approved by specially elected ratifying assemblies rather than, as required in the Articles, by the state legislatures). The latter act of disobedience is especially important. Since the proposed constitution would have reduced the power of the state legislatures, they would hardly have accepted it had they been allowed to act as judges in their own case. As Negretto explains in his chapter, a similar refusal to respect upstream constraints occurred in Colombia in 1990. In that case, however, it was the Supreme Court rather than the assembly itself that declared that the framers would be free to decide on the content of a new constitution. In her chapter, Malagodi shows that Nepal's constituent assembly ignored upstream instructions that imposed a two-year deadline on its work by extending its term four times.

Some cases contrast markedly with the sovereign assembly model. As noted, in 1958 the French parliament did not give de Gaulle a totally free hand to propose a new constitution. Several chapters in this volume also show the limitations of the alleged sovereignty of the constituent power. Gylfason's analysis of the obstructionist role of the Icelandic parliament offers the most striking example. Since a major aim of the committee that drafted the new constitution was to eliminate the overrepresentation of the rural districts in parliament, the majority of that body had an incentive to block the reform and did so. In his chapter, Negretto shows that the making of the 1994 Argentine constitution was substantively constrained by a congressional law based on a political pact between the government and the opposition. As Elster notes in his chapter on Norway, the framers respected procedural instructions laid down by the prince-regent.

A recurrent issue in constitution making is the *double role of electoral systems*. On the one hand, delegates are usually chosen by popular elections, the main exception arising in federal systems in which state legislatures may select the delegates. This was the case for the Federal Convention, for the German convention that adopted the 1949 constitution, and, as Bhatia explains in his chapter, for the 1946 elections to the Indian assembly. On the other hand, one of the central tasks of the assembly is to design or at least sketch in broad outline an electoral system for future legislatures. Although not all constitutions specify the system in great detail – the 1958 French constitution is very laconic on the subject – many do. Tensions may then arise if the franchise used in electing the framers differs from the franchise they write into the constitution. In France in 1789, Robespierre (1912–67, Vol. VII, 172) very effectively criticized the assembly for adopting stricter tax qualifications for suffrage than those under which they had been elected, arguing that in doing so they retroactively undermined their own legitimacy. As Elster notes in his chapter on 1814, a similar discrepancy arose in the Norwegian case, although nobody (to our knowledge) commented on it at the time. In his chapter, Bhatia notes a converse kind of tension between the qualified suffrage used in electing the provincial legislatures that nominated the delegates to the Indian assembly and the universal suffrage adopted in the constitution. How, some asked, could an elite body create a democratic constitution?

In his chapter, Bhatia also cites a somewhat similar puzzle, which to our knowledge has no parallel elsewhere: how could a unicameral assembly legitimately adopt a bicameral system in the constitution? If the delegates adopted bicameralism because of its superior cognitive features, would they not, as Robespierre argued with respect to the suffrage, retroactively undermine their own legitimacy? There are examples, however, of bicameral constituent assemblies: Japan 1946, Turkey 1961, Sweden 1974, Spain 1978, Romania 1991, and Poland 1992. With the exception of Sweden, none of these adopted a unicameral constitution.

In many countries, *constitutional amendments* require, for their adoption, a qualified majority. It might seem paradoxical, therefore, that the more fundamental decision to adopt the *constitution that is being amended* is virtually always done by simple majority voting. There is no paradox, however, if there is no constitution in place that can serve as a *default option* if a required qualified majority is not reached. (For a similar reason, parliaments always adopt budgets by a simple, and in some cases absolute, majority.) Conversely, the requirement, noted by Negretto in his chapter, that the 2007 Bolivian constitution be passed by a two-thirds majority in the assembly should not surprise us. This being said, we may well wonder why in other cases a simple majority is used even when a default constitution is in place. The answer may be found in the degree of malfunctioning of that default system.

The use of simple majority voting is consistent with a desire for a large consensus, to enhance the legitimacy of the new constitution. In 1949, for instance, the German framers set themselves – and achieved – the aim of adopting the constitution by an 80 percent majority. The nonconsensual adoption of a constitution can tear up the social fabric, as shown by the adoption of the violently anticlerical 1931 Spanish constitution by a 53 percent majority. In her chapter, Malagodi discusses how the constituent process in Nepal involved a baffling mix of simple majority voting, the requirement of two-thirds majority, and a demand for consensus.

III. SOCIAL AND INSTITUTIONAL CONTEXT

When do the people speak in the constituent process? According to the canonical formulation by Sieyes, the constituent power ultimately belongs to the Nation (as he said) or to the people (as we say). If the constituent assembly elaborates the constitution, how can the people at large shape it?

First, *the people can speak at the beginning* of the process, by choosing the delegates to the constituent assembly. In modern times, the choice is usually based on their programs or known opinions, but in some earlier assemblies (France 1789, Norway 1814) the deputies were elected on the basis of their *character*. As just noted, in India only some of the people spoke, and then only indirectly, through the provincial legislatures. In Norway, too, only some of the people spoke, but in direct elections. Today, universal suffrage ensures that the people as a whole talk when electing delegates to a constitutional convention or to a legislature that, as in France in 1946, is mandated also to propose a constitution. In his chapter, Negretto cites several other examples of such mandated assemblies, making the additional point that some may also be constitutionally authorized.

Speech at the beginning of the process can also take the form of *imperative mandates* from voters to their representatives. In constitution-making processes, this speech mode seems to be rare. As Elster discusses in his chapter on 1814, some of the resolutions of the Norwegian electoral assemblies had the flavor of mandates, but they were not binding. In 1787, the delegates to the Federal Convention from the small state of Delaware came with instructions not to assent to "the abolition of the fifth article of the confederation, by which it is declared that each state shall have one vote" (Farrand 1966, Vol. I, 6). The delegates followed the instruction, which was arguably decisive in forcing the large states to accept an equal number of senators for all states. It issued, however, from the state legislature, not from the voters. The grievance books that were written at the time of the elections to the Estates-General in France in 1789 contained many imperative mandates, which Louis XVI disallowed. They delayed the proceedings in the early stages, but probably did not shape the decisions (Hyslop 1968, 99–104).

Second, the people may *speak at the end* of the process, by ratifying assemblies (as in America in 1787) or in a referendum (as in many of the other cases discussed in this volume). In a nonnegligible number of cases, the proposed document was rejected by the people (see Elster 2013, 234 for some examples). In their chapter, Bucur et al. discuss what is arguably the most important case, the rejection of the first draft of the 1946 French constitution. One reason why it was rejected was probably the perceived importance of institutional interest behind the proposal: the constituent legislature created a "régime d'assemblée" that the voters found excessively legislature-centric. Yet even when the people speak approvingly at the end, its voice is not necessarily heard. When the referendum is purely consultative, the parliament may choose to ignore it, as happened in Iceland. As Gylfason recounts in his chapter, when Jon Elster visited Iceland in 2012 he confidently predicted that "If the people approved the constitutional proposal, Parliament would find it difficult to override the moral authority of the people." In making this claim, Elster was influenced by the fact that the Norwegian parliament had respected the negative outcome of two consultative referendums on Norwegian membership in the European Union, in 1972 and in 1994, despite the constitutionally required majority in the parliament in favor of entry.

Third, there is a recent tendency for the people to be allowed to speak *during the process*, by submitting proposals to the constituent body and even, as Gylfason explains in the case of Iceland, to engage with the framers through an interactive website. If, as seems possible, this procedure becomes the norm, it would contrast with the claim by Elster (2013, 234–6) that an optimal constitution-making process should be "hour-glass shaped," with upstream and downstream popular voices separated by an assembly deliberating behind closed doors. The proper mix of secrecy and publicity in debates and votes in the constitution-making process is a complex issue (Elster and Le Pillouer 2015).

Several contributors focus on the difficulties of constitution making in, "plural societies," that is, societies that are "deeply divided" on national, regional, ethnic, religious, or linguistic grounds. In his chapter, Gargarella distinguishes among four ways in which assemblies have addressed seemingly intractable issues: by the majority imposing its will, deferring the problem by dumping it on the future, by reaching a compromise based on an overlapping consensus, and by sweeping the conflict under the carpet by adopting mutually contradictory or ambiguous clauses. In addition to the Latin American cases he cites, the uneasy combination of regional autonomy and national unity in the 1978 Spanish constitution offers an illustration: "the price paid for such heavy compromise was that Spain, a country with relatively intense regional difficulties, was given a poor and incomplete territorial formula with the potential for worsening existing problems" (Bonime-Blanc 1987, 89–90). Gargarella also notes the illiberal and dangerous tendency, recently observed in some post-Communist constitutions (Elster 1993, 198–9), to limit the affirmation of rights by a blanket clause about the need to respect "public order and morality." Postcolonial constitution makers in India retained similar restrictions from the preceding regime.

In her chapter, Lerner affirms, as noted earlier, that the success of constitution making in deeply divided societies depends on prior informal deliberations between the conflicting sides. As she notes, an "overlapping consensus" may not be feasible, if liberal constitutionalism is seen as representing one side of the conflict rather than a neutral ground (echoing the saying that universalism is the particularism of the rich). While joining Gargarella in citing deferral and ambiguity among the "solutions" to conflict, she adds the technique of including nonjusticiable or "aspirational" clauses in the constitution. Examples include the guarantees of social and economic rights that were inserted in some post-Communist constitutions to placate the former Communists (Elster 1993, 198); and some "Directive Principles" in India's constitution. In the post-Communist cases, though, the constitutional courts took these "parchment rights" more seriously than the non-Communist framers intended them to be.

Several chapters discuss assemblies that were *simultaneously* constituent and legislative. In their chapters, Bucur et al. and Negretto address the claim by Elster (2006) that such mixed assemblies have a tendency to adopt legislative-centric constitutions, as illustrated by the Polish assembly of 1921 and the French assembly of 1946. Bucur et al. confirm the tendency for the case of investiture rules in government formation in European assemblies. Negretto is more skeptical, citing his finding that in the context of Latin American presidential regimes the choice between a pure and a mixed assembly makes no difference for the allocation of power among the branches of government. Even assuming he is right, it would still make sense, in the study of a given mixed assembly, to explore the hypothesis that its decisions might have been shaped by institutional interest. The mechanism is intelligible and testable.

Independently of this effect, mixed assemblies are easily distracted from their constituent task by other issues. As Madison wrote in his preamble to the Virginia resolution calling for the Federal Convention, it would be "preferable to a discussion of the subject in Congress, where it might be too much interrupted by ordinary business" (Farrand 1966, Vol. III, 560). Such interruptions occurred regularly if unpredictably in the French *Constituante*, where in a speech from 1789 Robespierre (1912–67, Vol. VI, 118–20) cited them to argue against a proposal to set aside all but two days of the week for constitutional matters only. In her chapter, Malagodi observes that the dual role of the Pakistani constituent assembly "led to inordinate delays" and, as noted later, a lack of "the constitutional moment." In times of transition, the dual role may be inevitable, but as we shall discuss shortly, legislative tasks can also be allocated to a separate body.

In some cases, constitutional conventions and legislative assemblies have operated *side by side*, as did for instance the Federal Convention and the Continental Congress. In his chapter, Negretto discusses the existence of parallel assemblies in Ecuador 1997–8 and 2007–8, in Colombia 1990–1, and in Venezuela 2007. As he writes, in a stark understatement, the conventions "had a difficult coexistence with the ordinary legislature." As he also notes, in the Colombian case one of the problems was solved or mitigated by a compromise banning members of the convention from competing in the forthcoming legislative elections. This measure echoes that taken by the (mixed) French *Constituante* on May 16, 1791, when the framers declared themselves ineligible to the first ordinary legislature, to prevent suspicions that they were carving out a place for themselves in that assembly. In both cases, decisions were taken to maintain some degree of separation of constituent and legislative powers. Although the French decision proved disastrous – the first legislature, filled with inexperienced men, was easily dominated by the Jacobin clubs – it did address a genuine problem.

IV. ADDITIONAL QUESTIONS

The present volume offers a number of case studies of *failures* of constitution making. Malagodi's chapter is explicitly devoted to two such failures, in Pakistan and Nepal. Gylfason's chapter details the mechanisms that have, so far at least, blocked the constituent process in Iceland. In her chapter, Lerner distinguishes among several mechanisms that led to failures of constitution making in Indonesia, Egypt, and Israel. Although she counts the process in Sri Lanka as a success, in the sense that it did lead to the adoption of a constitution, it might also count as a failure if the criterion for success is, as she also writes, the enactment of "an *enduring* democratic constitution" (our italics.) Finally, Elster's chapter on 1814 describes the near-miraculous self-fulfilling wishful thinking that enabled the Norwegian framers to avoid a failure that to sober observers seemed inevitable.

In his chapter on the political psychology of constitution making, Elster suggests that one cause of such failures might be the absence of a *crisis* that can generate the will to overcome partisan and short-sighted interests. (In a phrase attributed to Winston Churchill, "Never let a good crisis go to waste.") It is perhaps significant that the Icelandic process ran out of steam, as Gylfason explains in his chapter, when the economy improved. In her chapter, Malagodi suggests that the failures of constitution making in Nepal and Pakistan were due to delays and political infighting, leading to what she calls "an irrevocable loss of the constitutional moment."

The foregoing discussions have been mainly oriented toward explanatory issues, although occasionally we have also touched on normative questions. One may ask, more generally, about the *optimal design* of a constituent assembly. One approach might be to search for the design *most conducive to a good constitution*. Another might be to search for the design that is *least susceptible to distortion* by normatively irrelevant factors, such as self-interest, group interest, institutional interest, cognitive bias, passion, and prejudice. Elster (2013, chapter 4) opts in the main for the second approach, while also emphasizing the desirability of constructive designs that will enable framers to determine *where the shoe pinches* and *how to make good shoes*. The first task requires broad representation of citizens' interests, inducing a preference for proportional representation over majority voting in single-member districts. The second task might seem to require that delegates have some political experience, as was the case, for instance, of the American framers. As Gylfason explains in his chapter, the Icelandic selection of delegates *excluded* current MPs and cabinet ministers from the constitution-making body, while making mayors and other local politicians eligible. Although this proposal seemed attractive – mayors might be expected to know both where the shoe pinched and how to make better shoes – the twenty-five delegates included seven academics (two mathematicians!), five artists and persons associated with the media, as well as three lawyers. Three former MPs – but no local politicians – represented the political experience (complete list in Elster 2016, 193–5).

The paucity of accessible data makes explaining constitution making hard. Incomplete understanding results from insufficient documentation of plenary proceedings. James Madison's notes from the Federal Convention are not only unusually complete, but also unusually reliable, in that they were not written for an external audience or for posterity (but see Bilder 2015 for some nuances). Elster's chapter on 1814 relies on the letters by one framer, the History written by his son, the Recollections of another framer, the diary of the prince-regent, and on the official minutes. While extremely suggestive, these sources are also incomplete. In this respect, Gylfason's chapter is in a class by itself, as he received the largest number of votes in the elections to the Constitutional Council. His chapter would have found a natural place in *Constitution-Makers on Constitution-Making* (Goldwin and Kaufman 1988) if that volume were to be reedited. When there is a reasonably good record of the debates in the assemblies, supplemented and triangulated by letters and diaries of the framers, we can engage in the kind of *micropolitical analysis* pioneered by Ermakoff (2015).

Even in the best of cases, the reconstruction of the motives and beliefs of individuals, including their beliefs about the beliefs and motives of others, is an arduous and uncertain task. In his chapter on political psychology, Elster, following the French moralists as well as the framers at the Federal Convention, distinguishes among *reason*, *passion* (including prejudice), and *interest* as motivations of framers. In some cases, one may reasonably impute one of them to a given framer in a given situation, although the imputation is complicated by the fact that speakers, letter-writers and even diarists tend (like the rest of us) to profess noble motivations that they do not always harbor. Elster's most robust claim is that earlier writers on constitution making have overemphasized the causal efficacy of "ideas" (or reason) and interest, while neglecting that of passion. Hence, he suggests, the classical metaphor that constitutions are documents written by Paul when sober to restrain Paul when drunk should be turned upside down: *successful framers tend to be drunk*, that is, filled with passion. In particular, he endorses Kant's claim that without *enthusiasm* nothing great is ever achieved in history. Other emotions can, to be sure, undermine successful constitution making, in particular those generated by ethnic and especially religious conflicts.

REFERENCES

Amar, A. (2005). *America's Constitution: A Biography*. New York, NY: Random House.
Bilder, S. (2015). *Madison's Hand*. Cambridge, MA: Harvard University Press.
Bonime-Blanc, A. (1987). *Spain's Transition to Democracy*. Boulder, CO: Westview Press.

Choudry, S., and Ginsburg, T., eds. (2016). *Constitution Making*. Cheltenham: Edward Elgar.
Elster, J. (1993). "Constitution-Making in Eastern Europe." *Public Administration* 71, 169–217; reprinted in S. Choudry and T. Ginsburg (eds.), *Constitution Making*. Cheltenham: Edward Elgar.
(1995). "Forces and Mechanisms in the Constitution-Making Process." *Duke Law Journal* 45: 364–96.
ed. (1996). *The Round Table Talks in Eastern Europe*. Chicago, IL: University of Chicago Press.
(2006). "Legislatures as Constituent Assemblies." In R. Bauman and T. Kahana (eds.), *The Least Examined Branch*, 181–97. Cambridge: Cambridge University Press.
(2013). *Securities against Misrule*. Cambridge: Cambridge University Press.
(2016). "Icelandic Constitution-Making in Comparative Perspective." In V. Ingimundarson and P. Urfalino (eds.), *Iceland's Financial Crisis*, 187–202. London: Routledge.
Elster, J., and Le Pillouer, A. (2015). "Semi-public Voting in the *Constituante*." In J. Elster (ed.), *Secrecy and Publicity in Votes and Debates*, 52–71. Cambridge: Cambridge University Press.
Ermakoff, I. (2015). "The Structure of Contingency." *American Journal of Sociology* 121, 64–125.
Farrand, M., ed. (1966). *Records of the Federal Convention*. New Haven, CT: Yale University Press.
Goldwin. R., and Kaufman (1988). *Constitution Makers on Constitution Making: The Experience of Eight Nations*. Washington, DC: AEI Studies.
Hyslop, B. (1968). *A Guide to the General Cahiers of 1789*. New York, NY: Octagon Books.
Martin, S., and Rasch, B. E. (2013). "Political Parties and Constitutional Change." In W. C. Müller and H. M. Narud (eds.), *Party Governance and Party Democracy*, 205–29. New York, NY: Springer.
Maus, D. (1992). "L'institution présidentielle dans l'écriture de la constitution de 1958." In D. Maus, L. Favoreu, and J.-L. Parodi (eds.), *L'Écriture de la Constitution de 1958*, 261–77. Paris: Economica.
Miller, L., and Aucoin, L., eds. (2010).*Framing the State in Times of Transition: Case Studies in Constitution Making*. Washington, DC: United States Institute of Peace.
Morris, G. (1939). *A Diary of the French Revolution*, Vol. 1. Boston, MA: Houghton Mifflin.
Peyrefitte, A. (1994). *C'était de Gaulle*, Vol. 1. Paris: Fayard.
Robespierre, M. (1912–67). *Œuvres*. Paris: Presses Universitaires de France.
Sieyes, Abbé de (2014). "Reasoned Exposition of the Rights of Man and of Citizen." In O. Lembcke and F. Weber (eds.), *Emmanuel Joseph Sieyes: The Essential Political Writings*. Boston, MA: Brill.
Voigt, S., ed. (2013). *Design of Constitutions*. Cheltenham: Edward Elgar.
Young, A. (1794). *Travels in France*, Vol. 1. London.

1

Constitution Making in the Context of Plural Societies

The "Accumulation Strategy"

Roberto Gargarella

I. INTRODUCTION

The question that I want to explore in this chapter is the following: What should delegates in a constitutional assembly do in order to properly take into consideration the demands of rival groups, which are usually present in the context of divided societies?[1] In my analysis, I shall first assume that we want the constitution to last for a long period of time, setting the basis of the future national organization. Also, I shall presume that the constitution should be able to expose the convictions and ambitions of the entire society, rather than those of a small portion of it. In this way – I shall maintain – the constitution could be seen and recognized as the genuine expression of a compact between equals. But the problem is, again, how to do that, when the diverse groups that compose society are separated by profound differences, as is usually the case. Should the members of the assembly include in the constitutional text all their diverse views, so as to demonstrate the plurality of opinions existing in society? Should all groups be allowed to have their viewpoints stamped in the constitution, reflecting their most fundamental concerns? Should the different groups split their differences? Should the members of the convention try to navigate in between their disagreements? Should they put all their energies in trying to find common points of agreement?

In what follows I shall make reference to four different responses to the fact of pluralism, which we find in the history of constitutional conventions. I will call

[1] In my references to "divided societies" I will be thinking about societies characterized by "the fact of pluralism," by which I mean societies that are profoundly divided by the existence of a diversity of moral, political, religious, and philosophical doctrines. This understanding of the phrase is obviously related to the concept developed by John Rawls in his book *Political Liberalism* (Rawls 1991), although he concentrates his attention on views that are "reasonable." In addition, and contrary to what other doctrinaires suggest, I shall not propose a distinction between "divided" and "deeply divided," for example, which I find extremely difficult to maintain. See, for instance, Lerner in this volume.

them *imposition*, *silence*, *synthesis*, and *accumulation*. I will illustrate these four approaches with examples from early constitutional history in the Americas.

After describing these four different responses, I shall concentrate my attention on the analysis of the latter, that is to say, the "accumulation strategy." I shall do so because, in my opinion, it has been the more significant and influential approach, within the history of constitutionalism in the Americas, and also one very important in other parts of the world. Finally, I shall attempt to demonstrate why this understanding of constitutional creation is very difficult to defend, and illustrate the kinds of difficulties it tends to promote in actual practice.

II. INTRODUCING THE DIFFERENCES

Herein, I shall explore four different responses that may appear (and have actually appeared) in constitutional assemblies that are composed of groups with opposite views. In my presentation, I will be mainly taking into account the viewpoints of two opposite groups: liberals and conservatives. Liberals and conservatives were, in fact, the two main rival groups in most constitutional assemblies in the Americas, between the end of the eighteenth century and the mid-nineteenth century. Their rivalry may well illustrate the significance and implications of having a deeply divided constitutional assembly.

As we shall see, liberals and conservatives differed in many fundamental issues. And – what is more significant for our purposes – their disparities became reflected in the two main parts of the constitution, namely (what I shall call) (1) its *dogmatic* part, which is the one that includes the declaration of rights, and (2) its *organic* part, which is the one that organizes and divides power among the branches.

Generally speaking, *conservative* groups advanced a view of the constitution that combined *political elitism* (which became manifested primarily in the organic part of the constitutions that they promoted) and *moral perfectionism* (which became manifested primarily in the dogmatic part). Usually, they proposed concentrating power (favoring centralism over federalism) and strengthening the authority of the executive while, at the same time, making individual rights dependent on "external" values such as the values of a particular religion (Gargarella 2010, 2013). For instance, a conservative constitution may include in its text the right to publish ideas freely in the press, but make this right conditional upon not attacking the church.[2]

[2] This definition of conservatism gets very close to a standard definition of political conservatism. For example, the *Macmillan Encyclopedia of the Social Sciences* defines political conservatism as the ideology that "celebrate[s] inherited patterns of morality and tested institutions, that are skeptical about the efficacy of popular government, that can be counted upon to oppose both the reforming plans of the moderate Left and the deranging schemes of the extreme Left, and that draw their heaviest support

Meanwhile, *liberal* groups advanced a view of the constitution that combined *political moderation* and *moral neutrality*. Contrary to what conservatives preferred, liberals suggested limiting and controlling the exercise of power, ensuring equilibrium between the different branches of government. They wanted to avoid the risk of both "tyranny" and "anarchy" that, they assumed, derived from the absence of adequate institutional controls. That is why they usually favored a schema of "checks and balances." In addition, they tried to ensure a very particular protection of individual rights, which they reasonably assumed to be unprotected under the conservative program.[3] Liberals presented these rights as unconditional: in their opinion, rights should depend on the will of no one in particular, nor on any one person's conception of the good.[4]

III. FOUR DIFFERENT RESPONSES

Let me begin my exploration by examining the four different approaches concerning how to write constitutions in the context of plural and deeply divided societies.

1. **Imposition.** The first response that I shall explore, namely *imposition*, was frequent in socially and culturally heterogeneous countries that were controlled by one faction. Imposition implies that one of the involved groups manages to enforce its own will, thus displacing the demands of the rest. The response based on legal imposition was the most common among Latin American conservatives in the nineteenth century. During that century, particularly the first half of it, conservative groups managed to gain control over politics and thus enacted their favored constitutions, which unmistakably reflected their main concerns: the aim of averting anarchy and the need to avoid the decay of morals that they perceived in their respective countries. Frequently, these constitutions included a (super) strong executive;

from men who have a substantial material and psychological stake in the established order" (Sills 1968, Vol. 3, 291).

3 This definition of liberalism is also close to a standard definition of political liberalism. According to the *Macmillan Encyclopedia* "[liberal] thought and practice have stressed two primary themes. One is the dislike for arbitrary authority, complemented by the aim of replacing that authority by other forms of social practice. A second theme is the free expression of individual personality" (Sills 1968, Vol. 9, 276).

4 Given the weak influence they exercised in constitutional conventions, I shall not explore here a third position, namely political radicalism. This view, which has sometimes appeared in the history of constitutionalism in the Americas, was more related to French, early revolutionary ideologies. Radical constitutional thinkers proposed an alternative view of the Constitution, which could be characterized by the defense of *political majoritarianism* and *moral populism*. Radicals tried to strengthen the authority of the people, which conservative constitutions basically annulled. Radical constitutions also tend to include a list of rights in their texts but, as in conservative constitutions, these rights also seem conditional: they are defended as long as they do not contradict – or as long as they foster – the fundamental interests of the majority.

established an official religion; promoted a comprehensive moral view; and defined rights in consonance with the dominant moral project. In some more extreme and infrequent cases, those constitutions established a system of sanctions and rewards to those who behaved in ways rejected or favored by those in power.

One of the most extreme examples in that respect was the 1823 Chilean constitution, written by the conservative jurist Juan Egaña. Egaña and his constitution were enormously influential in Chile and, more generally, in the region, in spite of the fact that the peculiar constitution of 1823 was short lived. Egaña's constitution included a strong executive which, in Egaña's opinion, controlled "the entire administration, without the interference of the legislature, which has to enact only a few general and permanent laws and which will meet only after long intervals and during a very short time" (Silva Castro 1969, 86–7). One of the president's main functions was that of enforcing the Catholic religion, which was established as the country's official religion. Also, and to ensure the imposition of the official religion, the constitution created a "conservative Senate" in charge of controlling the "national morality and habits" and, more radically, accompanied its text with a substantive "Moral Code," directed at regulating the moral life of Chile's inhabitants even in its smallest details: in Egaña's opinion, the "Moral Code" represented the highest and most meditated expression of his life-long theoretical reflections on morality. The first part of the code was dedicated to religion and the need for protecting it (it regulated, for example, the way in which to celebrate the church's public festivities as well as the relationships between the individuals and their confessors). In its second part, the code analyzed the family, its composition, and the relationship among its members (it made reference to personal attitudes and behaviors including ingratitude, vanity, denigration, or the abandonment of one's parents). Its third part was related to education, which played a central role within Egaña's project. The code regulated the use of alcohol; provided for strict parameters to follow during private and public ceremonies; and established the prohibition of circulating pamphlets and leaflets without the previous authorization of a group of censors. The code also included strict sanctions against those citizens who "created political parties and frankly displayed their opinions, or those who gathered in public places" (Silva Castro 1969, 637–8). Extreme as it was, the 1823 constitution, and even more so the 1833 constitution, which could be seen as the continuation of the former, were enormously influential in the early constitutional history of Latin America.

2. **Silence/Deferral.** The second response, *silence* or *deferral*, may appear when the different parts recognize that they cannot reasonably solve their fundamental disagreements. In these situations participants may decide to leave the matter on which they disagree open, unresolved. Their decision is to not decide – to "leave things undecided." As Cass Sunstein has put it (making reference to judicial

decisions), sometimes people decide to "decide very little," to "leave things open," making "deliberate decisions about what should be left unsaid." This is, for him, "a pervasive practice: doing and saying as little as is necessary in order to justify an outcome" (Sunstein 1996, 2001, 3).[5] Also, studying the cases of "deeply divided societies," Hannah Lerner has shown the virtues of the choice of deferral. For her, "instead of seeing the making of the constitution as a moment of radical transformation, the framers [in Israel, India and Ireland] preferred to view the process ... as one of gradual transformation" (Lerner 2013, 194–5).

There is an interesting example of this "silent" response in the Mexican constitutional debates of 1857. One of the longer and more heated discussions during that convention referred to the place of religion and religious tolerance. In the face of that difficult issue, the delegates decided to go for inaction. The issue of religion was particularly pressing in light of the enormous privileges enjoyed by the Church at the time, which moved many liberals to reject any initiative aimed at ratifying the unfair advantages that it had acquired during so many years. For instance, the delegate Francisco Zarco, one of the most important figures of the convention, rejected the establishment of the Catholic religion, asserting that the role assumed by the Mexican Church during all those years had been unacceptable. "[I]t has denaturalized Christ's religion because it has declared itself the enemy of freedom; it has accumulated wealth impoverishing the country; it has deceived the people ... it has defended privileges and money, disregarding the truths of Catholicism" (Zevada 1972, 38–9). In the end, however, liberals did not manage to ensure religious tolerance through the constitution, given the differences that appeared not only with conservative representatives, but also even within the liberal group. What the delegates decided to do, in the end – making it manifest the transactional character of the constitution – was to *remain silent* concerning the religious question, preventing, at least, the constitution from becoming an *intolerant* document in this respect. They simply succeeded, in the end, in preventing the establishment of religious *in*tolerance.

In addition, one should not forget about the possible risks derived from the strategy of silence or deferral. For instance, the US Constitution included many things, and also, in some parts at least, an option for a strategy of deferral/silence. This is, for instance, what the American Framers decided to do concerning the divisive and conflictive issue of slavery: "Leave things undecided."Now, could one suggest that the outbreak of a civil war in 1861 was in some way related to this deferral strategy? I am not interested at this point in answering that impossible question about causality in the past, but I do want to raise that issue: Is it reasonable for a constitutional

5 Similarly, for Dixon and Ginsburg, "constitutional drafters often face constraints that cause them to leave issues to the future" (Dixon and Ginsburg 2011, 636).

convention to leave the most significant and divisive social questions undecided, as if that silence did not imply an "active" defense of a particular status quo? Is it reasonable to choose "silence" in the face of grave social conflicts, as if that silence implied peace or justice?

3. **Synthesis.** The third response, *synthesis*, can be related to the Rawlsian idea of an *overlapping consensus*. According to this approach, different groups support a common solution for different reasons – reasons that are internal to their own favored comprehensive views (Rawls 1991).[6] Reaching a synthetic agreement – an agreement that we can all share – may require from each part a significant effort: each part needs to leave aside or put between brackets some relevant aspects of its own claims. We find an interesting example of this response in the US initial constitutional debates concerning religion. The issue of religion was one of the most divisive matters among different groups, during the "founding period." Previous to the constitution, the prevailing situation looked like one of dire imposition: there was religious establishment in New England with the Congregational Church, and in the South with the Anglican Church. Different sects, who had suffered from religious persecution in England, were now making pressure for the advancement of their own views, through the use of the State coercive powers. In the end, however, most social groups accepted a nonestablishment clause (that was first accepted in Virginia and then incorporated into the Constitution),[7] because of different reasons, including self-protection, reciprocity, tolerance, secularism, etc. Not surprisingly, the case of the First Amendment became one of Rawls' main examples in order to illustrate his reflections on public reason, state coercion and the overlapping consensus.

4. **Accumulation.** The final response, *accumulation*, appears when the different participants, for some reason, find it too difficult to reach a common agreement, and at the same time reject remaining silent about the topics that divide them. In those cases, the convention's members may decide to simply sum or put together (one on the top of the other) their different claims, leaving their demands in tension – leaving all those tensions or even contradictions, totally or almost totally intact. Seemingly, this would appear as a way of reaching an agreement by "satisfying" all players,

6 For Rawls, this political conception needs to be such that there is some hope of its gaining the support of an overlapping consensus, that is, a consensus in which it is "affirmed by the opposing religious, philosophical, and moral doctrines likely to thrive over generations in a more or less just constitutional democracy, where the criterion of justice is that political conception itself" (Rawls 1987, 1).

7 The First Amendment of the US Constitution reads as follows: "Congress shall make no law respecting an establishment of religion, or prohibiting the free exercise thereof; or abridging the freedom of the press; or the right of the people peaceably to assemble, and to petition the Government for a redress of grievances."

giving each of them what they want. Arguably, the "accumulation approach" has been gaining importance in the Middle East, in the context of profound religious divisions. More significantly, this has been the most popular approach in Latin American constitutionalism, this is to say, in the region where I have been focusing my analysis so far. In what follows, I will present different examples related to the adoption of this strategy in Latin America, since its independence and until today, and examine them critically.[8]

IV. LATIN AMERICA'S "ACCUMULATION STRATEGY"

In the nineteenth century, and after the independence period, the "accumulation strategy" became particularly relevant in Latin America. The preference for "accumulation" became manifest in the two main areas of the Constitution, this is to say, the one related to the organization of powers, and the one related to the declaration of rights. Very commonly, and given the difficulties they found to combine their views and synthetize their frequently opposite claims, conservative and liberal delegates decided to put those conflicting claims together, including all of them in the same text.

Concerning the organization of powers, liberals proposed adopting a system of checks and balances (like the one that had been adopted in the United States), while conservatives preferred the creation of an overtly powerful executive (like the one it had been created, for instance, in the influential, stable and authoritarian Chilean constitution of 1833). Now, given the difficulties they found to negotiate their differences in this respect, liberals and conservatives in most Latin American countries decided to write constitutions that included both these opposite demands. In that way, they created constitutions that defined the creation of a system of "checks and balances" (allowing each branch to control the others), and at the same time established a hyperpowerful executive power (creating so-called hyperpresidentialist systems, Nino 1996). This latter choice was reflected through the fact that, according to the old conservative model of constitutionalism, they ensured special prerogatives for the president (related to the declaration of a *stage of site*, or the intervention into the affairs of local states). The decision was then taken to "accumulate" both opposing proposals in the same text. This peculiar combination would since then become the main and most distinctive feature of Latin American constitutionalism.

What Latin American constitutions did concerning the organization of power became reflected also in what they did regarding their declarations of rights.

8 It should be clear that the distinction among all these four different strategies does not imply saying that they are not interrelated, nor to deny that their effects, in some cases, may overlap.

A good example in this respect appears in Argentina's influential 1853 constitution. At the time, in Argentina, as in many other Latin American countries, liberal and conservative groups confronted each other violently, over a number of issues, particularly over religion. More specifically, liberals favored religious tolerance, while conservatives proposed religious imposition. In the face of those conflicts, Argentina's 1853 delegates (which included representatives of the liberal and the conservative groups) decided, first (and following the conservatives' demands), to provide a special status to the Catholic Church, through article 2 of the constitution ("The Federal Government supports the Roman Catholic Apostolic religion"), and at the same time (and following the liberals' demands) to adopt religious tolerance, through article 14 of the constitution ("All the inhabitants of the Nation are entitled ... to profess freely their religion"). This is to say, they included in the constitution both contradictory commitments at the same time.

We find exactly the same pattern in one of the most interesting articles of Argentina's 1853 constitution, article 19. This article was written mainly to put limits to the intervention of the state concerning issues of private morality. According to its initial formulation, which appeared in earlier constitutional documents, and also in the first draft of the 1853 constitution, the Argentinean delegates subscribed a typically liberal formula. According to this formulation, the State would ensure protection to private morality – the "private actions of men" – insofar as those actions did not harm others. This initial formulation represented what some could call the "dream of John Stuart Mill," and was advocated by numerous liberals, including Benjamín Gorostiaga. However, during the constitutional debates, representatives of conservative groups – led by conventional Pedro Ferré, from Corrientes – complained about the adoption of this and other liberal clauses. They affirmed that they would wholly reject the constitutional project, if it were not drastically changed in diverse aspects – most of them related to the treatment of the religious issue. Through such threats, conservatives managed to introduce numerous reforms in different parts of the draft, including the initial formulation of article 19. What they managed to do in this respect deeply damaged the original, liberal construction of the article, thus ruining John Stuart Mill's "dreamed" article. In its new formulation, the private actions of men would be respected to the extent that they did not affect "order and public morality." So, according to the final draft of article 19 (which is still in place in Argentina's constitution), "the private actions of men that in no way offend public order or morality, nor injure a third party, are reserved only to God, and are exempt from the authority of the magistrates." In its final presentation, the article did not become John Stuart Mill's "nightmare," but came close to it.

Even though the solutions implemented by Argentina's 1853 constitution were, in those respects, rather awkward, the fact is that they represented – as they still do – the main constitutional response advanced in Latin American constitutional assemblies, in situations of profound social pluralism.

The "accumulation strategy," which became so influential in nineteenth-century Latin America, was not abandoned in the following decades. By contrast, as we shall see, that strategy remained a crucial, distinctive feature of contemporary Latin American constitutionalism. Just as an illustration: the 1991 constitution of Colombia, or the prevalent Peruvian constitution, are constitutions that combine (what could be called) "socialist" and "neoliberal" economic commitments. They both include strong social clauses and at the same time offer firm protections to property rights, markets, and private investments.

However, as we shall see, the most significant examples of this peculiar "accumulation strategy" relate to the very structure of most Latin American constitutions. In fact, the vast majority of these constitutions combine modern, twenty-first-century-style declarations of rights (which include participatory rights and references to the rights of sexual, religion, ethnic, racial, or national minorities) with old-fashioned, eighteenth-century-style organizations of powers, which were based on a very restricted or elitist understanding of democracy. In my view, this combination represents the most worrisome aspect of contemporary Latin American constitutionalism, as will be explored in the following pages (Gargarella 2010, 2013).

V. WHY THE "ACCUMULATION STRATEGY"?

It is not clear what *explains* the usual Latin American preference for the "accumulation strategy." Perhaps it was just an exercise of "Peter when drunk legislating for Peter when sober," in other words, an expression of the passions that tend to emerge in times of crisis, like the ones that tend to be present during constitution-making periods (Elster 1995; see also Chapter 9 in this volume). My impression is that those choices do not express irrationality of any kind. Perhaps constitution makers chose to incorporate in the constitution values or rules that are in tension out of hypocrisy (i.e., they promised to do something that they were sure they would not fulfill in the future, just because they needed to satisfy or "calm down" their voters). Perhaps they did so because they preferred to "agree on something" rather than not to enact the constitution altogether; perhaps they did so because they simply could not resist the pressures they received from their voters; perhaps they preferred to bet on certain changes (say, new social rights), hoping for a change of external circumstances (Gargarella 2013); etc.

At this point, however, the most significant question for our purposes is a different one, namely one about the worth of choosing that peculiar constitutional model. More specifically: what, if anything, gives *value* to the "accumulation strategy"? What makes it an attractive option, given the tensions and contradictions that it promises to create at the interior of the constitution? Some people may say that those rich and contradictory constitutions manifest an understandable effort to deal with the differences that exist in modern plural societies. By subscribing different, somehow opposite principles, the legal document would allow either commitment to prevail through legal interpretation, depending on the relationship of the forces that dominate at any time. For instance, in situations of social fervor, the constitution appears capable of summoning the most advanced initiatives. Probably, in those situations judges would receive more demands from disadvantaged groups, and would be more sensitive to those claims.[9] Moreover – some may add – in modern, plural societies we do not want to have monolithic constitutions, that is, constitutions that are mainly organized around one single value or set of values, related to one particular conception of the good.

Still more interestingly, the creation of an ambiguous constitution may be considered a way of showing respect toward the different values existing in society. As some may put it, to quote Lerner, the presence of "competing perspectives expressed during open and free constitutional deliberation play an educative role, since they demonstrate the plurality of visions held by different parts of 'the people' and legitimate the exchange of opinions within an ongoing conversation, in place of violent conflict … constituent assembly debates in divided societies may provide a source of inspiration for further public and political discussion and deliberation around foundational issues" (see Chapter 3 by Lerner in this volume; see also Lerner 2013).[10] These arguments, however, seem substantially flawed for several reasons, as we shall explore in the text that follows.

VI. THE FAILURE OF THE "ACCUMULATION STRATEGY": CONSTITUTIONAL INTERPRETATION AND DELEGATION

Let me examine some reasons that run against the idea of choosing an "accumulation strategy" in what concerns the drafting of a constitution in a plural society. I have been making reference, once and again, to a general, fundamental problem, which is the following: the "accumulation" of opposite or conflicting demands represents

[9] In fact, empirical studies tend to support the claim that judges may become more socially active in the face of a greater number of demands coming from disadvantaged groups (Gargarella et al. 2006).

[10] For Lerner, "The incrementalist constitutional toolbox include[s] such strategies as avoiding clear-cut decisions, using ambiguous legal language, and inserting internally contradictory provisions into the constitution" (Lerner 2013, 7). In her view, ambiguities and contradictions may be deemed – in certain circumstances – proper constitutional responses. She states: "supporters of this approach have emphasized the advantage of such ambiguous arrangements for the purpose of maintaining stability and democracy at the foundational stage of the State" (ibid., 67). And also: "the adoption of incrementalist constitutional formulations in India in areas such as personal law and national language should not be seen as a failure. Rather, it was a conscious strategy of the Constituent Assembly in light of contemporary social and political circumstances. BN Rau, the key legal advisor of the constituent assembly, expressed this view when he stated, 'we have to bear in mind that conditions in India are rapidly changing; the country is in a state of flux politically and economically; and the constitution should not be too rigid in its initial years'" (ibid., 70).

an apparent way of unnecessarily introducing *tensions* and *inconsistencies* within the constitutional structure. These tensions and contradictions may be internal to one section of the constitution – call them *intrasectional* tensions (i.e., tensions that are internal to the "dogmatic" or "organic" parts of the constitution). In addition, these tensions can also emerge between the different parts of the constitution – call them *intersectional* tensions (tensions between the section dedicated to the organization of rights and the section dedicated to the organization of powers).

The difficulties generated by the "accumulation strategy" are diverse. First of all, there are problems of legal and *constitutional interpretation*. In this regard, the question is: How does one read a constitution that is at the same time committed to two opposite or conflictive claims? In the worst cases, a confusing constitutional text may become the object of purely manipulative readings (in fact, these are to be expected, particularly in more fragile legal communities, which are normally those that are more in need of stable legal interpretations). An extremely ambiguous document tends to restrict nothing, and appears to be compatible with almost any reading. All that seems to matter, in such circumstances, is what those occasionally in power want to do with the law.

In the face of this objection, someone could first reply something like the following: What is so strange about the "accumulation" solution (and what is the matter with it)? In fact, the preference for the "accumulation strategy" may be considered more normal or less problematic than I suggested, particularly in the context of modern, participatory democracies. Usually, in participatory democracies, every group wants to have its own views represented in the constitution, which in the end may affect the internal consistency of the document. For instance, according to Ginsburg et al., "participatory constitutional design processes may undermine textual coherence" (Ginsburg et al. 2009, 214).[11] Also, for Voigt, "if the public at large is called upon to actively participate in the constitution-making process … chances that it will be a coherent one will be lower than if the constitutional assembly is closed to active participation of the public" (Voigt 2003, 26–7). Similarly, for Horowitz "the constitution that emerges from this process will almost certainly be an ad-hoc creation, rife with internal inconsistencies and institutional mismatches" (Horowitz 2002, 18). Now, these legal inconsistencies – one could claim – should not necessarily (or only or mainly) be considered problematic. As Horowitz claimed, "the loss of design consistency may be offset by resultant gains in legitimacy" (Horowitz 2002, 18). It is important – one could add – that the constitutional assembly allowed

[11] They also affirm: "We know of no empirical study that has systematically analyzed constitutions for coherence or related concepts. That constitutions contain a complex array of institutions certainly poses a challenge to research design. Undoubtedly, one can find examples of poor drafting, internal contradictions, or errors, but no one has yet tied these directly to participation" (ibid., 215).

the different interested actors to form expectations concerning the final content and future practice of the constitution. In the end, it is not clear what is so wrong with the "accumulation" solution. Moreover, the "accumulation strategy" could be seen as just another illustration of the common phenomenon of *delegating power* to the judiciary or other actors. This is – one could add – a fairly normal strategy of dealing with conflict during constitution making, rather than a pathology.[12]

Now, contrary to this understanding of the phenomenon, I think that there are quite many and serious problems with the "accumulation" choice. Let me briefly examine some of those problems and also show how the "accumulation strategy" could be distinguished from normal tools of constitutional design such as delegation.

First, this kind of "delegation" is damaging in ways that other kinds of delegations of power are not. For instance, when the constitution asks judges to enforce social rights in a "reasonable manner," it offers them a criterion that is clear and important – one that encourages judges to construct their decisions through careful reasoning. If, by contrast, the constitution suggested the protection of a certain value, but also the defense of other values that are in tension with the first one, it in such a way offers judges confusing criteria, which good faith public officers would find difficult to honor. In Argentina, for instance, the same article 19 of the constitution (which I described as the "dream" and "nightmare" of John Stuart Mill) has been used to support and undermine the rights of homosexuals; to protect and condemn the right to consume personal drugs; and to allow and disallow the right to practice alternative forms of sexuality (participate in swingers' clubs, etc.).[13] To make the point more abstract: within judicial cultures that are so "textualist" (where the "words" of the constitution acquire a primary relevance, in what concerns constitutional interpretation) it does not seem a good idea to give judges textual support to adopt one legal solution and also the opposite one. This decision adds unnecessary confusion and complications to the already extremely complex task of interpreting the constitution.

Second, one could claim that by consciously incorporating in the final text of the constitution contradictory or ambiguous clauses, constitution makers show disrespect toward the citizenry. Constitution makers should try to use that unique opportunity they have – taking part in a constitutional convention – to overcome, remedy, or moderate fundamental social conflicts (say, religious or political tensions), rather than avoid those problems and throw them back to the electorate. Worse still, in this way constitution makers not only elude their constitutional duties and responsibilities, but also do so in an hypocritical way: this is – one could claim – what they do when they try to please all the different groups by telling each of them what it wants

[12] I thank one of the anonymous readers who reviewed this book for this comment.

[13] See, for example, Gargarella (2011).

to hear. Imagine, for instance, the case of an agnostic Argentine citizen, reading the 1853 constitution, which both subscribes a liberal principle of religious tolerances (article 14) and ensures the Catholic religion a privileged status (article 2). This person will then read article 2 with fear and anxiety and article 14 (which in parts refers to the same matter as article 2) with relief (something similar will happen, of course, if we took the example of a Catholic citizen reading the same constitution). To paraphrase Jacques Rousseau, in those conditions, it will be impossible for the committed citizen to look at the law and see him- or herself recognized and expressed by it: the voice of the law will sound to him or her as an alien voice that could not be his or hers. That same law would both express and repudiate his or her more profound commitments. As Ordeshook put it, the internal consistency of the constitutional document is an internal precondition for allowing citizens to recognize that their views are being taken seriously (Ordeshook 1993, 2001).

Finally, it is not true that constitutions that include contradictory clauses, or clauses that are ambiguous or in mutual tension, are in that way "neutral" and equally open to different interpretations – as defenders of the "accumulation strategy" may want to claim. Let me explain what I mean by this, through an example. Imagine a constitution that at the same time affirmed both strong social (occasionally socialist) commitments and a commitment to a free market economy (such as, perhaps, the Colombian 1991 constitution or Peruvian 1993 constitution). In defense of such a constitution with "two souls," one could say that in different historic periods, the legal practice could help activate one or the other "soul" of the document: that constitution would seemingly be a "neutral" document. For instance, in times of social crisis, judges would have reasons to emphasize the social aspects of the constitution, and in times of economic growth, they could put a stress on the free-market aspects of the document and be less concerned about its social clauses. This proposition, of course, faces numerous challenges, but here I will mention only one of them. That view – I submit – ignores that constitutions tend to subtly favor certain substantive solutions rather than others, in silent ways and through different means. In particular, such an approach ignores how much the actual life of the constitution and, particularly, the development of its *declaration of rights*, depends on the way the constitution organizes its *organization of powers* (I shall come back to this point in the text that follows). For instance, one can reasonably assume that strong executives will not accept being challenged by a socially active and politically autonomous civil society, such as the one that a constitution with numerous participatory clauses might want to encourage. Similarly, one could anticipate, a rather conservative and elitist body, such as the judiciary, would tend to be rather reluctant to enforce the social clauses of the constitution. In the end, in actual practice, supposedly "neutral" constitutions tend to reveal that they are actually partial rather than impartial.

VII. CONSTITUTIONAL TENSIONS

In the final section of this chapter, I shall illustrate the difficulties generated by the "accumulation strategy," first, at the intrasectional and then at the intersectional level. As Horowitz has put it, those internal contradictions included in the constitution "may ... render the constitutional scheme unworkable" (Horowitz 2002).

A. *Intrasectional Tensions*

Let me exemplify the case of intrasectional tensions by making reference to an example that recently emerged in the constitutions of Ecuador and Bolivia. Both constitutions tried to do justice to the demands of previously marginalized aboriginal groups. For that reason, both constitutions now make references to "communal property" and other aboriginal values, which were not recognized in previous legal documents. Now, this interesting decision brought with it more or less obvious interpretative problems, given that those constitutions did not abandon their old commitments to classical liberal rights. Of course, one can appreciate the intention behind incorporating new "interpretative principles" that are different from the traditional ones: constitutional delegates wanted to honor basic social values that for so long had been dishonored (also) at the constitutional level. However, it is hard not to wonder how these principles should be understood when the constitution does not repudiate principles and institutions that seem to run in the opposite direction, typically those associated with traditional (liberal or "classic") property rights. This seems a good illustration of what I called an *intrasectional* tension. It is also a good example of the problems that arise when we do not take the task of integrating the "old" and the "new" law seriously (in this case, the problem refers mainly to the need to carefully put together the remains of the "old constitution" with the "new articles" brought by the constitutional reform).

A dramatic example of the problems thus generated appeared in the context of the 2008 constitution of Ecuador. Probably, the most important innovation included in the Ecuadorian text, concerning the recognition of aboriginal values, was the "sumac kawsay," or principle of "Good Living." The concept of "sumac kawsay" is rooted in ancestral Quechua knowledge that "sets out a different vision of the cosmos than the Western vision, and arises out of communal, not capitalist roots" (Salazar 2015, 26). If the adoption of such a principle meant something, this was a firm decision to protect nature from capitalist devastation (similarly, the new constitution included the unusual idea that "nature has rights"). However, shortly after the constitution was thus modified, both the National Congress and the Supreme Court transformed those radical principles into empty ones, by privileging alternative constitutional commitments, which allowed the government to carry out harsh exploitative activities.[14] The contradictory character of the constitution obviously helped those in power to advance such a surprising reading of the constitution.[15]

Moreover, the "accumulation strategy" favors the creation of an unworkable, inefficient, or unnecessarily confusing constitution. The types of problems I am thinking about become particularly salient when the "accumulation strategy" is expressed in the organization of powers. A constitution that at the same time designs a system of "checks and balances" and a hyperpowerful executive branch, like most Latin American constitutions, is a constitution that affirms a functional commitment that is at the same time denied through another that runs in the opposite direction. Referring to these kinds of problems, nineteenth-century legal scholar Juan Bautista Alberdi criticized legal orders that "seized with one hand that which (they promised) with the other." They thus promoted – he concluded – "liberty on its surface and slavery in its depths" (Alberdi 1981, chapter 18). This inadequate institutional choice, I submit, has seriously affected the working and stability of Latin American constitutions since their origin.

In fact, the entire point of having a system of "checks and balances" is that of ensuring internal equilibrium between the branches, thus preventing mutual encroachments.[16] However, when a constitutional convention designs a system of mutual controls between the branches, and at the same time makes one of the branches more powerful than the others, it puts into question – if not directly undermines – what it did in the first place. A system of "checks and balances" wants to affirm precisely the kind of institutional commitments that (typically) hyperpresidentialist systems come to deny. In this way, the "balanced" constitution is suddenly transformed into an "unbalanced" one.

Not surprisingly then, and as a result of the special powers that they received, Latin American presidents usually interfered with the working of the other branches, gained control over Congress, and managed to create a politically dependent

[14] The controversy arose after the government decided to exploit petroleum in an area that was "not only home to the most important biodiversity on the planet, but was also territory of indigenous groups living in voluntary isolation" (Salazar 2015, 31). In the face of this conflict, the National Assembly maintained that the government's "Development Plan" did not seriously affect the realization of "Good Living," while helped to promote other fundamental commitments, such as those to promote national growth and promote sustainable development. Examining similar responses by the Constitutional Court, see for example Salazar 2015, 30.

[15] I write "surprising" because this interpretation came to directly and dramatically challenge one of the most remarkable innovations brought by the new Constitution.

[16] As James Madison put it, in *Federalist Papers* n. 51 "the great security against a gradual concentration of the several powers in the same department, consists in giving to those who administer each department the necessary constitutional means and personal motives to resist encroachments of the others. The provision for defense must in this, as in all other cases, be made commensurate to the danger of attack. Ambition must be made to counteract ambition. The interest of the man must be connected with the constitutional rights of the place."

judiciary. These outcomes can also be associated with the dramatic history of democratic instability that characterized the region during the entire twentieth century (Halperín Donghi 2007). In sum, the choice of an "accumulation strategy" has been far from innocuous in Latin American history.

B. *Intersectional Tensions*

Now, what has probably been the most important and grave failure of the "accumulation" strategy in Latin America relates to the case of *intersectional* tensions. The example that best illustrates these tensions is one that affects the vast majority of contemporary Latin American constitutions, namely the choice of hyperpresidentialist organization of powers, which comes *together with* the adoption of progressive declarations of rights (i.e., declarations of rights that include numerous new participatory rights; see Gargarella 2010,). Indeed, the very "double trademark" of the regional constitutionalism – branches of government arranged according to rules that prevailed in the nineteenth century and rights arranged following those that gained predominance in the regional twentieth century constitutionalism – reveals its unusual two-sided democratic commitment. The structure of power thus corresponds – as it still does – to the weak democratic understanding of the nineteenth century: low popular participation, exclusion of entire sectors, and limited political rights – the mechanisms emblematic of wealth-based democracy. The "engine room" of the constitution – the section dedicated to organizing powers – thus remains virtually untouched, in line with the constitutional model that prevailed in America since the end of the eighteenth century (Gargarella 2013). Meanwhile, the new declarations of rights appear linked to "next generation" democratic discourse and principles. These aim for broad popular participation, for which support is sought in various ways: institutional opportunities are opened to the public for increased decision making and control power (establishing recall elections, etc.); political rights are expanded; and, simultaneously, commitments are made to social rights with the aim of promoting even more political participation of majorities (all of which, I will insist, are subject to several limitations).

There is an obvious problem – I submit – when, seeking to promote popular participation, one relies on those whose power will be undermined, once such participation becomes effective.[17] To put it even more brutally: there is an obvious problem

[17] The problem identified is not dissipated by the allegation that the great "enemy" of popular political participation is "concentrated economic power" (Unger 1987). It is not only that a more extensive response to the problem is needed, it is also true that the response ignores, to begin with, the (cited) risks of maintaining concentrated political power (particularly in relation to the fore-mentioned objective of diluting political power) and, secondly, it ignores the ways that concentrated political power tends to interact with or favor directly economic concentration.

when you ask help from concentrated power to disperse it. It does not make sense to advocate for the democratization of power on behalf of the marginalized while maintaining concentrated political power. In those cases, one part of the constitution tends to begin working against the enforcement of the other part. Typically – one can anticipate it – a strong executive will tend to block all those initiatives capable of "empowering" the citizenry (or other breaches of power), and thus capable of questioning or undermining his or her own authority. In cases of this kind, more than in any other, the "accumulation strategy" shows its shortcomings. Moreover, those tensions help us explain and understand one of the main failures of contemporary Latin American contemporary, which relates to the following question: why do these generous lists of social, political, economic, and multicultural rights (rights that have been once and again included in these constitutions) still remain virtually unapplied?

VIII. CONCLUSION

In this chapter, I reflected on the drafting of constitutions in the context of divided societies, this is to say societies characterized by the fact of pluralism. In the first part of the chapter, I described four different drafting strategies, which have been present in the early history of constitutionalism: imposition, silence, synthesis, and accumulation. In the second part, I focused my attention on the analysis of the "accumulation strategy" that – I maintained – was the most important and influential choice adopted by constitution makers in the early constitutional history of the Americas. I critically examined that choice, which – I claimed – creates unnecessary and unjustified tensions and inefficacies in the actual working of constitutions.

REFERENCES

Alberdi, J. B. (1981). *Bases y puntos de partida para la organizaciónpolítica de la República Argentina.*Buenos Aires: Plus Ultra.

Dixon, R., and Ginsburg, T. (2011). "Deciding Not to Decide."*International Journal of Constitutional Design* 636.

Elkins, Z., Ginsburg, T., and Blount, J. (2008). "The Citizen as Founder: Public Participation in Constitutional Approval." *Temple Law Review* 81(2), 361–82.

Elkins, Z., Ginsburg, T., and Melton, J. (2009). *The Lifespan of Written Constitution.* New York, NY: Cambridge University Press.

Elster, J. (1995). "Forces and Mechanisms in the Constitution-Making Process." *Duke University School of Law* 45(1), 364–496.

Gargarella, R., Domingo, P., and Roux, T., eds. (2006). *Courts and Social Transformation in New Democracies.* London: Routledge.

Gargarella, R. (2010). *The Legal Foundations of Inequality.* Cambridge: Cambridge University Press.

(2011). *La justiciafrente al gobierno*. Quito: Corte Constitucional.
(2013). *Latin American Constitutionalism*. Oxford: Oxford University Press.
Ginsburg, T., Elkins, Z., andBlount, J. (2009). "Does the Process of Constitution-Making Matter?" *Annual Review of Law and Social Science* 5, 201–23.
Halperín Donghi, T. (2007). *Historia Contemporánea de América Latina*. Buenos Aires: Alianza.
Hamilton, A., Madison, J., and Jay, J. (1988). *The Federalist Papers*. New York, NY: Bantam Books.
Horowitz, D. (2002). "Constitutional Design: Proposals versus Processes." In A. Reynolds (ed.), *The Architecture of Democracy: Constitutional Design, Conflict Management, and Democracy*, 15–36. Oxford: Oxford University Press.
Lerner, H. (2013). *Making Constitutions in Deeply Divided Societies*. Cambridge: Cambridge University Press.
Nino, C. (1996). *The Constitution of Deliberative Democracy*. New Haven, CT: Yale University Press.
Ordeshook, P. (1993)."Some Rules of Constitutional Design." In E. Franker Paul, F. Miller, and J. Paul (eds.), *Liberalism and the Economic Order*, 198–232. Cambridge: Cambridge University Press.
(2001). "Are 'Western' Constitutions Relevant to Anything Other than the Countries They Serve?"In S. Voigt and H.-J. Wagener (eds.), *Constitutions, Market and the Law*, 3–24. Cheltenham: Elgar.
Rawls, J. (1987)."The Idea of an Overlapping Consensus." *Oxford Journal of Legal Studies* 7(1), 1–25.
(1991).*Political Liberalism*. New York, NY: Columbia University Press.
Salazar, D. (2015). "My Power in the Constitution: The Perversion of the Rule of Law in Ecuador." SELA, Yale University. Retrieved from: www.law.yale.edu/sites/default/files/documents/pdf/SELA15_Salazar_CV_Eng.pdf
Sills, D., ed. (1968). *International Encyclopedia of Social Sciences*. New York, NY: The Free Press.
Silva Castro, R. (1969). *Juan Egaña. Antología*. Santiago de Chile: Editora Andrés Bello.
Sunstein, C. (1996). "The Supreme Court 1995 Term: Foreword: Living Things Undecided." *Harvard Law Review* 110, 6.
(2001). *One Case at a Time*. Cambridge, MA: Harvard University Press.
Unger, R. (1987). "El sistema de gobiernoque le conviene a Brasil." In *Presidencialismo vs. Parlamentarismo*. Buenos Aires: Consejo para la Consolidación de la Democracia.
Voigt, S. (2003)."The Consequences of Popular Participation in Constitutional Choice: Towards a Comparative Analysis." In A. van Aaken, C. List, and C. Luetgeeds (eds.), *Deliberation and Decision*, 199–229. Aldershot: Ashgate.
Widner, J. (2008). "Constitution Writing in Post-Conflict Settings: An Overview." *William & Mary Law Review* 49(4), 1513.
Zevada, R. (1972). *La luchapor la libertad en el congresoconstituyente de 1857. El pensamiento de Ponciano Arriaga*. México: Ed. NuestroTiempo.

2

Constituent Assemblies in Democratic Regimes

The Problem of a Legally Limited Convention

Gabriel L. Negretto

The election or appointment of an assembly responsible for drafting a new constitution has historically been associated with episodes of deep political transformation, such as revolutions or regime change. However, these bodies are also invoked when it is necessary to replace a constitution within an established democracy. It is argued that compared to a constituent legislature, an assembly specially commissioned to write a constitution may better reflect citizens' preferences and promote an impartial constitutional design. From this perspective, conventions may help to create a more solid democratic foundation for new constitutions, contribute to a more balanced distribution of powers among state authorities, and ensure constitutional stability.

In this chapter, I make the central claim that these advantages are not inherent to conventions. Whether a constituent assembly is more or less able to reflect the diversity of interests and views of the electorate or prevent a partisan design depends on institutional rules unrelated to the nature of its task. I also propose that these bodies may incur significant risks when a constitution is replaced within a democratic regime. To preserve the stability and continuity of a democratic order, a constituent assembly must work within the limits of a preestablished legal regulation. Yet conventions often transgress their mandate by asserting their right to express or submit their decisions to the legally unbound power of the people. This claim to act on behalf of the people increases the likelihood of conflicts between the convention and established institutions and, more importantly, facilitates the use of this body by a dominant political group to legitimize its capture of state power. I support these arguments with a critical analysis of normative theories of constitution making, a review of the nature of conventions in American constitutional law and history,

I am grateful for the comments made by Jon Elster, Hélène Landemore, Hanna Lerner, Andrew Arato, José Antonio Cheibub, and the editors of this book on a previous version of this chapter.

and a comparative study of episodes of constitution making by conventions in Latin American democracies from 1900 to 2010.

The chapter starts with an analysis of the different bodies that may participate in constitution making. The second section discusses the relative benefits of constituent conventions vis-à-vis constituent legislatures. The third section assesses the problem of a legally limited convention in light of the history and theory of conventions in American constitutional law. The fourth section analyzes recent cases of constitution making by conventions in Latin American democracies. A brief conclusion follows.

I. CONSTITUENT ASSEMBLIES

A variety of collective bodies may be involved during a constitution-making process: constitutional commissions, executive bodies, round tables, national conferences, constituent conventions, and constituent legislatures. The last two, however, are the most common instances that work as true constituent assemblies where constitutional texts are deliberated, negotiated, and finally approved, particularly in democratic settings.[1] I will thus restrict my analysis to them.

Constituent conventions are collective bodies created for the sole or primary purpose of adopting or proposing a new constitution.[2] According to this definition, the key feature of these bodies is that they must be dissolved after the approval of a new constitutional text.[3] Although conventions can also be used to adopt or propose revisions to the existing constitution, throughout this chapter I will mainly focus on their constituent function.

In historical and comparative perspective, constituent conventions are rare. The paradigmatic example of this assembly, which inspired much of the existing theorization around it, was the Philadelphia Convention of 1787. Similar cases can be found in the Norwegian constituent assembly of 1814, the Danish constituent

[1] In an analysis of 411 episodes of constitutional replacement that took place around the world between 1789 and 2005, Ginsburg, Elkins, and Blount (2009, 213) found that in most cases the approval body was either a constituent convention (103 observations) or a constituent legislature (178 observations).

[2] Some authors use the term "constitutional convention," common in the American constitutional tradition, to denote constitution-making bodies commissioned to adopt a new constitution. See Elster (2006). As Roger Hoar points out, however, the adjective "constitutional" is confusing because it may refer to both the specific task of the assembly and its status within the existing legal order. Since special conventions may or may not be authorized by the existing constitution, it would be odd to distinguish between constitutional and extraconstitutional (or unconstitutional) constituent conventions (see Hoar 1917, 30). For this reason, throughout this text I will use the generic term "constituent convention" or simply "convention" to refer only to the nature of the task of this body.

[3] This includes as conventions assemblies whose central task was drafting a new constitution although they occasionally performed legislative activities for a short period of time, until a new legislature was elected. In this regard, I follow the view of historian Marc Kruman (1997, 15–33).

assembly of 1848–9, the German convention of 1948–9, and the Portuguese constituent assembly of 1976. In general, however, constituent conventions have been used in relatively few countries or regions. In fact, most of the constituent conventions that have existed in the world were created in the American states and in Latin American countries.

According to Hoar (1917, 4) the New Hampshire conventions of 1778 and 1781–3 and the Massachusetts convention of 1780 initiated the convention movement in the United States. The practice proliferated throughout the nineteenth century, and several states used these bodies during the twentieth century. Since the 1970s, however, there has been a sharp decline in the use of conventions for replacing or revising constitutions (see Williams 1996). Experts in American state constitutional law have counted 233 constituent conventions between 1776 and 2005 (Dinan 2006, 7–8).

At the national level, constituent conventions have also been frequent in Latin America.[4] Most of the first constitutions enacted after independence were made by assemblies that, along with framing a new constitution, were responsible for performing the role of an ordinary legislature. Constituent conventions emerged over time, however, with the adoption of the 1830 constitutions of Colombia and Venezuela, the 1853 constitution of Argentina, the 1857 constitution of Mexico, and the 1870 constitution of Paraguay. The use of these bodies continued well into the twentieth century and the first decade of the twenty-first century. According to Negretto (2017a), of a total of eighty-three constitution-making processes that took place in the region from 1900 to 2014, twenty-six (31 percent) used a special convention as a constituent body.

It is important to note that whereas conventions have been observed in a wide variety of political settings, they have rarely been used to replace a constitution within a democratic regime. From 1900 to 2015, twenty-five constitutions had been created in the world in the context of a democratic regime at least five years old.[5] Of these constitutions, only five, all located in Latin America, have been approved by

4 In a sample of 160 constitution-making episodes around the world from 1780 to 2012, Mendez and Wheatley (2013, 29) find that twelve of the twenty-three events that used constituent conventions were located in the Latin American region.

5 These constitutions are: Denmark 1915, Denmark 1953, Finland 2000, France 1958, Greece 1952, Iceland 1944, Ireland 1937, Sweden 1974, Switzerland 1999, Hungary 2011, Poland 1997, Ukraine 1996, Kenya 2010, Thailand 1997, Nepal 2015, Sri Lanka 1972, Bolivia 2009, Ecuador 1998, Ecuador 2008, Colombia 1991, Uruguay 1952, Uruguay 1967, Venezuela 1999, Dominican Republic 2010, and Trinidad and Tobago 1976. A constitution was considered to be new when its drafters claimed it was new and when state institutions and official sources in the country acknowledged the text as such (Negretto 2012, 2017b). Democratic years were coded based on Boix, Miller, and Rosatto's database (2010).

constituent conventions. Within this group, the oldest democracy in which a constituent convention was elected was that of Colombia, established in 1958.[6]

In contrast to conventions, assemblies that work as ordinary legislatures both during the drafting and after the approval of a new constitution are very common. These bodies differ from the point of view of the source of their constituent authority. Based on this perspective, Jon Elster (2006, 2013) has distinguished between three different types of mixed constitution-making bodies: mandated constituent legislatures, self-created constituent legislatures, and self-created legislating assemblies. Although this classification is very useful, it demands a few adjustments.

Mandated constituent legislatures are assemblies elected to enact a new constitution and pass ordinary legislation. They are frequently used in transitions to democracy where there is either no legislature at the beginning of the process or the existing one lacks legitimacy to assume a constituent function. Examples of these bodies can be found in the making of the 1975 Greek constitution, the first 1946 French constitution (rejected by voters), the 1931 and 1978 Spanish constitutions, the 1992 Slovakian constitution, and the 1946 and 1988 Brazilian constitutions.

Self-created constituent legislatures are ordinary legislatures that decide on their own authority to transform themselves into a constituent body. As regards these bodies, Jon Elster (2006, 182) does not clarify on what basis does a legislature decide to take on the task of writing a new constitution except that it is not derived from an electoral mandate. To make the adjective "self-created" as precise as possible, however, the term should be restricted to legislative assemblies that assume a constituent task following a political decision made by the incumbent government or existing legislative parties without any form of authorization, either electoral or legal.

These bodies have been common during revolutions and independence processes. For instance, legislatures self-appointed as constituent assemblies approved the 1776 constitutions of New Hampshire, South Carolina, and Virginia (see Kruman 1997, 22).[7] We may also find this type of body in the adoption of some independence constitutions in Eastern Europe, such as those of Croatia in 1990 and Estonia in 1992 (Kiris 1991; Mirth 1992). The drafting of a new constitution by a self-appointed constituent legislature also works as a nonlegal but politically expedient method of replacing constitutions in authoritarian regimes.[8] Constitution-making bodies of this type adopted most constitutions in Bolivia during the twentieth century and in Venezuela from 1904 to 1925.

[6] The 2010–11 Icelandic constitutional assembly is the only case of a convention elected outside Latin America and in a long-standing democracy for the purpose of replacing the existing constitution. So far, however, the constitution produced by this convention has not been put into force.

[7] Hoar (1917, 4) also includes in this category the 1776 constitutions of North Carolina, Georgia, and New Jersey.

[8] On constitution making in authoritarian regimes, see Negretto (2014).

Self-created legislating assemblies are a hybrid type of mixed body, intermediate between constituent conventions and ordinary legislatures. These are constituent assemblies that were supposed to dissolve after enacting a new constitution, but decided on their own authority to continue as ordinary legislatures. The Indian constituent assembly of 1946–50 and the 1934 constituent assembly of Brazil may fit this category.

Elster's classification is not exhaustive, however. A missing category of mixed constituent bodies is what we may call constitutionally authorized constituent legislatures. These are ordinary legislatures that can turn themselves into constituent bodies following a procedure established in the existing constitution or legal instrument of constitutional status. This occurs when the existing reform procedure enables the ordinary legislature to replace the constitution in force. Constitutionally authorized constituent legislatures have been used in some transitions to democracy where the old constitution was amended or an interim constitution was created to enable parliament to enact a new constitution.[9] This mechanism has been particularly important, however, in the adoption of new constitutions within established democratic orders. In particular, this type of legislature has been used to pass seventeen of the twenty-five constitutions enacted in a democratic regime from 1900 to 2015.

Some parliamentary systems have enabled the legislative assembly to adopt new constitutions because their revision procedure makes no distinction between piecemeal amendments and wholesale replacements. In 1953, the Danish parliament adopted a new constitution following the 1915 Constitutional Act, which established a uniform procedure of constitutional reform by the legislature (Krunke 2013). In 1974 the Swedish parliament replaced the 1809 instrument of government following the amendment process regulated in this document (Congleton 2003). The Finnish parliament passed a new constitution in 2000 using a reform process described in the 1928 Constitutional Act (Suksi 2011). In all these cases, the procedure required a new parliamentary election before the legislature could approve the desired constitutional changes and, in the case of Denmark, also ratification of the reform in a popular referendum.

A few separation-of-powers systems have also authorized the legislature to either amend or replace the constitution, sometimes distinguishing each procedure. In the case of Uruguay, all constitutions since 1934 have authorized the legislature to propose and pass either partial or total reforms, with ratification in a referendum. This provided the basis for the adoption of the 1942, 1952, and 1967 constitutions (see Negretto 2017a). The system is similar in Switzerland, although in this country

9 The enactment of Slovenia's 1991 constitution could be used as an example of the former and the 1998 Albanian constitution of the latter.

a clearer distinction exists between amendments and replacements. It was based on this distinction that the Swiss parliament adopted a new constitution in 1999 (see Biaggini 2011).

II. ARE CONVENTIONS INHERENTLY SUPERIOR CONSTITUENT ASSEMBLIES?

Constituent conventions have a privileged position within normative theories of constitution making. The traditional argument in favor of conventions derives from the theory of constituent power. This theory, as formulated by key participants of the American and French revolutions such as James Wilson, Thomas Paine, Thomas Jefferson, and Siéyes, postulates that the right to create and replace constitutions belongs to the people, not to government bodies. Given this right, constitutions should be adopted or altered only by special assemblies independent of constituted authorities, in particular of those responsible for enacting ordinary laws (see Colon-Ríos 2012). As Jefferson argued in his *Notes on the State of Virginia*, if the constitution is an act above the powers of the ordinary legislature, the legislature should not be allowed to alter constitutional provisions by its own decision. Otherwise, legislators would be judges in their own causes.[10]

Because their members are selected for the exclusive purpose of writing a new constitution, special conventions are also seen as producing documents with a high level of democratic legitimacy. Bruce Ackerman (1994) recommended using the American model of constituent convention in Eastern Europe to provide new constitutions in this region with a strong democratic foundation. More generally, Jon Elster has argued that "constitutions produced by conventions tend to have greater legitimacy and hence tend to enjoy greater stability" (2006, 185). In his opinion, conventions can be elected with a view to representing a variety of interests and programs rather than maximizing the representation of a particular group or ensuring stable governance, as might occur with a constituent legislature. A convention would also provide voters with the opportunity to elect delegates based on their reform proposals and not on other considerations (Elster 2006, 186–9).

A very different type of normative argument in favor of constituent conventions is epistemic in nature. According to Elster (2013,202), constituent conventions may promote active and moral aptitude in the framers by inducing full attention and concentration on the task they were commissioned to do and by reducing the impact of institutional interests on their decisions.[11] Unlike constituent legislatures, which take

[10] See *Notes on the State of Virginia*, in Jefferson (1984), 249–50.

[11] This argument derives from a more general position about procedural rules. According to Elster, these rules should be designed with an eye to removing obstacles to good decisions, without pursuing an ideal of what those decisions should be (Elster 2013, 3).

responsibility for legislative and constitutional decisions at the same time, constituent conventions enable the framers to hold sustained and focused deliberations on constitutional issues alone (Elster 2013, 212). In addition, members of a constituent legislature are more likely than delegates to a constituent convention to be biased toward the legislature in the design of the machinery of government. Just as an executive constitution-making body would write an important role for itself in the constitution, so a constituent legislature would give a preponderant importance to the legislative branch at the expense of the executive and the judiciary (Elster 1995, 2006, 2012, 2013).

From a normative point of view about the design of a democratic constitution-making process, it makes sense to choose a constituent body that gives more weight to the preferences of citizens than to those of state authorities and creates a sense of collective ownership over the new text. It is also defensible from an epistemic perspective to select a constituent assembly that removes cognitive biases and self-interest. It is not clear, however, that a constituent convention has an inherent advantage over any type of constituent legislature on these grounds.

The principle of separation between constituent and constituted powers demands that legislators should act within the limits of the powers that the people delegated to them under the constitution. This implies that they cannot alter those powers on their own authority. But why could legislators not have a constituent role if they are explicitly authorized by voters to adopt a new constitution? Moreover, popular ratification of the changes may also be required so that legislators' margin of autonomous decision is even more restricted. In the end, both constituent conventions and legislatures are representative bodies. So, unless one thinks that only the election of a special convention counts as an authentic expression of the constituent power of the people, there is no reason to think that constitutions should always be made by special conventions.

A constitution adopted by a popularly elected convention has an obviously stronger claim to democratic legitimacy than one produced by a legislature that appoints itself as constituent body. Yet it is not clear why a constitutional text approved by a legislature elected to have an initial constituent function or authorized to assume this role after an intervening democratic election would be any less legitimate. In the first case, one may argue that a body elected to have a legislative and a constituent function would lead voters to cast their votes based on considerations alien to the content of the new constitution, such as general party platforms or the personal traits of a candidate. A similar set of motivations, however, may explain voters' preferences when – as is often the case – those who compete for a position in a convention do not have yet well-formed preferences about their own reform proposals during the election. When the legislature is allowed to assume a constituent function only after an intervening election, the idea of a democratic deficit is even less persuasive because in this case the election of a new legislature should be determined primarily by public debates about constitutional reform.

It is true that unlike legislators, who are usually elected on a partisan basis, delegates to conventions may be partially elected, elected as independents, appointed, or randomly selected. This range of options enables conventions to enhance representation by incorporating ordinary citizens and traditionally excluded groups. In the vast majority of cases, however, constituent conventions (particularly after 1900) have been elected on a partisan basis, just like a constituent legislature.[12] In this situation, political diversity in the assembly hinges on the proportionality of the system under which its members are elected. The number of views that have an influence on final decisions also depends on the decision rule. If one party wins a bare majority of seats in the assembly, its influence over final decisions would be diminished if some form of qualified majority were required to pass the new constitution. From this perspective, a constituent legislature that is elected by a proportional formula and makes decisions by qualified majority is likely to be more inclusive in both representation and actual decisions than a convention that is elected by plurality and approves changes by simple majority.[13]

The proposal that conventions promote the active aptitude of framers to focus on constitutional issues alone is the most persuasive argument in favor of these bodies. Reformers who must divide their time between designing a constitution and making ordinary legislative decisions may not only confuse the two tasks, writing into the constitution matters that are better left to statute, but also have less time to concentrate on the discussion of constitutional provisions. This may detract from the quality of constitutional design. However, mixed assemblies may also achieve a relatively efficient division of labor between lawmaking and constituent activities. Just as ordinary parliaments have a committee system to promote the specialization of legislators on certain matters, nothing prevents a constituent legislature from creating an internal division of labor so that a subgroup of the assembly concentrates on the drafting of the constitution. For instance, during the making of the 1961 Venezuelan constitution a broadly representative bicameral commission was responsible for submitting

12 So far, assemblies entirely composed of randomly selected citizens have been used only in electoral, not in constitutional reform. The 2012–14 Irish convention, responsible for proposing amendments, had a mixed composition: two-thirds of its members were randomly selected citizens and one-third appointed politicians. The 2010 Icelandic convention is the only example of a convention elected on a nonpartisan basis.

13 Although qualified majority is rarely used as a threshold to pass a new constitution, it is more common among constituent legislatures than among conventions. In an ongoing research on the comparative features of constitution making processes across the world, I found that from a sample of 124 constitution-making bodies created between 1900 and 2015, only 32 used a qualified majority to pass the constitution. Among these cases, however, 27 correspond to constituent legislatures and only 5 to conventions. These data can be obtained from the author on request.

the draft of the new constitution to the plenary of Congress (see Planchart Manrique 1988).[14]

The idea that a legislature would be tempted to benefit itself at the expense of other branches of government is based on the assumption that the interests of existing institutions are articulated primarily through the organizational form of the constituent body. In most democratic contexts, however, popular representation in both constituent conventions and constituent legislatures is channeled through political parties. This means that the institutional preferences of constitution makers are more likely to be shaped by the concrete interests of their parties than by the abstract interest of the collective body in which they gather as representatives of the people. As politicians, constitution makers tend to defend the institutional interests of their parties because doing so benefits them individually, by helping them win office and have influence over important decisions (see Negretto 2013). For this reason, reformers who have a partisan link with the legislature or the executive are prone to making constitutional choices that favor these branches regardless of whether the constituent body is a legislature or a convention.

If the interests of existing institutions are represented through the parties that control or expect to control them, one way to induce impartiality in constitution making would be to forbid parties from participating in the constituent body. This would be the case of assemblies made up of randomly selected citizens or delegates elected on a nonpartisan basis. This solution, however, would imply that removing the influence of group and institutional interests does not depend on the type of body per se, but on its composition. Another possibility is to allow political parties to field candidates for the election of delegates but to postpone the implementation of the new constitution until some time after it was adopted. This would increase the level of uncertainty of constitution makers regarding which institutions would benefit them most, thus inducing a more impartial constitutional design (see Elster 1995, 1997).[15] However, if this impartial perspective effectively takes place it would derive from the delay in implementing the constitution, not from the nature of the constituent body.

Although many arguments in support of constituent conventions are based on principle and thus not subject to empirical validation, some make implicit or explicit causal claims that can be observed. For instance, if constitutions adopted by constituent conventions have a stronger democratic foundation than those written by constituent legislatures, then the former should last longer than the latter. More

[14] Something similar happened with the 1998 Albanian constitution, whose draft was made by a representative constitutional commission rather than by the parliament as a whole. See Carlson (2010).

[15] Prohibiting constitution makers from competing in future elections may reduce the influence of their personal interests in constitutional choice but is not likely to prevent them from advancing the interests of their parties.

explicitly, if constituent legislatures are prone to giving undue influence to legislative interests, constitutions produced by them should invest the executive and the judicial branch with less power than a convention would. There are several methodological problems in testing these claims, the most important of which is the large number of confounding variables potentially involved in measuring the causal effects of procedural rules. The empirical analyses performed so far, however, do not seem to validate those claims.

There is no cross-regional test available on the durability of constitutions under different constituent bodies. Yet the finding of recent empirical works that lengthier and more detailed constitutions survive longer (see Hammons 1999; Elkins et al. 2009) suggests the plausible hypothesis that legislatures, at least as regards the durability of the constitution, might be better constituent bodies than special conventions. Members of organized groups are likely to have stronger influence on members of a permanent legislature than on delegates to a temporary assembly. Being concerned with reelection, legislators are also likely to pay more attention to the interests of these groups than are delegates of a special convention. If this assumption is correct, then legislators may be more inclined to write longer and more detailed provisions into the constitution to make explicit to their constituents how their interests have been protected. These constituents, in turn, would have more incentives to support the constitution in the long run. In a more direct analysis of the impact of constituent conventions vis-à-vis constituent legislatures, but looking only at Latin American cases, Negretto (2017a) finds that there is no significant difference between the effects of these bodies on the durability of constitutions.

Whether constituent legislatures engage in self-dealing has been tested by Ginsburg, Elkins, and Blount (2009, 213), based on a sample of 411 episodes of constitution making around the world from 1789 to 2005. Correlating the use of pure and mixed constituent assemblies with an index of parliamentary powers, they conclude that there is no evidence to sustain the claim that constituent legislatures are more likely to strengthen the powers of the legislature. These results may be questionable, however. The sample used by Ginsburg et al. includes both democratic and authoritarian constitution-making episodes, so that the units of observation are too heterogeneous to make a reliable comparison possible (see Elster 2013). The same finding has been reported, however, in tests restricted to constitutions made under competitive conditions. Based on an analysis of thirty-one episodes of competitive constitution making in Latin America from 1900 to 2014, Negretto (2017a) shows that, at least in the context of presidential regimes, choosing a special convention or a constituent legislature does not make any difference to the allocation of powers between the different branches of government.[16]

[16] Although the number of observations in the competitive sample is small, the results also hold using the complete dataset of eighty-three episodes of constitution making in Latin America (both democratic

To sum up, the superiority of constituent conventions over constituent legislatures, regardless of the election, composition, or decision-making procedures of each body, has no support on theoretical or empirical grounds. A legislature explicitly authorized by voters to pass fundamental constitutional changes (either from the beginning or after an intervening election) can have the same democratic credentials as an elected constituent convention and both can represent a plurality of interests and views if they are elected by inclusive electoral rules or make decisions by qualified majority. A constituent legislature with an internal division of labor may also promote an adequate level of specialization on constituent tasks. As for the influence of group and institutional interests on design, the typical partisan convention is not more immune to them than a constituent legislature is.

In addition to the fact that constituent conventions have no inherent advantages, the usual convention made up of political parties may incur significant risks when a new constitution is adopted within an existing democratic regime. Constitutions adopted in a democratic regime may seek to overcome a political or institutional crisis, modernize existing structures, or further democratization.[17] Whatever the objective, however, the process should not have any feature that might jeopardize the stability and continuity of the political regime. This requires that the constitution-making body be able to coexist peacefully with the existing constituted powers and that its mission and powers are executed according to a preestablished legal regulation. Constituent conventions, however, are prone to violating these requirements.

A special convention is likely to enter into several types of conflict with the ordinary legislature. Some of these conflicts may refer to minor jurisdictional issues. A convention, for instance, may decide to modify the deadline the legislature imposed to approve the new constitution. Yet other conflicts could revolve around whether the convention has sovereign, legally unlimited power. If a statute regulates the tasks and powers of the convention, it may reject these limitations based on the idea that the legislature is politically inferior to the convention. A dominant political group could use this conflict to justify its usurpation of legislative functions or interference with the judiciary (see Partlett 2012; Landau 2013; Negretto 2016). To be sure, a legislature dominated by a single party or coalition can also act arbitrarily or transgress the constitution. Yet a legislative assembly cannot easily legitimize those actions by claiming to be outside and above the existing constitutional order, as conventions often do.

One possible way to minimize these risks in a democratic regime is making the convention a regular organ for the revision or replacement of the constitution. This

and authoritarian) from 1900 to 2014. In the few cases where the executive was directly involved in constitution making, there was an expected impact on design, namely toward the strengthening of executive powers.

[17] On the causes of constitution making in democratic regimes, see Negretto (2017b).

means, at a minimum, establishing the conditions and procedure under which a convention is called, but it can also include rules about the election, powers, and decision-making procedures of the assembly. The key objective of this regulation is to turn the convention into an institution regulated by and subordinated to the existing constitution and without jurisdiction over other state powers. Although most constitutions in the world do not foresee the election of a special convention for their replacement, that regulation could in principle be created. In this regard, the experience of American states shows that in the presence of a tradition of constitutional regulation of conventions, these bodies can in general fulfill a legally limited function. As we will see, however, the history of constituent conventions in America also shows the problems involved in subjecting a special convention to the existing legal order.

III. THE PROBLEM OF A LEGALLY LIMITED CONVENTION IN AMERICAN CONSTITUTIONAL LAW

According to some authors, the crucial distinction between democratic constitution-making bodies is not whether they specialize on writing a new constitution but whether they claim to embody sovereign power. In this vein, Arato argues that nonsovereign assemblies are normatively superior to sovereign bodies for the purpose of providing the constitution with a solid democratic foundation (see Arato 1995, 2015). He mentions as examples of the former the 1787 Federal Convention and some of the Round Tables that organized democratic transitions in Eastern Europe after 1989, and as example of the latter the 1789–91 *Assemblée Constituante* in France.[18] This distinction between sovereign and nonsovereign assemblies is consistent with the use of the term "constitutional convention" in American constitutional law, which refers not only to the specific mandate of this assembly but also to the execution of this mandate within the frame of existing laws.[19] However, a close analysis of that legal tradition at both the local and the federal level reveals that drawing a strict line of demarcation between a legally limited and a legally unbounded convention is problematic.

There are some issues on which all scholars on the use of conventions in American constitutional law seem to agree. One of them is that a convention is both "constitutional" and "legal" (rather than irregular, illegal, or revolutionary) if it is called

[18] In the end, and according to his theory of postsovereign constitution making, Arato considers that a two-stage process consisting of the drafting of an interim constitution by a nonelected round table followed by the drafting of the final constitution by a freely elected constituent legislature is normatively superior to a convention because the former is more effective in preventing authoritarian forms. See Arato (2015, 123–4).

[19] See Hoar (1917, 30) and footnote 2.

by the existing legislature following explicit constitutional provisions.[20] There also seems to exist a consensus that whenever the constitution is silent about revision procedures, a convention would still be legal if the legislature enables its election and regulates its operation through statutory law.[21] Based on this concept, one may distinguish among three types of conventions: constitutional, extraconstitutional but legal, and extraconstitutional and illegal.[22] In other words, only a convention called in the absence of constitutional provisions *and* without the consent of the existing legislature would be outside the existing legal order. The decisions of this convention could become valid only if a revolution eventually succeeds in imposing the new legality by force.

The archetypal example of an illegal or revolutionary convention is that of the 1841 "People's Convention" of Rhode Island.[23] In the absence of an amendment procedure in the state's colonial charter and in reaction to the government's opposition to revising the constitution to expand the franchise, members of the so-called suffrage movement called a convention commissioned to enact a new constitution. The assembly was elected in an irregular election and the constitution it enacted was ratified in an unofficial referendum. A majority of the total number of adult male residents of the state supported the constitution, but many of those who voted for it were not qualified to vote under the existing laws. Although new executive and legislative authorities were elected under the new constitution, the rebel government failed to impose itself. The federal government sided with the Charter government, and members of the suffrage movement were put in jail or forced to leave the state (see Thompson 2001). Although it did not rule on the merits of the case, the US Supreme Court implicitly acknowledged the illegality of the People's Convention based on the recognition that the courts of Rhode Island and the president of the United States made of the Charter government as the only legal authority in the state.[24]

Beyond this case, however, the legal foundation of a wide variety of conventions and convention acts is uncertain. Can a convention be legal if it is convened by the legislature against explicit constitutional provisions regulating a different mode of revision? The 1789 Pennsylvania Convention, the 1791 Delaware Convention, and the 1850 Maryland Convention were all called by the legislature in transgression of the existing revision procedures. Some scholars regard these bodies as irregular and illegal because in their view the legislature had no power to contravene the Constitution (see Jameson, 1887, 216–18). Others, however, argue that these

[20] See Jameson (1887, 209–69) and Hoar (1917, 30–7; 38–57).

[21] Ibid.

[22] See the Pennsylvania Supreme Court ruling *Wells v. Bain* (1872), in Hoar (1917, 16–17).

[23] See Jameson (1887, 218–37), Dodd (1921, 498), and Hoar (1917, 20–2).

[24] See *Luther v. Borden* (1849), in Jameson (1887, 224–42).

conventions are extraconstitutional but legal nonetheless because the electorate supported them either before the legislature decided to call the convention or at the time of voting for its delegates (see Hoar 1917, 51–7).[25] Given these contradictory interpretations of the same episodes, one is forced to conclude that the history of conventions in American constitutional law does not provide unambiguous guidance to the use of conventions outside the amendment procedures in force.

Although this might seem a technical matter, at its root the problem revolves around an important normative question: where does the authority of conventions come from? If their authority originates in the constitution or, in case of no regulation, in a legislative act, then popular approval cannot validate a transgression of the legal framework. If, however, the authority of conventions comes directly from the people speaking through the electorate, then it does not matter whether the constitution is silent or establishes a different procedure: a convention would still be legal if it is approved by voters. Neither the practice nor the jurisprudence on constituent conventions provides decisive support to either theory.[26] Yet the position one takes on this issue is crucial because it will also determine how we assess the case of a convention that after being called regularly and according to existing procedures makes decisions that violate the legal limits imposed on its commission.

Most state conventions elected since the nineteenth century have submitted their proposals of reform to popular approval (see Dodd 1921, 68–70). Some authors even think that conventions have the duty to ratify their revisions in a referendum if the constitution or the law is silent about it (see Jameson 1887, 490–7). Consider now the effect of legal transgressions of the convention in the light of popular ratification. If the authority of conventions comes directly from the people speaking through the electorate, then any violation of the legal limits imposed on their tasks can be validated ex post if voters ratify the decisions of the convention in a referendum. These limits may refer to its commission to amend the constitution rather than to create a new one, the timeframe of its work, its decision-making procedures, or the prohibition of engaging in ordinary lawmaking.[27]

There is no better example of the ambiguity of the subjection of constituent conventions to the law than the actions of the Federal Convention of 1787.[28]

25 Whereas the 1789 Pennsylvania Convention was called after the legislature made an informal inquiry to determine whether the people wanted a convention, the 1791 Delaware Convention was called by the legislature and elected by the people without any initial authorization. See Jameson (1887, 213–16).

26 See the different views of Dodd (chapter 3) and Hoar (chapter 5) in analyzing the precedents about who has the authority to call and bind conventions.

27 Hoar shows that in several cases where the convention engaged in ordinary lawmaking, state court decisions invalidated those acts not because the convention had no power to do so but because it did not submit the decision to popular approval. See Hoar (1917, 144).

28 On the legality or illegality of the actions of the Federal Convention, see Kay (1987), Amar (1994), and Ackerman and Kaytal (1995).

This convention produced a new constitution instead of amending the Articles of the Confederation as mandated. It also violated the existing amendment process by requiring ratification by nine instead of thirteen states and replacing state legislatures by popularly elected conventions as ratification bodies. Although the Continental Congress and state legislatures implicitly acquiesced to these actions, it was apparent that the convention exceeded its mandate. Madison justified the convention with two central arguments. The first was that since the people are unable to act spontaneously and universally to alter or abolish their government when they deem it necessary, great constitutional transformations usually depend on irregular and unauthorized propositions made by a group of representatives. The second argument was that these actions entail no risk as long as the people themselves are the ones who decide whether to approve the proposed changes.[29] Popular ratification, in other words, removes any preceding errors or irregularities.

The distinction between a French, "legally unbound" model, and an American, "legally limited" type of constituent assembly is blurred if the latter is assumed to be free to do anything, even breaking the law, as long as the sovereign people ratifies its decisions ex post. The potentially arbitrary power of a convention explains why Madison considered Jefferson's idea of using periodical conventions a risky method to alter the constitution or resolve constitutional controversies.[30] It also explains why the convention mechanism mentioned in Article V of the US Constitution has never been used at the federal level. It is not only unclear how but whether the tasks and powers of this assembly could be legally limited (see Dellinger 1979; Vile 1991, 1993).

It is true that with the exception of the secession and reconstruction periods, most conventions elected in the American states after 1787 were called regularly and did not claim sovereign powers to invade or usurp the functions of constituted authorities (see Dodd 1921, 188). However, two circumstances peculiar to the American states account for this result. The first is that over time most state constitutions regulated the convention mechanism of revision. In spite of the ambiguities discussed earlier about the convention's source of authority, a tradition of legal regulation provided state courts with some guidance as to how to decide on constitutional controversies regarding the powers and decisions of these bodies. The second reason is that while a state convention might claim a direct relation to the sovereign people of the state and demand freedom from legal regulation by the legislature, it still remains subordinated to the federal constitution and federal authorities. In other words, the existence of a federal government above state governments provides a check and an effective limit on what state conventions can do.

29 See Madison, Hamilton, and Jay (1788 [1987], 264), Federalist Paper No. 40.

30 See Federalist No. 49, 313–14, and Letter to Thomas Jefferson, February 4, 1790, in Madison (1999, 474–7).

IV. CONVENTIONS IN LATIN AMERICAN DEMOCRACIES

Unlike American state constitutions but similar to the American federal constitution and the position of Madison on this issue, most national constitutions do not have provisions regulating their own replacement. Those that do include such provisions usually authorize the legislature, not a special convention, to replace them. Given this legal vacuum and the uncertainty associated with calling a special convention working in parallel with an ordinary legislature, it is not surprising that most democratic regimes in the world have rejected the convention mechanism to adopt a new constitution.

The fact that it was only in Latin American democracies that constituent conventions have been used and led to different political results makes the analysis of these cases particularly interesting for comparative purposes. Between 1990 and 2010, six conventions were elected in the context of a Latin American democracy: one in Colombia (1991), one in Argentina (1994), two in Ecuador (1997-98, 2007-08), one in Venezuela (1999), and one in Bolivia (2006-08). Only in Argentina was the convention created to amend rather than to replace the existing constitution.[31] The case is relevant for comparative analysis, however, because in spite of being called under the constitution in force, it was initially uncertain whether this body would comply with its legal mandate.

Figure 2.1 illustrates the source of regulation of Latin American conventions, which fit the categories of constitutional, extraconstitutional but legal, and extraconstitutional and illegal assemblies already discussed. It is important to consider the origins of these assemblies because the most problematic conventions were those located in the extraconstitutional and illegal category. As I will show, however, whether conventions fulfilled their initial commission or jeopardized democracy depended crucially on the level of partisan conflict about the organization and goals of the constitution-making process and the distribution of power among the parties represented in it.

Both the Argentinian and Bolivian conventions were called under the existing constitution. The 1853 Argentine constitution contained a revision procedure that made possible its total or partial reform. According to this procedure, the legislature should first affirm the necessity and scope of reform by at least two-thirds of each chamber and then call for the election of a national convention to adopt the changes. Following this mechanism, a congressional law passed in 1993 called for the election of delegates to a convention, established the timeframe of its work,

[31] In previous works, I considered the outcome of the 1994 constitutional reform in Argentina as another instance of democratic constitutional replacement in Latin America. A reconsideration of the evidence, however, has led me to conclude that it should be coded as a constitutional amendment.

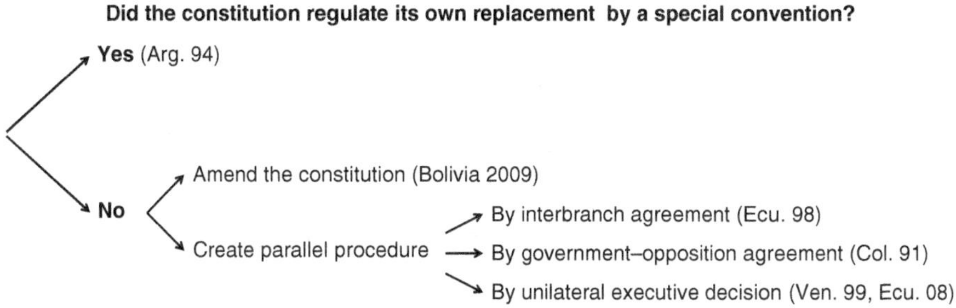

FIGURE 2.1. Democratic constitution making in Latin America, 1990–2010. Did the constitution regulate its own replacement by a special convention?

and constrained the changes the assembly could approve. Although the convention would be free to write the final text, the congressional law severely limited its powers by indicating the content of most reforms based on a previous political pact between the government and the main opposition party (see Negretto 2013).

The 1967 Bolivian constitution only allowed its partial revision through amendments whose necessity had to be first declared in the congress and then passed in a subsequent legislature, in both cases by two-thirds of the members present and voting in the session.[32] In the midst of mounting social mobilizations in favor of replacing the old constitution, the latter was reformed in February 2004 to allow the congress to convene a constituent convention and regulate its internal procedures. Based on this reform, in 2006 the congress passed a law regulating the election of delegates to the convention; the decision-making process of the assembly, which required a two-thirds majority to pass the constitution; the relationship between the constituent convention and the congress; and final ratification of the constitution by referendum (see Böhrt Irahola 2013).

The 1997–8 constituent assembly of Ecuador serves as an example of an extraconstitutional but legal convention. The 1978 Ecuadorean constitution did not have a procedure for its replacement. However, after congressional removal of the incumbent president in 1997, an interim president, using constitutional powers and in agreement with the congress, convened a referendum asking for authorization to elect a convention (see Negretto 2013).[33] As a result of popular support obtained in the referendum, the congress passed a transitory constitutional provision to regulate the election and tasks of the convention.

[32] This procedure was amended in 2002, but only to include a popular referendum to ratify amendments.

[33] The president had the power under the existing constitution to call a referendum on matters of national importance, which clearly included submitting the question of whether the existing constitution should be replaced and whether a constituent convention should be elected to perform this task.

The remaining conventions were both extraconstitutional and illegal. Even within this category, however, one can observe two different alternatives. Colombia illustrates a consensual option, because in spite of its illegality the convention was regulated via a political agreement made between the government and opposition parties. After an unofficial referendum in the March 1990 congressional elections provided support for the election of a special convention, President Barco issued an emergency decree calling a new, but this time official referendum in the May presidential election. As this referendum again supported the election of the convention, on August 2, 1990, the president-elect, Cesar Gaviria of the Liberal Party, signed an agreement with the leaders of the main political forces on the procedures by which the convention would be elected and the aspects of the constitution that should be reformed (see Negretto 2013). Based on this agreement, Gaviria used his state of siege powers to issue a decree (of very dubious legality) that determined the mode of election, rules of operation, and areas of reform that the convention could consider.[34]

Venezuela and Ecuador represent cases of legal break by the executive without the consent of the legislature or a political negotiation with opposition parties. In both cases, the president unilaterally convened a referendum – without constitutional authorization or forcing the interpretation of existing rules – so that citizens would vote on whether an elected convention should replace the constitution. Following this authorization, an assembly selected under the rules decided by the executive passed a new constitution subject to final ratification in a referendum (see Bejarano and Segura 2013).

Regardless of how they were called into existence, all conventions except that of Argentina in 1994, entered into conflicts of various levels of intensity with the legislature. At the same time, most of these conventions attempted to transgress the limits of their commissions. Yet only two actually usurped legislative or judicial functions. Partisan conflicts over the process or the content of the constitution and, crucially, the number of parties with control over the decision rule seem to explain these outcomes. Table 2.1 illustrates this association.

In the case of Argentina, the constituent convention complied with the core of the congressional law that regulated its powers. During the first sessions there was a heated debate between the two main parties that organized the process, on the one hand, and the rest of political organizations, on the other, about whether the assembly should accept the limits imposed on the content of the reforms to be adopted. During the debate, several delegates cited the authority of noted Argentine constitutional theorists who argued that the congress was able to suggest

[34] See Decree 1926 of August 24 1990, in http://www.suin-juriscol.gov.co/viewDocument.asp?id=30014406 (accessed January 2018).

TABLE 2.1. *Legal Regulation, Convention–Legislature Conflicts, and Convention Powers in Latin America, 1990–2010*

Cases	Source of Regulation	Convention–Legislature Conflict	Legal Mandate	Convention Control	Attempt to Transgress Legal Mandate?	Interference with Legislative or Judicial Functions?
Argentina	Constitution/ congress	No	Adopt specific reforms	Two parties	No	No
Bolivia	Constitution/ congress	Yes (high)	Draft constitution	Two parties	Yes	No
Ecuador I	Executive/ congress	Yes (low)	Draft constitution	Three parties	No	No
Colombia	Executive/ interparty agreement	Yes (medium)	Draft constitution[a]	Two parties	Yes	Partial[b]
Ecuador II	Executive	Yes (high)	Draft constitution	One party	Yes	Yes[c]
Venezuela	Executive	Yes (high)	Draft constitution	One party	Yes	Yes[d]

[a] The Supreme Court invalidated the initial restriction to adopt specific reforms and enabled the convention to have full powers to decide on the content of the new constitution.
[b] Drafted the constitution but also decided to call early congressional elections.
[c] Drafted the constitution but also assumed legislative functions, and claimed discretion to intervene other constituted powers.
[d] Drafted the constitution but also interfered in the activities of Congress and the judiciary.

the content of reforms without the convention being legally bound to accept them (see Alfonsín 1996).

In the end, however, a majority of delegates supported the restrictions imposed by the legislature (see Negretto 2013). The 1994 Argentine convention executed its task within the timeframe established beforehand and did not interfere with the functions of any other branch of government. The main factor underlying this outcome was the fact that although they initially disagreed on reforms, both the government and the main opposition party obtained important concessions and neither won enough seats to control the assembly. They thus needed each other to reach a majority and obtain their share of the agreement that constrained the convention.

In Bolivia, most parties agreed on the need to call a convention but disagreed deeply on how to regulate the assembly and on the content of the future constitution. In this context, making the convention sovereign and "above" constituted powers was one of the central demands of the government party.[35] Since this party won a majority of delegates in the convention but was unable to reach the two-thirds required by the congressional law that called it into existence, the convention's claim to have sovereign power could be used by the government to violate that requirement (see Lehoucq 2008).[36] Several conflicts took place between the convention and the congress and between government and opposition around this issue. In the end, however, the government party (which also lacked a majority in the upper chamber of the bicameral legislature) backtracked from its attempt and the convention did not usurp or interfere with congressional functions (see Böhrt Irahola, 2013).

Both the need for a convention and the procedure to call it into existence was widely agreed among the bigger parties in the case of the 1997–8 constitution-making process in Ecuador. Most parties also agreed on the general content of the future constitution, although there were disagreements between large and small parties about the machinery of government and the electoral system (see Negretto 2013). Coexistence between the legislature and the convention was relatively peaceful in spite of some conflicts between these two institutions regarding the term limits imposed on the writing of the new constitution. The convention was supposed to have full powers to freely decide the content of the revisions but no authority over the existing branches of government. In the execution of its mandate the assembly never attempted to transgress these limits. As in Argentina, no party was able to win

[35] In September 2006 the government party managed to impose as the first rule of procedure that the assembly was the holder of national sovereignty. See also the regulation of this issue in the enabling congressional law, in http://pdba.georgetown.edu/Electoral/Bolivia/Leyes/LeyConvocatoria.pdf (last accessed January 2018).

[36] There were also conflicts regarding the timeframe imposed on the convention, which the latter transgressed.

a majority of seats in the convention and the same parties that called this body into existence were the ones that had more influence during its deliberations.

In Colombia there was an initial inclusive agreement on calling the convention as well as on the general content of reforms. In addition, no single party or coalition won a majority of seats in the convention. The executive decree that called for the election of the convention attempted to impose on this body the content of the reforms it should implement. In reviewing this decree, however, the Colombian Supreme Court upheld its legality as regards the mode of election, timeframe, and composition of the assembly, but declared the convention free to decide on the content of the new constitution.[37] Although this did not imply that the convention could interfere with the normal functioning of constituted powers, opposition parties in the assembly nevertheless claimed that this body had the power to call for the anticipated election of a new congress. The main reason for this move was that opposition parties had increased their support in recent elections and expected to repeat that result in a new congressional election (see Negretto 2013, 186). The initiative to end the terms of legislators elected in 1990 created a severe conflict between the two bodies, which could be solved only after a compromise between the government and opposition parties. The compromise accepted the right of the assembly to call for the election of a new congress after the approval of the constitution, provided that members of the convention did not compete in this election (see Negretto 2013).[38]

A very different structure of conflicts and balance of forces characterized the cases of conventions called by unilateral executive decision. Although few parties rejected calling a convention, in both Venezuela and Ecuador (2007) the procedure to call a convention, the nature of this body, and the content of the new constitution were highly controversial. In the case of Venezuela, one of the provisions issued by the national electoral commission, to be included in the referendum to authorize the calling of the convention, declared this body to be sovereign. Ruling on the constitutionality of these rules, however, the Supreme Court declared the sovereignty provision invalid (see Viciano Pastor and Dalmau 2001).[39] In spite of this, one of the first acts of the convention after the government party won an overwhelming

37 Based on the distinction between constituent and constituted powers, the court argued that the authority of the convention came directly from the nation as the holder of popular sovereignty. See Ruling 138, in http://www.suin-juriscol.gov.co/viewDocument.asp?id=30014406 (last accessed January 2018).

38 From July 15 to December 1, 1991, a thirty-six-member commission appointed by the assembly was in charge of exercising legislative functions until the members of the newly elected congress took office.

39 Somewhat contradictorily, however, in January 1999 the court had already decided that calling the convention through a referendum outside the mechanisms of revision of the existing constitution was valid because the constituent power of the people could not be limited by amendment procedures meant to be observed by the constituted powers. See Viciano Pastor and Dalmau (2001).

majority in the election of delegates was to declare itself above the constituted powers. Following this declaration, it intervened in the judiciary and restricted the activities of the congress (Brewer-Carías 2011).

In Ecuador between 2007 and 2008, a government-dominated convention also claimed sovereign powers to absorb legislative functions even though it lacked a mandate to do so. Article 1 of the executive decree that called this convention into existence stated that the convention had "full powers" (*plenos poderes*) to adopt a new constitution. Yet it also stated that any change that the assembly introduced in the institutional structure of the state could become effective only after the new constitutional text was approved (see Brewer-Carías 2007). Once elected, however, the assembly passed a resolution asserting that its powers were above any of the existing branches of government, including the congress and the judiciary. Based on this decision, it explicitly assumed the power to legislate and declared the existing congress in recess (Wray Reyes, "El Proceso Constituyente Ecuatoriano," unpublished manuscript, 2013).[40]

To sum up, regardless of their origin most conventions had a difficult coexistence with the ordinary legislature and claimed special powers to act beyond their commission. Whether they succeeded in their attempt, however, was related to the level of partisan conflict about the organization and goals of the process and depended ultimately on the balance of political forces in the assembly. Whenever a party or coalition had the resources to manipulate the convention to its own advantage, they did so using the purportedly superior democratic legitimacy of this body to mask arbitrary decisions.

These processes have not been neutral for democracy. Political conflicts associated with the coexistence of special conventions and legislatures were in most cases only temporarily disruptive, although in at least one case (Bolivia) were associated with high levels of political confrontation that arguably affected the quality of the democratic regime.[41] Some of these conflicts, however, had a more negative and lasting political effect when a dominant political force used them strategically to usurp legislative and other government functions, as in Venezuela and Ecuador (2008). In these two cases, the country ceased to be democratic at the time or a few years after adopting the new constitution.[42]

40 As regards the judiciary, the constituent assembly established that the Supreme Court, the Supreme Electoral Court, and the Constitutional Court would continue in their functions unless it decided otherwise.

41 On the high levels of political confrontation and even violence between opposing parties during Bolivia's constituent process, see Böhrt Irahola (2013).

42 Such is the case of Venezuela after 2006, and Ecuador after 2007, according to the Polity IV index (2015).

V. CONCLUSION

This chapter has argued that constituent conventions are not inherently superior to all forms of constituent legislatures, whether from the point of view of democratic legitimacy or rational decision making. It has also proposed that partisan conventions may entail significant political risks when used to replace a constitution within an established democratic regime. Given their claim of being an instrument of the legally unbound power of the people, conventions tend to enter into conflict with the ordinary legislature and, more consequentially for the continuity of democracy, may be used by a partisan majority to legitimize acting beyond their commission.

There clearly are circumstances in which calling a constituent convention may be appropriate. This is the case when the lack of legitimacy or suboptimal performance of the existing institutions and the demand for a new constitution are closely associated with the way the legislature works. In this situation, since the legislature itself needs to be reformed, an independent convention may be more likely to enhance public trust in the process. However, there are no easy solutions for the problem of how to subject the convention to a preestablished legal regulation.

Since the key political problem of conventions is that a partisan majority can use their supposedly higher democratic credentials to capture state power, one option is to call an ad hoc citizen assembly or an assembly with a mixed composition in which citizen representation prevails. The little experienced accumulated so far on these types of conventions suggests that in most political contexts these bodies are likely to be initially rejected or their decisions blocked ex post by established political parties.[43] Another alternative is to regulate the way in which the convention comes into existence by the constitution in its original or amended form. Constitutional and legal conventions may in general entail fewer risks than revolutionary ones. Election rules and decision-making procedures can also be designed to foster cooperation and consensus in these bodies. However, as this chapter has shown using evidence from Latin America, whether the convention is effectively limited by its commission may in the end be determined by the actual balance of partisan power among the political forces that organized and controlled the process.

REFERENCES

Ackerman, Bruce. (1994). *The Future of the Liberal Revolution*. New Haven, CT: Yale University Press.

Ackerman, Bruce, and Neal, Katyal. (1995). "Our Unconventional Founding." *The University of Chicago Law Review* 62(2): 478–573.

[43] See Renwick (2014) on this point.

Alfonsín, Raúl. (1996). *Democracia y Consenso: A Propósito de la Reforma Constitucional*. Buenos Aires: Corregidor.
Amar, Akhill. (1994). "The Consent of the Governed: Constitutional Amendment Outside Article V." *Columbia Law Review* 94: 457–508.
Arato, Andrew. (1995). "Forms of Constitution-Making and Theories of Democracy." *Cardozo Law Review* 17(2): 191–232.
(2015). *Post-Sovereign Constitution Making*. Oxford: Oxford University Press.
Bejarano, Ana María, and Renata Segura. (2013). "Asambleas Constituyentes y Democracia: Una Lectura Crítica del Nuevo Constitucionalismo en la Región Andina." *Colombia Internacional* 79: 19–48.
Biaggini, Giovanni. (2011). "Switzerland." In Carlo Fusaro and Dawn Oliver (eds.), *How Constitutions Change*, 303–28. Oxford: Hart Publishing.
Böhrt Irahola, Carlos. (2013). "El Proceso Constituyente Boliviano." Available from the author on request.
Boix, Carles Michael K. Miller, and Sebastian Rosato. (2013). "A Complete Data Set of Political Regimes, 1800–2007." *Comparative Political Studies* 46(12): 1523–54.
Brewer Carías, Allan. (2007). "El inicio del proceso constituyente en Ecuador en 2007 y las lecciones de la experiencia Venezolana de 1999."*Iuris Dictio* 7(11): 71–94.
(2011). *Dismantling Democracy in Venezuela: The Chávez Authoritarian Experiment*. New York, NY: Cambridge University Press.
Carlson, Scott. (2010). "The Drafting Process for the 1998 Albanian Constitution." In Laurel E. Miller (ed.), *Framing the State in Times of Transition: Case Studies in Constitution Making*, 311–31. Washington, DC: United States Institute of Peace Press.
Colon Rios, Joel. (2012). *Weak Constitutionalism: Democratic Legitimacy and the Question of Constituent Power*. New York, NY: Routledge.
Combellas, Ricardo. (2003). "El Proceso Constituyente y la Constitucion de 1999." *Politeia* 30(30): 183–208.
Congleton, Roger D. (2003). *Improving Democracy through Constitutional Reform. Some Swedish Lessons*. Boston, MA: Kluwer Academic.
Dellinger, Walter E. (1979). "The Recurring Question of the "Limited" Constitutional Convention." *The Yale Law Journal* 88: 1623–40.
Dinan, John. (2006). *The American State Constitutional Tradition*. Lawrence, KS: Kansas University Press of Kansas.
Dodd, Walter F. (1921). *The Revision and Amendment of State Constitutions*. Baltimore, MD: Johns Hopkins University Press.
Elkins, Zachary, Tom Ginsburg, and James Melton. (2009). *The Endurance of National Constitutions*. New York, NY: Cambridge University Press.
Elster, Jon. (1995). "Forces and Mechanisms in Constitution-Making." *Duke Law Review* 45: 364–96.
(1997). "Ways of Constitution-Making." In Axel Hadenius (ed.), *Democracy's Victory and Crisis*, 123–42. Cambridge: Cambridge University Press.
(2006). "Legislatures as Constituent Assemblies." In Richard W. Bauman and Tsvi Kahana (eds.), *The Least Examined Branch. The Role of Legislatures in the Constitutional State*, 181–97. New York, NY: Cambridge University Press
(2012). "Clearing and Strengthening the Channels of Constitution-Making." In Tom Ginsburg (ed.), *Comparative Constitutional Design*, 15–30. New York, NY: Cambridge University Press.

(2013). *Securities against Misrule: Juries, Assemblies, Elections*. New York, NY: Cambridge University Press.

Ginsburg, Tom, Zachary Elkins, and Justine Blount. (2009). "Does the Process of Constitution-Making Matter?" *American Review of Law and Society* 5: 201–23.

Ginsburg, Tom, and Alberto Simpser (eds.). (2014). *Authoritarian Constitution-Making: The Role of the Military in Latin America*. New York, NY: Cambridge University Press.

Hammons, Christopher W. (1999). "Was James Madison Wrong? Rethinking the American Preference for Short, Framework-Oriented Constitutions." *American Political Science Review* 93(4): 837–49.

Hoar, Roger Sherman. (1917). *Constituent Conventions: Their Nature, Powers, and Limitations*. Boston, MA: Little, Brown, and Company.

Jameson, John Alexander. (1887). *A Treatise on Constituent Conventions; Their History, Powers and Modes of Proceeding*, 4th edn., revised and enlarged.

Jefferson, Thomas. (1984). *Writings*. New York, NY: The Library of America.

Kay, Richard. (1987). "The Illegality of the Constitution." *Constitutional Commentary* 4: 57–80.

Kiris, Advig. (1991). *Restoration of the Independence of the Republic of Estonia: Selection of Legal Acts, Ministry of Foreign Affairs of the Republic of Estonia*. Tallinn: Estonian Institute for Information.

Kruman, Marc W. (1997). *Between Authority and Liberty: State Constitution Making in Revolutionary America*. Chapel Hill, NC: University of North Carolina Press.

Krunke, Hellen. (2013). "Formal and Informal Methods of Constitutional Change in Denmark." In Xenophon Contiades (ed.), *Engineering Constitutional Change: A Comparative Perspective on Europe, Canada and the USA*, 73–92. Oxon: Routledge.

Landau, David. (2013). "Abusive Constitutionalism." *UC Davis Law Review* 47: 1–58.

Lehoucq, Fabrice. (2008). "Bolivia's Constitutional Breakdown." *Journal of Democracy* 19(2): 46–60.

Madison, James. (1999). *Writings*. New York, NY: The Library of America.

Madison, James, Hamilton, Alexander, and Jay, John. (1788) [1987]: *The Federalist Papers*. London: Penguin.

Mirth, Karlo. (1992). "Croatia's Independence." *Journal of Croatian Studies* 32–33: 5–9.

Negretto, Gabriel. (2012). "Replacing and Amending Constitutions: The Logic of Constitutional Change in Latin America." *Law and Society Review* 46(4): 749–79.

(2013). *Making Constitutions: Presidents, Parties, and Institutional Choice in Latin America*. New York, NY: Cambridge University Press.

Negretto, G. (2016). Constitution Making in Democratic Constitutional Orders. The Challenge of Citizen Participation. In Saskia Ruth, Yanina Welp, and Laurence Whitehead (eds.), *Let The People Rule? Direct Democracy in the Twenty-First Century*, 21–40. University of Essex: ECPR Press.

(2017a). Constitution Making and Constitutionalism in Latin America: The Role of Procedural Rules. In T. Ginsburg and R. Dixon (eds.), *Comparative Constitutional Law in Latin America*, 17–56. Northampton, MA: Elgar.

(2017b). "Constitution Making in Comparative Perspective." In William R. Thompson (ed.), *Oxford Research Encyclopedia of Politics*. Available at http://politics.oxfordre.com/view/10.1093/acrefore/9780190228637.001.0001/acrefore-9780190228637-e-66?rskey=M8Ivuc&result=2 (accessed January 2018).

Parlett, William. (2012). "The Dangers of Popular Constitution-Making." *Brooklyn Journal of International Law* 8: 193.

Planchart Manrique, Gustavo. (1988). "The Making of the Venezuelan Constitution." In Robert Goldwin and Art Kaufman (eds.), *Constitution Makers on Constitution Making: The Experience of Eight Nations,* 353–96. Washington, DC: American Enterprise Institute for Public Policy Research.

Renwick, Alan. (2014). *After the Referendum: Options for a Constituent Convention.* London: The Constitution Society.

Suksi, Markku. (2011). "Finland." In Carlo Fusaro and Dawn Oliver (eds.), *How Constitutions Change. A Comparative Study*, 87–114. Oxford: Hart Publishing.

Thompson, Paul. (2001). "Is There Anything Legal About Extralegal Action? The Debate over Dorr's Rebellion." *New England Law Review* 36: 385–431.

Viciano Pastor, Roberto, and Rubén Martínez Dalmau. (2001). *Cambio Político y Proceso Constituyente en Venezuela (1998–2000).* Valencia: Tiranto Lo Blanch.

Vile, John R. (1991). "American Views of the Constitutional Amending Process: An Intellectual History of Article V." *American Journal of Legal History* 35: 44–69.

Wheatley, Jonathan, and Fernando Mendez. (2013). *Patterns of Constitutional Design: The Role of Citizens and Elites in Constitution-Making*. London: Ashgate.

Williams, Robert F. (1996). "Are State Constituent Conventions Things of the Past? The Increasing Role of the Constitutional Commission in State Constitutional Change." *Hofstra Journal of Public Policy* 1: 1–26.

3

Constituent Assemblies and Political Continuity in Divided Societies

Hanna Lerner

I. INTRODUCTION

What can we learn from past and more recent experience of constituent assemblies in divided societies? Most research on constitutions in divided societies tends to focus on the outcome of the drafting process, extensively studying the type of institutions and compromises included in formal constitutional documents.[1] Yet a growing consensus seems to emerge recently concerning the importance of investigating the process of constitution making, both theoretically and empirically.[2] This chapter aims to contribute to the evolving discussion by questioning the role constituent assemblies play in societies divided over foundational identity issues.

The extent to which "divided societies" should be regarded as a separate category in the context of constitution making may be seen as a contested question. Certainly, all societies may be considered divided along identity or ideological lines, and constitutional debates usually revolve around contentious foundational issues

[1] For example, Sujit Choudhry, *Constitutional Design for Divided Societies* (New York, NY: Oxford University Press, 2007); Donald Horowitz, "Democracy in Divided Societies," *Journal of Democracy* 4:4 (1993), 18–38; Arend Lijphart, "Constitutional Design in Divided Societies," *Journal of Democracy* 15:2 (2004).

[2] Andrew Arato, *Civil Society, Constitution and Legitimacy* (Lanham, MD: Rowman & Littlefield, 2000); Jon Elster, "Forces and Mechanisms in the Constitution Making Process," *Duke Law Journal* 45:3 (1995), 363–96; Tom Ginsburg, Zachary Elkins, and Justin Blount, "Does the Process of Constitution-Making Matter?" *Annual Review of Law and Social Science* 5 (2009), 201–23; Donald Horowitz, "Constitutional Processes for Severely Divided Societies," paper presented at the Department of Political Science, Tel Aviv University (March 2015); John Carey, "Does It Matter How the Constitution in Created?" in Zoltan Barany and Robert G. Moser (eds.), *Is Democracy Exportable?* (Cambridge: Cambridge University Press, 2009), 155–77.

I am grateful to the participants of the conference on Perspectives on Constituent Assemblies, Columbia University, April 2016, for helpful comments and suggestions, and to Donald Horowitz, Alfred Stepan, Rohan Edrisinha, Ben Schonthal, Asli Bali, Andrew Arato, and Karen Barkey for invaluable advice on this project.

that divide any given society. A growing number of scholars, however, have recognized that some societal schisms are more intense, comprehensive, and enduring than others.[3] The type of schisms that characterize divided societies under study here are substantively different and more severe than those that characterize heterogeneous or multicultural societies such as the Canada or Belgium, in which the majority of the population shares the fundamental principles of political liberalism.[4] In divided societies, frictions extend beyond the kind of tensions that could be bridged by "overlapping consensus."[5] They often concern deep disagreement over the religious, national, ethnic, or linguistic identity of the state that are difficult to resolve by mechanisms of resource or power allocation, because they usually involve competing perception regarding the fundamental norms and values that should guide state policies for the entire population. In deeply divided societies, conflicts over the shared vision of the state often occur along interreligious or interlinguistic lines; but such conflicts may also cut across ethnic, religious, or linguistic divisions and involve intraethnic or intrareligious debates. Such cross-cutting cleavages can be found, for example, in Egypt, Turkey, India, Indonesia, and Israel, where tensions exist between those who hold a fundamentalist/conservative world view and those that adhere to a more moderate/liberal/secular approach, within the different religious or ethnic groups. Albert Hirschman termed these types of conflicts as "non-divisible," characterized by the unwillingness of the parties to compromise.[6] By contrast, "divisible" conflicts are easier to settle because the warring parties can agree to "split the difference" or compromise.[7]

When divided societies engage in drafting a constitution, ideological disagreements are imported into the constitutional debate, as each side seeks to express its aspirations and goals in the constitutional document. Yet in the absence

3 Ian Lustick, "Stability in Deeply Divided Societies: Consociationalism versus Control," *World Politics* 31:3 (1979), 325; Eric A. Nordlinger, *Conflict Resolution in Divided Societies* (Cambridge, MA: Center for International Affairs, Harvard University, 1972), 9; Arend Lijphart, *Democracy in Plural Societies: A Comparative Exploration* (New Haven, CT: Yale University Press, 1977); Nathan Glazer, "Democracy and Deep Divides," *Journal of Democracy* 21:2 (2010), 14; Choudhry, *Constitutional Design for Divided Societies*, 5.

4 Defined in terms of distinction between individuals' private cultural/religious/linguistic identity and the shared civic identity of the citizenry. See John Rawls, *Political Liberalism* (New York, NY: Columbia University Press), 1996.

5 Rawls, *Political Liberalism*, chapter 6.

6 Albert O. Hirschman, "Social Conflicts as Pillars of Democratic Market Society," *Political Theory* 22:2 (1994), 203.

7 A somewhat similar distinction has been made by Yael Tamir, who distinguished between "thin" and "thick" multiculturalism. For Tamir, "thin" multiculturalism relates to two or more liberal cultural communities within one state, such as the English- and French-speaking communities in Canada, while "thick" multiculturalism involves cultures of which at least one is illiberal. Yael Tamir, "Two Concepts of Multiculturalism," *Journal of Philosophy of Education* 29:2 (1995), 161.

of consensus on the character of the state, this importation makes it difficult to draft definitive constitutional principles to guide future legislative and judiciary decision making. In the context of such deep disagreements, especially when religious or nationalist demands clash with basic rights and principles of minority rights or gender equality, the option that many liberal constitutionalists advocate, of writing a "thin" procedural constitution, faces substantial challenges and may ultimately prove unattainable.[8] Under such conditions, not all drafters perceive liberal constitutionalism as a neutral ground intended to allow future democratic deliberation on controversial issues. Rather, liberal constitutionalism represents one side in the conflict over the religious identity of the state – the liberal side. Given the deep disagreements over identity issues, the expectation that constitution making in divided societies would represent a moment of "new beginning" or a "founding moment" of "higher lawmaking"[9] is misleading. Precisely because society is divided over core questions concerning its shared credo and identity, at the moment in which this credo or shared identity is to be formulated in a written document, it becomes impossible to separate between the drafting of the polity's ultimate "rules of the game' and the type of contestation involved in "regular" politics – or to distinguish between "higher" and "ordinary" lawmaking.

How does such political diffusion between ordinary and constitutional politics affect the working of constituent assemblies in divided societies? The chapter tackles this question by exploring six democratically elected constituent assemblies, in Egypt, India, Indonesia, Israel, Sri Lanka, and Tunisia. Its main finding is that, in contrast with common views among international advisors and constitution-making experts who claim that internal procedures of decision making have a determinant impact on the assembly's ability to achieve its goals, in deeply divided societies, external political factors –particularly the existence of predrafting agreements between the leading political parties concerning controversial identity issues – are crucial in facilitating the enactment of a democratic and inclusionary constitution.

It is important to emphasize that this chapter does not intend to advocate for consociationalism (and political pacts) as the appropriate method for constitution making in divided societies. I also do not mean to suggest that the preconstitutional agreement is the only factor that explains the success or failure of constituent assemblies, or that constituent assemblies have no significant role in the drafting process. Rather, constituent assembly members play an important role in formulating the wording of the constitution and delineating the scope of issues it entrenches.

8 For more on the challenges of a "thin" constitution, see Hanna Lerner, "The Political Infeasibility of a 'Thin' Constitution: Israel's Recent Attempt to Draft a Constitution (2002–2006)," *Transnational Law and Policy* 22 (2012), 85–121.

9 Bruce Ackerman, *We the People: Foundations* (Cambridge, MA: Belknap Press of Harvard University Press, 1991).

Similarly, constituent assemblies in divided societies may have an important long-term impact that goes beyond the immediate and direct influence of the constitutional text, for example, as a significant reference point for future political debates.

Most importantly, this chapter seeks to highlight the difficulty in separating between political processes that occurred prior to the drafting by constituent assemblies from the procedures of its deliberation and decision making, and the need to "zoom out" and analyze constituent assemblies as part of a broader political process of political negotiations. Those studying the work of constituent assemblies in divided societies should pay close attention to the politics that preceded the formal stage of drafting. Scholars of constitution making tend to focus on the question of legal continuity of the drafting process – whether the drafting of a new constitution represents a legal break with the past and what that means in terms of the legitimacy of the new constitution. But in deeply divided societies it seems that considerations of *political continuity* are of no less (and maybe greater) importance. The controversial issues that are dividing the society in the predrafting stage continue to divide the society during the drafting process as well as in the postdrafting stage of constitutional implementation and interpretation. "Hot potatoes," such as questions of religion–state relations, definition of national identity or decisions concerning the use of formal language, tend to persist on the political agenda before, during, and after the constitution is written. The drafters are challenged with task of mitigating them or creating the institutions that would allow further discussion.

The preliminary observations included in this chapter draw on the experience of six constituent assemblies that operated in divided societies in Asia and the Middle East, including Egypt 2012, India 1946–50, Indonesia 1955–7, Israel 1948–present, Sri Lanka 1972, and Tunisia 2011–14. In all these countries democratically elected (directly or indirectly) constituent assemblies have freely and openly debated the drafting of a new constitution at a foundational moment of the state (either postcolonial or postauthoritarian). In all these cases, the debates occurred under conditions of deep societal disagreement over the state's religious, national, or linguistic identity, yet within an institutional framework of a relatively stable state. Thus, recent constitutional debates in countries that are generally described as postconflict or failed states (e.g., South Sudan or Yemen), which often require the intervention of international actors in the drafting process, are excluded from the discussion. In the cases under study, the declared goal of the constituent assemblies was to draft a democratic constitution that would protect individual and minority rights. In all these cases, constitutional drafters were concerned with the need to increase political and legal unity (for various purposes including economic development, regime change, immigration absorption, etc.), and the question of whether such unity implied the enforcement of cultural, religious, or linguistic uniformity comprised one of the central areas of controversy in the constituent assembly. Yet, as demonstrated in the text that follows, not all debates ultimately yielded the drafting of a formal democratic constitution.

II. PREDRAFTING AGREEMENTS

International advisors often pay close and meticulous attention to the rules of conducts in constituent assemblies and to the design of the assemblies' procedures of deliberation and decision making.[10] This close attention is often based on the assumption that the procedures of deliberation and decision making within a constituent assembly have a determinant impact on the success of the assembly's debates. One of the most comprehensive reports written by international advisors to constitution-making processes stated:

> If the idea of the constitutional moment has any significance, it is probable that the really key moment is when the process is being designed, rather than when the design is being applied. This may be the moment of greatest optimism; it may be the moment when concessions will be most readily made. This gives particular importance and responsibility to the designers.[11]

The authors use the example of Nepal to illustrate how ill-designed constituent assembly procedures contributed to the failure of the drafting process, since "little attention was given to the issues of how the constituent assembly would work, or the participation of the public in the deliberations."[12]

However, an overview of the role constituent assemblies play in various divided societies suggests that factors concerning *internal* functioning of constituent assemblies – such as the size of the assembly, whether it is directly or indirectly elected, the committee's structure, the discussions' timeframe, the extent of public input, or the dominance of a leading political party – are less substantial in facilitating the enactment of a democratic and inclusionary constitution, compared with the influence of political factors *external* to the assembly discussions. In particular, one of the most important factors in determining whether constituent assemblies succeed in achieving their declared goals – namely, the enactment of a formal constitution that establishes the state's democratic institutions and includes a bill of rights – is the existence of predrafting agreements concerning controversial identity issues, negotiated between leaders of the competing camps prior to the initiation of the formal drafting process. In other words, the "success" of a constituent assembly

[10] Bill Proctor and Ikbal Ben Moussa, *The Tunisian Constituent Assembly's By-laws: A Brief Analysis* (Stockholm: International IDEA, 2012); Michele Brandt, Jill Cottrell, Yash Ghai, and Anthony Regan, *Constitution Making and Reform: Options for the Process* (Geneva, Switzerland: Interpeace, 2011).

[11] Brandt et al., *Constitution Making and Reform*, p. 52.

[12] Ibid.

in enacting a democratic and inclusionary constitution seems to be affected less by the particularities of the assembly's design and more by the political mitigation of identity conflicts during the period that preceded the assembly's formation.

The idea that preconstitutional negotiations allow for democratic constitution making and successful transition toward democracy has been advocated by prominent political theorist Andrew Arato.[13] Indeed such theories underplay the significance of deliberations during the constituent assembly stage in the constitution-making process and put greater emphasis on legal and political developments that occur prior to the constituent assembly debated. However, predrafting agreements differ from interim constitutions or from political pacts that determine power allocation between the competing parties involved in the constitutional negotiations. In contrast with interim constitutions, which are usually perceived as formal legal documents enforceable by courts (e.g., in the case of South Africa),[14] preconstitutional agreements play no formal role in the process of constitutional drafting. They also differ from political pacts that define – often in great detail – the governmental structure and other central elements in the final constitutional document. In contrast with such pacts – sometimes achieved through round table negotiations – preconstitutional agreements do not necessarily carry a formal role in the process and hence their impact may be less direct. They usually result from coalitional negotiations held months, years, and even decades before the formal deliberation by the constituent assembly begun. Preconstitutional agreements may be reflected in "objective resolutions" that are often adopted during the first stage of the constituent assembly debates as a set of general guidelines indicating the direction to which the constituent assembly should go.[15] Yet, again, in contrast with preconstitutional agreements, objective resolutions comprise part of the formal process of constituent assembly deliberation and may be adopted in the absence of preconstitutional political agreement.

Examples for the significant role of preconstitutional agreements in influencing the constitutional drafting can be found in the cases of postpartition India (1947–50), Sri Lanka (1972), and in Tunisia (2011–14). In all three cases, provisions formulated in the written constitution were based on a general framework of principles delineated by political negotiations that occurred years before the formal drafting process began. In the remaining cases under study here – prepartition India (1946–7),

[13] Andrew Arato, *Post Sovereign Constitution Making: Learning and Legitimacy* (Oxford: Oxford University Press, 2016); Andrew Arato, "Conventions, Constituent Assemblies, and Round Tables: Models, Principles and Elements of Democratic Constitution-Making," *Global Constitutionalism*, 1:1 (March 2012), 173–200.

[14] Ibid.

[15] Such objective resolution was adopted, for example, at the opening session of the Indian Constituent Assembly debates.

Israel (1948–present), Indonesia (1955–9) and Egypt (2012) – the elected constituent assembly failed to enact a formal liberal-democratic constitution. While each of these four episodes failed in its own way, one of the only commonalities between them was the lack of preconstitutional political agreements concerning the shared norms and values that should underpin the state. In other words, the political stories unfolding beyond the constituent assemblies seem to influence the outcome of the drafting process more than the nature or the procedures of the debates taking place within the three assemblies.

In India, the drafting process may be divided into two separate stages: the first stage began on December 1946 with the convening of the constituent assembly in New Delhi and lasted for seven months, until July 1947, when the country was violently partitioned between two independent states: India and Pakistan. The second stage of drafting began after partition and lasted for nearly two and a half years, until January 1950, when the new constitution was promulgated. Whether the partition of India was inevitable or not is a question long debated by historians.[16] Nevertheless, the failure to draft a constitution for a united India demonstrated the limitations of constitutional procedures in divided societies and the importance of predrafting political agreements between the conflicting parties concerning the shared vision of the state. The Indian story illustrates how political disputes may be imported into the constitutional debate and how procedural disagreements concerning the constituent assembly's design may be used to emphasize the ideological differences between the competing positions. Whereas the first stage of constituent assembly debates did not rely on a predrafting political agreement between the two conflicting parties – the Hindu-dominated Congress Party and the Muslim League – the second stage of constituent assembly debates drew to a large extent on a predrafting program that had been envisioned particularly by leaders of the Indian national movement for two decades.

In the summer of 1946, almost a year before partition, a British Cabinet Mission had determined the procedures for selecting the constituent assembly members.[17] The Cabinet Mission Plan also designed the federal structure for the

[16] For example, Mushirul Hasan (ed.), *India's Partition: Process, Strategy and Mobilization* (Oxford: Oxford University Press, 2001); C. H. Philips and Mary Doreen Wainwright, *The Partition of India: Policies and Perspectives 1935–1947* (London: Allen & Unwin, 1970); Anita Inder Singh, *The Origin of the Partition of India 1936–1947* (New Delhi: Oxford University Press, 1999).

[17] According to the Cabinet Mission Plan, the members of the constituent assembly were to be elected by legislative assemblies of the provinces included in British India, which themselves were elected according to the 1935 Government of India Act. The Congress Party, which had an overwhelming majority in most provincial legislatures, filled 208 seats out of the total of 296 seats allotted to these provinces. The Muslim League won all but seven seats reserved for Muslims, and overall had 73 seats in the assembly. Granville Austin, *The Indian Constitution: Cornerstone of a Nation* (Oxford: Oxford University Press, 1999), 9.

soon-to-be-independent India (based on three provincial groupings), and defined specific procedures for deliberation and decision making in the constituent assembly. These arrangements did not rest on long-term negotiations but rather were drafted hastily, as the British government was preparing to end its rule in India. Indeed, both the Congress Party and the Muslim League were reluctant to fully accept the terms delineated by the British plan. The intense negotiations among the Congress, the League, and the British government on the procedures of the constituent assembly and the form of India's federal system continued for several months. The letters exchanged among the three parties, as well as protocols of the tripartite meetings, reveal how the dispute over the proposal of provincial grouping heightened the tensions and exposed fundamental disagreements between the Congress and the League. The leaders of the two parties used the Cabinet Mission Plan and its legal formulations as a battering ram, rather than as a vehicle for compromise. Both parties utilized the disagreement over constitutional procedures for political advantage. While historians still debate the main causes of the country's partition, clearly instead of bringing the sides together, the debates over the constitute assembly turned into a focus for political tension that emphasized the differences between the two sides.[18]

Even after partition, India was still one of the richest countries in the world in terms of its linguistic, ethnic, and religious diversity. The Muslim minority remained significant, encompassing around 10 percent of the population. Nevertheless, partition increased the dominance of the Congress Party in the constituent assembly, which in turn made it easier for its leadership to incorporate in the constitution elements of its vision of Indian unity. This vision was based on a decades-long period of Congress-led consultation concerning the future independent constitution. Most importantly, it rested on a detailed draft constitution adopted in 1928 by the All Parties Conference that met in Lucknow. The draft, known as "the Nehru Report," was written by a seven-member committee, chaired by Motilal Nehru.[19] The document defined the principles of a future constitution for India, including its parliamentary system and a detailed list of civil, political, social, and economic

[18] For a detailed analysis of this exchange see Hanna Lerner, *Making Constitutions in Deeply Divided Societies* (Cambridge: Cambridge University Press, 2011), chapter 5.

[19] The committee was appointed during the May 1928 meeting of the All Parties Conference, which included representatives of all the major political organizations in India, including the All-India Hindu Mahasabha, the All-India Muslim League, the All-India Liberal Federation, the States' Peoples Conference, The Central Khalifat Committee, the All-India Conference of Indian Christians, and others. See Niraja Gopal Jayal, *Citizenship and Its Discontents: An Indian History* (Cambridge MA: Harvard University Press, 2013), 306, n. 5. For the text of the report see "Report of the Committee Appointed by the All India Conference to Determine the Principles of the Constitution for India, 1928," in Ravinder Kumar and Hari Dev Sharma (eds.), *Selected Works of Motilal Nehru*, Vol. 6 (New Delhi: Vikas, 1995).

rights. While named after the committee's chair, Motilal Nehru, in many ways the report mirrors the views of his son, Jawaharlal Nehru, who played a central role in its drafting, and who later became India's first prime minister. The Nehru Report prefigured many of the guiding principles concerning the structure of government, which were embedded in the final constitutional draft.[20] Similarly, the Fundamental Rights and Directive Principles of State Policy sections of the final constitution rested heavily on the list of basic rights included in the Nehru report.[21] Another influential document was the "Resolution of the Fundamental Rights and Economic Changes," which was adopted during the Karachi session of the congress in 1931, and often viewed as representing a political compromise between Nehru's and Gandhi's perspectives.[22]

The influence of preconstitutional agreement regarding divisive issues on the final constitutional document is also apparent in the case of Tunisia. Part of the success of the Tunisian 2011–14 constituent assembly debates is attributed to preconstitutional agreements achieved between the secular and Islamist opposition groups nearly a decade before the uprising against the authoritarian rule of Zine El Abidine Ben Ali. Under Ben Ali's regime, much of the leadership of both the Islamist *Ennahda* and the secular Congress for the Republic (Congrès pour la République, or CPR) groups relocated overseas. Beginning in May 2003, they held clandestine meetings in Aix-en-Provence, France, led by the Tunisian human rights lawyer Moncef Marzouki.[23] These meetings allowed the parties to develop habits of trust and compromise despite ideological differences and facilitated the emergence of pragmatic and strategic alliances, particularly surrounding human rights issues.[24] Some observers consider the political solidarity formed during these meetings to

[20] One may wonder whether the guiding principles included in the Nehru Report would have been as influential if the Muslim League would have remained in the constituent assembly and partition prevented. However, such "what if" questions are difficult to answer in retrospect.

[21] Jayal, chapter 5. See also Neera Chandhoke, "The Antecedents of Social Rights in India," in Udit Bhatia (ed.), *The Indian Constituent Assembly: Deliberations and Democracy* (London: Routledge, 2018), 83–102.

[22] Jayal, 139–42. See also Rohit De "Constitutional Antecedents," in Sujit Choudhry, Madhav Khosla, and Pratap Bhanu Mehta (eds.), *Oxford Handbook on the Indian Constitution* (Oxford: Oxford University Press, 2016), 32.

[23] Nadia Marzouki, "Dancing by the Cliff: Constitution Writing in Post-Revolutionary Tunisia 2011–2014," in Aslı Bali and Hanna Lerner (eds.), *Constitution Writing, Religion and Democracy* (Cambridge: Cambridge University Press, 2017), 343–69.

[24] On the importance of building trust during preconstitutional negotiations see also Wiktor Osiatynski, "The Roundtable Talks in Poland," in Jon Elster (ed.), *The Roundtable Talks and the Breakdown of Communism* (Chicago, IL: University of Chicago Press, 1996), 32 on the case of Poland's 1989 roundtable talks that preceded the constitution drafting and paved the way to Poland's transition to democracy. As Osiatynski claims, the "by-product of the length of the talks was that, over time and with repeated meetings, fear, anger, and hatred declined and resentments [between the communist government and Solidarity-led opposition, HL] melted."

have been crucial in enabling meaningful coalition politics among the opposition groups in the postrevolution constitution-drafting period and to have facilitated many of the compromises achieved during the constituent assembly debates, for example, concerning the role of religion in the Tunisian state.[25]

A third example of constituent assembly debates that were significantly impacted by predrafting political agreement can be found in 1972 Sri Lanka. The first autochthonous constitution of Sri Lanka is considered by many to represent a failed project of nation-building.[26] The constitution failed to facilitate national unity between the Sinhala majority and other minorities, particularly the Tamils. Yet the written constitution drafted by the constituent assembly was not a result of unplanned process. Quite the opposite. The fundamental principles that guided the drafting of the 1972 Sri Lankan constitution resulted from political intracoalitional negotiations that preceded the drafting process by more than half a decade. The United Front (UF) coalition, which was formed during the 1960s and comprised the three opposition parties at the time – the Sri Lanka Freedom Party (SLFP), the Lanka Sama Samaja Party (LSSP), and the Communist Party (CP) – initiated and led the constitution-making project. In 1968 the three parties set a committee on constitutional reform, chaired by Colvin de Silva.[27] The promise to draft a new constitution for the island of Ceylon formed part of the UF election campaign. In May 1970, the UF coalition won a sweeping electoral victory, securing 115 out of the 151 parliamentary seats. Two months later, in July 1970, the drafting process began with the appointment of a twelve-member Drafting Committee of senior lawyers and governmental legal experts. The Drafting Committee composed a list of thirty-eight core constitutional principles as an outline of the new charter, termed Draft Basic Resolutions (DBRs).[28] In January 1971, the legislature, sitting as a constituent assembly, began debating the DBRs. Between July 1971 and January 1972, the Drafting Committee had transformed the DBRs into a draft constitution, which the assembly discussed again. The new constitution was ratified in May 22, 1972. One of the most controversial questions debated by the constituent

[25] Ibid. See also Alfred Stepan, "Tunisia's Transition and the Twin Tolerations," *Journal of Democracy* 23 (2012), 89–103.

[26] Rohan Edrisinha, "Sri Lanka: Constitutions without Constitutionalism. A Tale of Three and a Half Constitutions," in Rohan Edrisinha and Asanga Welikala (eds.), *Essays on Federalism in Sri Lanka* (Colombo: Center for Policy Alternatives, 2008), 7–8.

[27] The three parties agreed on a common program for a new constitution that "will secure fundamental rights and freedoms to all citizens." See Nihal Jayawickrama, "Reflections on the Making and Content of the 1972 Constitution: An Insider's Perspective," in Asanga Welikala (ed.), *The Sri Lankan Republic at 40: Reflections on Constitutional History, Theory, Practice* (Colombo: Centre for Policy Alternatives, 2012), 58.

[28] The DBRs were also reviewed by the prime minister's cabinet and by a seventeen-member Steering and Subjects Committee, composed of government and opposition parliamentarians.

assembly concerned the proposal to include in the new constitution an ambiguous phrase concerning the "rightful place of Buddhism." Despite demands to specify the legal implications of the ambiguous phrase on the one hand, and protest from non-Buddhist minorities and secular opposition on the other, the early compromises agreed on by in the UF manifesto were embedded in the final constitutional text. As Benjamin Schonthal showed, none of the proposed amendments to the draft constitution discussed by the constituent assembly was accepted.[29] Similarly, the UF coalitional agreement affected the constituent assembly debates on the Language Clause much more profoundly than did proposals or criticism voiced by participants in the debate itself.[30] Tamil representatives walked out of the constituent assembly, as the government insisted on retaining the existing legislation, providing special status to Sinhala.[31] Indeed, with a two-third majority in the parliament (and in the constituent assembly), the UF coalition was not required to reach out to either opposition parties of minority parties. Critics have considered the adoption of the 1972 constitution a major landmark in the process of Sri Lankan national disintegration.[32]

In three other cases – Egypt (2012), Indonesia (1955–9), and Israel (1948–present) – the elected constituent assembly failed to achieve its declared goal of enacting a formal permanent democratic constitution. Although, as elaborated below, the three cases differ in the type of "failure" of the constituent assembly, in all three of them the absence of predrafting political agreements seems to have played a significant role in the story.

In Egypt, an indirectly elected constituent assembly that followed democratic parliamentary and presidential elections wrote the short-lived 2012 Egyptian constitution. Nevertheless, the legitimacy of the drafting process was contested, and its debates were characterized by deep distrust between the various factions. The need to draft a new constitution emerged on February 17, 2012, two days after Mubarak's resignation, with the suspension of the 1971 constitution by the Supreme Council of the Armed Forces (SCAF), the country's interim military leadership. At no point during the transition period (or prior to it, as in Tunisia), did the Islamist and secular

29 Benjamin Schonthal, *Buddhism Politics and the Limits of Law: The Pyrrhic Constitutionalism of Sri Lanka* (Cambridge: Cambridge University Press, 2016), 96.

30 Radhika Coomaraswamy, "The 1972 Republican Constitution in the Postcolonial Constitutional Evolution of Sri Lanka," in Asanga Welikala (ed.), *The Sri Lankan Republic at 40* (Colombo: Center for Policy Alternatives, 2012), 126–7; R. Sampanthan, "Interview: The Ilankai Thamil Arasu Katchi (Federal Party) and the Post-Independence Politics of Ethnic Pluralism: Tamil Nationalism Before and After the Republic," in Asanga Welikala (ed.), *The Sri Lankan Republic at 40*, 953–4.

31 The 1972 constitution recognizes Sinhala as the official language of Sri Lanka "as provided by the Official Language Act, No. 33 of 1956" (Article 7). It also stated that "The use of the Tamil language shall be in accordance with the Tamil Language (Special Provisions) Act No. 23 of 1958" (Article 8).

32 Edrisinha, "Sri Lanka: Constitutions without Constitutionalism," 22, 30.

leadership achieve any kind of agreement concerning controversial fundamental issues such as the role of Islam and the secular identity of the state. The continuous distrust between the conflicting groups was reflected throughout the negotiations on the design of the constituent assembly and its deliberations. The first stage of the process included a SCAF-appointed committee of legal experts' drafting of amendments to the 1971 constitution. These amendments were approved by a referendum on March 19, with 77 percent support. However, eleven days later, on March 30, SCAF decided to officially repeal the 1971 constitution and replaced it with a provisional Constitutional Declaration, which delineated new guidelines for the transitional period.[33] Despite its procedural and substantive inconsistencies,[34] the Declaration determined a new procedure for constitutional drafting that included indirect elections of a 100-member constituent assembly.[35]

In the parliamentary elections held in January 2012, the Muslim Brotherhood's (MB) Freedom and Justice Party received the largest number of seats. Owing to its large parliamentary bloc, the MB dominated the selection process for the 100-member assembly. The non-Islamist camp sharply objected the assembly's composition and boycotted the discussions. Consequentially, Cairo's Administrative Court dissolved the first constituent assembly on the grounds that it was unrepresentative.[36] In the absence of consensus among the parties in the parliament, the second constituent assembly resembled the first in composition and conducted its work under threat of another court-ordered dissolution. Following the success of Mohammad Morsi in the presidential elections in June 2012, the MB commanded full control over the drafting process. While several non-Islamist groups withdrew from the debates, the final constitutional draft produced by the assembly was approved by a referendum in December 2012, with support of 64 percent of the voters and a turnout of 33 percent. However, six months after the enactment of the 2012 constitution, the Egyptian military removed Morsi from office and suspended the constitution. Ultimately, the 2012 constitution was too short lived to be tested against the

33 Tamir Moustafa, *Drafting Egypt's Constitution: Can a New Legal Framework Revive a Flawed Transition?* Brookings Doha Center – Stanford Project on Arab Transitions, Paper Series No. 1, March 2012.

34 Nathan Brown and Kristen Stilt, "A Haphazard Compromise," Carnegie Endowment for International Peace, April 11, 2011.

35 The text of the Constitutional Declaration is available at www.egypt.gov.eg/english/laws/constitution/default.aspx. According to Article 60, the two houses of the legislature were to convene within six months after their election to elect a 100-member constituent assembly. The Assembly was given six months to complete the draft constitution, which would then be submitted (within fifteen days after its completion) to the citizenry for approval in a referendum.

36 "Egypt Court Suspends Constitutional Assembly" *BBC News*, 10 April 2012. Retrieved from: www.bbc.com/news/world-middle-east-17665048

fears of the secular camp that it would lead to creeping Islamization or the worries of the Salafi camp that it would prove a dead letter.[37]

Israel provides another example of constituent assembly debates occurring under conditions of broad political disagreement over the religious and national identity of the state, which failed to yield a formal democratic constitution. In contrast with Egypt, where the failure of the 2012 process led to the establishment of an authoritarian regime and the adoption of a new constitution two years later, Israel managed to consolidate its democracy without a written constitution. Nevertheless, the ongoing failure of the elected constituent assembly to fulfill the task of drafting a written constitutional document, as was explicitly mandated in Israel's Declaration of Establishment, may be explained by the lack of political preconstitutional agreement among Israeli lawmakers concerning the basic constitutional principles.

The debates on the Israeli constitution began in July 1948, two months after independence, with the appointment of the Provisional Council's Constitution Committee. The committee deliberated the future constitution for nearly seven months until the elections for the constituent assembly in February 1949. During the discussions, a consensus seemed to emerge on institutional and governmental issues; however, bitter conflicts arose on the question of religion–state relations. The committee was divided between those who held a more secular vision of Israel as a Jewish state, and those who held more religious perspective. The tensions over the role of religion and religious law in the newly established state "for the Jewish people"[38] led the committee chairperson, Zerach Varhaftig, to conclude that the differences of views on this issue were impossible to bridge and hence the constitution-writing project should be postponed.[39] After the elections of the constituent assembly, which transformed itself during its second meeting into Israel's first legislature, the Knesset,[40] the debates on the constitution focused not on its content but rather on the question of whether a constitution should be written at all. Prime Minister David Ben-Gurion was one of the main objectors to the drafting of a written constitution, for various reasons still debated by historians.[41] In June 1950, after only nine sessions devoted to the topic of the constitution, the Knesset decided

37 Nathan Brown, "Islam and Constitutionalism in the Arab World: The Puzzling Course of Islamic Inflation," in Hanna Lerner and Asli U. Bali (eds.), *Constitution Writing, Religion and Democracy* (Cambridge: Cambridge University Press, 2017), 289–316.

38 At the early debates, the Palestinians were completely excluded from participating in the discussions on the constitution.

39 Zerach Varhaftig, *A Constitution for Israel: Religion and State* (Jerusalem: Medilot 1988) (Hebrew).

40 For the text of the Transition Law see Divrey Hakneset, *Knesset Record*) 1 (1949), 52.

41 For the various reasons behind this objection, see Lerner 2011, chapter 3. See also Nir Kedar, *Ben-Gurion and the Constitution* (Ramat Gan: Bar-Ilan University Press & Dvir Press, 2015) (Hebrew).

to refrain from drafting a formal constitutional text. Instead, it agreed to enact the constitution through a series of basic laws to be adopted separately over the years.[42]

The next attempt to draft a complete constitutional document occurred between 2003 and 2006 when, influenced by civil society initiatives calling for the drafting of a formal constitution,[43] the Knesset's Law, Constitution and Justice Committee, chaired by Knesset Member Michael Eitan of the Likud Party, led a two-year process of intense discussions on a draft constitution. The Committee submitted to the Knesset plenary a constitutional report, titled "Constitution by Broad Consent," which included a constitutional draft for further debate by all Knesset members.[44] Notably, rather than resolving the disputes that arose during the committee discussions, the draft submitted to the Knesset incorporated all the competing positions and the Committee charged the Knesset with the task of transforming this multiversioned document into a comprehensive constitutional formula. During one session of discussion on the topic, in February 2006, representatives across the political spectrum expressed reservations concerning the need to draft a new constitution, calling for the preservation of the existing, ambiguous, informal constitutional arrangements, rather than the enactment of a constitution reflecting the worldview of one particular sector of the population. At the end of the discussion, the Knesset passed a declaratory resolution stating that after the coming elections it would "continue this effort, aiming at presenting a proposed constitution, based on broad consent, for Knesset decision and the people's ratification."[45] Nevertheless, the project disappeared from Israeli political and public agenda. The Knesset discussion, as well as the draft prepared by the constitutional committee, reflected the deep disagreement in Israeli society on fundamental constitutional principles, particularly regarding religious and national identity, and the absence of a political "broad consent" or preconstitutional agreement that could have facilitated the enactment of a formal constitution.

The third example of a democratically elected constituent assembly that failed to draft a democratic constitution is found in Indonesia. During half a decade following its independence, Indonesia had adopted three constitutions designed as provisionary arrangements until a democratically elected constituent assembly

42 The Knesset decision, known as "the Harari Resolution," did not specify whether the basic law legislation requires special procedures. It also failed to detail the content of the future basic laws or when will they be collected into a single constitutional document. Between 1958 and 2014, the Knesset adopted only thirteen basic laws.

43 Particularly, efforts led by the Israeli Democracy Institute. See Arye Carmon, *Building Democracy on Sand: An Israel Story* (Jerusalem: Israel Democracy Institute, 2012).

44 "*Constitution in Broad Consent: Report of the Constitution, Law and Justice Committee Regarding Proposals for the Constitution of the State of Israel*" (Jerusalem: Knesset, 2006) (Hebrew).

45 Divrey Hakneset (Knesset Records) (2006), 70. The resolution passed by a majority of thirty votes, with nineteen opposed and one abstainer.

would draft a permanent and more comprehensive constitution. The first constitution was written in 1945 by a sixty-two-member committee appointed by the Japanese, recognizing the imminent end of their rule in Indonesia at the last stages of World War II.[46] Second, in 1949 a federal constitution of the United States of Indonesia was adopted as part of the Hague Agreement between Indonesia and the Netherlands. It survived only a few months, until the summer of 1950, when Indonesia withdrew from the Agreement and enacted a unitary constitution of the Republic of Indonesia. The 1950 constitution established Indonesia's parliamentary system. Accordingly, in December 1955, free and open elections for Indonesia's Konstituante (constituent assembly) were held. Thirty-four parties were listed in the elections. Forty million citizens (about 90 percent of the registered voters) participated, electing 514 representatives out of 544 members of the Konstituante. The additional thirty members represented minority groups (Chinese-, Indo-European-, and the Dutch-occupied territories of West Irian).[47] For two and a half years, the Konstituante debated the new constitution and discussed key questions such as what should be the "philosophy of the state" (Dasar Negara) and how to define the relations between Islamic law and state legislation. The main division in the Konstituante was between those who wished Indonesia to be an Islamic state, and the nationalists, who envisioned an all-inclusive Indonesian national identity rather than an exclusively Islamic identity.[48] While the Konstituante continued its debates, without arriving at a seemly solution, the Indonesian economy continued to deteriorate, national conflicts intensified, and the army increased its interference in politics and in the economy. In May 1957, President Sukarno declared martial law and began creating the institutional framework of Guided Democracy, which was allegedly intended to restore stability and prevent the disintegration of the republic. In June 1959, after the Konstituante's failure to achieve consensus, Sukarno dissolved it by a presidential decree and reinstated Indonesia's initial 1945 constitution.

The cases described in the foregoing suggest that the political compromises on contentious ideational issues achieved by constituent assemblies largely depend on predrafting political agreements between the conflicting sides, negotiated prior to the beginning of the formal drafting process. However, this analysis does not intend to suggest that constituent assemblies have no significant role in the drafting process.

[46] The Investigative Committee for Preparatory Work for Indonesian Independence (BRUPK), comprising mainly the older generation of Indonesian leadership from Java. See R. E. Elson, "Another Look at the Jakarta Charter Controversy of 1945," *Indonesia* 88 (October 2009), 109. M. C. Ricklefs, *A History of Modern Indonesia since 1200*, 4th ed. (Stanford, CA: Stanford University Press 2008), 245.

[47] Adnan Buyung Nasution, *The Aspiration for Constitutional Government in Indonesia: A Socio-Legal Study of the Indonesian Konstituante 1956–1959* (Jakarta: Pustaka Sinar-Harapan, 1992), 30–5.

[48] On the Konstituante debates, see Adnan Buyung Nasution, *The Aspiration for Constitutional Government in Indonesia*, chapter 2.

As the following section illustrates, constituent assembly members play an important role in formulating the wording of the constitution and delineating the scope of issues it entrenches. And as discussed in the last section of this chapter, constituent assemblies in divided societies may have an important long-term impact that goes beyond the immediate and direct influence of the constitutional text.

III. POSTDRAFTING POLITICAL CONTINUITY

The intense religious, linguistic, or national conflicts that often characterize deeply divided societies are not always resolved by the formal process of constitutional drafting. As the previous section demonstrated, some constituent assemblies in divided societies fail to enact an enduring democratic constitution. In other cases, where a formal constitution is written and democratic institutions are established, drafters often adopt incrementalist constitutional strategies in order to circumvent potentially explosive conflicts. Such strategies may include the deferral of controversial decisions, the use of ambiguous and vague language, or the inclusion of conflicting provisions, or even nonjusticiable sections, in the written constitutions. Such incrementalist strategies allow the constituent assembly to shift the burden of resolving – or even further discussing – contentious issues to the new political institutions created by the constitution. The adoption of incrementalist constitutional arrangements is often meant to afford the political system greater flexibility for future decisions about controversial ideational questions, because the formal constitution refrains from setting legal limitations on the range of political possibilities to be decided by future legislatures.[49] In other words, incrementalist constitutional formulations in the areas of religious, linguistic, or national identity transform controversial choices from the level of entrenched constitutional "higher lawmaking" to the level of ordinary lawmaking.

Examples for incrementalist constitutional strategies can be found across a range of identity conflicts. The Indian constituent assembly, for example, chose to defer choices regarding the contentious question of the country's national language to

[49] Strategies of constitutional ambiguity and deferral have been documented and analyzed recently by a number of scholars. See, for example, Rosalind Dixon and Tom Ginsburg, "Deciding Not to Decide: Deferral in Constitutional Design," *International Journal of Constitutional Law* 9:3–4 (2011), 636–72; Stephen Holmes, "Gag Rules of the Politics of Omission," in Jon Elster and Rune Slagstad (eds.), *Constitutionalism and Democracy* (Cambridge: Cambridge University Press); Cass Sunstein, *Designing Democracy: What Constitutions Do?* (Oxford: Oxford University Press, 2001), 50–6 (writing about "incompletely theorized agreements"). Often, however, such studies refrain from theorizing the difference between incompletely theorized agreements that address institutional or governmental procedural aspects of the constitution (e.g., electoral laws, structure of the judiciary), and those that address disagreements on on ideational or foundational issues, which are the central concern in this chapter focusing on divided societies.

future legislators. The constitution explicitly postponed the decision by fifteen years, determining that at the end of the interim period a parliamentary committee would examine the issue (Article 344).[50] Similarly, following three years of controversies over the formulation of the Hindu Code, which was meant to regulate Hindu family law, the drafters decided to leave this controversial issue to be further deliberated and decided on by the parliament, on the level of ordinary legislation.[51] Ambiguous language with regard to the religious or secular identity of the state was intentionally used in the constitutions of Tunisia (2014),[52] Egypt (2012),[53] and Sri Lanka (1972)[54] as a form of compromise between the competing religious-fundamentalist and liberal-secular camps. Nonjusticiable provisions were adopted in the constitutions of India, Sri Lanka, and Pakistan as a separate section termed "Directive Principles of State Policy," which addresses controversial socioeconomic and religious issues.[55]

Whether or not the adoption of incrementalist arrangements should be encouraged depends on one's perspective concerning the risks and opportunities the incrememntalist constitutional approach involves. On the one hand, when the conflict is about "non-divisible" issues and none of the sides is willing to compromise,

50 Meanwhile, Hindi was labeled the "official language of the Union" (Article 343), while English was to continue to be used "for all official purposes" (Article 351). In addition, the constitution recognized fourteen other languages for official use (listed in the Eighth Schedule of the Constitution).

51 Reba Som, "Jawaharlal Nehru and the Hindu Code: A Victory of Symbol over Substance?" *Modern Asia Studies* 28 (1994), 165–94.

52 The preamble, for example, includes references to both Islamic identity and human civilization: "Expressing our people's commitment to the teachings of Islam, to their spirit of openness and tolerance, to human values and the highest principles of universal human rights, inspired by the heritage of our civilization … based on the foundations of our Islamic-Arab identity and on the gains of human civilization…" For the English language text of the 2014 Tunisian constitution, see www.constituteproject.org/constitution/Tunisia_2014?lang=en

53 Although drafted by a constituent assembly with an Islamist majority, the provisions concerning the role of Islam left much room for legislative and judicial interpretation. Article 2 defined Islamic Shari'a as the principal source of legislation, yet was copied from the 1971 constitution that is considered a secular constitution. Similarly, while the new constitution also included Article 219, which widened the scope of the definition of the principles of Islamic Shari'a to include Sunni jurisprudence, in accordance with Salafi demands, the definition remained broad enough to "include various opinions (some moderate and others more severe) about most issues." Brown, "Islam and Constitutionalism in the Arab World," 289–316.

54 Article 6, known as "the Buddhist Chapter," was intentionally designed as a compromise between two conflicting views regarding the role the state should take in protecting Buddhism: "The Republic of Sri Lanka shall give to Buddhism the foremost place and accordingly it shall be the duty of the State to protect and foster Buddhism while assuring to all religions the rights granted by section 18(1) (d)." See Schonthal, *Buddhism Politics and the Limits of Law*, chapter 4.

55 Notably, incrementalist arrangements are adopted most frequently with reference to particular identity conflicts. Regarding other issues, the same drafters may adopt a reformist approach, using the constitution as a vehicle for social reconstruction. In India, for example, B. K. Ambedkar, who supported the inclusion of the "directive principles" section, advocated for the inclusion of radical provisions concerning caste equality.

transferring the "hot potato" of contentious identity-related choices from the constitutional to the more flexible arena of ordinary politics may avert fierce and even violent conflict. Furthermore, in accommodating the citizenry's competing views, such formulations promote consensual – rather than majoritarian – democracy. Incrementalist strategies thus allow the deescalation of what could become an explosive conflict. By defusing the pressure to make permanent decisions on divisive issues, strategies of deferral or constitutional ambiguity may allow the drafters to create consensus around institution-building measures and other elements in the formal constitution.[56]

On the other hand, incrementalist arrangements are often criticized as an ideological compromise and a failure to achieve a more liberal constitution.[57] Moreover, they risk a permanent preservation of the conflict, or even its exacerbation.[58] In Sri Lanka, for example, many view the refraining of the 1972 constitution's drafters from reforming the 1956 Language Act as one of the central reasons for the outbreak of the civil war with the Tamil minority.[59] But even in the absence of violent outbreaks, legislators' continuous deferral of decision making on controversial issues may pose a potential danger to democratic stability. The political inability to settle controversies over ideational conflicts tends to invite judicial intervention. Such interventions may create tension between the legislative and judicial branches, which may be particularly problematic if the Supreme Court and the parliament hold opposing ideologies regarding controversial foundational issues, such as religion–state relations. A direct conflict between the two branches of government may lead to public delegitimation of both institutions: the judiciary might lose its legitimacy as a neutral arbitrator in legal issues and the parliament might lose its legitimacy as an organ representative of the various interests in society. Such developments have occurred in Israel: given the great political power that religious parties held in the Knesset, the secular-liberal camp turned to the Supreme Court to rule against the existing religious regulations. However, the court's increasing

56 Aslı U. Bali and Hanna Lerner, "Constitutional Design without a Constitutional Moment: Lessons from Religiously Divided Societies," *Cornell Journal of International Law* 49:2 (September 2016), 227–308.

57 See, e.g., On India: Anuradha Dingwaney Needham and Rajeswari Sunder Rajan (eds.), *The Crisis of Secularism in India* (Durham, NC: Duke University Press, 2007). On Israel: Mordechai Kremnitzer, "Between Progress towards and Regression from Constitutional Liberalism: On the Need for Liberal Constitution and Judicial Review of Knesset Legislation," in Yoav Dotan and Ariel Bendor (eds.), *Zamir Book: On Law, Government and Society* (Jerusalem: Sacher Institute for Legislative Research and Comparative Law, Hebrew University, 2005) (Hebrew). On Tunisia: Zaid Al-Ali and Donia Ben Romdhane, "Tunisia's New Constitution: Progress and Challenges to Come," *Open Democracy*, February 16, 2014. Retrieved from: www.opendemocracy.net/north-africa-west-asia/zaid-al-ali-donia-ben-romdhane/tunisia%E2%80%99s-new-constitution-progress-and-challenges-to-

58 For additional analysis on the disadvantages of incrementalist constitutional strategies see Chapter 1.

59 Sampanthan, "Interview," 953–4.

intervention in the religious status quo (and the celebration in the 1990s of a "constitutional revolution" by the Supreme Court Chief Justice at that time, Aharon Barak) led to religious leaders' public refusal to abide by the Supreme Court's decisions and ultimately resulted in the obstruction of the constitution-making process. As one religious Knesset member said: "Even if the Ten Commandments would be proposed as a Basic Law, the religious parties would object. Because if the Ten Commandments became a law of the state, the Supreme Court would interpret them and change them."[60] These developments explain the lack of political will to complete the constitution-drafting project that was initiated in the early 2000s.[61]

In sum, critics of the incrementalist approach often claim that constitutional indecisiveness or ambiguity dismantle the distinction between "higher lawmaking" and "ordinary lawmaking," which is a cornerstone of liberal constitutionalism.[62] However, as noted earlier, this distinction is by definition challenged when constitutions are debated in divided societies. At the same time, it is important to distinguish here between the drafters' approaches toward decision making in issues concerning the institutional as opposed to the foundational (or symbolic) aspect of constitutions. While the establishment of governmental mechanisms requires clarity with regard to the "rules of the game," the foundational/symbolic aspect, which reflects the citizens' ultimate goals and shared identity, must convey the possibility of inclusion, rather than finality. Therefore, the drafters of incrementalist constitutions, seeking to circumvent explosive conflicts, often choose to include ambiguous or fuzzy provisions regarding the constitution's symbolic and normative aspect.

Sometimes it is difficult to separate between debates concerning the constitution's procedural or institutional aspects and those that concern ideational issues. Moreover, in some cases, the exportation of controversial issues from the constitution-drafting process does not rest on a genuine intention to pursue further political deliberation but rather represents an instrumental strategy aimed at guaranteeing favorite decisions in a more politically convenient setting. Given predictions on how political forces will congeal into the institutional arrangements in the postdrafting phase, drafters may prefer to transfer decision making to political bodies that would favor their positions. By that, they pursue in fact a strategy of restriction of future political choices rather than aim at permit flexibility. Similarly, constitutional deferral may go hand in hand with strict negotiations concerning the structure of future judicial institutions (e.g., nomination procedures for the supreme/constitutional court) that

60 David Tal of Shas Party, Divrey Hakneset, *Knesset Record* 184 (1999), 537.

61 For a more detailed discussion on the political obstacles to the completion of the constitution-writing project in Israel see Lerner, "The Political Infeasibility of 'Thin Constitutions'."

62 Ackerman, *We the People*, 85–121.

would guarantee certain judicial interpretations on issues left open by the constitutional drafters. Indeed, whether drafters' choices are underpinned by a genuine intention for further deliberation or by a more instrumental/strategic motivation is a question often difficult to investigate by empirical means. Furthermore, even when the adoption of vague constitutional formulations or the deferral of choices was initially motivated by instrumental intentions, the political or legal outcomes may not always meet the intended consequences predicted by the drafters. In some cases, the indecision on the constitutional level yielded an unintended institutional trajectory that was difficult to change in later decades (for example, in the case of Orthodox monopoly on marriage and divorce and the prevention of civil marriage for more than six decades in Israel).

IV. CONCLUDING REMARKS: POTENTIAL LONG-TERM INFLUENCE OF CONSTITUENT ASSEMBLY DEBATES

While preconstitutional political agreements have a significant influence on constituent assemblies' success in achieving their explicitly declared goals, I do not wish to claim that the deliberations and decision making taking place in constituent assemblies in divided societies is insignificant. Rather, constituent assembly members often play an important role in formulating the provisions and exact phrases included in the formal constitutional text, whether through committees work or in the plenary discussions. Similarly, they may decide which controversies are settled through constitutional provisions and which are left outside the formal constitutional text, thus determining the scope of issues entrenched by the constitution. Moreover, constituent assemblies in divided societies may have an important long-term impact that goes beyond the immediate and direct influence of the constitutional text. Representing a significant reference point for future political debates, minutes of constituent assembly debates may have an enduring educative and instructive influence on legislative and judicial branches as well as on the general public.

Elsewhere, I have written about the educative role incrementalist constitutions play in deeply divided societies, where the embrace of conflicting visions enables these arrangements to maintain constitutional legitimacy. Consent, which is a necessary condition for meaningful and legitimate constitutions, is usually achieved by giving the polity a sense of authorship and ownership, a sense that they are included in the constitutional "We the People."[63] In deeply divided societies, incrementalist

[63] Daniel J. Elazar, "Constitution-Making: The Pre-Eminent Political Act," in Keith G. Banting and Richard Simeon (eds.), *The Politics of Constitutional Change in Industrial Nations: Redesigning the State* (London: Macmillan, 1985), 233.

constitutions achieve legitimacy and consent by representing the identity of the people as it really is – a deeply divided one.[64] In many respects, under conditions of deep disagreement over the vision of the state, the protocols of constituent assembly debates may play a similar role in representing and giving voice to the competing perspectives concerning the norms and values that should underpin the state.

Reading the controversies and opposing arguments during constituent assembly debates may be as important as reading dissenting opinions written by the Supreme Court in foundational constitutional decisions. In both cases, giving voice to minority or opposing opinions increases the legitimacy of the existing institutions, and even facilitates a process of peaceful constitutional change. Dissent is often regarded as an essential safeguard of democracy.[65] While, as Mark Tushnet said, "The fate of a dissent lies in the hands of history,"[66] dissents allow courts to express internal opposition and appeal to future potential corrections of previous decisions. As Benjamin Cardozo wrote, "The voice of the majority may be that of force triumphant, content with the plaudits of the hour and recking little of the morrow. The dissenter speaks to the future, and his voice is pitched to a key that will carry through the year."[67] Similar words can describe dissenting views of minority perspectives in constituent assemblies.

Inclusive constituent assembly debates, where both majority and minority groups freely voice their positions, may influence the way future legislatures or courts interpret constitutions. Judges may use ideas expressed during the drafting debates to limit reformist constitutional interpretation. Alternatively, conflicting views argued during the assembly debates, similarly to court dissenting opinions, may serve as a reasoned basis for a reformist legislation. Competing perspectives expressed during open and free constitutional deliberation demonstrate the plurality of visions held by different parts of "the people" and legitimate the exchange of opinions within an ongoing conversation, in place of violent conflict. The US *Federalist Papers* are often cited as sources of inspiration for future legislators and judges in their interpretation and implementation of constitutional principles. Similarly, constituent assembly debates in divided societies may be a source of inspiration for further public and political discussion and deliberation around foundational issues. The *Federalist Papers* provide an explanation and justification for the particular choices

[64] Hanna Lerner, *Making Constitutions in Deeply Divided Societies*, chapter 9.

[65] William O. Douglas, "The Dissent: A Safeguard of Democracy," *Journal of the American Judicature Society* 32 (1948), 105.

[66] Mark Tushnet (ed.), *I Dissent: Great Opposing Opinions in Landmark Supreme Court Cases* (Boston, MA: Beacon Press, 2008), 221.

[67] Benjamin N. Cardozo, *Law and Literature and Other Essays and Addresses* (1931), 36. Cited in Melvin I. Urofsky, *Dissent and the Supreme Court: Its Role in the Court's History and the Nation's Constitutional Dialogue* (New York, NY: Pantheon Books, 2015).

the drafters made. By contrast, constituent assembly debates in divided societies sometimes yield no clear resolution and leave certain constitutional formulations ambiguous. As opposed to the *Federalist Papers*, constituent assembly debates in divided societies may not present a particular credo, a coherent set of norms and values, but rather the disagreement that underpins state institutions. The record of constituent assembly debates may delineate the contours of the dispute and the scope of possibilities and choices the drafters had faced. This scope may be different and broader than the way a particular constitutional principle had been interpreted or implemented in the postdrafting stage. Further deliberation and discussion of these disagreements comprises part of the postdrafting constitutional heritage in divided societies.

4

Constituent Assembly Failure in Pakistan and Nepal

Mara Malagodi

I. INTRODUCTION

The present chapter compares the experiences of the only two failed constituent assemblies in South Asia in order to explain the reasons of Pakistan and Nepal's aborted constitution-making processes and reflect on the long-term impact on later legal and political developments.[1] Such experiences are those of the first Constituent Assembly of Pakistan (CA1P) and the first Constituent Assembly of Nepal (CA1N). CA1P operated from 1947 until 1954; in October 1954, the governor general dissolved it and in March 1955 the federal court legalized his intervention. CA1N, instead, operated from 2008 until 2012, when Nepal's Supreme Court prohibited further extensions of its term leading to the assembly's dissolution by the president on the advice of the prime minister. Both Pakistan and Nepal's first constituent assemblies were dissolved by executive action before they succeeded in completing and promulgating the new constitution, notwithstanding their many delays and extensions. Moreover, in both cases, the judiciary played a key role in legitimizing the assembly's dissolution in legal terms. Thus, this chapter aims to answer the two following questions through a comparative analysis of these case studies: first, why did the first constituent assemblies of Pakistan and Nepal fail? Second, to a more limited degree, what has been the impact of the failure of these bodies on constitutional developments and democratic politics in both countries? In this respect, it is

1 The expression "South Asia" indicates the eight countries that are the member states of the South Asian Association for Regional Cooperation (SAARC): Afghanistan, Bangladesh, Bhutan, India, Maldives, Nepal, Pakistan, and Sri Lanka. It is important to highlight that during the life of Pakistan's first constituent assembly, Pakistan still comprised the East wing, which then seceded and became the independent Republic of Bangladesh in 1971.

I am very grateful to my Research Associate Khem Shreesh for his invaluable assistance, and to the volume editors, Vatsal Naresh, Matthew Nelson, Maya Tudor, and Tarunabh Khaitan for their helpful comments.

important to consider the diachronic essence of the comparison between the case studies and the very recent nature of Nepal's events.

It is argued that there are important merits in the diachronic comparison between Pakistan and Nepal's failed constituent assembly experiences. Notwithstanding the sixty-year temporal gap, the extensive similarities between the case studies allow for more generalizable comparative insights and lessons. The bases of this comparison are as follows:

- Pakistan and Nepal's dissolved assemblies were in both countries the first representative (whether directly or indirectly elected) institutions charged with the drafting of permanent constitutions that were expected to usher in a new regime and consolidate democratic politics. As such, the sense of anticipation was enormous: these constituent assembly processes were originally thought of as "gatherings of the nation." As such, the expectation that these would be foundational constitutional moments and critical junctures that would firmly set Pakistan and Nepal on the path of constitutional democracy made the impact of their failure all the greater.
- Both Pakistan and Nepal's constituent assemblies operated in polarized postconflict political contexts: after Partition (1947) in Pakistan and after the People's War (1996–2006) in Nepal. Both countries featured deep-rooted legacies of authoritarian government, executive dominance, disregard for constitutional praxis, and militarized state institutions, which in turn had been legitimized by a perceived need for unity vis-à-vis internal strife and the threat of obliteration from neighboring India. As both countries emerged from violent conflicts, group polarization on the basis of identity steadily increased in what were already deeply divided societies with competing visions of the nation and the organization of the state. Moreover, both Nepal and Pakistan featured a great degree of sociocultural diversity that their monolithic ethnocultural forms of nationalism struggled to accommodate both in ideological and institutional terms.
- Both constituent assemblies were unicameral chambers that fulfilled the double function of ordinary legislatures and extraordinary constitution making bodies – a situation that considerably delayed the process of constitution drafting as the majority of the assemblies' session were dedicated to ordinary law making. Moreover, bitter political conflict stemmed from the fact that both Pakistan and Nepal featured a parliamentary form of government with its intimate link between the executive and the legislature through the mechanism of confidence, especially in the context of the frequent changes at the helm of the government in both countries during the work of the assemblies. Thus, this double function engendered another level of political conflict within the

constituent assemblies and between the assemblies and other state bodies. In particular, the work of both constituent assemblies was marred by continuous tensions with the executive in both its elected and unelected forms over the direction of constitution making. Thus, the assemblies became progressively marginalized as sites of constituent power and key decisions were increasingly brokered outside of the legislative forum.

- Both in Pakistan and Nepal deep political fragmentation and the lack of a strong, well-organized national party negatively impacted the work of the constituent assemblies and their relationship with other government branches. In Pakistan, while the Muslim League controlled CA1P, it progressively lost its role as the party driving national and regional politics alongside the constitution drafting process. This is in stark contrast with the experience and role of the Congress Party in India. In fact, the League, even if it controlled the majority of CAP1 seats, was eventually supplanted by a number of smaller regional parties in all other representative institutions outside of the assembly and in the executive bodies, thus increasingly isolating CA1P. In Nepal, the composition of CA1N was such that a broad coalition of political parties was necessary to achieve the two-thirds majority necessary to pass the document, even if the Maoists were the biggest party. As a result, no single political party controlled the drafting process and cross-party alliances on an identity basis started to form within the assembly's committees and through the caucuses. The direction of constitution making toward inclusive state restructuring met with the opposition of the more conservative political forces and led to the marginalization of the assembly as the center of deliberative politics.
- Both Pakistan and Nepal's constituent assemblies featured profound internal disagreements over key aspects of the new constitution draft, such as the role of sociocultural identity and religion vis-à-vis national identity, political representation, and the territorial organization of political power.
- The same accusation of working with no end in sight was leveled at both assemblies in order to justify their dissolution. On the one hand, Pakistan's assembly had no fixed term statutory basis; on the other hand, Nepal's 2007 interim constitution prescribed a fixed term of two years for the body, but the assembly extended its own term four times by way of constitutional amendment. In reality, CA1P had a complete draft ready for promulgation on the eve of the dissolution, while CA1N had reached important compromises and agreements within the various committees as early as 2010, as evidenced by their reports, even before the assembly's first extension of its term.
- The judiciary played a pivotal role in sealing the fate of both assemblies and in providing a justification in legal form to their untimely demise. The involvement of Pakistan and Nepal's apex courts in the politically controversial

litigation over the dissolution of the assemblies considerably weakened the legitimacy and standing of the higher judiciary in both countries.

- The demise of Pakistan and Nepal's first constituent assemblies was followed by the formation of new constituent assemblies featuring a very different political makeup whereby the dominant forces in the first assemblies were consistently downsized in the second. These new bodies succeeded in completing their work in less than two years, but they were sidelined and ended up rubber-stamping a constitutional deal made outside the deliberative legislative forum. As a result, the constitutions that they produced proved to be unstable political settlements.

The notion of "failure" of Pakistan and Nepal's first constituent assembly experiences is key to understanding the wider implications of this comparison. Both bodies were dissolved before succeeding in promulgating a new constitution, even if they were close to completing their task. Therefore, the dissolution of the assemblies represents an obvious failure to produce a constitution at all. The complete failure of a constituent assembly process merits particular attention because it consists of a failure of extraordinary constitutional politics – more specifically, of the highest modality of constitution making. In this respect, Andrew Arato explains that constituent assemblies are the archetype of revolutionary constituent power: they are sovereign institutions with unlimited powers embodying the unified will of the people and promising a total rupture from the old regime through a foundational moment.[2] Clearly the political stakes in a constitution-making process via the constituent assembly procedure are extremely high, and conversely so are the risks inherent in the potential failure of such a process. The inability of the body conceived as a gathering of the nation to ink the constitution bears profound enduring consequences for the polity's sense of national unity and for subsequent attempts at constitution making.

The central argument that this chapter puts forward is that the failure of Pakistan and Nepal's first constituent assemblies and the implication of the judiciary in their demise bore long-term destabilizing effects on constitutional politics and democratic governance in both countries. In Pakistan, the dissolution of CA1P led in the immediate term to a bout of emergency rule, to the promulgation of the short-lived 1956 republican constitution passed by a second constituent assembly, which was de facto controlled by the unelected executive (the governor general supported by the army), and eventually to the country's first military coup in 1958. In the long term, Pakistan embarked on a cycle of recurring praetorian rule and political instability, while the political cleavage between East and West Pakistan deepened. In 1971,

2 A. Arato, *Post Sovereign Constitution Making* (Oxford: Oxford University Press, 2016), 91, 108.

civil war eventually broke out between the country's two wings, which led to the secession of East Pakistan in 1971 and the creation of independent Bangladesh. In Nepal, the dissolution of CA1N was followed by a period of eighteen months of government with no legislature in place in a parliamentary system, the appointment of the Supreme Court's chief justice as the interim prime minister, and the promulgation of a new contentious constitution in 2015. The new document, however, while eventually passed by the second assembly, was largely agreed by the leadership of the main political parties outside of the legitimate democratic forum of the constituent assembly. The new constitution was finalized in a fast-track exclusionary process amidst violent protests by Madhesi communities in the Terai and an unofficial Indian blockade, ultimately leading to further polarization along ethnic lines, increasing secessionist threats, and enduring political instability.

These observations form the basis of a more generalizable conclusion: the process of constitution making has an intimate relationship with its outcome, and the interplay of process and outcome within a specific historical and social context bears long-term consequences for constitutional democracy and political stability in any given country. Based on a close reading of archival material and legal documents alongside academic commentaries, this chapter advances the following hypothesis with regard to the failure of Pakistan and Nepal's first constituent assemblies. It is argued that the direction of constitution making taken by both CA1P and CA1N threatened to fragment further Pakistan and Nepal's dominant groups, hence their ability to control crucial strategic state institutions and economic resources. As a result, key political actors mobilized against the assemblies and sought to obstruct their proceedings and put an end to their constitution-making endeavors. More specifically, both assemblies failed because of the specific interplay of certain structural and contextual factors in the constitution-making process (the CA as constitution and ordinary lawmaking body in a parliamentary system, the fragmentation of a dominant national party, the authoritarian political legacies, regional and international political pressures) with the behavior of the political actors fragmented and polarized along a combination of ideological and identity lines in a postconflict scenario.

The essay contributes to the burgeoning literature on constitution making by shedding light, first, on the circumstances and concomitants that led to the failure and untimely demise of these democratic constitution-making processes; and, second, on the impact of such failure on Pakistan and Nepal's constitutional and political trajectories. The chapter is divided into two parts each analyzing the context and background of CA1P and CA1N respectively, their institutional set up, the actors involved, the decision-making processes, and the circumstances and impact of their untimely demise. Finally, a brief section offers some concluding remarks and comparative lessons.

II. PAKISTAN

This section examines the failed constitution making experience of Pakistan's first constituent assembly, and the aftermath of its dissolution. It is argued that the issues of executive dominance and incomplete ethnocentric nation building have remained critical even in Pakistan's contemporary constitutional politics, partly as legacies of the failed constitution-making experience of its first constituent assembly.

A. *Pakistan's Period of Constitutional Engagement (1947–1954)*

Pakistan, like India, acquired independence from the United Kingdom in August 1947 through legislation passed in Westminster, the India Independence Act 1947, which granted Dominion status to both countries. They retained the British monarch as their head of state until the promulgation of their permanent republican constitutions. From August 1947 onwards, Pakistan's first constituent assembly began preparing the new constitution, while the country was still ruled under the framework of the Government of India Act 1935, amended over the years to suit the new Dominion constitutional framework. Jinnah's became Pakistan's first governor general and president of the constituent assembly. CA1P was created under the India Independence Act and originally featured sixty-nine members. The work of the assembly proceeded slowly, with many interruptions and delays. However, by mid-October 1954, CA1P had a full draft ready for promulgation, while opposition to the dispensation mounted outside the assembly. On October 24, the governor general suddenly issued a proclamation dissolving the assembly. The CA1P president, Tamizuddin Khan, swiftly moved to the courts to challenge the legal validity of the governor general's intervention. While the Chief Court found for the assembly, the Federal Court reversed the decision of the lower court and condoned Ghulam Mohammad's dissolution, providing a cloak of legality to the governor general's executive intervention. Ghulam Mohammad then convened a second assembly, and Pakistan's new constitution was eventually promulgated in 1956. It proved, however, a short-lived experiment. The steady erosion of Pakistan's democratic process paved the way to General Ayub Khan's military coup in 1958 and the suspension of constitutional government, leading to a recurrent cycle of praetorian politics.

B. *Context and Background of CA1P*

This section analyzes the historical legacies and political context in which CA1P operated after independence in order to understand how these elements constrained the agency of Pakistan's constitutional actors and contributed to the failure of CA1P.

First of all, Pakistan acquired independence in 1947 on the basis of an awkward geographical configuration comprising the Muslim majority areas of British India (aside from Kashmir) with two noncontiguous wings separated by thousands of miles of Indian territory: East and West Pakistan. It also faced major economic and strategic imbalances because of the smaller share of the economic, military, and institutional assets at partition. Thus, it needed to build its state structure and institutional framework nearly from scratch, an additional burden for CA1P in its ordinary legislative capacity, hence delaying its constitution-making work.[3]

Second, Pakistani nationalism was ethnocentric, but it did not contain any guiding programmatic principles like Indian nationalism with its reformist commitments to political equality and economic self-sufficiency.[4] Pakistan was to be a "homeland to protect Indian Muslims," hence merely defined in terms of religious identity and lacking any specific territorial and institutional dimension.[5] As such, CA1P did not have a strong, unifying ideological blueprint – aside from the "Ideology of Pakistan" delineated during a national education conference in November 1947 – that could guide the constitution-making process. Similarly, it could not forge a sense of national identity capable of superseding the various regional identities, bridging the territorial and political cleavages between the two wings, and establishing the egalitarian basis for liberal democracy to sink roots. To add further to Pakistan's structural imbalances, the East wing contained the majority of the country's population (East Pakistan, 42 million and West Pakistan, 33.7 million), but the West wing's territory was more than five times that of the East wing.[6] Additionally, while at independence the majority of Pakistanis were indeed Muslim, about 22 percent were Hindu (mostly in East Pakistan); 1.3 percent Christian; and Sikhs, Zoroastrians, Buddhists, and Bahá'ís respectively constituted less than 1 percent of the population.[7] Pakistan featured an even greater degree of linguistic diversity at independence: Urdu – the national language – was the mother tongue of only 7.3 percent of the total population. The biggest language was Bengali, with 56 percent of the total population concentrated entirely in the East wing. The West wing, instead, was linguistically much

3 I. Talbot, *Pakistan: A Modern History* (New York, NY: St. Martin's Press, 1998), 95–124.

4 M. Tudor, *The Promise of Power: The Origins of Democracy in India and Pakistan* (Cambridge: Cambridge University Press, 2013), 67–99.

5 Jalal argues that "proclaiming itself an Islamic State created on the bedrock of a non-territorially defined Muslim Nation or *ummah*, the architects of Pakistan embraced the idea of the nation-state without conceding space to territorial nationalism in their official ideology," in A. Jalal, "Conjuring Pakistan: History as Official Imagining," *International Journal of Middle Eastern Studies* 27 (1995), 74.

6 See http://121.52.153.178:8080/xmlui/bitstream/handle/123456789/14515/Census%20of%20Pakistan%20%2c%201951%20Urban%20%26%20Rural%20Population%20%26%20Area%20%28Table%201%20%26%201%20A%29.PDF?sequence=1&isAllowed=y (accessed January 26, 2017).

7 S. Sheikh, "Religious Minorities in Pakistan: Aspirations and Challenges," in M. Joseph (ed.), *Understanding Pakistan* (London: Routledge, 2016), 220.

more diverse and featured Punjabi as the biggest regional language and the mother tongue of 29 percent of the total population (67.08 of West Pakistan), Sindhi as the mother tongue of 5.9 percent of the total population (12.85 of West Pakistan), Pashtu as the mother tongue of 4.9 percent of the total population (8.16 of West Pakistan), and Baluchi as the mother tongue of 1.5 percent of the total population (3.04 of West Pakistan).[8] Ultimately, the two pillars of Pakistani ethnocultural nationalism proved to be either insufficient as national glue (Islam) or exceedingly divisive (Urdu) as reflected in the protracted deliberations of CA1P over their controversial position in the drafting of the new constitution.

Third, the political legacies of colonialism in East and West Pakistan proved difficult for CA1P to overcome. On the one hand, the markedly different historical experiences of the two wings during colonial times deepened the already profound political cleavages between the two areas of the country, as reflected in the difficulties encountered by CA1P in trying to bridge them. On the other hand, the authoritarian legacy of colonial governance, coupled with the dominance of Punjabis in the army and bureaucracy vis-à-vis the Bengali numerical dominance in CA1P, intensified the standoff between the assembly and the military-bureaucratic axis. In East Pakistan the exposure of the Bengali population to representative institutions and their higher attainments in Western-style education had produced a radical critique of the British Raj. As such, Bengal was the epicenter of the nationalist and revolutionary independence movement; it featured well-established networks and ideological coordinates for oppositional politics, activism, and resistance to state oppression. Moreover, Bengal had an old proud tradition of language nationalism since colonial times and independent Pakistan's Urdu-only policy at the center proved extremely contentious. Instead, West Pakistan's autocratic political culture was rooted in paternalism, wide discretionary powers, and the personification of political authority – all features of the colonial government that remained persistent in the postcolonial political system. In the Punjab, the British had sought partial collaboration from the rural elites and established a more paternalistic rule in the region by creating a deep-rooted culture of clientelism and a symbiotic relationship with colonial state structures.[9] Since its annexation to British India in 1849, the Punjab had also become pivotal to imperial governance: the province was regarded as British India's "granary" (by the 1920s the Punjab produced one-third of British India's total wheat) and "garrison" (by 1875 the Indian army drew a third of its recruits from the Punjab). Moreover, the support lent by the Punjabi military forces to the colonial establishment during the 1857 revolt further reinforced the

[8] M. Brown and S. Ganguly, *Fighting Words: Language Policy and Ethnic Relations in Asia* (Cambridge, MA: MIT Press, 2003), 52–4.

[9] See www.global.ucsb.edu/punjab/14.1_Talbot.pdf (accessed March 12, 2016).

alliance between British rulers and Punjabi landlords. As a result, the Punjab's privileged relation with the colonial structure laid the foundations for its preponderant position within the administration of postcolonial Pakistan.

Fourth, CA1P had to operate in a difficult postconflict context of deepening communal tensions within the country, growing militarization of the state, and increasing tensions with India. In fact, Pakistan had emerged as a sovereign state from the bloodshed of the partition of the Indian subcontinent. The communal nature of partition led to approximately 1 million casualties and the migration and displacement of more than 10 million people between the two newly created states. In 1948, violence resumed when India and Pakistan went to war against each other over the disputed territory of Kashmir. The violence of partition and the war further deepened the politicization of communal identities and heightened the tension with the Indian neighbor. The threat posed by India to Pakistan's very existence and the inequitable division of the British Indian Army between the two countries resulted in a substantive commitment of Pakistan's budget to military expenses.[10] Pakistan's "economy of defense" in turn led to a progressive centralization of state authority, which was accompanied by a further "Punjabization" of nonelected executive institutions, in particular the army and civil bureaucracy. Thus, the already influential Punjabi-dominated Pakistan Army acquired a greater role in the country's government. Conversely, the mounting concentration of power at the center engendered further executive dominance and disrespect for constitutional boundaries, while growing dissatisfaction in the provinces produced increasingly strong centrifugal tensions, especially in East Pakistan.

Fifth, Pakistan's fear for survival shaped the country's first decade of postcolonial politics and inevitably affected the work of CA1P. The Indian threat and the Cold War scenario incentivized Pakistan's military establishment to strengthen the alliance with the USA, contributing to the formation of the South East Asia Treaty Organization (SEATO) Pact in September 1954. The focus on national security brought greater political emphasis on national unity at all costs. As a result, the constitution-making direction that CA1P had taken on the issues of political representation and federal restructuring displeased the military-bureaucratic axis, who opposed popular politics in any ideological or identitarian form. The work of CA1P was increasingly perceived as a challenge to the hegemony of the nonelected executive bodies controlled by Punjabi groups. Rapidly, Pakistani politics took an authoritarian turn.

Sixth, key constitutional conventions were disregarded in the appointments for Pakistan's top political posts since independence (including Jinnah's appointment as governor general in 1947), weakening the rule of law. The turn toward

[10] Talbot (2000), 218.

authoritarianism sharply accelerated after the death of Liaquat Ali Khan. He had attempted to undermine the power of the traditional elites and reform the Pakistani state, but he was assassinated in October 1951. After that, the unconstitutional game of "musical chairs" with the appointments in the highest offices of the state continued unabashed: Khawaja Nazimuddin was transferred from the governor general's seat to the prime minister's, while Malik Ghulam Mohammad became Pakistan's third governor general.[11] As Jalal highlights, the disarray in Pakistan's political arenas was an opportunity for the military and bureaucratic axis to advance their own institutional interests by virtually equating these with the imperative of the state.[12] CA1P was soon to be the main casualty of this realignment.

Seventh, the increasing disregard for constitutional practice was accompanied by a steady polarization along identity lines that directly affected CA1P. "After the assassination of Liaquat, Pakistan began choosing its leadership on a geographical basis. No longer did the nation have Jinnah or Liaquat, associated with neither the West nor the East wing. Kwaja Nazimuddin was a Bengali and Ghulam Mohammad a Punjabi."[13] On the one hand, Ghulam Mohammad emerged as the steward of the bureaucratic faction and developed closer ties with the army, while working internationally to deepen the relationship with the United States. On the other hand, Nazimuddin buoyed the Bengali cause for equal legislative representation, which culminated with the assembly passing the Basic Principles Committee Report in December 1952 with the support of the Islamic factions, and rejected the One Unit Plan for West Pakistan.[14] The Punjabi dominated military-bureaucratic axis then started equating the work of CA1P with Bengali majoritarianism and Islamism; as such the constitution draft that the assembly had prepared was perceived as antinational and a threat to Pakistan's national unity and national security. As a result, CA1P became an obstacle that had to be removed.

Eighth, while the Muslim League dominated CA1P, outside of the Assembly the party progressively failed to gain the necessary popular support to function as a unifying political force akin to the Congress in India and became progressively obliterated in the various provincial elections. As a result, the constituent assembly became increasingly isolated. In fact, the early years of Pakistan's independent history saw the proliferation of regional parties and deepening political fragmentation, forcing the central state to rely increasingly on the army and the bureaucracy to exercise its authority effectively. When Prime Minister Nazimuddin decided to impose martial rule throughout the Punjab in March 1953 and dismiss the chief minister of Punjab

[11] Talbot (1998), 139–40.

[12] A. Jalal, *The State of Martial Rule: The Origins of Pakistan's Political Economy of Defence* (Cambridge: Cambridge University Press, 1990).

[13] McGrath (1996), 80–1.

[14] L. Binder, *Religion and Politics in Pakistan* (Berkeley, CA: University of California Press, 1963).

because of the anti-Ahmadi riots, the crisis offered the ideal opportunity for the governor general to move against the prime minister. On April 17, 1953, Ghulam Mohammad issued a proclamation dismissing Nazimuddin. Virtually no protests followed what was essentially a coup d'état, even if presented in the guise of a "cabinet reshuffle" on the basis that the British constitutional conventions pertaining to cabinet government did not apply in Pakistan.[15] On the same day, the governor general "reshuffled" the cabinet, recalled the Pakistani ambassador from Washington, DC – the Bengali politician Mohammad Ali Bogra – and appointed him as the new prime minister, while purging the cabinet of all the other Muslim League members.[16] The governor general had become active in politics and effectively abandoned his super partes' constitutional role. The sacking of Nazimuddin, a prime minister who commanded the confidence of the legislature, was only the first of many instances in Pakistani history in which the unelected executive thwarted democratic politics. It is in light of this incomplete constitutionalization of executive power together with growing identity politics that the experience of CA1P, and its untimely demise, ought to be analyzed.

C. *Institutional Setup, Actors, and Decision Making in the CA1P Process*

Pakistan's first constituent assembly featured the same institutional foundations of India's constituent assembly, but the outcome of the two processes could have not been more divergent. Both bodies received their powers under the India Independence Act 1947 and were indirectly elected by the provincial legislatures in 1946 on the basis of communally defined separate electorates. Originally composed of sixty-nine members, by 1948 CAP1 grew to seventy-nine members. The seats were allocated on the basis of provincial representation: East Bengal, forty-four seats; Punjab, twenty-two seats; Sindh, five seats; NWFP, three seats; Baluchistan, Baluchistan states, Bahawalpur, Khairpur, and NWFP states, one seat each. Territorially, the representatives of the East wing had a clear majority in the assembly, almost 60 percent, while Punjabi representatives controlled slightly less than 30 percent of the total seats. In terms of political affiliation, most CA1P members (fifty-nine seats) went to the Muslim League.[17]

CA1P became gradually marginalized and the difficult political circumstances facilitated the dominance of the executive over the legislative branch. As Talbot explains, "the Constituent Assembly was in theory a crucial cog in the political process at the centre. The national cabinet was responsible to it ... and it also possessed

[15] McGrath (1996), 117.
[16] Ibid., 97–8.
[17] A. Jalal, *The State of Martial Rule* (Cambridge: Cambridge University Press, 1990), 63.

the authority to restrict the Governor General's powers. In reality authority lay in descending order with the Governor General, the Prime Minister and the central cabinet. The Assembly's muted legislative role was seen in the frequent recourse to rule by ordinance."[18] Two factors in relation to the composition of the assembly became pivotal to its marginalization and untimely demise. First, as the political cleavages between the East and West wings deepened, the Punjabi-dominated military-bureaucratic axis at the center increasingly worried about the Bengali majority in the assembly. Second, Muslim League politicians dominated the assembly, but by the early 1950s the influence of the League had progressively started to wane at both the national and provincial levels, leaving the assembly members even more isolated from both the other state bodies and the electorate. The Muslim League did not have a rooted territorial organization in the provinces that became Pakistan, apart from East Bengal. Moreover, the League's leadership and the demand for Pakistan itself had originated in the Muslim minority areas of British India, not in the Muslim majority ones.[19] Following partition, the party leaders had moved to Pakistan and the Muslim League lost the organizational support and local link it had created in the United Provinces. Moreover, since the Muslim League saw linguistic divisions as irrelevant, linguistic regionalism was forced to express itself in regional parties outside the guidance of the national party.[20] The Muslim League's leaders could not enforce their plan for national consolidation. Ultimately, they were forced to compromise with the increasingly powerful regional parties and concede a great deal of autonomy to the administrative bureaucracy in order to consolidate state authority.[21]

CA1P functioned both as ordinary legislature and constitution-making body, and this configuration led to inordinate delays on the drafting front. As Sir Ivor Jennings, the British constitutional expert engaged to assist with the drafting, commented: "Until 1953, when the Basic Principles Report came up for consideration, the sessions of the Constituent Assembly, as such, were few and short. For the most part, too, they were taken up with the alteration of the transitional constitution."[22] On August 12, 1948, the Committee on Fundamental Rights of Citizens and Minorities was established. It was only on March 12, 1949 that the Basic Principles Committee was set up, when the assembly accepted the Objectives Resolution presented by Prime Minister Liaquat Ali Khan. The Resolution committed the new constitution to Islam as the core element of both its legal framework and national

[18] Talbot (1998), 134.

[19] K. Adeney and A. Wyatt, "Democracy in South Asia: Getting Beyond the Structure-Agency Dichotomy," *Political Studies* 52 (2003), 1, 19.

[20] Ibid., 20.

[21] Talbot (1998), 100.

[22] *Sir Ivor Jennings Private Papers* ICS/125/B/15/8ii, Constituent Assembly of Pakistan.

identity. The text of the Resolution, however, remained vague and most importantly nonjusticiable.[23] The Basic Principles Committee comprised twenty-five members and was led by Tamizuddin; the Committee was then divided into three thematic subcommittees (constitutional structure, judiciary, franchise), of whose work little is known except for sporadic statements in the media and the Jennings' Private Papers.[24]

There were many delays in the work of the Committee and it was only on December 19, 1952 that the Basic Principles Report was signed. Jennings described the Report as such:

> It provided a scheme not for a "Dominion of Pakistan" but for a "Republic of Pakistan"; and by resolution of the Constituent Assembly the formula became "the Islamic Republic of Pakistan." There was no controversy over the republican character of the constitution, but there was much argument over the relations between East and West Pakistan. A formula [for political representation] was invented by the new Prime Minister, Mr. Mohammed Ali, ... and the greater part of the Report of the Basic Principles Committee was adopted by the Constituent Assembly between September 1953 and July 1954.[25]

Then, the Constitution Drafting Committee met for the first time on November 16, 1953 and it started to consider drafts only on June 27, 1954. In July 1954, Jennings arrived in Karachi at the invitation of the assembly's Drafting Committee, which had finalized the draft and gained the assembly's vote of approval on September 21. On October 15 the document was submitted to Jennings, who made only minor changes to it.[26]

In 1953, the assembly had adopted the Mohammad Ali formula for parliament under the new constitution. The formula established a bicameral legislature, with the lower house consisting of 300 members elected on the basis of population, thus giving a clear majority to East Pakistan, and the upper house consisting of 50 members equally divided among the five provinces.[27] Significantly, in September 1954 the assembly rejected the governor general's One Unit plan to merge the four provinces of West Pakistan into one, which had been envisaged by West Pakistan's elites to counter the numerical superiority of Bengal. After this, CA1P swiftly moved to finalize the constitution. The draft featured the Objectives Resolution as Preamble, a republican and parliamentary democratic framework in which the president was reduced to "a mere figurehead," a federal structure, a bicameral legislature organized on the basis

23 M. Lau, *The Role of Islam in the Legal System of Pakistan* (Leiden: Martinus Nijhoff, 2006), 8.

24 McGrath (1996), 7–75.

25 *Sir Ivor Jennings Private Papers* ICS/125/B/15/8ii, Constituent Assembly of Pakistan.

26 McGrath (1996), 121–4.

27 Ibid., 112.

of the Mohammad Ali formula, concessions to the Islamic factions, a section on fundamental rights, a Supreme Court empowered to strike down primary legislation on the basis of unconstitutionality, and extensive emergency provisions.[28] CA1P was able to finalize the draft constitution thanks to the alliance between the Bengali and the Islamist CA members. As a result, the draft represented a compromise between different concerns and ideologies, and was unpalatable to many.

In particular, the governor general and the bureaucratic-military axis were displeased with the draft constitution. As Jalal elucidates,

> a federal constitution with a Bengali majority in the lower house was anathema to the civil bureaucracy and the defence establishment, and not simply because a lot of them belonged to the Punjab ... politicians were seen as a danger to the larger imperative of streamlining the state and inserting it into the international system. So it was not provincial but institutional interests that demanded a unitary instead of a federal form of government ... state-building [was placed] on a collision course with the political process.[29]

Moreover, the concessions to the Islamic factions with regard to judicial reviews of laws repugnant to Islam opened the way to the religious groups to interfere with governmental affairs.[30] Opposition to the draft also came from East Bengal, where the Muslim League politicians in the assembly faced great hostility from the regional parties, especially since the League's electoral debacle in 1954 at provincial level.

The assembly was aware that a standoff with the governor general was becoming inevitable. Thus, it went on the legislative offensive and actively attempted to curb executive power and entrench the principle parliamentary supremacy by codifying constitutional conventions into statute to limit royal prerogative powers.

> On 21 September [1954], the Constituent Assembly amended the Government of India Act. The amendments precluded the Governor General from acting except on the advice of his ministers. All ministers had to be members of the Assembly at the time of their selection and continue to hold office only so long as they retained the confidence of the legislature. The Cabinet was declared to be collectively responsible to the Assembly, and would be required to resign if any one of its members lost the confidence of the Assembly. The Assembly stated that their purpose was to give legislative sanction to certain accepted principles and conventions connected with the formation and working of government in a parliamentary system.[31]

[28] Ibid., 124–5.
[29] Jalal (1990), 175.
[30] Ibid., 185.
[31] McGrath (1996), 123.

The new statutory basis of the conventions effectively meant that a breach of those conventions could be litigated in court. As a result, the assembly's attempt to constitutionalize executive power was met by a swift realignment of the forces opposing the nascent constitutional settlement. This eventually led to the governor general's dissolution of the constituent assembly on October 24, 1954 by use of his prerogative powers.

D. *The Constituent Assembly's Demise and Aftermath in Pakistan*

The growing political tensions between Ghulam Mohammad and the assembly culminated in the governor general's dissolution of CA1P. The response of the assembly's president, Tamizuddin Khan, was swift and on November 8 he filed a petition in the Chief Court of Sindh claiming that the governor's dissolution was unconstitutional. As Jalal succinctly elucidates, "the petition was a test of the judiciary's independence from the executive."[32] The assembly engaged British barrister Denis Nowell Pritt QC to represent them, while the governor general engaged Jennings QC, who returned to Karachi on November 26. Jennings played an ambiguous role in Pakistan; in fact, recent research has demonstrated that he remained in close contact with British diplomats even when instructed on the cases effectively passing key information to Western governments at a critical time in the Cold War.[33]

At first instance, the Chief Court rejected the government's submissions that the court had no jurisdiction to decide the matter and that the governor general's dissolution of the constituent assembly was within the lawful exercise of his royal prerogative powers, and found in favor of the assembly.[34] Ghulam Mohammad then swiftly appealed to the Federal Court and brought in Kenneth Diplock QC (later Lord Diplock) alongside Jennings, while the constituent assembly did not even have sufficient funds to agree to the offer by Pritt to act pro bono, but conditional on the reimbursement of his living expenses.[35] In March 1955, the Federal Court reversed the decision of the Chief Court and found for the government. Jennings had advanced the following argument: as Pakistan was a Dominion, the assembly's amendments to the Government of India Act 1935 were invalid because they did not receive the assent of the governor; thus, in such circumstances the dissolution was lawful. One of the key points raised by Jennings was that all legislation passed

32 Jalal (1990), 197.

33 M. Malagodi, "Dominion Constitutionalism and the Royal Prerogative in Pakistan." Paper presented at the Modern Law Review seminar Dominion Constitutionalism at the Twilight of the British Empire, City Law School, University of London, June 10, 2016.

34 *Maulvi Tamizuddin Khan v. Federation of Pakistan* PLD 1955 Sindh 96.

35 McGrath (1996), 175.

by the constituent assembly, not just ordinary legislation but also constitutional legislation, necessitated the governor general's assent to be legally valid under English law as the governor general represented the British monarch.[36] Jennings argued that Pakistan's Dominion status required that the constitutional basis of the country, the Government of India Act and the India Independence Act, be interpreted in light of the English common law position on prerogative powers.[37] The Federal Court's decision to accept Jennings' submissions engendered further political instability in Pakistan. It undermined the sovereignty of Pakistan's constitution-making body, questioned the country's political basis of independence, and threw the nation into legal uncertainty by invalidating much of the legislation previously passed by the assembly. The court's decision also gave a cloak of legality to what was effectively a coup d'état by the governor general. In fact, Ghulam Mohammad had intended to take control of the constitution drafting process since the beginning of the court proceedings, which he was in any case prepared to ignore had the court ruled against him.[38] As Chief Justice Munir recalled later in his memoires, the president of CA1P had lost his case even before entering the courtroom.[39]

Six days after the judgment of the Federal Court, the governor general declared a state of emergency and promulgated an Emergency Powers Ordinance.[40] A string of constitutional cases ensued, shaking the legal and political foundations of the Pakistani state. In *Usif Patel*, a challenge to the validity of the governor general's emergency order, the apex court sought to restore its reputation and ruled that the federal government was required to call for a second constituent assembly.[41] In *Special Reference No. 1 of 1955*, instead, the Federal Court found for the government on all issues: invoking the "doctrine of necessity" it ruled that the governor general's dissolution of CA1P was lawful and that while a second assembly had to be convened, the life of the assembly could not be "indefinite."[42] Significantly, the government made the factual assertion that CA1P had failed to produce a constitution at all. Lawyers for CA1P sought to challenge this blatantly false assertion on the basis of evidence, but the court sidestepped the issue and maintained they were unable to go into questions of fact, thus legitimizing the allegation that CA1P had not performed its task.[43] As a result, the court became complicit in the myth that CA1P had failed to draft the constitution, and provided a cloak of legal legitimacy to the governor

36 Section 6(3), India Independence Act 1947.

37 *Federation of Pakistan and Others v. Maulvi Tamizuddin Khan* PLD 1955 Federal Court 240.

38 *Sir Ivor Jennings Private Papers* ICS 125/B/15/7/1.

39 McGrath (1996), 216–17.

40 H. Khan, *Constitutional and Political History of Pakistan* (Karachi: Oxford University Press, 2001), 143.

41 *Usif Patel* PLD 1955 FC 387.

42 *Special Reference* No. 1 PLD 1955 FC 435.

43 K. J. Newman, *Essays on the Constitution of Pakistan* (Dacca: Pakistan Co-operative Book Society, 1956), XLVIII.

general's executive intervention. In the short term, the court seemed to succeed in preserving a semblance of constitutionality and avoiding an outright executive takeover. In reality, the apex court's decisions had compromised the judiciary's independence and contributed to craft a narrative in which elected officials were corrupt, inefficient, and partisan political actors incapable and unwilling to serve the people by producing a constitution in a timely fashion, while at the same obliterating the enormous impact of structural constraints on the work of CA1P. In the end, this judicially sanctioned narrative that devalued deliberative politics, delegitimized representative bodies, and bolstered the executive progressively became Pakistan's dominant political discourse.

Eventually, on May 10, 1955, the governor general summoned a second indirectly elected constituent assembly. CA2P featured eighty members, forty for each wing. While the Muslim League still remained the largest party in CA2P with twenty-five seats (notably with only one from East Pakistan), it had lost the majority it had enjoyed in CA1P.[44] CA2P was fragmented along both ideological and regional lines, and more pliant to executive influence than its predecessor. In the meantime, General Iskander Mirza had been appointed governor general as Ghulam Muhammad's health was rapidly deteriorating. The new assembly's first actions were to validate the laws passed by CA1P and then to enact the One Unit Plan merging the territories of West Pakistan into a single province in line with the government's wishes. Eventually, the coalition between the Muslim League and the United Front succeeded in agreeing a draft. Pakistan's first Constitution was adopted on March 23, 1956: it featured a parliamentary form of government with a unicameral legislature of 300 members elected half from each Wing irrespective of proportional representation on the basis of population, an unusually powerful president reflecting the postindependence aggrandized role of the governor general, and a highly centralized federal structure. The most contentious issues in CA1P had been resolved in favor of the military-bureaucratic axis. Jalal describes the document as "a veritable time bomb with the fuse box in the custody of the president."[45] In fact, the new constitution paved the way for an authoritarian executive intervention. In October 1958 the military coup led by General Ayub Khan put an end to this fragile experiment in constitutional democracy: it was the first of the many recurring cycles of praetorian rule in Pakistan.

III. NEPAL

This section examines Nepal's failed constitution-making experience under CA1N between 2008 and 2012, and the aftermath of its dissolution. The assembly was

[44] Khan (2001), 157.

[45] Jalal (1990), 215.

expected to complete the peace process and deliver radical state restructuring, "build a New Nepal," and craft state institutions based on the principle of social inclusion. It is argued that the issues of executive dominance and ethnocentric nation building have remained critical in Nepal's constitutional politics, partly as legacies of the failed constitution-making experience of its first constituent assembly.

A. *Nepal's Period of Constitutional Engagement (2006–2012)*

In 2006, Nepal emerged from a ten-year-long armed insurgency in which more than 17,000 lives were lost and more than 3,100 Nepalis "disappeared."[46] The peace process essentially entailed two steps: the integration of the Maoist combatants into the Nepal army, which was eventually completed by April 2012, and the drafting of a new constitution – Nepal's seventh – by a directly elected inclusive body. After a number of postponements, in April 2008, the elections for CA1N were peacefully held.[47] The 601-member unicameral assembly operated both as the country's legislature and constitution-drafting body. To the surprise of many, the Maoist emerged as the largest party, with 35 percent of the seats in a body of more than thirty parties. On May 28, 2008, at CA1N's first meeting, Nepal was proclaimed a federal republic putting an end to more than two and half centuries of monarchical government. However, CA1N remained deeply divided and even with four extensions to its term, it was unable to agree on a new constitution, especially with regard to the modalities of federal restructuring. Hence, CA1N was dissolved in May 2012, leaving Nepal with neither a legislature nor a constitution-drafting body in place for more than a year. In November 2013, CA2N elections signaled the electorate's change of mood – and a new trajectory for the country's path to constitutional restructuring. Following the disastrous earthquakes of 2015, a new constitution, which was not in line with many decisions taken within CA1N and ultimately far less inclusive, was "fast-tracked" and eventually promulgated in September 2015 amidst violent protests in the Terai and profound disillusionment for many Nepalis.

B. *Context and Background of the CA1N*

This section analyzes the historical legacies and political context in which CA1N operated in order to understand how these structures constrained the agency of Nepal's constitutional actors and contributed to CA1N failure.

46 International Committee of the Red Cross; see: www.icrc.org/eng/resources/documents/news-footage/2012/nepal-tvnews-2012-03-06.htm (accessed February 13, 2018).

47 The Carter Center, 2008. "Observing the 2008 Nepal Constituent Assembly Elections." See www.cartercenter.org/resources/pdfs/news/peace_publications/election_reports/FinalReportNepal2008.pdf (accessed February 13, 2018).

First, Nepal's first constituent assembly had to operate in a difficult postconflict political setting and seek to overcome a long history of authoritarian politics in the country linked to the role of the national Shah monarchy and its support base. Unlike Pakistan, Nepal was never colonized. The creation of modern Nepal dates back to the late eighteenth century, when the military conquests initiated by King Prithvi Narayan Shah of Gorkha, a small kingdom lying west of the Kathmandu Valley, led to the annexation of many small principalities and kingdoms under Gorkhali sovereignty.[48] In this respect, Hinduism and its association to the Shah monarchy were used as a key tool to legitimize governmental authority and executive dominance.[49] This continued under the later regime of the Rana line of hereditary prime ministers (1846–1951), which assumed the powers of the monarch without displacing him. Nepal's first experiment with constitutional democracy lasted for less than a decade (1951–60) and saw the direct involvement of Sir Ivor Jennings in the drafting of Nepal's first permanent constitution (1959), where he deployed the so-called "Pakistan formula."[50] The experiment was, however, short lived. In 1960, King Mahendra Shah abruptly brought it to an end with the support of the Army. The royal coup inaugurated three decades of monarchical Panchayat autocracy (1960–90) under the legitimizing umbrella of ethnonationalist propaganda, centered on the Shah monarchy, Hinduism, and the Nepali language, thus further reinforcing patterns of exclusion within the country's population dominated by ethnolinguistically and religiously defined Parbatiya groups close to the monarchy.[51]

The period between 1990 and 2006 was Nepal's second experiment with democracy. In 1990, an alliance of banned and underground political parties succeeded in putting an end to the autocratic monarchical Panchayat regime through a popular movement. Pro-democracy leaders sought to institutionalize a constitutional monarchy and parliamentary democracy through the promulgation of the 1990 constitution;[52] however, for many Nepalis this was an unsatisfying settlement. Moreover, political instability marred the country's parliamentary politics from 1994,[53] and the beginning of the People's War in 1996 led to an escalation of political violence and a progressive militarization of the state. The royal massacre of 2001, combined with

48 P. Pradhan, *The Gorkha Conquest* (New Delhi: Oxford University Press, 1991).

49 R. Burghart, *The Conditions of Listening: Essays on Religion, History and Politics in South Asia* (New Delhi: Oxford University Press, 1996).

50 M. Malagodi, "Constitution Drafting as Cold War Realpolitik – Sir Ivor Jennings and Nepal's 1959 Constitution," in H. Kumarasingham (ed.), *Constitution-Making in Asia* (London: Routledge, 2016), 154–71.

51 R. Burghart, "The Political Culture of *Panchayat* Democracy," in M. Hutt (ed.), *Nepal in the Nineties: Versions of the Past, Visions of the Future* (New Delhi: Oxford University Press, 1993), 1–13.

52 M. Hutt, "Drafting the Nepal Constitution, 1990." *Asian Survey* 31: 11 (1991), 1020–39.

53 J. Whelpton, et al., *People, Politics and Ideology: Democracy and Social Change in Nepal* (Kathmandu: Mandala Book Point, 1999), 187–214.

the growing military successes of the Maoists, who by 2002 controlled roughly half of Nepal's territory, led to a further erosion of democratic politics.[54] Newly crowned King Gyanendra proclaimed two bouts of emergency rule in 2002–3 and 2005, but an alliance between the mainstream political parties and the Maoists succeeded in restoring democratic politics in April 2006.

Second, the expectations that ordinary Nepalis had placed in CA1N were enormous given the many historical efforts at democratizing the country. The decision that Nepal should have a new constitution, which would meet the longstanding Maoist demand for a constitution drafted by the People's elected representatives, was taken in the last phase of Nepal's civil war. On November 25, 2005, the Twelve Point Agreement was reached in India between the Maoists and the mainstream political parties with the support of the international community.[55] It included a commitment to elect a constituent assembly. The promise of a constituent assembly made by King Tribhuvan in 1951 was finally going to be met, even if half a century later. The success of the pro-democracy movement against King Gyanendra's authoritarian rule in April 2006 led to the restoration of the House of Representatives (the parliament's Lower house), which had been dissolved in 2002 to have a legislature while the constituent assembly's elections were being organized. Nepal's return to parliamentary politics inaugurated a phase of exhilarating optimism for the advancement of democracy and social inclusion, and the beginning of what appeared to be a genuine constitutional moment to "build a New Nepal."

Third, CA1N had to contend with the divisive legacy of Nepal's ethnocultural nationalism anchored in the prominence of the Shah monarchy, Hinduism, and the Nepali language amidst a startling level of sociocultural diversity. The 2011 Census illustrates the varied composition of Nepal's population with 125 caste and ethnic groups, of which only the largest six are above 5 percent of the total population and they are not territorially concentrated. The two biggest groups are the Chetri, i.e., Kshatriyas of local Khas origins (16.6 percent) and Bahun, i.e., Hill Brahmins (12.2 percent); together they constitute the Parbatiya group. Similarly, while Nepali remains the lingua franca of the majority, only 44.6 percent named it as their mother tongue, alongside ninety-one other mother tongues. Like in Pakistan, Nepali nationalism is vague; in fact, it is a state-framed ideology that has served over the years to defend the status quo. Unsurprisingly, the main grievances with regard to the 1990 constitution were the semiconstitutional position of the Shah monarchy, a strong

[54] G. Lakier, "After the Massacre: Secrecy, Disbelief, and the Public Sphere in Nepal," in W. Mazzarella & R. Kuar (eds.), *Censorship in South Asia: Cultural Regulation from Sedition to Seduction* (Bloomington, IN: Indiana University Press, 2009); D. Thapa (ed.), *A Kingdom under Siege: Nepal's Maoist insurgency 1996 to 2003* (Kathmandu: The Printhouse, 2003).

[55] See http://peacemaker.un.org/sites/peacemaker.un.org/files/NP_051122_12%20Point%20Understanding.pdf (accessed March 12, 2016).

executive dominance, the overly centralized nature of state institutions, and the ethnocentric institutionalization of the nation at the constitutional level to enshrine *Parbatiya* dominance also on a symbolic level.[56] In substantive terms, this hegemony was reflected in the underrepresentation of Janajati, Madhesi, Dalit, religious minorities, lower castes, and women in all the branches of the Nepali state leading to clear exclusionary patterns on the basis of identity. Furthermore, the 1990 constitution banned the formation of political parties on a communal basis,[57] and retained the thirty-year-old ban on proselytism.[58] After the redemocratization of 1990, the Nepali state became even more Kathmandu-centric, with Parbatiya males even more overrepresented in state bodies (parliament, government, judiciary, civil service, police, army, universities, etc.), especially in their higher echelons.[59]

Fourth, CA1N operated in a context of profound political fragmentation and lacked a national political force with a unifying ideology to guide the constitution-making process. On the one hand, radical constitutional change was widely viewed by the Maoists and ethnolinguistic minority groups as the primary vehicle for state restructuring to address the peace process' mantra of "building a new Nepal." A new constitution written by elected representatives would "deepen democracy" by securing the inclusion of marginalized groups in state institutions and break the hegemony of Parbatiya elites. Significantly, the demand for federalism came from the Madhesi and Janajati communities. In fact, in January 2007, the *Madhesi Andolan*, a mass protest movement against governmental discrimination of the Madhesi population in the Terai, led to prolonged strikes and violence. To appease the protestors, the interim government eventually accepted their demand for the federalization of the country and amended the interim constitution accordingly, committing CA1N to draft a federal constitution. On the other hand, the old mainstream political parties viewed the politics of recognition of federal restructuring along identity lines, electoral quotas for marginalized groups, and positive discrimination for government posts as a threat to both national unity and their own hegemony. As a result, their leadership opposed the direction of constitution making in CA1N and worked to delay and eventually derail the process, leading to further polarization along identity lines. The issues of federalism and representation for Madhesi present a deepening political cleavage with the potential of mirroring the developments in East Pakistan.

56 M. Malagodi, *Constitutional Nationalism and Legal Exclusion. Equality, Identity Politics, and Democracy in Nepal* (Delhi: Oxford University Press, 2013), chapters 3 and 4.

57 Article 112 (3) Constitution of the Kingdom of Nepal, 1990.

58 Article 19 (1) Constitution of the Kingdom of Nepal, 1990.

59 D. Kumar, "Social Structure and Voting Behaviour," in L. R. Baral (ed.), *Elections and Governance in Nepal* (Delhi: SAGE, 2005), 210–11.

Fifth, the international context in which CA1N operated had a profound impact on the constitutional process. While the majority of Western donors had supported the Nepali government and the king during the conflict, in 2005 they started pushing alongside India for an alliance between the mainstream parties and the Maoists. International donors were committed to the progressive agenda of state restructuring, and millions of dollars flooded into Nepal during the early years of the peace process. However, as the CA1N process had started to falter, by 2011 the tide had changed. The mandate of the United Mission in Nepal (UNMIN) was not renewed and it ceased its operation. Similarly other agencies and organizations started to roll back their programs as the political opening of 2006 began to close at alarming speed. Lip service to the issue of social inclusion remained, but it effectively fell off the political agenda with the dissolution of Nepal's first constituent assembly. It is in light of this incomplete constitutionalization of executive power and political equality that the experience of CA1N, and its untimely demise, ought to be analyzed.

C. *Institutional Setup, Actors, and Decision Making in the CA1N Process*

Following the promulgation of the interim constitution on January 15, 2007, Maoist delegates joined the interim parliament and then the cabinet, opening the way to the final preparations for the CA1N elections, which – after a few postponements – were held on April 8, 2008. The process was conducted in a reasonably free and fair manner, with a turnout of above 60 percent of eligible voters.[60] CA1N featured 601 seats, with 240 (42 percent) allocated by first-past-the-post in single-member territorial constituencies and 335 seats (58 percent) allocated by proportional representation in which the entire country functioned as a single constituency and the electorate voted for political parties, not individual candidates. The PR mechanism gave parties a free hand in the selection of candidates, subject only to the legal quotas relating to identity, 13 percent Dalits, 37.8 percent marginalized groups, 4 percent backward regions, 31.2 percent Madhesi, and 30.2 percent Other Groups.[61] The remaining twenty-six seats were reserved for appointments made by the cabinet after the election. Twenty-five of the fifty-seven parties contesting the election found representation in the CA1N, alongside two independent candidates. The Maoists won almost double the seats of each mainstream party: the Nepali Congress obtained

60 See www.cartercenter.org/resources/pdfs/news/peace_publications/election_reports/FinalReportNepal2008.pdf (accessed March 30, 2016).

61 The sum of these percentages is more than 100 percent. "Explanation – As a number of candidates represent more than one group, the sum total of the percentage of the candidates of all groups appears to be more than one hundred"(Schedule 1, Election to Members of the CA Act, 2007). Thirty-three percent of the total seats were also allocated to women.

19 percent, while the United Marxist-Leninist (UML) 18 percent. The fourth biggest party, the Madhesi People's Rights Forum (MJAF), captured 9 percent, the fifth, the Terai Madhes Loktantrik Party 3.49 percent. Only five other parties controlled more than 1 percent of the seats; sixteen parties fell below that threshold.[62] The uneven distribution of seats, the fragmentation of Nepal's political spectrum, and the polarization of diametrically opposed and competing visions of the Nepali polity within CA1N set the stage for many rounds of political maneuvering.

The assembly held its first meeting on May 28, 2008, and in a historic proclamation declared Nepal a "Federal Democratic Republic," putting an end to the 265-year-old Shah monarchy. Having done so, its first task was to create its Rules of Procedure and in its second meeting a forty-four-member CA Rules Committee was established. Significantly, no records of the CA1N debates were kept. By November, both the Rules and an 82-week timetable for the CA were approved. Then in December, the constitution-drafting work was organized into committees: the Constitutional Committee, ten Thematic Committees, and four Procedural Committees. For proposals to pass within a committee a simple majority vote was required. All the Thematic Committees concluded their work and submitted their reports and concept papers for discussion by the full assembly between May 2009 and January 2010.[63] The reports gave a clear indication that CA1N was moving toward an inclusive constitution openly recognizing identity as its organizing basis. For instance, the report of the Committee on State Restructuring and Distribution of State Power featured a federal model with fourteen provinces based on the criteria of "identity" as well as "capability," with the names and boundaries of the provinces mostly along ethnic lines and preferential political rights (*agradhikar*) as temporary reservations of a share of political offices for the majority group in each province.[64] Crucially, four UML members voted for the proposal in the Committee against the party line, allowing it to pass at the committee stage.

The life of CA1N was marred by political instability from its inception. The relative Maoist majority resulted in them obtaining key posts, including that of the Prime Minister with the support of the Madhesi parties, UML, and a number of smaller parties, while the Nepali Congress remained firmly in opposition. However, Prime Minister Dahal was forced to resign in May 2009 after a row with the president over the sacking of the Chief of Army Staff. He was succeeded by the UML leader Madhav Kumar Nepal, who was in office a little over a year. Another UML

62 See www.uio.no/english/research/interfaculty-research-areas/democracy/news-and-events/events/conferences/2010/papers/Vollan-SystemOfRepresentationNepal-2008.pdf (accessed February 13, 2018).

63 See www.asd.org.np/en/transition/constitution/chrono (accessed January 10, 2016).

64 CA1, Report of the Committee for Restructuring the State and Distribution of State Power 2010. See www.ccd.org.np/resources/Concept_Paper_Restructuring_State_GTZ_ENG.pdf

leader, Jhalanath Khanal, took the helm of the government in February 2011, after seventeen unsuccessful rounds of votes within CA1N. His tenure was particularly short lived, and in August 2011 he was again replaced by Maoist ideologue Baburam Bhattarai, who remained in office until CA1N dissolution in May 2012. Throughout the life of CA1N, Nepali party leaders mostly concentrated on political power play for governmental posts and on the army integration process. They did not give the constitution-making process their personal time or priority, which meant that CA1N could not finalize a draft. Leaders turned to constitution drafting only at the last minute, but by then they were unable to reach an agreement before the assembly's dissolution.

Significantly, in 2008 the electorate had rejected a number of old party leaders, even though the electoral law allowed them to run in up to two first-past-the-post constituencies. However, former Prime Minister Sushil Koirala and Madhav Kumar Nepal – to mention just two examples – still managed to secure seats in CA1N as part of the twenty-six cabinet appointed posts. The appointment of leaders who had been rejected by the electorate was indicative of the attitude of the main political parties toward democratic decision making and the assembly itself. The party leaders were always confident that they would have the last word on any question of constitution making in the name of taking decisions by "consensus" (*sahamati*). As a result, decisions on key constitutional matters became the exclusive purview of the political leaders outside of CA1N itself. This delegitimized the drafting process in CA1N, and the leaders remained unable to reach a consensus even outside the Assembly.[65] The commitment to "consensus" decisions was built into the interim constitution in all the clauses related to decision making in the constituent assembly. However, the constitution provided for voting procedures for all the decisions to be taken by the assembly, and most of them required a simple majority of members present in the House. Only constitutional amendments and the passing of the new constitution required a two-thirds majority. While legally, two-thirds of the constituent assembly members could, under the interim constitution, declare a new constitution, politically it proved impossible to do so without the support of all the main political leaders, i.e., "by consensus," which would secure the legitimacy of the new document.

Even if the CA1N rules were silent on the issues of caucuses and party whips, these institutions played a fundamental role in the work and demise of the assembly. CA1N Speaker Subhash Chandra Nemwang allowed for the spontaneous creation of cross-party caucuses along identity and gender lines.[66] The formation of

[65] Martin Chautari, *The Debilitating Dynamics of Nepal's Constituent Assembly (2008–2012)*. Briefing Paper No. 8 (March 2013). See www.martinchautari.org.np/files/BriefingPaper8_EngVer.pdf (accessed January 11, 2016).

[66] See www.ekantipur.com/2014/03/08/top-story/ca-caucus-debate-rages-parties-divided/386395.html (accessed January 11, 2016).

the Women, Janajati, Dalit, and Madhesi caucuses demonstrated that other bonds of solidarity and political cooperation existed in CA1N beyond party affiliation. In fact, on numerous occasions, assembly members voted according to their conscience, ignoring party lines. The party leadership responded by unleashing their whips on the defiant constitutional assembly members. However, the use of party whips in CA1N not just on ordinary legislative matters, but also on votes on constitutional issues when rebellious members were subjected to a three-line-whip, effectively curbed many cross-party initiatives. This was especially significant for the rebellious members elected under proportional representation, as expulsion from their parties would result in the loss of their seat.[67] Thus, the main three political parties, including the Maoists – all dominated by upper caste Pahari Hindu men – succeeded in silencing voices of dissent and demands for inclusion within their own party. This severely limited the availability of "systemic" ways through which the demands of the marginalized groups could be accommodated within the institutional process.

The committees' reports had all been discussed in plenary sessions by May 2010, but no consensus could be reached on the most contentious issues: federal restructuring, presidential versus parliamentary government, and the judiciary. As a result, the new constitution could not be finalized even if agreements had been reached at committee stage with a few members dissenting. CA1N then bought more time by amending the interim constitution to extend its own term in May 2010. At this point, the task of resolving these issues was removed from the open public debates of the body directly representative of the Nepali people and put into the hands of the old guard of leaders of the main parties. These men negotiated crucial decisions about Nepal's new constitutional settlement, mostly through the High Level Political Committee (HLPC), which had been set up by G. P. Koirala in January 2010. As a result, no inclusive and transparent deliberations within CA1N were allowed to iron out the differences between the various political forces.

Ultimately, the modus operandi of backdoor secret negotiations and opaque deals outside the assembly undermined the legitimacy of the constitution-making process itself. At the same time, the political leaders failed to forge a compromise solution, notwithstanding three further extensions of CA1N's term in May 2011, August 2011, and November 2011. "Postponing," or rather "delaying," the entire constitution-making process was the strategy adopted by the political parties in opposition, since no consensus could be found on key issues.

67 K. Khanal, Frits Sollewijn Gelpke Uddhab, and Prasad Pyakurel 2012. *Dalit Representation in National Politics of Nepal*. See www.idsn.org/fileadmin/user_folder/pdf/New_files/Nepal/2013/Dalit_Representation_in_National_Politics_of_Nepal_-_2012.pdf (accessed January 11, 2016).

D. *Demise and Aftermath of the CA1 Process in Nepal*

After the third extension of CA1N, on November 26, 2011 a full bench of the Supreme Court comprising then Chief Justice Khil Raj Regmi and Justices Damodar Prasad Sharma, Rajkumar Prasad Shah, Kalyan Shrestha, and Prem Sharma ruled on the writ petition filed by Advocates Bharat Jungam and Balkrishna Neupane on September 21 arguing that it was a violation of Article 64 of the interim constitution to extend again the assembly's term. The bench asked the government to complete the drafting of the new constitution before the expiry of the six-month extension, i.e., before May 2012. In his respect, the court issued an order stating that "if the Constituent Assembly fails to promulgate the new constitution within the next six months, its term would automatically end after six months."[68] CA1N was unable to complete the new dispensation within the extended timeframe. Then Prime Minister Bhattarai tabled a bill supported by the main four political parties to amend further the interim constitution and secure another three-month extension of the assembly's term.

In response to the attempted extension, Advocates Rajkumar Rana, Kanchan Krishna Neupane, and Bharat Mani Jangam filed a writ petition in the Supreme Court seeking a stay order on the 13th amendment bill tabled in CA1N. The single bench made up of Chief Justice Khil Raj Regmi found for the petitioners and issued a stay order on the amendment bill, effectively disallowing any further extensions of the assembly's term. The chief justice found the government to be in violation of the Supreme Court order issued in November 2011 and to be in breach of their duty to complete the drafting of the new constitution by May 2012.[69] Last-minute negotiations took place among the main political party leaders outside the assembly, "even on 27 May, the CA members were kept waiting since the morning in the CA hall for the final and decisive session to start – it never did as the party leaders were busy in together discussing the final constitution outside the parliament."[70] When the leaders failed to reach a compromise on federalism on May 27, Prime Minister Bhattarai advised the president to dissolve the assembly and called for new elections.

The dissolution of CA1N in May 2012 left Nepal with neither a legislature nor a constitution-drafting body in place for more than year. On March 14, 2013, a new "consensus government" was constituted. It was composed of ministers appointed

[68] *Adv. Bharat Mani Jangam and Adv. Bal Krishna Neupane v Prime Minister and Cabinet Office et al.* Writ N. 068-WS-0014. See http://ncf.org.np/ca-archives/ca_updates7.htm (accessed March 11, 2016).

[69] *Adv. Rajkumar Rana, Adv. Kanchan Krishna Neupane and Adv. Bharat Mani Jangam v Prime Minister and Cabinet Office et al.* Writ N. 068-WS-1085, 1086, 1087. See http://webcache.googleusercontent.com/search?q=cache:QvKwEOGuf4UJ:www.supremecourt.gov.np/download/068-WO-1085_1086_1087.pdf+&cd=2&hl=en&ct=clnk&gl=uk&client=safari (accessed March 11, 2016).

[70] See www.idea.int/asia_pacific/nepal/no-constitution-yet-for-nepal.cfm (accessed March 11, 2016).

by the political parties and headed by the Supreme Court Chief Justice Khil Raj Regmi. Ironically, it was named "Nepal Interim Election Council" to obscure the fact that Nepal's key executive institution was led by the head of Nepal's judiciary (only on temporary leave from his judicial post and the adjudicator on both constitutional cases that led to the dissolution of CA1N) – a blatant violation of the doctrine of separation of powers. Moreover, the new government remained unburdened by any form of parliamentary accountability since no legislature was in place, a particularly pernicious situation for a parliamentary democracy. Unsurprisingly, this interim period undermined the constitutionality of the political process by implicating the Supreme Court in executive politics and further eroded public trust in state institutions and political actors, both perceived as caught up in partisan politics and incapable of delivering institutional reform. Officially, such a manipulation was justified as an exceptional measure for exceptional circumstances, but Nepal's constitutional moment became irremediably lost.

The elections of CA2N eventually took place on November 19, 2013, after two postponements. The assembly's composition mirrored the one of its predecessor: a 601-seat unicameral legislature functioning both as the country's parliament and its constitution-drafting body. The elections brought the main centrist parliamentary parties back to the political forefront as the Nepali Congress (34 percent) and UML (30 percent) emerged as the biggest two parties, while the Maoists (14 percent) were relegated to the third position. A further twenty-eight parties secured representation in CA2N, but they all won less than 5 percent.[71] In March 2014, CA2N finally succeeded in readopting the many agreements on the new constitution previously reached by the CA1N. However, the thorny issues that caused CA1N to be dissolved without a new constitution proved divisive. The questions of federal restructuring and form of government continued to polarize Nepal's political spectrum. CA2N did not succeed in promulgating the new constitution within its original deadline of January 2015.

The new government attempted to prohibit the formation of cross-party caucuses in the CA2N, while the use of party whips continued. In the wake of the 2015 earthquakes, Nepal's political elites vowed to "fast track" the drafting of the new document and complete the peace process. The four main parties represented in the assembly reached a number of agreements outside of CA2N that made little effort to include representation from the marginalized groups and sought to postpone the naming and demarcation of the federal units until the promulgation of the new constitution and new elections. The postponement immediately sparked protests and litigants took to the Supreme Court, which issued an interim order against the

[71] See http://election.gov.np/CA2070/CAResults/reportBody.php?selectedMenu=5 (accessed September 11, 2016).

implementation of the agreement.[72] Politicians accused the court of overreaching and the assembly's Constitution Drafting Committee pressed on with the preparation of the draft on the basis of agreement defying the court order. Protests grew increasingly violent and the security forces' response heavy handed, especially in the Terai, where the demands for federalism and equal citizenship have been historically the strongest among Madhesi communities. In the meantime, the assembly opted for a fast-track procedure to pass the new constitution, allowing for a very brief period of public consultation over the draft.[73] Amidst mounting tensions, the political leaders eventually relented and agreed on a new seven-province federal deal.[74] On August 23, the draft constitution (with the seven-province model) was tabled in the CA2N for approval as the MPs representing the marginalized groups walked out in protest.[75] Violent demonstrations and communal violence erupted across the Terai, leading to the death of security forces and protestors in Kailali, the imposition of a curfew, and the deployment of the Army.[76] While a constitution was eventually framed, it did not bring about radical institutional restructuring: proportional representation was reduced, federal restructuring not carried out along identity lines, secularism ambiguous, and citizenship discriminatory on the basis of gender. The new constitution was promulgated on September 20, 2015, but in January 2016 it was already amended once and at the time of writing a second amendment is in the pipelines. These measures, however, have failed to quell protests and further heightened Pahari–Madhasi polarization. A new phase of political instability and polarization along identity lines has begun in Nepal.

IV. CONCLUSIONS

The present chapter sought to answer two key questions. First, why did the first constituent assemblies of Pakistan and Nepal fail? In both countries, significant segments of the political establishment felt threatened by their deliberations and the direction of constitutional restructuring they were driving. Thus, key political actors mobilized against the assemblies, sought to obstruct their proceedings and put an end to their constitution-making work. Both bodies were trying to accomplish two key tasks: to constitutionalize the powers of the executive and establish

[72] See https://twitter.com/dipjha/status/612139709553229824 (accessed January 11, 2016).

[73] See http://thewire.in/2015/08/01/nepals-fast-tracked-constitutional-process-trades-rights-for-speed-7673/ (accessed January 11, 2016).

[74] See www.karma99.com/2015/04/proposed-federal-structures-of-nepal.html (accessed January 13, 2016).

[75] See http://thehimalayantimes.com/kathmandu/ca-on-cusp-of-promulgating-constitution/ (accessed January 13, 2016).

[76] Human Rights Watch, October 2015. "Like We Are Not Nepali." See www.hrw.org/report/2015/10/16/we-are-not-nepali/protest-and-police-crackdown-terai-region-nepal (accessed January 13, 2016).

their primacy as lawmaking and constitution-drafting bodies; and to accommodate regional ethnolinguistic demands for representation and inclusion through federal arrangements and inclusive political representation. Concerns about national unity, preservation of the status quo, and survival vis-à-vis the external threat posed by India prevailed in both countries at the expense of democratic engagement and deliberative politics. Second, what was the impact of the failure of these bodies on constitutional developments and democratic politics in both countries? It has been argued that the dissolution of the Assemblies bore long-term destabilizing effects in both countries, bolstering the unaccountable arms of the state, weakening the judiciary and public confidence in the democratic process, and deepening the political cleavages on identity basis, which in Pakistan proved fatal to its territorial integrity and in Nepal represent a major concern.

In terms of comparative lessons, three main insights can be gained from the comparison of the failed constituent assembly experiences of Nepal and Pakistan:

1. Constituent assemblies as the highest form of constituent power conjure dramatic expectations with regard to their transformative potential of the constitutional process and outcome. Therefore, this modality makes the task of constitution making even more arduous. With regard to the political process, constituent assemblies represent a "gathering of the nation" and as such they are expected to produce through deliberations a document that permanently and authoritatively encapsulates and affirms the unity of the nation. This approach is particularly problematic in deeply divided societies where different actors and groups hold competing visions of the polity's very nature and raison d'être. Hanna Lerner has convincingly demonstrated that an open-ended incrementalist method of constitution making can offer a durable solution in highly diverse societies as in independent India.[77] This was, however, not the case in Pakistan and Nepal, with their commitments to a monolithic ethnocultural attitude toward nation building. With regard to the legal outcome, constituent assemblies are expected to engineer a document that represents a radical break from the previous regime. In Pakistan and Nepal those bodies set out to formulate the legal basis of constitutional democracy and, as such, to constitutionalize the executive and create an inclusive institutional framework. However, the hegemony of the Punjabi-dominated military-bureaucratic axis in Pakistan, and of the Parbatiya-dominated political and institutional elites in Nepal prevented both assemblies to generate such transformations. As a result, the dramatic expectations raised by the

[77] H. Lerner, *Making Constitutions in Deeply Divided Societies* (Cambridge: Cambridge University Press, 2011).

constituent assembly mode of constitution making were frustrated in both countries, leading to an irrevocable loss of the constitutional moment, which was never quite regained during the second constituent assembly experiences.

2. The fact that the first constituent assemblies of Pakistan and Nepal functioned both as extraordinary constitution-making bodies and ordinary legislatures within a parliamentary form of government led to further delays and complications, adding another layer of difficulty to an already complex task. The entanglement of the assemblies in the day-to-day political business contributed to a progressive isolation and marginalization of these bodies as sites of constitution making. As a result, in Pakistan the constituent assembly became increasingly disconnected from both the other state bodies and the electorate, while in Nepal the assembly's constitution-making function was progressively outsourced to the political parties' leadership outside of the assembly. In both countries, the delays in constitution drafting helped forces outside the assemblies to undermine the authority and finality of constituent power, thus paving the way to their dissolution.
3. Constituent assemblies are bodies with extraordinary legitimacy and purpose; therefore their untimely demise ought to take place through similarly extraordinary means. The opposition to the assemblies, however, did not stem from the judiciary. Institutionally, the tension between the executive and the legislature represented the fault line of the first constituent assembly experiences in both Pakistan and Nepal. When the assemblies came at loggerhead with vested interests and powerful established elites operating through executive, institutional and extraconstitutional channels, executive action alone was not sufficient to seal their fate and reboot the constitution-making process. It was imperative to have the stamp of approval of the apex judiciary because it was essential to lend extraordinary constitutional legitimacy to the demise of assemblies. In the end, the courts simply rubber-stamped in legal form a political decision that had already been taken. However, by doing so, the courts had implicated both the judiciary and the constitutional machinery as a whole in the sordid tale of the constituent assemblies' failure in both countries. It is because of the extraordinary nature of this failure and the extraordinary extent to which the state went to justify it that its consequences have been so profound and pervasive.

5

Precautions in a Democratic Experiment

The Nexus between Political Power and Competence

Udit Bhatia

The Indian constituent assembly, which undertook the task of framing a constitution for independent India, voted to establish universal adult suffrage for the new republic. This decision was historic, reversing decades of qualified suffrage under the colonial government. It was particularly significant because such transfers of power do not always end in the decentralization of political power. Indeed, many post-colonial governments, including neighbouring Pakistan, declined to conduct elections soon after independence. Moreover, this also marked the first transition to adult suffrage through a constituent assembly mandated to establish the constitutional framework for a polity. Everywhere else before this, the move towards adult suffrage had come about only through gradual political developments and legislative change. Where revolution had resulted in the establishment of new constitutions, for instance, in the United States and France, these had continued to fall short of enfranchising everyone.

This chapter addresses a gap in the dominant narrative on the Indian constituent assembly. According to that narrative, India's historic transition after independence marked a clear break from the colonial past. This meant that the constituent assembly abandoned the rhetoric favoured by colonial officials that the Indian people were in the 'waiting room of history', gradually transitioning towards the full realization of democratic freedoms. Instead, it affirmed its faith in the political capacities of Indians, voting to immediately operationalize democratic institutions. I will argue that this view hides the variety of ways in which anxieties about citizens' inability for self-government continued to play a role in the assembly's deliberations. This argument is particularly relevant in light of recent events in Indian politics. In 2015, the Indian states of Rajasthan and Haryana enacted laws that required candidates for election to local councils in villages to have completed a high school education. Critics of these laws argued that they were unfair because a large proportion of potential candidates did not have access to education. In particular, they were criticized for their disparate impact on disadvantaged sections of the population – such as women and members of disadvantaged castes. When the case found its way to the Supreme Court, the judges argued that the laws were justified because education was essential to sensible political judgment.[1] My chapter contributes to the debate by suggesting that this argument is not novel to the Indian constitutional scene. Nor is it a resurrection of a colonial tradition that attempted to posit education as a prerequisite for wielding political power. Rather, I suggest that one finds various forms of this argument at the very inauguration of India's constitution.

This constitutional moment in India comes at a time when 'epistocracy' – rule by experts – has begun to find contenders in normative political theory.[2] A second contribution of this chapter lies in expanding our understanding of ways in which epistocracy can be incorporated by authors of democratic constitutions. I highlight two such approaches. The first, competence as prerequisite, insists that only persons above a certain threshold of competence ought to have political power. The second, competence as advantage, urges that even if less competent persons hold political power, more competent persons ought to enjoy a greater share of it. 'Competence as prerequisite' must be understood as a broad category, embodying restrictions other than those on the exercise of suffrage. As such, I explore mechanisms advanced as necessary concomitants of the right to vote and how epistocratic arguments were deployed in resisting them. I examine the treatment of two mechanisms that were advanced as critical to the proper actualization of democracy: (1) special provisions for indigenous persons and (2) proportional representation as the appropriate electoral mechanism. I also attempt to contribute to our understanding of the 'competence as advantage' approach. I argue that the second chamber can be conceptualized as an epistocratic mechanism, aimed at conferring power on epistemically superior individuals. The Indian constitution attempted to do so through three mechanisms: (1) indirect elections, (2) nominations for 'experts' and (3) graduate constituencies.

I. BACKGROUND TO THE ASSEMBLY'S PROCEEDINGS

In September 1945, the newly elected Labour Government in Britain, headed by Clement Atlee, announced its intention to hold elections to India's provincial legislatures which would act as electoral bodies for a constituent assembly. This assembly would be responsible for framing a constitution for an independent India.

The Labour government dispatched a mission commonly called the 'Cabinet Mission' and charged it with facilitating negotiations between the Indian National

1 *Rajbala v. State of Haryana* (2016) 1 SCC 463.

2 Jason Brennan, *Against Democracy* (Princeton, NJ: Princeton University Press, 2016); Ilya Somin, *Democracy and Political Ignorance: Why Smaller Government Is Smarter* (Stanford, CA: Stanford University Press, 2013).

Congress and the Muslim League. However, the Muslim League under Mohammad Ali Jinnah was distrustful of the Congress, and equated it with the dominance of Hindus. It called for the creation of a constituent assembly for Hindustan and another for Pakistan – a state they asked to be carved out for Muslims. The Congress, on the other hand, insisted that the people of India were Indians, regardless of their religion. It saw itself as an umbrella party, consisting of Hindus, Muslims and many communities of India, committed to self-determination by India and overthrow of the imperial British government.[3]

The Cabinet Mission arrived at a compromise plan, announced in May 1946, according to which the Indian provinces were to be geographically grouped into those which were predominantly Hindu; those which were predominantly Muslim; and finally, others where the population of Hindus and Muslims was equal.[4] The plan recommended that representatives from these provinces meet in three separate groups to frame the constitutions for their respective provinces. These groups would later meet together to settle the Union Constitution. Both the Congress and the Muslim League accepted this plan even as they held strong reservations.[5]

By August that year, elections to the constituent assembly took place under the terms of the Cabinet Mission's plan. The members of this assembly were elected by the provincial legislatures, with the provinces represented in the assembly at a ratio of approximately 1 to 1 million of their population. The provincial legislatures were elected by qualified franchise and communal electorates.[6] These legislators, belonging to three communal categories – Muslims, Sikhs and General (Hindus and all other communities) – would elect members of the constituent assembly separately, according to their percentage in the province's population and their proportion of the provincial delegation. The princely states were to elect ninety-three representatives in the assembly, selected through consultation between the assembly and the rulers of the states.[7]

Eventually, talks between the Muslim League and the Congress broke down even as the assembly was convened on 9 December 1946. In December, the members of

3 Granville Austin, *The Indian Constitution: Cornerstone of a Nation* (Oxford: Oxford University Press, 1999), 5.

4 The first group included Madras, Bombay, Central Provinces, United Provinces, Bihar and Orissa. The second group was made up of Punjab, Northwest Frontier Province and Sindh. The final group included Bengal and Assam.

5 Austin, *The Indian Constitution*, 6.

6 Only about a quarter of the population was entitled to a vote, which depended on the ownership of property. Though the Congress was keen on a universal franchise, it accepted the principle of a qualified vote for the moment because preparations for general elections would have delayed the creation of the assembly.

7 The princely states were nominally sovereign monarchies, which were not directly ruled by the colonial government. Instead, these were governed by their local ruler under a subsidiary alliance agreement with the British government.

the assembly still hoped that the League would join them, but this began to look like a very distant possibility by the time they met next in January 1947.[8] Partition was imminent by the end of April, when the assembly met for the third time and it became a reality on 3 June 1947. The India Independent Act passed by the British Parliament came into force on 15 August 1947, and the constituent assembly set out to draft the Indian constitution.

The dominant view within scholarship on the Constituent Assembly Debates is that their participants were more or less unanimous in their endorsement of adult suffrage in India, without any qualifications on sex, property or education. Granville Austin argues that 'Belief in the principles of parliamentary democracy appears most strikingly in the nearly universal approval of adult suffrage – which had come during the years of the independence movement to mean direct elections.'[9] He suggests that 'Since the nineteen twenties, the Congress had demanded adult suffrage for the people of India; it had become a *sine qua non* of independence.'[10] Similarly, Ingrid Creppell urges that 'It is clear from the Constituent Assembly Debates that granting the franchise to India's entire adult population appeared, for the most part, a foregone conclusion.'[11] Three lines of arguments can be found explaining how this position came about.

The first line of argument emphasizes the *ideological* commitment of the Indian leadership to the democratic process with unqualified suffrage. Such commitment is seen as a product of acceptance of modernist premises by members of the constituent assembly. Modernity here was understood as implying democracy underpinned by political equality. It was an idea whose 'time had come'.[12] The rhetoric of democratization that spurred the Second World War contributed to the solidification of this ideological framework. The arrival of democracy, however, was not merely an inevitability; it was also aspirational. The Indian constitution was viewed as an instrument for overcoming a traditional, hierarchical order with a modern and egalitarian one. It involved constituting citizens as bearers of liberal rights that they were previously denied by both the colonial government and social elites in the pre-colonial era. In particular, adult suffrage was seen as a way of overcoming the emphasis on ascriptive identities that had been perpetuated by the colonial government in its engagement with Indian people.[13] Rather than attempting to negotiate, as

8 Austin, *The Indian Constitution*, 9.

9 Ibid., 46.

10 Ibid., 58.

11 Ingrid Creppell, 'Democracy and Literacy: The Role of Culture in Political Life', *European Journal of Sociology* 30:1 (May 1989), 40.

12 Christopher Alan Bayly, *Recovering Liberties: Indian Thought in the Age of Liberalism and Empire* (Cambridge: Cambridge University Press, 2011), 308–9.

13 Rajeev Bhargava, *The Promise of India's Secular Democracy* (New Delhi: Oxford University Press, 2010), 28–33; Rochana Bajpai, *Debating Difference: Group Rights and Liberal Democracy in India* (New Delhi: Oxford University Press, 2011), 91–2.

colonial officials had done, a fair balance of political power between communities, adult suffrage would provide a simple mechanism for establishing a fair and equitable political system.

Even where elements of the old order were retained, a discursive shift accompanied its justification. Previously, for instance, intervention by the state in regulation of speech was justified by reference to incapacities of the natives. Unlike British subjects, Indians could not act as proper autonomous, self-governing agents. This justified a range of restrictive legislations, such as the law on sedition. Now, the same legal code was justified by the constituent assembly by appealing to the identity of those who would operate it: Indians, rather than alien officials. Thus, even illiberal governmental mechanisms now eschewed the notion that its subjects were 'unfit' for enjoying certain kinds of freedoms.[14]

A second argument emphasizes *strategic* considerations that went into the award of adult suffrage with the inauguration of the new constitution. Years of having opposed the colonial government for curtailing political rights meant that it would be politically unwise for framers of the constitution to backtrack on adult suffrage. After all, this opposition was developed in the form of a mass movement with the Indian National Congress at its forefront, claiming to fight for political power on behalf of the disenfranchised masses. Not only was it politically inexpedient to backtrack on the franchise; rather, strategic considerations weighed in favour of adopting universal suffrage in the new constitution. This could help institutionalize the de facto authority that the Congress held among the masses. Mohammad Ali Jinnah, leader of the Muslim League, viewed this strategic consideration as crucial to the Congress' stance on adult suffrage:

> There are in India roughly 400,000,000 souls who, through no fault of their own, are hopelessly illiterate and consequently priest and caste-ridden. They have no real conception of how they are being governed even to-day and it is proposed that to the elected representatives of such should India's future constitution be entrusted. Is it too much to say that, since the vast majority of the elected representatives will be illiterate Hindus, the Constituent Assembly will be under the influence of Mr. Gandhi and the Congress leaders ...?[15]

The hegemonic status of the Congress at the time of independence also provided 'insurance' against possible side effects of granting the franchise.[16] The partition of

[14] Gautam Bhatia, 'The Conservative Constitution: Freedom of Speech and the Constituent Assembly Debates', in Udit Bhatia (ed.), *Deliberations on Democracy: The Indian Constituent Assembly Debates* (London: Routledge, 2017), 103–29.

[15] Cited in Anil Chandra Banerjee (ed.), *Indian Constitutional Documents 1757–1947*, Vol. IV: 1935–1947 (Calcutta: A Mukherjee & Co., 1965).

[16] Christophe Jaffrelot, *La democratie en Inde: Religion, caste et politique* (Paris: Fayard, 1998).

India and the formation of Pakistan strengthened its hegemonic status, as its primary competitor in the electoral arena, the Muslim League, no longer posed a serious threat. The Congress's dominance reflected in elections to the constituent assembly, which was aptly described by Graneville Austin as a 'one party body' in a 'one party country': 'The Assembly was the Congress and the Congress was India.'[17]

A third argument emphasizes *cultural* reasons for eschewing qualifications such as those based on education in the award of the franchise. Ingrid Creppell argues that widespread literacy is a necessary condition for an endogenously held cultural valuation of literacy. That is, for literacy to be projected as a prerequisite for a vote, it must be internally valued by members of a particular polity as something indeed worth having. But in India, literacy was not widespread enough to be valued as a cultural norm. Barely 10 per cent of the population at that time was literate, and therefore, a literacy qualification would have 'functioned as too crude a political device, providing no sticking point'.[18] This explanation finds resonance in a telling statement by a member of the constituent assembly, who argued that a literacy qualification would have been desirable for the franchise, but because too many people would be excluded by it, such a move would render democracy in India entirely meaningless.

Despite the force of these suggestions in explaining the adoption of adult suffrage, I argue that they tend to make invisible ways in which this move was still seen as suspect in the Indian constituent assembly. In the following sections, I demonstrate how debates over the exercise of the franchise and bicameralism in the assembly were influenced in significant ways by concerns about citizens' political incompetence.

II. COMPETENCE AS PREREQUISITE

On 4 January 1949, Thakurdas Bhargava, a member from East Punjab, argued that the constitutional provision requiring adult suffrage be amended to disqualify illiterate members from the vote.[19] Without such qualifications, elections in India would be a 'farce'. Bhargava proposed that such disqualification ought to be implemented for the first ten years. Interestingly, a draft provision entitling every citizen to free primary education within a period of ten years from the operation of the constitution had earlier been rejected by the Advisory Committee of the constituent assembly. Thus, Bhargava's proposal sought to institute a qualification, which, by

[17] Austin, *The Indian Constitution*, 10.

[18] Creppell, *Democracy and Literacy*, 42.

[19] *Constituent Assembly Debates* (Official Report) (New Delhi: Government of India Press) 7.2: 1245, 4 January 1949. All references to the debates are provided by volume, page number and date, to this edition.

the assembly's own admission, the state was unable to ensure it could assist citizens satisfy. Other members also explicitly voiced their criticism of adult suffrage during the assembly's proceedings. Hriday Nath Kunzru, for instance, suggested that the franchise ought to have been postponed for a period of fifteen years, restricting it to less than 50 per cent of the population for the time being. He suggested that the ignorance of the electorate meant that a gradual expansion of the franchise was needed in order to prevent demagoguery.[20] Kunzru's argument found support from Frank Anthony, who suggested that a largely illiterate electorate would be 'predominantly unaware of exercising the franchise on a basis of being able to analyse political issues in a rational way'.[21] Both proposals were underpinned by the notion that literacy served as a proxy for rational reflection, which was necessary for judging political issues and voting appropriately.

Indeed, none of these members formally pressed an amendment against the universalization of the franchise. But it is worth looking beyond explicit criticism of adult suffrage per se. Some have argued that the history of India's nationalist discourse had constrained the constituent assembly's functioning such that its members found it incumbent upon themselves to institute adult suffrage. But did all members find these constraints acceptable? Prabhu Dayal Himatsinghka's statement points to why we might doubt this: 'But there it is, having advocated adult suffrage, it has become impossible for the leaders to say that they do not like it. *I know many do not relish the provisions of adult suffrage but they dare not say so*' (emphasis mine).[22] Similarly, Ayyangar argued that adult suffrage had been adopted 'in keeping with the times', but left to himself, he would have sought alternatives until adult education became available to all persons.[23]

There were undertones that questioned the wisdom of the franchise in India. One finds several references to adult suffrage in the context of the franchise as a 'risk', or an 'experiment'.[24] This vocabulary was adopted even by some who otherwise endorsed the principle of adult suffrage.

[20] Quoted in CAD 11: 939, 25 November 1949 (Frank Anthony).

[21] Ibid. Similarly, M. Thirumala Rao argued in favour of a 'graded' expansion of the franchise. Referring to adult franchise as a 'dangerous weapon', Rao pointed to the lack of education and insufficient development of patriotism to support his statement. Unlike the middle classes and intelligentsia, others had not sufficiently imbibed the values necessary for the proper exercise of the franchise. See ibid., 818, 22 November 1949.

[22] Ibid., 669, 18 November 1949.

[23] Ibid., 663, 18 November 1949. Lok Nath Mishra, too, argued in favour of indirect elections, with representatives to the legislature chosen by members of the *Panchayat* (governing council) for each village (CAD 7.1: 648, 20 November 1948).

[24] See CAD 5: 300 (DH Chandrasekharaiya), 28 August 1947; ibid., 302 (Vallabhbhai Patel); CAD 7.1: 960 (KT Shah), 10 December 1948; CAD 7.2: 1255, 4 January 1949 (Biswanath Das); CAD 10: 271 (Shibban Lal Saksena), 14 October 1949; CAD 11: 963 (Mahavir Tyagi), 25 November 1949.

> Another redeeming feature is the adult franchise. The adult franchise is the greatest risk which the Constituent Assembly has taken. I may tell the House it is the greatest risk for this reason that 85 per cent of our population is illiterate and it is even now doubted whether the adult franchise will be successful. Whatever it may be, Sir, successful or not successful, we have taken the risk rightly. We had to take the risk and we have taken the risk. A democracy without adult franchise would have no meaning and, therefore. I am very glad and the House is proud that we have in this Constitution put in 'Adult Franchise.'[25]

The notion of an experiment implies a departure from tried and tested ways. The Indian masses had been previously ruled only by monarchs and colonial governments. The adoption of democracy, then, marked a break from their past into an uncertain future. But there was another crucial sense in which the democratic system in India constituted an experiment. Here, the point of reference was not its own past, but that of the modern West. There, democracy had emerged only with the rise of mass literacy. Thus – the argument went – India had gambled by choosing to take the unprecedented step of enfranchising illiterate citizens whereas industrialized societies had adopted a very different political trajectory.

In what follows, I attempt to trace various ways in which such undertones, voicing anxieties about peoples' incapacities for self-rule, played a role in the Indian constituent assembly. These include, first, suspicion of capacity for self-government within indigenous persons (*adivasis*); and second, appeals to persons' lack of education in the design of the electoral procedure.

A. *Governance of Indigenous Areas*

Scepticism over the political capacities of adivasis had a wider history in India, evident in the way they were approached by the constitutional framework under the colonial state. Under that framework, certain areas had been marked as indigenous areas, where ordinary laws would not apply. Instead, the governor general was given discretion to determine policy for such areas either directly or through his agents. This framework was projected, first, as having established British authority as a paternalistic guardian of adivasi interests against exploitation by non-tribal persons. Second, it was defended as necessary in enabling the colonial government to undertake a program of reform, intended to exert a civilizing influence on adivasis. Third – and most crucially, for our discussion – the colonial framework was underpinned by the assumption that tribes could not cope with the complexity of representative institutions. This assumption was further based on two kinds of arguments. The first emphasized indigenous persons' lack of prior engagement with political institutions.

[25] CAD 11: 624, 17 November 1949 (RK Sidhva).

For instance, the Montague–Chelmsford Report, on which the Government of India Act 1919 was based, had suggested that 'there was no political material on which to found political institutions' in areas dominated by adivasis.[26] A second defence pointed to the lack of formal education among indigenous persons, and urged that this indicated their incompetence for representative government. On this point, the constituent assembly's sub-committee on indigenous persons quoted the findings of David Symington, the author of a report commissioned by the colonial government:

> They are not only illiterate but also ignorant of everything outside their daily run. They are contemptuous of education which they regard as a degrading and senseless waste of time. They have more faith in witchdoctors than in pharmacopoeia. They live near the border-line of starvation. They are inveterate drunkards. It was not surprising that they take no interest in the local boards elections or local board administration.[27]

In sum, indigenous persons were historically viewed with suspicion on account of their lack of education, which stood as a *proxy* for political intelligence, as well as their inability to *demonstrate* prior political participation.

Before proceeding, it is worth briefly examining Bhimrao Ambedkar's view on adivasis and their political competence. Ambedkar was the chairman of the constituent assembly's drafting committee, and is widely seen as one of the most pivotal individuals in the formulation of the constitution. His views on this subject are important not merely because of his prominence in the constitution-making process, but also given his strong, theoretically rich writings on suffrage. As a leader of the Dalit community, disproportionately affected by educational qualifications for the franchise, Ambedkar championed the idea that the franchise was pivotal in obtaining resources for education in the first place. Presently, I wish to highlight his views on the suffrage for adivasis, presented during his submissions before the Simon Commission in the run up to the Government of India Act 1935. In his statements before the commission, Ambedkar began by discussing both hill tribes and criminal tribes in the same breath, suggesting that he did 'not think it would be possible to allow them the privilege of adult suffrage'.[28] Later in his testimony, he reiterated his commitment to adult suffrage, inviting a direct question on whether he was willing to 'extend adult suffrage to the aboriginal tribes and to the criminal and hill tribes'.[29] At this point, Ambedkar responded in the affirmative.[30] But almost immediately,

[26] Report on Indian Constitutional Reforms (Calcutta: Superintendent of Government Printing, 1918), 129.

[27] Cited in CAD 7.1: 147–8, 4 November 1948.

[28] *Report of the Indian Statutory Commission: Selections from Memoranda and Oral Evidence*, Part I (London, His Majesty's Stationery Office, 1930), 53 (column 20).

[29] Ibid., 56 (column 110).

[30] Ibid. (columns 110–11).

he drew a distinction between his stance on 'criminal tribes' and 'aborigines'. The former, he argued, ought to be excluded from the franchise 'because by occupation they are a people who have more the interest of their own particular community in their mind, and they are not very particular as regards the means whereby they earn their living'.[31] In other words, Ambedkar viewed criminal tribes' purported engagement with crime as an occupation as a proxy for their inability to act morally if granted the franchise. As for the hill tribes, he did not see any 'harm' in granting them the franchise. However, it is worth noting that this endorsement about the *permissibility* of enfranchising the hill tribes marked a sharp departure from his categorical affirmation of the suffrage for Dalits. Indeed, it is quite possible that Ambedkar's views had changed by the time he was elected to serve in the constituent assembly. Yet, it is worth acknowledging that even a prominent defender of universal suffrage, sensitive to social and economic deprivation, was not always immune from endorsing exclusions, particularly with respect to adivasis.

Let us now return to the constituent assembly's treatment of provisions concerning adivasis. Provisions on the administration of indigenous areas were listed in the fifth and sixth schedules of the constitution. Here, I examine debates over the fifth schedule, which governs a large majority of indigenous areas. The original draft of the schedule gave considerable autonomy to 'Tribes Advisory Councils' (TACs).[32] These councils were to be made up primarily of indigenous members of state legislatures. The initial constitutional provision permitted the TACs, in collaboration with the state's governor, to determine whether or not laws made by the legislature in a state would apply to, or needed modification for, places designated as indigenous areas.[33]

The councils were not intended to bypass the democratic process in order to boost the overall influence of adivasis in a state's political affairs. Rather, they were intended as a device to secure self-governance of adivasis over matters that primarily concerned them. Note three important features of such councils in the original constitutional proposal. First, they were to be chosen primarily from elected state legislators, who were also indigenous persons. Second, the initial provision gave revising powers to the TAC in consultation with the governor (who was appointed by the central government). It allowed these authorities to revise or withhold the implementation of legislation with respect to indigenous areas. The power afforded was stronger than a mere veto in that it allowed modification of legislative decisions. The power of the governor, in consultation with the TAC, to make new regulations was limited to matters in indigenous areas which were 'not provided for by any law for the time being in force in such area'.[34] Moreover,

[31] Ibid. (column 112).

[32] Constituent Assembly of India, 'Draft Constitution Prepared by the Drafting Committee', in B. Shiva Rao (ed.), The *Framing of India's Constitution*: Vol. III (New Delhi: Universal Law Publishing, 1967[1948]), 651.

[33] Ibid. See Clause 5 in Part II of the Fifth Schedule.

[34] Ibid., Clause 5(2).

a decision taken under the revising powers would be binding on the state legislature, rather than just recommendatory. However, it did not institute an alternative source of original political decisions. Third, the governor was required to act in consultation with the TACs. In particular, the power to revise or withhold legislation could be exercised by the Governor only if he was 'so advised by the Tribes Advisory Council for the state'.[35]

The final constitutional provision adopted by the assembly involved important changes.[36] It granted the power of revising and withholding legislation in indigenous areas exclusively to the governor, dispensing with the need for the TAC's consent. Further, it expanded the governor's ability to frame regulations by removing the limitation stipulated in the initial provision. The governor now did not need to limit herself to areas where laws did not already exist. Rather, he could make regulations 'for the peace and good government of any area' designated as an indigenous area. Thus, an *unelected figure* chosen by the national government, rather than *elected legislators* appointed by the state government, was made the locus of power. Further, recall that legislators serving in the TACs were to be primarily adivasi legislators. As such, the previous draft of the fifth schedule had given power to *indigenous persons*. By contrast, the governor's office could be taken up by a *non-indigenous person*. So the final provision dispensed with the necessity that the powers awarded by the fifth schedule would lie primarily with indigenous leaders. In sum, the original draft of the fifth schedule had made it (1) mandatory that the locus of power was indigenous legislators, and (2) likely that such legislators were largely accountable to indigenous voters. The final provision retained neither of these features.

In the light of these changes, it is worth highlighting the assembly's concerns about, both, indigenous lawmakers and voters. First, adivasis were singled out by the constituent assembly's members in criticism against the adult suffrage. Brajeshwar Prasad, for instance, urged that elections were particularly unsuitable for adivasis because they exposed them to exploitation: 'The tribal people being ignorant, being backward, being down-trodden, will be exploited by powerful groups during the times of election. I hold that the principle of election is not at all suitable to these people'.[37] For Prasad, the answer to the exceptional situation of adivasis, its delicate and complex nature, required not the centralization of political power, but a delegation of such power to experts who could study, assess and offer prescriptions for their problems. Thus, anthropologists, doctors and scientists, rather than politicians or legislators, ought to play a greater role in administering tribal affairs.[38] Biswanath

35 Ibid., Clause 5(1).

36 See Article 244 in the Constitution of India.

37 CAD 9.1: 664 (Brajeshwar Prasad), 24 August 1949.

38 Ibid., 282 (Brajeshwar Prasad), 9 August 1949.

Das raised similar concerns, classing hill tribes with women and scheduled castes, as groups incapable of exercising their vote properly:

> As regards literacy among the hill tribes whom you have enfranchised in full and given the right to vote, it is practically next to nothing. What a tremendous risk you have taken? You are calling upon them to vote, but who are they? A very highly inflammable class of people who have up to date absolutely no experience either of propaganda or of voting in elections.[39]

Second, it was not just indigenous voters, but also their elected legislators who were viewed as epistemically unable to engage with the 'complex' task of administration. KM Munshi insisted that the TAC would be unable to determine whether an 'elaborate' act of parliament ought to apply to indigenous areas.[40] Kuladhar Chaliha criticized the delegation of political power to elected representatives to indigenous persons on similar grounds. He insisted on eliminating 'the trouble of the primitive people from framing rules for these very cumbrous and complex things'.[41] Note that the complexity of legislation did not prevent proponents of such arguments from vesting discretionary power with a single, unelected figure. Thus, the governor was nevertheless viewed as competent enough to determine whether or not some law should apply to indigenous areas. However, a body of elected indigenous legislators was epistemically incompetent relative to such a figure.

B. *Illiteracy and the Electoral System*

Some members of the constituent assembly argued that the Indian constitution ought to adopt a system of proportional representation for elections. Like safeguards for adivasis, proportional representation was defended as necessary to operationalize genuine democracy in India. Rochana Bajpai's work highlights three distinctive arguments of this kind. First, it was argued that the first-past-the-post system effectively disenfranchised voters who did not vote for the winning candidate. On this account, proportional representation was more democratic because it gave each person an equal chance of winning. It was, therefore, more consistent with political

[39] CAD 7.2: 1255, 4 January 1949.

[40] Munshi pointed to the Money Lenders' Act as an example: 'Take for instance, money-lending. It is such difficult subject and I am sure some of the tribals on my side would not be able to understand the implications of Money- lenders' Act, and if their advice is sought, I am sure, they would say that they do not understand a word of it. The word "consulted" therefore has been put in the place of "advice" purposely' (CAD 9.2: 998–9, 5 September 1949).

[41] CAD 11: 569 (Kuladhar Chaliha), 16 November 1949.

equality, understood as the right of every individual to be represented by a person of her choice:

> The twin principles of democracy are that everybody has a right of representation and the majority has the right of govern (sic). The electoral system must be such as to ensure representation to everybody. This is the significance of adult franchise but the method adopted really amounts to the disenfranchisement of 49 per cent of the voters ... I am talking of political minority. Even political minorities are entitled to be represented in representative institutions ... It is better for us to adopt this principle (Proportional representation by single transferable vote) which is more progressive in instinct and which is really democratic.[42]

Second, proportional representation was also favoured by some as a way of making legislative assemblies more representative of the diversity of political opinions in society. In particular, it would allow minority political opinion to be represented in legislatures. Proportional representation, then, was more democratic because it allowed the legislative assembly to mirror political opinions in proportion to their strength in society. One member drew on Mill's writings on proportional representation in making this argument:

> ... Those who have read the writings of Mill must have been impressed by his advocacy of fundamental principle of democracy, that every political opinion must be represented in an assembly in proportion to its strength in the country, and naturally so ... But if you adopt a method by which only 51 percent of the people alone are represented in the legislature, it ceases to be the mirror of the nation. Now the question is, does the method of representation adopted by this House give effect to or rather does it implement the principles of democracy?[43]

Third, Bajpai argues that proportional representation was also endorsed as a mechanism for preventing the concentration of power in any single party. This account suggested that first-past-the-post hand exposed the polity to threats of totalitarianism.[44] On the other hand, proportional representation would help restrain majorities by encouraging a stronger opposition, greater likelihood of coalition governments, and establishing the need to consult minority political opinion in the formulation of

[42] CAD 7: 299 (ZH Lari), 8 November 1948, cited in Bajpai, *Debating Difference*, 151.

[43] CAD 8: 283 (ZH Lari), 25 May 1949, cited in Bajpai, *Debating Difference*, 153.

[44] Mahboob Ali Baig Sahib Bahadur's, for instance, stated that: 'Can you think of any parliamentary democracy where there is no opposition? Unless there is opposition, Sir, the danger of its turning itself into a Fascist body is there. An opposition can come into existence only if persons holding different views from the majority are enabled to be returned to the legislature ...' (CAD 7: 1245, 4 January 1949, cited in Bajpai, *Debating Difference*, 154).

policy. Here, the traditional failing of proportional representation—the weakness of governments it produces—was advanced as a strength.[45]

However, the constituent assembly rejected the demand for proportional representation. On one line of argument, it was viewed as a divisive move, aimed at strategically bringing in religious minorities through the back door.[46] It was also seen as potentially obstructing the formation of a strong and stable government. Ambedkar, for instance, argued against proportional representation on the grounds that 'whether it relieves the people from the wants from which they are suffering now or not, our future government must do one thing, namely it must maintain a stable government and maintain law and order'.[47] Significantly, epistemic arguments played an important role in the assembly's dismissal of proportional representation.

Firstly, some emphasised that literacy was a *precondition* for marking the ballot correctly under a system of proportional representation:

> Now, I do not think it is possible to accept this amendment, because, so far as I am able to judge the merits of the system of proportional Representation, in the light of the circumstances as they exist in this country, I think, that amendment cannot be accepted. My Friend Mr. Karimuddin will, I think, accept the proposition that proportional representation presupposes literacy on a large scale. In fact, it presupposes that every voter shall be literate, at least to the extent of being in a position to know the numericals, and to be in a position to mark them on a ballot paper. I think, having regard to the extent of literacy in this country, such a presupposition would be utterly extravagant. I have not the least doubt on that point. Our literacy is the smallest, I believe, in the world, and it would be quite impossible to impose upon an illiterate mass of voters a system of election which involves marking of ballot papers. *That in itself, would, I think, exclude the system of proportional representation* (emphasis mine).[48]

Further, others appealed to the absence of education, understood as a *proxy* for the kind of intelligence needed to engage with a complex system such as proportional representation. This electoral system required more intelligence on behalf of voters, as they would have to mark multiple preferences, and make difficult calculations: 'To work this system properly, the electorate must be well educated, because the voters has to give his preferences and illiterate person will not be able to understand the significance of the various preferences'.[49] The fact that even legislators had found it difficult to understand the system was cited as evidence that this was beyond the

45 CAD 7: 1234 (Kazi Syed Karimuddin), 4 January 1949.
46 CAD 8: 325 (Rohini Chaudhari), 26 May 1949.
47 CAD 7.2 1262 (BR Ambedkar), 4 January 1949.
48 Ibid., 1261 (BR Ambedkar), 4 January 1949.
49 CAD 8: 320 (Shibban Lal Saksena), 26 May 1949.

abilities of uneducated persons.[50] Where the system had worked, for instance, in Switzerland, Belgium or Ireland, its success was attributed to the small size and educated electorate.[51] Such was the purchase of this argument that even proponents of proportional representation had to acknowledge its force.[52]

Here, let me emphasise that arguments about the size and illiteracy of India's electorate had been mobilized previously in order to urge that the democratic process would be unworkable there. These arguments had played a pivotal role in the colonial government's justification for deferring democracy in India, and establishing limited representative institutions with a qualified franchise.[53] In debates leading to the Government of India Act 1935, such arguments were repudiated by those who favoured a more extensive democratic regime. First, critics of the colonial government argued that the purported inability of illiterate persons to understand the electoral process meaningfully was overstated.[54] Even illiterate persons possessed adequate ability to comprehend the significance of their vote, and how it ought to be used. Through the use of common sense, and the insight obtained from their attempts to earn a living, they possessed the abilities presupposed by democratic citizenship. Second, critics also argued that any potential difficulties were surmountable through innovation with the ballot itself.[55] This was achieved in the first instance by placing separate ballot boxes with pictures of every candidate in the election. Voters could register their preference by dropping the ballot paper in the box marked for their preferred candidate. Later, party symbols on the ballot were used as a way of allowing voters to register their preferences. This allowed persons to participate in the elections regardless of their ability to read or write. Thus, the dismissal of similar arguments earlier ought to be borne in mind when one reads the assembly's appeal to the incapacities of uneducated persons to work a purportedly complex system such as proportional representation.

50 CAD 7.2: 1259 (M. Ananthasayanam Ayyangar), 4 January, 1949.

51 CAD 8: 320 (Shibban Lal Saksena), 26 May 1949.

52 DH Chandrasekharaiya, a proponent of proportional representation argued that: 'The only objection to it may perhaps be that it is a little complicated system'. Nevertheless, he went on to argue that 'we are now trying big experiments in democracy, I think that no difficulty should be considered as too great for us to, solve. In our country 90 per cent of the population is illiterate, nevertheless elections are being held and political institutions are being run without any serious difficulties. Similarly, I feel that the system of proportional representation can get on every well notwithstanding the illiteracy of the masses' (CAD 5: 299–300, 28 August 1947).

53 See, for instance, *Report of the Indian Franchise Committee*: Vol. I (Calcutta: Government of India, 1932), 18–20.

54 'Sub-committee Reports', in *Indian Round Table Conference*: Vol. XII. (London: His Majesty's Stationery Office, 1931), 228, 230.

55 Ibid., 223.

III. INTERLUDE

Despite misgivings from certain quarters, the constituent assembly did proceed to institutionalize adult suffrage. The first elections under universal adult franchise took place in India only in 1952, once the constitution framed by its constituent assembly had come into operation. The assembly itself was constituted through indirect elections by the provincial legislatures. Further, provincial legislatures had been elected on the basis of qualified suffrage which had been put into force by the Government of India Act 1935. The irony of a body chosen under such limitations framing democratic institutions for independent India was not lost on members of the assembly. Some members even proposed postponing the assembly's proceedings until such time as direct elections had been held. But a decision was made to vest constituent power in the assembly because hosting fresh elections would involve postponing the transfer of power. At its very inception, therefore, a compromise was made in postponing adult suffrage in India.

More crucially, the scope of citizens' involvement was limited to adult suffrage exercised in two elections – for selecting representatives to the state legislative assembly and the first chamber of the parliament. The lack of consideration given to greater political involvement of citizens is significant. In what follows, I examine the constituent assembly's treatment of referendums, which offered a way in which such involvement could have been institutionalized.

Before examining proposals placed before the assembly, it is worth highlighting the different types of referendums that are possible. First, they can be either *mandatory* or *voluntary*. In the voluntary type, legislative assemblies have the option of calling on voters to express their preferences through a referendum, but are not required to do so. On the other hand, mandatory referendums take place when the constitution provides that certain decisions must involve a referendum either in addition to, or in place of, the legislative body. For instance, a referendum might be mandated in the case of an initiative, whereby a legislative proposal that enjoys the support of a certain number of voters is subject to either a confirmatory or legislative referendum (see later). Second, referendums can be *binding* or *non-binding* on the legislative assembly. Legislative assemblies have the option of not acting on a non-binding referendum, treating them merely as inputs into their own final decisions, whereas the verdict of a binding referendum cannot be thus set aside. Third, referendums can be either *confirmatory* or *legislative*. A confirmatory referendum is one where electors are directly called on to ratify or reject legislation enacted by the legislative body. Here, the role of the referendum is limited to assenting or rejecting the bill rather than amending it. Further, the role of the electorate in relation to the legislative assemblies is non-reversible. The former cannot initiate legislation, but can only affirm (or deny) it. Legislative referendums give electors the power to vote on legislation. A matter might be brought to a referendum – ordinarily through recall measures – without its having been enacted by the legislative body. It is also possible that the legislative body may voluntarily ask for a measure to be decided through a referendum without having taken a decision on that measure itself. Fourth, referendums can be held on either *ordinary* legislative matters or *constitutional* ones.

Consider KT Shah's proposal for incorporation of referendums in the Indian constitution.[56] He urged that the constitution ought to provide for voluntary referendums. His proposal would have had the effect of allowing the executive to call for any referendum: binding or non-binding, confirmatory or legislative, on ordinary as well as constitutional issues. Here, one might object that constitutions do not need to allow a voluntary referendum. After all, even in the absence of such a provision, it is always open to the parliament to opt for a referendum on any measure that falls within its jurisdiction. What, then, would have been added by Shah's proposed amendment? But a closer look shows that Shah's proposal was not entirely vacuous. It sought to give the power to hold a voluntary referendum to the *executive* rather than the legislature. Thus, the executive could without consulting the legislature, have asked for a referendum to confirm or deny the parliament's decisions, or even transferred decision making from the parliament to a referendum altogether. Indeed, the close relationship between the executive and the legislature in a parliamentary system implies that the government is unlikely to transfer a matter to a referendum if such a move antagonizes the majority in the first chamber. However, transferring the power for a voluntary referendum to the government, nevertheless, would allow it to circumvent having to obtain approval for such a measure from the second – and in India's case, indirectly elected – chamber. A second proposal on referendums by Brajeshwar Prasad urged the assembly to mandate a confirmatory and binding referendum for amendments to the constitution.[57] Under his proposal, any constitutional amendment that secured the requisite majority in both houses of the parliament would have to gain the subsequent approval of a majority of the electorate through a referendum. This sought to substitute the proposal, eventually adopted, to give confirmatory power to state legislatures.

Both proposals for referendums, then, subordinated the potential exercise of direct democracy to representative institutions. Shah's proposal, in being voluntary, left the decision to move a referendum on the government – which further derived its existence from the majority in the first legislative chamber. Prasad's proposal, by limiting itself to a confirmatory role, sought to allow referendums only on decisions enacted by both legislative chambers. I do not highlight this in order to criticize their proposals; after all, it remains far from clear that direct democracy is

[56] CAD 7.1: 980, 10 December 1948.
[57] CAD 9: 1646–7, 17 September 1949.

an advancement over representative institutions.[58] My point is merely to emphasize that as far as referendums go, Shah and Prasad were not particularly ambitious in devolving power directly to the people.

Yet, their proposals received almost no attention from colleagues in the constituent assembly. Not only did the constitution not provide for any form of referendum, but even proposed amendments to that effect received no engagement whatsoever. Some indication about how other members felt can be found in Shah's comments just days ahead of the adoption of the constitution.[59] Criticizing the Indian constitution's reliance on representative institutions to the complete exclusion of any form of direct democracy, Shah complained:

> Several suggestions had been brought forward at the proper movement regarding, for instance, the right to consult the people by means of a Referendum or the power of the people to initiate radical legislation to make the Constitution really democratic. But they have been all negatived. The excuse has been given that we are not yet ready for such methods of working democracy in all its fullness. We would need, we were told, greater experience, better education, and more widespread consciousness of political power in the masses as well as its responsibilities, to be able to work with success such radical forms, of democratic government. I am afraid, Sir, I cannot quite accept and endorse such a, view of our people's capacity, or of a working democracy in this country … Had we agreed to such arguments in the past, had we accepted the suggestion of the British that the people of India were not educated enough and aware enough of their rights and obligations to be able to work a democratic Government of their own, we should never even now have obtained our independence, and the right to self-government which is now our proud possession.[60]

IV. COMPETENCE AS ADVANTAGE

In the second half of the chapter, I explore how the constituent assembly sought to confer greater political power on persons deemed more competent. Here, I focus on ways in which the second chamber in India's bicameral legislature was designed to serve an epistocratic purpose. Three such mechanisms of second chambers in India are examined: (1) indirect elections, (2) nominations and (3) graduate constituencies.

58 Nadia Urbinati, *Representative Democracy: Principles and Genealogy* (Chicago, IL: University of Chicago Press, 2006).

59 As a secondary report on his colleagues' (non)response, this statement ought to be read with some scepticism. It is entirely possible that Shah was attributing certain grounds for the exclusion of his proposal, whereas these were not offered to him. It is also quite possible that his colleagues did not really articulate any reasons for ignoring proposals for referendums. In the absence of any further engagement on this from the assembly, Shah's own views on such treatment are, nevertheless, important.

60 CAD 11: 619.

These mechanisms share the premises that (1) the electoral process is insufficient in bringing into the legislature adequately competent persons[61]; (2) and that it is permissible to bypass the normal electoral process to vest competent persons with legislative power equal to those elected by the people.

The constituent assembly voted to institute a bicameral legislature at the Centre. The first chamber (*Lok Sabha*) would consist of members directly elected on the basis of universal adult suffrage, while the second chamber (*Rajya Sabha*) would derive its members on the basis of indirect elections through the legislative assemblies of various states. At the provincial level, it provided for the bicameralism in some states, while leaving the legislative assembly in other states with the choice to create a second chamber.

The justifiability of a second legislative chamber is by no means uncontroversial. The framers of the Indian constitution were well aware of this, and cited arguments by figures such as Emmanuel Joseph Sieyès and Harold Laski[62] against bicameralism. Several members criticized the proposal for a second chamber on the ground that it would 'clog in the wheel of progress', delaying legislative action and preventing speedy transformative decisions.[63] Mohd. Tahir argued that it was paradoxical for a body like the constituent assembly to insist on a bicameral legislature. If faith could be reposed only in decisions that had been approved by two separate legislative chambers, then what authority did a unicameral legislature have in insisting on the creation of a second legislative house? Others also expressed anxiety about the representation of vested interests through the second chamber.[64] In particular, they urged that the second chamber would give disproportionate representation to the interests of the landed classes and block attempts at redistribution of wealth.

There are various arguments one might offer for the desirability of a second chamber in the democratic process. First, a second legislative chamber can allow for the representation of groups that are absent from or disadvantaged by arrangements in the first legislative chamber. This argument applies particularly

[61] The precise conception of competence expected of legislators was left unspecified by members of the assembly. Competence in relation to legislators can be conceptualised in various ways. Jeremy Bentham, for instance, distinguished three dimensions of competence: virtue, ability, and energy. John Stuart Mill, on the other hand, separated 'talking' from 'doing', or deliberative competence from technical competence. See Jon Elster, *Securities Against Misrule* (Cambridge: Cambridge University Press, 2013), 141–2; Nadia Urbinati, *Mill on Democracy: From the Athenian Polis to Representative Government* (Chicago, IL: University of Chicago Press, 2002), 60–4.

[62] See statements by HV Kamath (CAD 9.1: 16) and Damodar Swarup Seth (CAD 7.1: 988) respectively.

[63] CAD 4: 926–7 (Shibban Lal Saksena). Also see statements by Kuladhar Chaliha (CAD 7.2: 1310) KT Shah (ibid., 1305–6); NG Ranga (CAD 9.1: 53–4). Renuka Ray (CAD 9.1: 56) also argued that the second chamber was redundant since the president at the Centre and governors in the states could act as a check on hasty legislation.

[64] HV Kamath (CAD 4: 679); Saranghar Das (CAD 4: 682).

in the case of minority groups disadvantaged by electoral procedures that prioritize rule by majority in the first chamber. This function is best served when the second chamber adopts a different electoral procedure than that present in the first: for instance, when members are chosen through proportional representation rather than first-past-the-post or even indirect rather than direct elections. A second way of defending bicameralism is by emphasising its role in supporting a federal arrangement. This argument is closely related to the previous one since it highlights the role of the upper chamber in ensuring better representation of the people. However, rather than better representing groups of persons, the upper house is expected to represent provincial units. Third, one might defend a second chamber on epistemic grounds: for its ability to revise or re-examine decisions adopted by the first chamber. On this argument, the need for a second chamber stems from the fallibility of all political decisions. This particular strand of argument can pull in three further directions, calling for a second chamber comprising (1) A different set of individuals, (2) different institutional features or (3) different kinds of individuals.

(1) **Different Set of Individuals:** Bicameral legislatures can be used to multiply opportunities for rectifying errors, and delaying the legislative process in the hope that temporary surges of passion could be overcome. The idea is not that the second set of individuals who occupy another chamber is epistemically superior. As another representative assembly, constituted of persons also subject to epistemic deficiencies, it, too, can commit mistakes. However, the idea here is that having two chambers affords *two opportunities* for detecting such error. Moreover, by requiring both houses to pass the same bill, it injects a degree of *delay* into the legislative process. The idea is that the introduction of this delay can lead to deeper examination. In particular, this delay could help mitigate the effect of momentary passions, preventing these from getting embedded in the content of laws. This is best instantiated by the fabled conversation between Thomas Jefferson and George Washington – a conversation that was narrated in the Indian constituent assembly by L. Krishnaswami Bharathi:

> It appears that Thomas Jefferson was protesting very strongly against the idea of a Second Chamber, to Washington. Mr. Farrand reports this incident very interestingly: they were taking coffee at breakfast time. Suddenly George Washington asked: 'Why, Mr. Jefferson, why are you pouring the coffee into your saucer?' Jefferson replied: 'To cool it'. Even so, we want to cool legislation by putting it into the saucer of the senatorial Chamber. That is a forceful way of expressing the idea and as we are going to be constituted, it is to check or prevent hasty legislation and not at all to impede progressive legislation. There shall be no mistake about it; the idea is not to check progressive legislation but to have some time so that cool, calm and deliberate conclusions may be arrived at.[65]

[65] CAD 7.2: 1308 (L. Krishnaswami Bharathi), 6 January 1949.

Of course, it is quite possible that both houses, composed as they are, of fallible beings, may commit the same error despite two opportunities for reflecting on it. It is also possible that the delay introduced by the second chamber does not lead to further reflection leading to detection of the error. Here, a comparison with the multiple locks on doors is helpful. It is not absurd to put two or more locks of the same kind on one's door while leaving the house. The idea here is not that the second lock is a better lock, but that it is better to have at least two locks rather than one. A determined or skilled robber may nevertheless manage to break in, but one hopes that the second lock makes the process harder, and delays it, giving more time for someone to notice and possibly intervene.

A crucial feature of argument (1) in favour of second chambers is its reversibility: the presence of the lower chamber can be defended with the same arguments in relation to the upper chamber. It is not just that the Senate is a body for revising and reconsidering decisions made by the House of Representatives. The House of Representatives, too, can be seen as a chamber that is able to provide a second opinion and delay in decisions adopted by the Senate.

(2) Different Institutional Features: Recognition of our epistemic deficiencies might lead in a second direction – one that calls for a chamber with institutional features designed to overcome, or mitigate, such deficiencies. The arguments made for a second chamber in the Federalist Papers exemplify this strand of argument. The longer terms of the Senate allowed its members to accumulate expertise better than representatives in the lower house, who were engaged in lawmaking only for short periods of time. As a result, the Senate's longer terms for its members helped improve the quality of legislation. Further, longer terms meant that members of the Senate did not need to give in to short-term demands of their constituents. Instead, unlike representatives in the House of Representatives, they had more time to convince their constituents about the need for laws that required the sacrifice of present interests for a greater good in the long run. Finally, the smaller size of the Senate also enhanced the quality of its legislation, as passionate surges were more likely in large assemblies such as the House of Representatives.

In argument (1), what necessitated the presence of a second chamber was merely the need for an additional body comprising different sets of persons to those who exercised power, and the presence of delays in the passage of legislation. In argument (2), the second legislative chamber was justified, again, not by a deficiency in the people who elected members to the first chamber, but by institutional features of the House of Representatives: the shorter terms of its members and the larger size of the assembly. The two arguments are related insofar as institutional features can exacerbate or fail to address deficiencies that arise from our shared epistemic limitations. For instance, we may worry about the inability of an institution to provide ample time for pooling expertise because we recognize that persons generally require time to acquire new knowledge. Or we may worry that larger assemblies are likely to give impetus to passionate surges to which all persons are vulnerable.

(3) **Different Kind of Individuals:** Contrast these with a third justification one might offer for revising decisions through a second chamber – an argument offered by members of the Indian constituent assembly for bicameralism. This justification argued that the second chamber offered a way of introducing epistemically superior persons into the legislature. In this argument, unlike (1) discussed earlier, the second chamber *is* more epistemically superior. But, on the other hand, unlike (2), this epistemic superiority is not a function of its institutional features, but of the prior competence of persons who constitute the second house. In other words, the argument here was individual-oriented, rather than institution-oriented. The attempt to secure such individuals was operationalized in three ways: indirect elections, nominations and graduate constituencies. In what follows, I explore debates over these three mechanisms in greater detail.

A. *Indirect Elections*

The Indian constituent assembly adopted indirect elections for the Rajya Sabha. Members of the second chamber were to be chosen by elected representatives in the state legislatures. This mirrored the composition of the American Senate before it was amended by the 17th Amendment. Significantly, arguments for indirect elections, such as those found during the establishment of the American Senate, viewed these as a way of 'refining the popular appointments by successive filtrations'.[66]

It is worth highlighting that indirect elections were proposed not just for the second chamber, but for the first legislative chamber as well. Consider Loknath Mishra's amendment to establish indirect elections for the Union as well as provincial legislatures.[67] Mishra argued that indirect elections offered an opportunity to mitigate the epistemic costs associated with large constituencies associated with direct elections. Mishra's argument relied, first, on the suggestion that ordinary citizens were epistemically inadequate: 'they are not as clever or as intelligent as the diplomats or the members that will be coming to represent them in the many Houses'.[68] Further, he urged that it was the task of elected represents to educate their

[66] James Madison, *Notes on Debates in the Federal Convention of 1787*, edited by Adrienne Koch (Athens, OH: Ohio University Press, 1984[1840]), 40.

[67] CAD 7.1: 646, 29 November, 1948.

[68] Ibid., 647.

constituents.[69] However, this process of instruction was unlikely in large electoral constituencies, comprising several thousand persons. If elections were mediated through village councils, who would elect legislators, persons could be grouped into smaller units. This would enable village councils to educate epistemically deficient citizens.

Similarly, others highlighted the illiteracy of the population as a reason for preferring an indirectly elected second chamber. Thus, Ayyangar stated that he had doubts about the workability of adult suffrage in India as a result of its large illiterate population.[70] Under such circumstances, he would have preferred to adopt indirect elections, mediated through village councils. Brajeshwar Prasad argued that the Lok Sabha, elected by people who 'are not only illiterate, but narrow-minded, steeped in fanaticism and superstition' would 'release forces of violence and of disorder' on an unprecedented scale.[71] The second chamber could operate as a check on the vagaries of adult suffrage, introducing persons who were wise and literate.[72] Therefore, such proposals viewed literacy as a proxy for the kind of intelligence necessary to vote directly for competent representatives.

Before proceeding, it is worth emphasizing a curious feature of indirect elections in the Indian case. The constitutional provision on elections to the Rajya Sabha did not specify whether voting ought to take place through open ballot.[73] The Representation of the People Act (RPA) adopted by the provisional parliament, also did not prescribe the nature of the ballot. As a result, Rajya Sabha elections continued to be conducted through secret ballot until as recently as 2003. An amendment to the RPA mandated that elections to the Rajya Sabha would henceforth be conducted through an open ballot.[74] Until the 2003 amendment was enacted, the secrecy of votes added a further layer of insulation for the second chamber by rendering state legislators unaccountable for their choice of representatives in the Rajya Sabha.

69 Ibid.

70 CAD 11: 669, 18th November 1949.

71 Brajeshwar Prasad stated that: 'With the inauguration of the new Constitution on the basis of adult franchise, it is risky to vest all powers in the hands of the Lower House … I believe that power must be vested in the hands of those who are literate; not only literate but wise too. I believe that power must be vested in the hands of those who are not only wise but who have got a sense of justice. I have no faith that the Lower House, constituted on the basis of adult franchise, will be able to do justice to anybody. People in India are not only illiterate, but narrow-minded, steeped in fanaticism and superstition' (CAD 9.1: 45–6, 1 August 1949); also see ibid., 20.

72 Another member, PS Deshmukh also attributed the preference for second chambers among his colleagues to 'distrust of adult franchise' (ibid., 49). Also see CAD 8:182 (S. Nagappa), 20 May 1949.

73 *Representation of the People Act, 1951* (India).

74 Ibid., Section 59. Inserted by Inserted by Act 40 of 2003.

B. *Nominations*

Consider four proposals in the constituent assembly for nominations to the second chamber of the union parliament:

1. Election of 25 legislators in two stages:
   The first stage would consist in nomination of persons to five panels: (i) National language and culture, literature, art, education and other professional interests; (ii) Agriculture and allied interests; (iii) Labour; (iv) Industry and commerce; and (v) Public administration. Registered associations from these vocations, and the national assembly were eligible for nominating members for such panels.
   The second stage would consist in an electoral contest between nominees with the national assembly as the constituency.[75]
2. Nomination of ten members nominated by the executive in consultation with universities and scientific bodies.[76]
3. Nomination by the executive of twelve members who have 'special knowledge or practical experience in respect of such matters as literature, science, art and social service'.
4. Nomination by the executive of three members to assist and advise the parliament on specific bills.[77]

I begin by discussing the assembly's adoption of the third provision over the first and second, before then examining the fourth proposal. The first draft provision tried to establish nomination through vocational panels, which mirrored those found in the upper house for the Irish legislature. This proposal was later dropped after the constitutional advisor, B. N. Rau, was advised during his visit to Ireland that this mechanism had posed several problems there.[78] The assembly's decision to adopt the third proposal represented a contraction in the leeway afforded to nominated members in some respects. The number of nominees dropped from twenty-five to twelve. Further, proposal (2) required the president to consult with scientific bodies and universities in nominating members to the upper house. This requirement was removed after objections that expertise relevant to legislative affairs could exist outside such formal institutions.[79]

[75] Benegal Narsing Rau, 'Draft Constitution by the Constitutional Adviser', in B. Shiva Rao (ed.), *The Framing of India's Constitution: Select Documents, Part III* (New Delhi: Universal Law Publishing, 1967[1947]), 22.

[76] CAD 4: 928 (Gopalaswami Ayyangar), 28 July 1947.

[77] CAD 8: 82 (BR Ambedkar), 18 May, 1949.

[78] Ibid., 83.

[79] CAD 4: 1029–30 (Gopalaswami Ayyangar), 31 July 1947.

One might argue that the constituent assembly's adoption of nominations should not be treated as an epistocratic measure. Rather, it ought to be treated as an attempt to rectify shortcomings of *representation*, rather than epistemic capacity. Here, representation is understood as valuable for non-epistemic reasons, like providing persons with the ability for self-governance (whether or not they do so in an epistemically optimal way). On this reading, nominations from experts in certain fields is merely a way of ensuring that members of those domains are not left unrepresented because of their numbers, and instead find a voice in decision making. Nominees' expertise in the defined fields does not give them any privileged claim to wider competence with respect to legislation relative to any other set of individuals.

Examining reasons offered for the provision on nomination confirms the idea that this was meant as a device for by-passing the ordinary electoral process in order to secure epistemically superior persons as legislators. As one member argued, the provision was a way of providing safe passage for experts who would feel 'shy' in contesting elections.[80] Naziruddin Ahmad put this explicitly when he defended nominations on the grounds that:

> It may be that at any future election we may lose Dr. Ambedkar himself, and there should be some means of bringing him in by a presidential nomination. Then there is the Rt. Honourable Mr. Jayakar. These are really great men of the Law and their addition, or rather the choice of the President in their selection should be very useful.[81]

Further, a closer look at the constitutional provision on nominations provides more evidence that it was intended to improve the legislature's epistemic competence, rather than merely improve its representative character. First, the choice of fields chosen as relevant for overriding the electoral process is crucial. The constitutional provision on nominations suggests that knowledge of 'literature, art, science and social service' and not, for instance, agriculture, industry or labour, trigger claims for representation. In other words, only particular kinds of knowledge were picked out as relevant in defining what must be represented. Here, it is worth noting that the rejected proposal on vocational panels was more inclusive with respect to the categories for which it demanded representation, encompassing fields such as agriculture and labour.[82] Further, in the case of categories of persons that were awarded

80 CAD 7.2: 1220 (Rohini Kumar Chaudhari), 3 January, 1949. Also see CAD 4: 927–8 (N Gopalaswami Ayyangar), 28 July 1947; CAD 9.1: 487 (PS Deshmukh), 19 August 1949.

81 CAD 7.2: 1213, 3 January 1949.

82 Indeed, the final provision did not provide an *exhaustive* list of categories for nomination. Rather, the fields mentioned there were *illustrative*. However, the illustrations did serve to constrain the vocations from which nominated members could be drawn. For instance, it would be hard to argue that the nomination of a farmer was possible under the final provision.

legislative quotas – such as certain backward castes and tribes – the legislators chosen under these safeguards would nevertheless need to prove their popularity among the group they stood for. In the case of literature, art, science and social service, however, members could be appointed without requiring that they undergo any process of elections at all. Even in the case of proposal (1) on vocational panels, nominated persons were required to participate in an electoral contest, with members of their respective professions as the constituencies. If representation, rather than expertise were the purpose of nominations, candidates ought to be required to demonstrate that their perspectives were *representative* of those held by others in the fields of literature, art, science and social service. Instead, allowing the executive to appoint members seems to prioritize prominence or excellence over representativeness in those fields as a prerequisite for serving as a legislator.

Let me now say more by way of comparison between the final constitutional provision and the third proposal highlighted earlier. I begin by distinguishing two dimensions along which the contribution of actors to legislative discussion might vary. First, the legislative role of agents varies in the *scope of decisions* upon which their preferences are considered. Their role may be restricted, for instance, to providing inputs on proposed legislation where vital interests of their group are affected. On the other hand, they may be given a wider mandate of participating on all issues that lie within the ambit of the assembly. Second, the legislative role afforded to political agents might vary on the dimension of *weight afforded to their preferences*. Political players might be given a veto, vote or rights to be consulted on matters. The *veto* might be restricted to particular matters, as when minority representatives are given the right to reject proposed legislation that affects their vital interests. On the other hand, a presidential veto is not restricted to legislation that covers only a particular set of subjects. *Rights to consultation* might again be specific to some subject, or general. As an example of the latter, consider the British monarch's right to be consulted, as well as aid and advise ministers. However, rights to consultation might be limited, as when a group must be asked for its views when a proposed policy is likely to affect its interests. The *vote* is a weaker mechanism than a veto because a political agent shares power with other agents, and cannot herself determine the decision. But it is stronger than mere rights to consultation where she can only try and influence primary agents whose vote or veto determines the outcome.

Proposal (4) had proposed permitting the executive to nominate three members whose role would be restricted in both scope and weight. Such members would 'assist and advise the Houses in a particular measure that may be before the House'. Their terms were to be 'co-terminous with the proceedings with regard to a particular Bill in relation to which they are nominated by the President to advise and assist the House'.[83] Further, their contribution was limited to taking 'part in

[83] CAD 8:83 (BR Ambedkar), 18 May, 1949.

the debate, whether the debate is taking place in the House as a whole or in a particular committee to which they are nominated by the House as a whole or in a particular committee to which they are nominated by the House as members thereof'.[84] Yet, the final provision adopted by the Assembly expanded the power available to nominated members in both respects.

C. *University Constituencies*

There was yet another – and more significant – way, though, in which bearers of knowledge were afforded a special place in democratic politics by the constituent assembly. This was through upper chambers in certain legislatures of the states, also known as State Legislative Councils. Article 171 of the constitution provided for one-twelfth of the seats in these councils to be filled by persons who were graduates, and an identical proportion by those who were engaged in teaching in educational institutions above the secondary level.

Interestingly, the Indian constituent assembly chose to incorporate university constituencies at the same time that such constituencies were being abolished by the British Parliament. Although previous attempts had been unsuccessful in 1931 and 1936, the amended Representation of People Act of 1948 finally abolished university constituencies in Britain. Critics emphasized that such constituencies were incompatible with the principle of one person, one vote. More importantly, they rejected, both, the idea that university constituencies were instrumental in protecting the interests of education, or that they could enhance the epistemic quality of legislative discussion:

1. The first line of criticism refuted the suggestion that graduates had some common interests which needed representation. Rather, graduates were further made up of several communities: 'a professor here, a clergyman there, a stockbroker or a Member of Parliament'.[85] Further, others denied that members from the universities had played any significant role in representing the domain of education. Their positions on educational policy had demonstrated that they were poor representatives of that domain.[86]
2. A second criticism also rejected the epistemic case for university constituencies as an inadequate one. Herbison argued that the education obtained at university was oriented towards vocational training, rather than cultural

[84] Ibid.
[85] HC Deb 16 February 1948, Vol. 447 col. 938 (Hugh Dalton).
[86] HC Deb 17 February 1948, Vol. 447 col. 1076 (Peggy Herbison).

education, which was relevant for good political judgement.[87] Note that this critique was modest insofar as it only highlighted the *inadequacy* of university education as a proxy for good political judgement. In previous parliamentary debates on the subject, others had argued that the reactionary environment of universities rendered such constituencies epistemically *worse off* than ordinary ones. Such critics had pointed to how their 'aloofness and divorcement from the actualities of life'[88] meant that universities were not capable of independent political thought. Their traditions and 'powerful reactionary influence' resulted in a muzzling of political agents and hampered progressive political thought.[89]

3. Yet another strand of criticism against the epistemic case in the 1948 debates was directed at the benefits of the purported independence of legislators belonging to university constituencies. This argument on the partisan nature of such constituencies, pointing out how Conservative politicians who had failed in ordinary elections got themselves elected through the university seats.[90] On the other hand, others argued not that university MPs lacked independence, but that this characteristic was undesirable. Not associating themselves with a party like other members demonstrated indecisiveness, spinelessness.[91]

Having examined the British case against university constituencies, let me return to their treatment in India at more or less the same time. Such constituencies had been represented, among other civic interest groups, since 1887 when they had been introduced by Dufferin. In the first place, the Indian constituent assembly removed all special seats, including university constituencies, from the directly elected houses of provincial legislatures.[92] Further, the principle of awarding votes to organized corporate interests was also explicitly rejected.[93] Members of the assembly agreed that 'There is to be no special representation in the Legislative Assembly either for

87 Ibid., Vol. 447 col. 1076.

88 HC Deb 16 March 1931, Vol. 249 col. 1752 (James Barr).

89 Ibid.

90 HC Deb 17 February 1948, Vol. 447 col. 1015 (Arthur Woodburn).

91 HC Deb 14 June 1948, Vol. 452 col. 194–5 (Richard Crossman).

92 Under the Government of India Acts enacted by the British Parliament, there were university constituencies for the directly elected house of provincial legislatures. Members elected from university seats sat alongside, and enjoyed the same legislative privileges, as those directly elected through the qualified suffrage.

93 In addition to university constituencies, the Government of India acts provided for range of other special seats, arranged for the representation of communal and corporate interests. There were seats for scheduled castes, backward areas and tribes, Sikhs, Mohammedans, Anglo-Indians, Europeans, Indian Christians, representatives of labour as well as commerce, industry, mining and plantation, landholders and women.

universities, or for labour, or for women'.[94] This resonated with the line of reasoning prominent in the Indian constituent assembly that the adult franchise was the best way to distribute political power, establishing a fairness of equality that eliminated the need for further mechanisms such as quotas or special representation. Yet, in the state legislative councils, matters were different. If previously recognized corporate interests – those of commerce, mining, plantation – were eliminated, the second chamber in the states extended the franchise to more members within the educational establishment than before. Departing from the emphasis on universities, teachers in secondary and senior-secondary schools were extended similar privileges as graduates. The underlying assumption here was that such persons would, in their choice of a representative, prefer someone like them in the relevant respect: education. Some argued that the legislative council's role was to bring into the legislature wise persons – 'real intelligentsia, men of real opinion'[95] – who would otherwise not subject themselves to the 'rough and tumble of active politics.[96] Thus, a graduate education or a career in education served as a proxy for the kind of epistemic competence needed to elect intelligent representatives.

V. CONCLUSION

I have tried to demonstrate that the Indian constituent assembly's break from the colonial past, and suspicions about peoples' capacity for democratic citizenship, was not as clear as some have suggested. Nervousness about the democratic 'experiment' meant that the founders tried their best to institute what they viewed as necessary precautionary measures. These measures modified democratic mechanisms to deprive purportedly incompetent citizens of political power, or tried to bolster the degree of power available to those deemed more competent than others. This approach towards constitution making was far from unique to the Indian case. Rather, as I have shown, the founders drew on provisions found in American, British and Irish constitutions to achieve their aims. The Indian case, then, emphasizes a tension found in constitutional thought across time and political space, between respect for democratic decisions and anxieties about the competence of decision makers.

94 Constituent Assembly of India, '*Report of the Provincial Constitution Committee*', in B. Shiva Rao (ed.), *The Framing of India's Constitution*: Vol. II (New Delhi: Universal Law Publishing, 1967[1947]), 671.

95 CAD 9.1: 26–8 (Mahavir Tyagi), 30 July 1949.

96 Ibid., 33 (Purnima Banerji), 30 July 1949. Also see statement by Shibban Lal Saksena (ibid., 24–5, 30 July 1949).

6

A Race against Time

The Making of the Norwegian Constitution of 1814

Jon Elster

On May 17, 1814, the Norwegian constituent assembly adopted the constitution that, interrupted only by the German occupation from 1940 to 1945, has been in continuous force up to the present. Although it has been amended many times, the amendments have, with one exception discussed later, followed the amendment clause in the constitution itself. Next to the American constitution, it is the oldest in the world. Although mildly interesting, this fact in itself does not call for a chapter. I believe, however, that the process of preparing the assembly and its subsequent proceedings have several interesting features that can shed light on constitution making more generally.[1] In particular, it illustrates how unrealistic beliefs about what is politically possible can, in a limited but very real sense, be self-fulfilling.

I shall proceed as follows. In Section I, I survey the main primary and secondary sources on which I shall draw. Section II sketches the all-important international context. Section III discusses the convocation of the constituent assembly and the election of the delegates. Section IV discusses the two main groupings of the assembly, those who wanted full independence and those wanted union with Sweden. Section V considers the voting procedures of the assembly. Section VI discusses a crucial vote that took place on April 19 and its implications. Section VII briefly summarizes the events that led up to the revised constitution of November 1814. A final section concludes.

[1] I shall only briefly consider the substance of the constitution, which is often considered to be the most liberal and democratic among early constitutions, notably with respect to the freedom of expression and voting rights. However, its second paragraph is very illiberal, excluding Jesuits, monastic orders, and Jews from the kingdom. There were no Jews or Jesuits in Norway at the time. Henrik Wergeland, whom I cite in the text that follows, worked hard to abolish the clause concerning the Jews, which his father Nicolay Wergeland, also cited later, had defended in the assembly. It was abolished in 1851, after the death of Henrik Wergeland. The clause concerning Jesuits was abolished only in 1956.

I am grateful to my coeditors and to Eirik Holmøyvik for comments on earlier drafts.

I. BIBLIOGRAPHICAL OVERVIEW

The four volumes of the Proceedings of the Constituent Assembly (*Riksforsamlingens Forhandlinger*, available on-line) include the following:

- Instructions of the prince-regent (and would-be king of Norway) Christian Frederik about how to elect the delegates
- Mostly anodyne but occasionally interesting resolutions from the electoral assemblies
- The names of the delegates
- The procedural rules of the assembly
- The names of the fifteen members who were elected to the drafting committee of the constitution
- Eleven "basic propositions" formulated by the drafting committee and voted on by the assembly
- The most important of the numerous (private) drafts of the constitution
- The two drafts from the constitutional committee
- The comments of the prince-regent on the first of these drafts
- Important but tantalizingly brief summaries of the debates and votes in the assembly.

Although incomplete in the last-mentioned respect, the documentation is otherwise very full. Compared to other constitution-making processes, the numerous private drafts were a unique feature. Holmøyvik (2012) provides a superb analysis of many of the substantive issues that were presented in the drafts and debated in the assembly. As noted, I shall focus on procedure rather than on substance.

Among contemporary and near-contemporary sources, four stand out. Two are documents written by a father and his son, Nicolai and Henrik Wergeland. The former was among the most active framers and the author of a full constitutional draft. (His rigid and pedantic cast of mind is reflected in the fact that it has exactly 100 paragraphs.) For my purposes, the "Letters to a Friend" (Wergeland 1830) that he wrote during the sitting of the assembly are more important than the substantive ideas in his draft. Henrik Wergeland (1857) wrote the first full history of the constituent process, with valuable analytical insights. The third source is the relevant part (about 250 pages) of the Recollections (*Erindringer*) by the framer Jacob Aall (1859), for a large part based on notes that he took during the assembly. They constitute by far our most important first-hand document. While they do not come close to matching the richness of James Madison's notes from the Federal Convention, their value exceeds, in my judgment, Tocqueville's brilliant, caustic, and biased account of the 1848 French constituent assembly. In addition to providing many factual observations and acute psychological insights, Aall delights the reader with his dry humor.

The last source is the journal (Linvald 1943) that the Prince Regent Christian Frederik kept during most of the year 1814, from the Treaty of Kiel (January 14) to the revision of the Norwegian constitution that cemented the contested alliance with Sweden. It is not always easy to infer the true beliefs of the regent from his journal, but some entries suggest that he shared (or at least encouraged) the beliefs of many framers that a completely independent Norway, with himself as king, was within the realm of the possible. I return to this question below.

Later Norwegian historians have of course covered the events at great length. I rely mainly on the standard accounts by Bergsgård (1943, 1945) and Steen (1951). Unlike the scholarly work by Holmøyvik (2012), which has 2,194 footnotes, many of them quite extensive, these earlier accounts are written for a general audience and are virtually devoid of references. Their authors had certainly mastered the most important sources, however, and their books are generally considered to be trustworthy. On one crucial point, I shall nevertheless question the judgment of Steen.

II. THE INTERNATIONAL CONTEXT

Constituent assemblies often operate in a turbulent and uncertain environment: after the implosion of an autocratic regime, in an economic crisis, in the wake or in the middle of a revolution, or after a defeat in war (see Chapter 9 in this volume). The Norwegian context was unusually complex. For a short time, the country seemed to be in a vacuum, separated from Denmark, but not yet united with Sweden nor independent.

In the Treaty of Kiel, concluded on January 14, 1814 between Sweden and Denmark with England as a guarantor, Denmark conceded Norway to Sweden in exchange for concessions elsewhere. The Norwegians would retain the "laws, rights, liberties and privileges" they had at the time. As Denmark–Norway was an absolute monarchy, these did not amount to much, and certainly not to a constitution.[2]

The previous year, Prince Christian Frederik, first in line for the Danish throne, had been appointed viceroy or governor (*stadtholder*) of Norway. When he received

[2] The Danish Regal Law (*Kongeloven*) from 1665 is an unusually explicit statement of absolutism. It affirms that among the major rights of the king is that of "after his own will and pleasure to explain, multiply, diminish, yes even purely and simply abolish laws previously given by himself or his ancestors, and to exempt what and whom he pleases from the general command of the law." The only exceptions were the king's confession of the Lutheran religion, the inalienability of the domain and of the king's own powers, and the laws of succession to the crown. Any separation or delegation of powers was thus explicitly forbidden. The king had the power to do essentially anything, except limiting his own powers. Holmøyvik (2012), 3 shows, however, the existence of proto-constitutional norms during the reigns of the alcoholic Frederik V (1746–66) and the insane Christian VII (1766–1808).

news about the Treaty of Kiel on January 24, 1814, with instructions from the Danish king to surrender the Norwegian fortresses and return to Denmark, he decided to disobey and carve out a space for himself in Norway. Before he got fully underway, however, the Swedish king signed a proclamation on February 8, asking the Norwegians to welcome the Swedish troops as "brothers" and assuring them that "Our Governor General will … listen to Your most eminent men and then submit to Us for Our approval a draft of a constitution that will correspond to Your needs and protect Your happiness. We promise in advance that this constitution will be based on the two beautiful rights that belong to a courageous and noble people, that of expressing itself (*yttra sig*) through its representatives and that of taxing itself." Although minimal, these guarantees at least went beyond the Danish regal law. I shall refer to this document as a "counterfactual constitution."

The Swedish troops were, however, occupied elsewhere. The Swedish crown prince and de facto ruler, Bernadotte, was involved, with his army, in the final stages of the struggle against Napoleon, which ended with the latter's abdication in early April. Christian Frederik stepped into the vacuum. After testing the waters in Trondheim, on February 16 he met with fifteen civil servants and six landowners and merchants at Eidsvold, a small town close to Oslo, to ask their advice about how he might accede to power in Norway. Once his attempt to claim the throne on the basis of his royal inheritance right had failed to persuade his interlocutors, he accepted a proposal to call a constituent assembly within eight weeks. He also proclaimed himself regent, in the firm expectation that he would later be chosen as king.

Christian Frederik's ambitions were complex and are hard to determine with precision. He may have wanted to become king of an independent Norway, to reunite Norway with Denmark, or to become king in a union between Norway and Sweden. Perhaps he even saw himself as king of a union of all three countries. According to Aall (1859, 403), "there was no doubt that he preferred Denmark's throne to Norway's" and that he saw the latter merely as a step toward the former. It is also hard to determine whether his personal ambitions counted for more than an impartial concern for the welfare of the peoples involved. Fortunately, these questions are irrelevant for my purposes. Whatever the motivations for his plans, they were apparently based on massive wishful thinking.

> It is hard to say what was the most unreasonable part of [his] plans, either that the English government would help Norway against the Kiel peace, although all the English words and actions said the opposite, or that the Swedes should make a new revolution [following a previous change of reign in 1809] and replace Carl Johan with Christian Frederik, at the very moment when Carl Johan had brought Sweden from debasement to new glory among the European powers. Taken separately, each idea is wishful and fantastic; taken together they amount to sheer fairy-tale politics. (Bergsgård 1945, 21–2)

The second idea was unrealistic given Sweden's participation in the defeat of Napoleon on April 6. This fact was not known in Norway until May 1 (Wergeland 1857, 206). The first idea, however, was unrealistic once news of the Treaty of Kiel reached Norway on January 24.

Christian Frederik's journal shows him to be out of touch with the political realities.[3] On the basis of various reports from England, he writes on March 5 and March 18 that the English people experienced a "pleasant feeling" or "joy" (CF, 357, 361) on learning the determination of the Norwegians to defend themselves, as if this popular opinion could sway the government. On the latter date, he also reports that British newspapers "unanimously say that Sweden cannot demand the help [of the English] against Norway [and] that the efforts [of Sweden during the Napoleonic wars] could be rewarded by a colony that Great Britain might cede or by Finland, which one could expect from Russian magnanimity" (CF, 361). When on April 14 he heard about a letter that reported total failure in London for the Norwegian envoy who was trying to negotiate better conditions, he refused to believe it, adding that "the only thing that does not indicate favorable dispositions of England [towards Norway] is the embargo … on all ships headed for Norway; but still some ostensible measures are necessary even if England wants to favor us" (CF, 376). On June 6, when war with Sweden was looming, he suggested in a conversation with an English envoy that "a bloody war between the Scandinavian peoples … would give Russia the means of taking both" CF p. 405). He returns repeatedly to the fantasy of his being chosen king of Sweden (CF, pp. 370, 380, 385). A majority of the framers seem to have shared this wishful thinking (Aall 1859, pp. 350, 354, 380). The paradox, to which I shall devote considerable space, is that their delusion proved to be largely self-fulfilling. Had Christian Frederik and the framers been more realistic, they would have achieved less.[4]

I should add, nevertheless, that Christian Frederik's *beliefs* are as hard to determine as his ambitions. His journal suggests that at some times at least he was caught up in the wishful thinking he did so much to encourage. At other times, he may have assessed the international situation more accurately. As we shall see, as early as April 2 he formed a back-up plan based on more realistic assumptions about the intransigence of the signatories to the Treaty of Kiel. He did not, however, share his (perhaps intermittent) mental reservations with the framers. For my purposes, the crucial causal factor was the perception that the framers had of the regent rather than his actual psychological make-up, which remains somewhat inscrutable.

[3] Here and later referred to as CF, with page numbers in parentheses being those of the edition by Linvald (1943).

[4] A considerable psychological literature (summarized in Section II of Weinberg 2009) suggests that moderate overconfidence enhances performance. These findings are irrelevant for my case, I believe, as the Norwegians benefited from sheer *luck*, not from any systematic tendencies.

On the military side, the balance of forces was in favor of the Norwegians while Carl Johan and the bulk of the Swedish army were fighting on the Continent. Bergsgård (1945, p. 62) asserts that the Swedes "were afraid that Christian Frederik should learn how weak they really were, tempting him to attack; in that case they could offer little resistance." One Swedish politician even said that if Norway had attacked at that time, "Sweden would have ceased to exist" (*ibid*, p. 63). Once Carl Johan came back on May 28, joined by his army over the following month, an offensive war by Norway was out of the question. The mountainous terrain of Norway might have favored a defensive guerrilla war, which might have dragged on for years until Sweden's will to fight was exhausted (*ibid*, pp. 68–70). Yet with an English embargo on grain, the Norwegians *capacity* to fight might have been exhausted even earlier. These military issues are well beyond my competence. It seems, though, that both Christian Frederik and the framers counted more heavily on the benevolence of England than on the offensive or defensive strength of the Norwegian army.

III. CONVOCATION AND ELECTIONS

The convener of the constituent assembly was Christian Frederik, who in circular letters of February 19 laid down rules of suffrage and eligibility, as well as rules of apportionment that created an assembly of 112 members. Without affirming that this is an optimal assembly size, it seems to lie between the upper and lower limits defined by James Madison in *The Federalist* No. 55: "a certain number at least seems to be necessary to secure the benefits of free consultation and discussion, and to guard against too easy a combination for improper purposes; as, on the other hand, the number ought at most to be kept within a certain limit, in order to avoid the confusion and intemperance of a multitude."

The rules for the (indirect) elections ensured that out of the 112 deputies, 33 would be chosen by and from the military (with equal numbers of officers and soldiers) and also that a substantial minimum would be farmers. This created an assembly consisting of 25 civil servants, 21 of them lawyers; 14 priests; 18 officers, 5 large landowners; 13 merchants; 22 farmers; 10 noncommissioned officers; and 5 enlisted soldiers. (The sum exceeds 112, since some categories overlap.) Broken down differently, 53 came from the countryside, 33 from the army and navy, and 26 from the towns.

One may ask why the regent chose these rules, which are surprising both in their (for the time) democratic character and in the uniquely high proportion of military men. Bergsgård (1943, 172) suggests two explanations for the large number of farmers. First, Christian Frederik wanted the majority of the population to be represented; second, the farmers were also the most nationally minded. To ensure their representation, each electoral district had to send at least one farmer to the assembly. Fewer farmers would have been elected if their representation had not been mandatory, because among the eighteen electoral districts, sixteen chose only the one farmer that the rules obliged them to elect. Steen (1951, 116) suggests that Christian Frederik believed that "farmers and the lower classes more generally were most susceptible to influence, and therefore could easier be persuaded to adopt the [regent's] policy of independence," adding, somewhat incoherently, that this belief reflected a "romantic attitude" toward the peasantry.

Steen (1951, 116) also suggests that the main reason for the high proportion of officers, soldiers, and seamen was the fact that independence would have to be defended with arms. By contrast, Aall (1859, 381) argues that the regent had chosen so many from the army and the navy because they would be "dependent on his will or at least share his views." Another framer, Nicolay Wergeland (1830, 38), reports that some military deputies told him that "under the existing circumstances it would be inappropriate for our order to favor peace (*at være fredeligsindede*) or to oppose the belligerent plans of the prince-regent: we would be blamed, misunderstood, and affected in our honor." Although he does not affirm that the regent had *chosen* them for this reason, that hypothesis cannot be excluded. Langslet (2014, 107) offers a pragmatic explanation: "large parts of the adult male population were under arms and would otherwise have been excluded from the elections"; see also the regent's retrospective statement in Linvald (1943, 485). Whichever of these (mutually compatible) explanations one prefers, they converge to the conclusion that the strong military presence strengthened the independence party (see the next section).

Concerning the overall character of the elections, Aall (1859, 381) writes that

> The people's choice of its representatives was in general made very carefully and with the purest concern for the task itself (*Sagen selv*), without any of the passions that later so often governed these choices. For this important duty one chose men who were the most trusted of their fellow citizens and considered as the most competent. In these elections, wealth was for the most part a secondary criterion. Nor did one consider political opinions, partly because their importance was little known outside of the capital, and partly because the nation's men were not yet clearly divided into the previously mentioned parties [the independence party and the union party]. The very first steps on the road to our new constitution were simple, calm, and free from the fermenting passions that usually reign under great revolutions.

As far as I know, this characterization is accurate. Social status certainly mattered in the elections, but not wealth and political views. There was no organized campaigning. To Aall's last phrase, we might add that the *later* steps were not free from passions (see the next section).

To my knowledge, no primary or secondary assemblies tried to impose strict imperative mandates on the deputies, perhaps because the issues to be debated and decided were, as Aall claims, as yet poorly defined. The issue of national independence seems to have completely overshadowed internal constitutional issues. Freedom from foreign domination loomed much larger than freedom from arbitrary government. Some primary assemblies explicitly gave full powers to the deputies, using phrases such as "We will accept their decisions as if they were our own." Although the address of one municipality (Hitra) enters into some details about the constitutional machinery, such as the need for a quorum in decision-making bodies, it does so in the form of wishes (*Gid!*), not of instructions. Another municipality (Høle) authorizes (*befuldmægtige*) the deputies to choose a form of government "that will ensure our political, civil, and religious freedom." Although this authorization could be understood as an instruction to guarantee these freedoms, the language is too vague to be constraining. By contrast, the four deputies from Bergen to the parliament that would act as a de facto constituent assembly in adopting the November constitution (see later) came with a bound mandate not to accept a union with Sweden (Steen 1951, 233–4). They tried to be untied, but their constituents refused. A member of the delegation from Bergen, Wilhelm Christie, who was elected as president of the assembly and was instrumental in bringing about the union, had to vote against it.

Many deputies from rural districts were somewhat *rustic*, that is, unfamiliar with the operation of a political assembly. In one of the gently ironical observations with which his *Recollections* are spiced, Aall suggests that this fact may have been important for the rapid march of the assembly. With only five weeks from beginning to end, it was the shortest constituent assembly on record. Just on May 10, the assembly adopted 33 of the 110 clauses in the constitution. Given the extreme pressures from the international environment, this brevity was indispensable for its success. Aall cites two mechanisms by which *rusticity led to brevity*.

First, the internal "interim rules" of the assembly (never superseded by permanent rules) were prepared very quickly, leading to brief and simple regulations.[5] "*The untrained hand was quicker than the trained hand would later become*. In the subsequent ordinary sessions of parliament, the preparation of the rules and the

[5] The principle that the office of the president should rotate every eight days was imposed by the prince-regent (Aall 1859, p. 393) and faithfully followed to the end. This issue is not trivial. Sieyès advocated a very rapid turnover in the presidency of the *Constituante* to prevent capture by one fraction, whereas Bentham argued, on the basis of English experience, that the president of an assembly had to be permanent so that he could acquire the necessary experience (references in Elster 2013, 12). I do not know what the regent's motives were in imposing the rule of rotation. It turned out to matter, although not in a way he could have foreseen (Aall (1859, 433). His intervention is an interesting exception to the generally valid proposition that constituent assemblies tend to ignore upstream attempts to constrain them.

debates over them" would take up a considerable amount of time (Aall 1859, 393; my italics). As we shall see, the rules were not only brief and simple, but also, crucially, incomplete.

Second, "for the cause as a whole it must be esteemed *useful that the ability to speak in public was yet poorly developed* among the representatives at Eidsvold. One can just imagine how these important objects of deliberation would have been treated in later parliaments. The ability to express one's ideas and the courage to let oneself be heard in public assemblies has in later parliaments often led to *excessive delays*" (Aall 1859, 429–30; my italics). To this observation we may add the fact that since the Eidsvold proceedings – unlike later parliaments – were closed to the public, the temptation to "speak to the gallery," which could also have delayed the proceedings, was absent.

A further, unrelated cause of the brevity of the proceedings was that the regent himself verified the credentials of the delegates. "In this way one simplified and shortened the work of the constituent assembly, since the verification in later parliaments was often difficult and time-consuming" (Aall 1859, 387).[6]

IV. INDEPENDENCE PARTY AND UNION PARTY

None of the delegates had been elected on a party platform. Yet in the first days of the assembly, they crystallized into what came to be called the "independence party," because its members demanded full national independence, and the "union party," because its members demanded union with Sweden. They were "parties," however, only in the sense of informal groupings around a few leaders. The "unionist" N. Wergeland (1830, 44) wrote that "I do not know if the term [party] is appropriate. 'Fractions' would be even more incorrect, that I know for certain, at least with respect to those with whom I keep company. We do not conspire, we hold no meetings, prepare no plans, and do not impose on ourselves any obligations to use our common forces to achieve anything or work for a goal." There were only accidental and informal discussions among like-minded delegates, although "others suspect us of the activities I have been denying." The regent sometimes refers to parties, for instance when referring to the election on April 12 of the members of the drafting committee: "The opposed [union] party had plotted during the night by sending voting tickets to the peasants, who understand nothing of this; the wise (*sensé*) party therefore did the same, fortunately with success" (CF, 374). It seems likely, however,

6 By contrast, in the French *constituante* of 1789 the verification took six weeks. It is arguable that the French monarchy would have survived if the credentials had been verified immediately, as the long delay enabled the deputies from the third estate to get to know each other and to overcome their deference to the nobility.

that these manipulations were the work of individual delegates acting more or less on their own, rather than a concerted plot. The comments by Aall (1859, 417) on similar efforts to manipulate the crucial vote on April 19 support this impression.

The terms "*independence* party" and "*union* party" are also misleading. According to Steen (1951, 142), many – perhaps most – members of the independence party anticipated a subsequent reunion with Denmark. Among them, he writes, "some wished for reunion, others merely saw it as a political necessity." The same distinction between wish and necessity applies to members of the union party. Some, like its main spokesman Count Wedel, had worked for union with Sweden for many years (Bergsgård 1943, 189). He might also have viewed it as inevitable. Others, such as Jacob Aall, had strong affiliations with Denmark and viewed the union merely as a necessity imposed by the great powers. Hence we can redefine the opposition as turning on the factual question *whether independence was politically possible*. If union was inevitable, independence was impossible. If independence was thought to be desirable, it had to be possible, since "ought implies can."

Yet it would also be misleading to think that the differences concerned *purely* factual matters, since some of the beliefs were rooted in emotions. The French moralist La Fontaine wrote that "Each believes easily what he fears and what he hopes." In the 1814 assembly, hope took the form of *enthusiasm*, defined by the *Oxford English Dictionary* as "Rapturous intensity of feeling in favor of a person, principle, cause, etc.; passionate eagerness in any pursuit, proceeding from an intense conviction of the worthiness of the object."[7] Although enthusiasm is neglected in the scholarly literature on emotions, it is the subject of some brief and penetrating remarks by Kant (summarized in Elster 2013, 90, 205). He distinguishes it from what he calls *Schwärmerei*, an unambiguously pejorative term that can perhaps be translated as "visionary derangement." Enthusiasm, by contrast, is highly praised, since, Kant asserts, "nothing great is ever done without it." Yet, he also says, it is not unambiguously praiseworthy, since (like many other emotions) it distorts rational belief formation. Going beyond Kant, we can distinguish between two distorting mechanisms. First emotions generate *wishful thinking*: factual constraints are ignored, and implausible scenarios appear as highly likely. Second, they generate *urgency*: the enthusiast wants to act immediately, and does not take the time to gather relevant information (Elster 2009).

According to Steen (1951, 143–4), the Norwegian framers of 1814 were characterized by "an incredibly vitality and restless activity" – "enthusiasm was their normal state of mind." His words suggest that the emotion of enthusiasm may be similar to the state of *hypomania*, "characterized by elation and a feeling of well-being together with quickness of thought" (*Oxford English Dictionary*). We can most easily

7 See also Elster (2017) and Elster (forthcoming b).

recognize the emotion by its behavioral effects: supernormal energy and subnormal need for food and sleep. Although most emotions are thought to decay quickly, or have a "short half-life," the enthusiasm of the 1814 framers seems to have sustained them from mid-April to the end of May, but perhaps not for much longer (see note 14). Jacob Aall often refers to this emotion as motivating his opponents, sometimes calling it by the pejorative term *svermeri* (Aall 1859, 359, 361, 422), sometimes by *enthusiasme* (Aall 1859, pp. 372–4). The most important reference occurs when he discusses the "excesses" that must inevitably arise in "a sudden transition from a complete exclusion from the government to … the participation of the people in legislation through its representatives" (Aall 1859, 431). He asserts that "[P]roofs of these excesses are evident in the constitutional drafts that were presented to the Eidsvold assembly, both by those who could not be assumed to have the requisite knowledge and political understanding and by *insightful men who were in a kind of exalted mood* that does not allow for calm deliberations" (Aall 1859; my italics). The excesses he had in mind took the form of *aversion to incrementalism* (Aall 1859, p. 431–2). For the enthusiast, the best is often the enemy of the good (Allouche-Pourchel 2010, 105).

The enthusiastic advocates of independence at Eidsvold overlooked the fact – obvious to us and to the sober advocates of a union with Sweden – that England would never allow a retreat from the Treaty of Kiel. Aall (1859, 409) reports that the independence party "consistently believed that the voices raised in England for Norway's cause would bring about England's neutrality, or even its support for the Norwegian struggle for independence." Conversely, the independence party followed the regent (CF, 376 cited earlier) when it dismissed a letter with unwelcome news as "a lie invented to scare us" (Aall 1859, 423).

The enthusiasm was reinforced by *anger*. For many Norwegians, being a pawn in the game of the great powers, without being consulted, was insufferable. Commenting on the emergence of the independence party after the regent's declaration of February 19, Aall (1859, 354) writes that its views "spread increasingly in greater and greater circles from the seat of the regent to the nation as a whole, and nurtured the patriotic mind with high-flying rhetoric taken from Norway's distant past and from *the violence with which a foreign will wanted to impose a hated yoke*" (my italics). Similarly, Steen (1951, 111) writes that "what perhaps created the most fertile soil for the policy of independence was the *indignation* of the Norwegians over the way in which the old union had been dissolved and the new one created … Without consulting the Norwegian people, [the Danish king] had broken a bond that was four centuries old and handed Norway over to Sweden, which in Norway was hated rather than loved" (my italics).

Unlike enthusiasm, anger has been extensively studied by psychologists. Two findings (Lerner and Keltner 2001) stand out. On the one hand, anger changes an agent's *beliefs* by making her risk assessment more optimistic, compared to those of a neutral observer (or perhaps to her nonemotional assessments). On the other hand, anger changes an agent's *preferences* by making her less risk averse, compared to her nonemotional risk preferences.[8] Although one may not always be able to tell whether an observed increase in risk-taking behavior has a cognitive or a motivational basis, I believe that the framers of 1814 were mainly subject to a cognitive bias. Jennifer Lerner (personal communication) agrees with my conjecture that enthusiasm will have the same effects as anger. When both emotions are triggered, as they were in the 1814 assembly, they will presumably shift risk assessment strongly toward the optimistic end of the spectrum.

Lerner and Keltner (2001) find that *fear* has the opposite effects, making people both more pessimistic and more risk averse, compared to the same baselines. Before pursuing this issue in the context of 1814, I want to note the semantic ambiguity of "fear." *Prudential fear*, as when we say "He took an umbrella because he feared it might rain," is simply a belief–desire complex. No emotion is involved. *Visceral fear*, as when we say "He ran away from the snake on the path because he feared it would bite him," is a gut feeling that can arise even before explicit cognition. In the political context, it can be difficult to distinguish between visceral panic and rational prudence, just as it can be hard to distinguish between motivational and cognitive effects of the former.

After a talk with Jacob Aall on February 28, Christian Fredrik wrote in his journal that Aall "shows a pusillanimous character," adding that "he wants to *calculate* our forces and our dangers" (CF, 354; my italics). The first comment might refer to visceral fear, whereas the latter seems to refer to prudential fear. Other remarks suggest, however, that the regent accused the unionists of cowardice, that is, of visceral fear. On March 3, he asked the unionist Count Wedel whether he was "afraid," to which the latter answered that "one has to be of royal blood to ask me that question" (editorial note in Aall 1859, 362). In a journal entry from the same day, the regent wrote that Wedel's language "was that of Aall, that one has to *calculate* one's forces and foresee the ills that might arrive" (CF, 356; my italics). In the opening session of the assembly on April 11, the regent "blamed the lack of spirit (*kleinmodighet*) of those who do not think Norway strong enough to persist as an independent state" (Aall 1859, 392), reflecting a journal entry on February 7 in which he castigates "the weak in spirit" (CF, 337).

Overall, it seems that Christian Frederik was subject to what one might call a "bias of enthusiasm," that of accusing one's opponent of being viscerally afraid rather than rationally prudent. To my best understanding, however, the unionists were in fact

8 We cannot use risk neutrality as a baseline for comparison, as the agent might be risk averse even in a nonemotional state.

not subject to excessive pessimism. They assessed the situation coolly and correctly. Although both Aall (1859, 420) and Steen (1951, 164) claim that each side interpreted information about the international situation according to what suited it, this symmetry claim seems questionable. For the most part, members of the union party based their policy preferences on their beliefs, whereas members of the independence party were more likely to base their beliefs on their preferences and emotions.

The unconditional proponents of independence and the unwavering advocates of union with Sweden did not exhaust the assembly. Aall (1859, 418–19) distinguishes three groups: advocates of independence (subdivided into extremes and moderates), advocates of a union with Sweden, and those in the middle (subdivided into the undecided and what one might call the "weathervanes"). In his view, the middle group was "perhaps the most numerous." The role of the weathervanes, who "anxiously listen to what the dominant tone might be, so that they would not hurt their foot on any stone" (Aall 1859, 419), is especially interesting. If Steen (1951, 142) based his estimate that about 80 among the 112 delegates belonged to the independence party on their votes, it would be consistent with Aall's statement.

V. VOTING IN THE ASSEMBLY

On the first working day of the assembly, April 11, the delegates elected a committee to propose procedural rules, which the assembly adopted with a few modifications the following day.[9] The most interesting issues concern the voting rules. Article 10 states that "All questions that, after oral discussion, can be reduced to a Yes or No, are decided by secret ballot (*ballottering*), unless one fifth of the members present require written votes, which shall then take place under the names of the voters and be entered into the protocol. The majority decides." (The text has "plurality," which in the terminology of the time meant majority.)

I have translated "ballottering" as "secret ballot," which is the meaning given in the dictionaries I have consulted. Yet this reading of the article might seem hard to square with the complaint by N. Wergeland (1830, 19) about the voting practice: "The mode of voting used here, by roll-call (*oppraab*) in alphabetical order, does not seem so good in all respects. Someone always has to cast the first vote, but it is not good that some *always* are the first and others always the last. There ought to be some alteration. One should also be allowed to vote after others or at the end. The letter A may already have had, and may in the future also have, a greater influence than it should" (his emphasis). Although it is indeed true that sequential public voting may induce undesirable effects (cascades, conformism,

9 Unless otherwise noted, my sources for the proceedings of the assembly are the four volumes of Olafsen et al. (1914–18).

path dependence), the order in which *secret* ballots are handed in cannot have any of these consequences. I note in passing that the second sentence in the quote from Wergeland is inaccurate, as deputies can in fact cast *public* votes *simultaneously*, making it impossible for an individual member to know, *at the moment of voting*, how others are voting. Bentham (1999, 106) argued strongly and, in my view persuasively, for this system (extensively discussed in Elster 2013).

Wergeland's complaint was made in a letter dated April 17. It clearly refers to the vote on April 16 on the first of the eleven "principal propositions" that the drafting committee had proposed, namely that Norway should be a "limited and hereditary monarchy." The reference to the excessive influence of the letter A was not to a person, but to the first-voting electoral district Aggershuus Amt, in which Wergeland's opponent Falsen cast a vote that probably influenced subsequent opinions. The issue was not decided by secret ballot, perhaps because its conjunctive form made it impossible to reduce it to a yes-or-no question.[10] Instead, the delegates stated their views orally and publicly, in the alphabetical order of the electoral districts. After Falsen changed the motion by adding that "the regent take the name of king," it was adopted by 78 votes to 33. Wergeland had proposed that the head of state bear the title of king "only if the state can sustain the dignity of this name as well as its independence." As a unionist, he did not believe it could.

In his letter, Wergeland seems to assume that roll-calls rather than secret ballot would be the dominant, or at least an important, mode of voting. Whatever his assumptions, it seems highly likely that this was in fact what happened. Voting by secret ballot is time consuming. The members have to line up for the vote, and the ballots have to be opened, counted, and sometimes recounted. The intense time pressure under which the assembly found itself after May 1 (see later) would have counted heavily against using this procedure. It is hard to believe that the secret ballot was used for each of the many votes in which the minutes from the assembly say that the Eidsvold assembly "unanimously" adopted proposals from the constitutional committee. Some votes, though, were very close, 56 to 55 in one case, 53 to 52 in another. Some votes that were not close are also recorded with the precise numbers, e.g., 82 to 18 or 62 to 39. In such cases, individual voting and counting must have taken place. Yet even these votes were so numerous that it is unlikely that the assembly respected its own rules and used the secret ballot rather than the less time-consuming – but public – roll-call vote. The question matters, since the importance of the weathervanes and of soldiers concerned with their honor depends on the

[10] Hommerstad (2015, 111) claims that secrecy was rejected because "the independence party needed the social control of a public vote." If this is true, we should expect Wergeland to have expressed a preference for secret voting rather than, as he did, for public voting in random order.

secrecy or publicity of the vote. Nobody could be ostracized or criticized for their vote if it remained unknown. It also mattered, of course, in the race against time.

There is a further puzzle that arises in this context. Although the rules said that decision were to be taken by (simple) *majority*, the assembly also decided, on the very day it adopted the rules, that any proposal from the constitutional committee that is debated in plenum and adopted by *two-thirds* of the members who are present "is valid" (*er gjeldende*). Plausibly, the latter rule means that a two-thirds majority ensures the definite and final adoption of the clause in question, whereas a clause adopted by simple majority may be subject to revision. If this interpretation is correct, the Norwegian assembly deviated from the general practice of constituent assemblies, that "nothing is decided until everything is decided." A constitution forms a whole, where the effects of one clause may depend crucially on the others.

For some votes with more than a two-thirds majority, the protocol gives the exact numbers, as in the 82–18 example already cited. For many other votes, however, the minutes simply report that *more than two-thirds* approved, without giving the numbers. (On one occasion, it was also reported that a proposal had been *rejected* by more than two-thirds majority, implying presumably that it could not be brought up again.) To me, this fact suggests a vote by standing or sitting or by raising one's hands, practices used in many assemblies (see, e.g., Elster and Le Pillouer 2015). The president of the assembly would then visually inspect the situation, and either declare that the requisite majority had clearly been obtained or clearly not been obtained, or decide that there was enough doubt for a count to be required. The phrase "more than two-thirds" supports this conjecture, as it goes beyond what the assembly had decided. If all votes were decided by counting, a majority of *exactly two-thirds*, as actually happened in one vote (72 out of 108), would have been good enough.

The internal rules of the assembly were adopted in a hurry. One effect of this haste was observed in the crucial vote on April 19 when the assembly discovered that it had no rule for how to break a tied vote. (The result was 55 votes on either side.) It adopted on the spot the English practice of a double vote for the (independence-friendly) president Hegermann, whose vote caused the proposal to pass. Nicolai Wergeland (1830, 34) claims that "the No-voters, at least a large part of them" approved of the new rule even though they knew that on this occasion it would work against them. He also asserts (Wergeland (1830) that the seemingly counter-interested behavior of these deputies was due to "haste and thoughtlessness," a claim that is hard to square with his statement that they *knew* what the effect of the vote would be.

Wergeland (1830) observed correctly that the reference to the English model was misleading, since the Speaker in the House of Commons does not take part in debates and votes, *except* to break a tie. If Hegerman had not voted, there would not have been a tie. It is also tempting to speculate about what would have happened if the tie on April 19 had been broken by another procedure, which might have led to the opposite outcome. Ties are often broken by a *lottery*. On February 12, the assembly had in fact used this procedure to break a tie in the election of the members of the constitutional committee. Except for the Swedish parliament between 1973 and 1976, however, lotteries are never used to make substantive political decisions, only procedural ones. To decide the fate of the nation by the flip of a coin was probably unthinkable, in the sense that the idea did not occur to anyone. If the defeated group had been quicker on their feet, however, they could have proposed that the *oldest* member be given a double vote. This member, Peder Klaumann, belonged to the union party in the assembly, and would have tipped the balance in their favor. The English practice was certainly a focal-point solution, in the sense of Schelling (1960), but it was not the only one.

If the vote on April 19 was as important as I think it may have been (see the next section), the fate of the country could have been different – and Norway might perhaps have remained in a union with Sweden to the present day – if one of three procedural choices had been made differently.[11] First, the assembly could have used a different method for breaking ties. Second, it could have taken the votes in a different order (Wergeland's proposal). Third, it could have voted by secret ballot. Accident or luck, not the general will, shaped the outcome.

The regulations had another gap: they did not state how to vote when the decision could not be reduced to Yes or No. Although almost all votes on specific clauses in the constitution were in the Yes–No format, a vote on May 5 opposed *three* proposals for the king's majority age. Fifteen members voted for nineteen years, fifty-one for twenty years, and forty-four for twenty-one years. The age of twenty was adopted. In this case, the assembly decided by (what we call) plurality, not by majority voting. One could also, however, have held up two alternatives against each other in majority voting, and then held the winner up against the third. In this case, the outcome would have been the same, regardless of which options were held up against each other, since we can safely assume that preferences were single-peaked. Any delegate who preferred twenty-one years to twenty would prefer twenty to nineteen. This was the only nonbinary choice in the proceedings.

When a proposal can be stated in a way that allows for a Yes–No vote, it can sometimes be restated in a more complex form. In a journal entry for May 8, Christian Frederik wrote that "§ 51 [§ 22 in the final text] was rejected by the plurality [majority]

[11] Some might claim that structural forces would have proven stronger even had this razor-thin majority been reversed. Although this claim is impossible to prove or disprove, we may note that at the Federal Convention in Philadelphia, some important votes were definitely decided by the barest possible majority.

of votes, but the President managed to have it adopted in its entirety by repassing it point by point" ("*la § 51 a été rejetée à la pluralité des voix, mais en la repassant de points en points le Président est parvenu à la faire accepter en entier*"). The phrasing seems to suggest agenda manipulation, although it is hard to tell. His statement is surprising, as the minutes of the assembly give a completely different version of the vote. Without trying to resolve the discrepancy, let me just note that the mathematician Poisson (1837, 21) showed that under majority voting a complex proposal can indeed be rejected as a package while each of its components would be accepted in separate votes.

VI. THE VOTE ON APRIL 19

I have cited several times the framer Nicolay Wergeland. His son Henrik, a legendary poet and public intellectual, was the author of a history of the constitution that draws heavily on his father's manuscripts. In the introduction to the work, he offers (Wergeland 1857, 13 ff.) eight reasons to explain how a small, uneducated, and isolated people could produce a constitution with the outstanding qualities of the 1814 document. The third reason is stated as follows:

> *The constituent assembly made the constitution and the election of the king the only objects of its deliberations.* The assembly was active, in agreement on the principal propositions, and respected the procedural simplifications that that could bring it to its goal ... That the constituent assembly, although with authority to do so, refused itself the examination of whether its work could be upheld and defended, and to that end itself undertake negotiations with powers that would deny the nation its independence (*forbyde Nationen enhver Selvstændighedshandling*), turned out to be one of those heavenly fingers that intervened in Norway's destiny.

A few pages later, Wergeland (1857, 17) adduces, as a possible ninth explanation, the *haste* of the proceedings. Earlier, I have cited several causes of the extremely rapid pace. First, as Aall observed, the sheer lack of experience of the delegates accelerated the process. Looking backward, Wergeland (1857, 17) asserted that these procedural defects were "justified in light of the result." Looking forward, the prominent unionist Løwenskiold asserted on April 19 that "it was more important *act well than to act quickly*" (Aall 1859, 414; his italics). Also, the strong emotions of many members seem to have induced a feeling of urgency and a need to act immediately.[12] Thus on April 16 the assembly debated a proposal by Falsen on the very day it was made, although the rules it had just adopted stated that any motion had to be

[12] By contrast, Wergeland (1857, 142) refers to Aall as a "temporizer," perhaps alluding to the Roman general Fabius "the hesitator" whom Seneca (*On Anger* I, xi) celebrated for his self-control.

announced on the previous day (Aall 1859, 410).[13] But when Falsen tried to spring another surprise on April 18 he was met with strong reactions, and the vote on his motions postponed to the following day.

To these causes of haste, I shall add a third one, linked to the most important of these motions: "This assembly must be considered as dissolved once the constitution has been adopted and the king been elected." To understand this somewhat enigmatic proposal, it must be seen in the context of a debate that began on April 16 over a proposal to create a committee of foreign affairs, with the task of gathering information about the international situation and perhaps even conducting diplomacy. "The president cut off the debate, which began to deteriorate into a dangerous intensity, [but] the interrupted struggle continued in private after the meeting, and there was a loud murmur in the assembly that indicated how unruly the session would be where these questions were to be discussed" (Aall 1859, 412). Falsen's proposal on April 18 was intended and understood as an attempt to block any information-gathering or contact with foreign powers. Against Nicolai Wergeland's objection that "the assembly should not tie its hands" by refusing to gather information about international affairs (Aall 1859, 415), the proposal was adopted with, as noted, the vote of the president as a tiebreaker. Unfortunately, we do not know the identity of the voters on the two sides. It is interesting, though, that in this (public) vote the members of the independence party did not achieve the large majority they had on April 16.

A tentative reconstruction of the *motives* of the framers on this point points to several factors that may have been at work. First, as noted, in their urgent wish for an immediate decision some framers may have been reluctant to accept time-consuming processes of information gathering and negotiations. Second, the fear that the favorable but fluid military situation might not last probably counted for something. To the unknowable extent that this reasoning was decisive, their hurry was based on a correct perception of objective haste, not on an emotion-based subjective urgency. (This mind-set may have been that of the regent.) Third, some framers may have feared, more or less consciously, that the knowledge they could gather about the international situation was likely to undermine the prospect of independence. Like some individuals who suspect that they have a fatal disease, the framers may have preferred not to find out. (Conversely, Løwenskiold and Nikolai Wergeland were – justifiably – confident that by gathering more information the assembly would have realized that the prospect of independence was a pipe dream.)

13 It is natural to draw an analogy with the emotionally charged night of August 4, 1789, when the French *Constituante* abolished feudalism overnight. In doing so, the assembly violated the rule it had adopted on July 29 that "Any proposal in legislative or constitutional matters must be brought to discussion on three different days" (see Elster 2007 for discussion).

Fourth, other framers may have been so firmly in the grip of wishful thinking that they saw no need to gather information which, they assumed, would simply favor their plans. Finally, a forceful and demagogical speech (Aall 1859, 415–16) by Jonas Rein, assimilating unionists to traitors, probably swayed some minds.

One can be more confident concerning the *effects* of the vote. Steen (1951, 158) underestimates its importance when he states that "it meant that the assembly would not debate foreign policy, but it did not mean anything more." It is very likely that had the framers engaged in time-consuming international investigations before achieving their work, Sweden would have been in a position to impose a counterfactual constitution much less favorable to Norway. Commenting on the draft proposed by the constitutional committee, Steen (1951, 163) observes that "in the debates it encountered certain political and social facts, that led to modifications on some points. Although it does not belong to history, it is natural to speculate about *the much more violent political reality* the draft would have encountered if it should have been negotiated immediately with the Swedish authorities and confronted with the Swedish constitution" (my italics). Aall (1859, 407) also writes: "Under the auspices of independence and shaped by the nation's own representatives, the work took *a much more liberal form* than if it had been carried out under the impressive influence of Sweden, itself supported by the most powerful states of Europe" (my italics).

The news on May 1 about Napoleon's fall crystallized the minds of the framers. As Wergeland (1857, 206) reconstructs their thinking, "moments have become scarce. The events that are about to unfold must encounter our work in its completed state." His father wrote in a letter from that day that "the fall of the emperor and the ensuing continental peace cannot be happy events for the cause of our independence" (Wergeland 1830, 50). By coincidence, that was also the day the drafting committee submitted its text to the assembly. The race against time began.

VII. FROM MAY TO NOVEMBER

The assembly voted over the clauses in the constitution from May 4 through May 11. Unlike the procedure in previous weeks, there was no break on Sunday (May 8). Although many members stated that they would not show up on that day, in the end only two abstained (Aall 1859, 430): the assembly was in a hurry. The document was formally adopted on May 17, followed by election of the regent as king. Both votes were unanimous.

Whereas enthusiasm – the alliance of passion with (cognitively defective) reason – was the driving force in the struggle for national independence, the organization of the constitution itself owed a great deal to group interest and, possibly, personal interest. Two issues that obviously affected class interests – the question of obligatory military service and the abolition of economic monopolies and privileges – were left to future legislation. By contrast, issues of suffrage, eligibility, and apportionment could not be postponed. Although a draft submitted by the constitutional committee on May 4 had quite democratic and egalitarian provisions in these respects, the final document was more restrictive. A number of groups that would have had the right to vote if the draft had been followed were now excluded (Steen 1951, 170–1).

Estimates suggest that around 45 percent of adult males would be entitled to vote, if they registered (Kuhnle 1972). Although the right to vote in the elections to the electoral assemblies was poorly defined and practice varied, it appears that the framers were elected under a larger franchise than the one they adopted for the future. In many of the addresses adopted by the primary voting assemblies, the voters are referred to simply as homeowners (*husfedre*). This discrepancy could, potentially at least, have undermined the legitimacy of the assembly.

On May 21, Aall had a meeting with the regent at which he presented him with a document (reproduced in Aall 1859, 761–4) that he had prepared during the sitting of the assembly but that circumstances had prevented him from reading. He recounts that in response to his warnings, Christian Frederik responded that "he did not at all doubt that England would issue threats, but was equally convinced that it would not execute them" (Aall 1859, 452). If he made that statement, it was disingenuous, as news about the English blockade or Norway had reached him the day before (CF, 397).

On June 6, the regent met with the English diplomat Morier, who told him in no uncertain terms that England stood by the Treaty of Kiel. He also asked whether "it would not be appropriate to convene a new constituent assembly to communicate the declarations of the allied powers, [since] the first assembly doubtless was not aware of them" (CF, 405). The regent's answer, as reported by himself, was evasive. I believe he must have understood that full independence was impossible, and that only the terms of capitulation remained to be settled. His task now was to save the constitution, with the inevitable adjustments needed by a union with Sweden. In fact, this outcome may have been at the back of his mind even before the assembly met. On April 2, after the Danish king had told him that the situation for independence was hopeless, he answered by stating that "if all of Europe is allied against Norway, only this constituent assembly or another one can determine whether the nation, compelled by necessity, shall enter into a union with Sweden; but in that case the constitution shall be maintained and the conditions be settled under English mediation" (cited after Steen 1951, 128; a slightly different version is in CF, 367). On April 9, after a discussion with an envoy carrying a letter from the Swedish governor-general of Norway who had been appointed after the Treaty of Kiel, he wrote in his journal that he was "convinced that the Swedes do not think of attacking us *during the sitting* of the constituent assembly" (CF, 371; my italics). His "back-up plan" (Redvaldsen 2014, 188) was to present Sweden with a fait accompli.

The scenario sketched in the letter of April 2 is pretty much what happened. Although Sweden wanted to impose its own conditions, with no regard for the constitution (Bergsgård 1945, 56–8), the allied mediators negotiated internal home rule for Norway, maintaining the constitution modified to take account of the fact of the union. A brief military skirmish between Norway and Sweden ended with the convention of Moss on August 14, in which the Swedish promised to respect the Eidsvold constitution, with the necessary modification.[14] After further negotiations, brilliantly conducted on the Norwegian side, the minimal necessary changes were incorporated in the November constitution enacted by a second constituent assembly (not elected, however, according to the procedures laid down in the constitution). The details are complex, but irrelevant for my purpose, which has been to show how Christian Frederik and the framers won the race against time.

VIII. CONCLUSION

Consider again the idea of a counterfactual constitution. Either of the various counterfactual constitutions mentioned earlier would have conferred a much smaller degree of self-government on Norway than the *November* constitution did. As the counterfactuals mentioned by Aaal and Steen are only hinted at, let me focus on the one promised by Carl XIII on February 8. If he had sent troops immediately and handed down a constitution according to the procedures described in the proclamation, it would probably not have given Norway any effective rights beyond that of taxing itself. There is a clear parallel between the proposed procedure for adopting the constitution and the substance of the proposed constitution itself. The Swedish king promised that his envoys would "listen" to the Norwegian notables before drafting a constitution, and that the constitution would grant the Norwegian populace the right to "express itself," perhaps in the form of petitions, through its representatives. Neither promise would ensure an effective influence of the Norwegian people in matters affecting them, other than taxation. As the most important example, Sweden might retain for itself the right to conscript Norwegian soldiers for its own wars. One may also question whether the right of the Norwegian people to determine their own taxes would have been effective, notably in wartime.

14 In a discussion of a previous version of this chapter, Øystein Sørensen suggested that the Norwegian enthusiasm and anger had run out of steam by the summer of 1814, thus preventing a serious military confrontation that would have led to an imposed Swedish constitution. If that hypothesis were to be confirmed, *both the eruption of the emotions and their abatement were crucial for the happy outcome.*

Nicolai Wergeland was wrong, and his son was right. Had the union party had its way, the union would have been much less favorable to Norway. Blind enthusiasm, in Kant's words, led to an outcome that prudent and realistic considerations, *aimed at the same ends*, could never have produced. Rubenfeld (2001, 129) argues, quite generally, that "constitutional provisions tend to be enacted at times *not of sober rationality, but of high political feelings* … For if the legitimate authority of constitutionalism is conceptualized in the Ulyssean terms of 'Peter sober' legislating for 'Peter drunk,' the world is turned upside down when we seem to find, in actual constitution making, Peter drunk legislating for Peter sober" (his italics). Enthusiasm, aided by luck, may work wonders. It may also produce disaster, as when the French framers on May 16 1791, "drunk with disinterestedness" (Lebègue 1910, 261), declared themselves ineligible to the first ordinary legislature. Since the new assembly, filled with only inexperienced members, was easily dominated by the Jacobin clubs, the road was open for the Terror.

REFERENCES

Aall, J. (1859). *Erindringer*. Christiania: Cappelen.

Allouche-Pourcel, B. (2010). *Kant et la Schwärmerei*. Paris: Harmattan.

Bentham, J. (1999). *Political Tactics*. Oxford: Oxford University Press.

Bergsgård, A. (1943). *Året 1814: Grunnlova*. Oslo: Aschehoug.

(1945). *Året 1814: Unionen*. Oslo: Aschehoug.

Elster, J. (1995c) "Forces and Mechanisms in the Constitution-Making Process." *Duke Law Journal* 45, 364–96.

(2007). "The Night of August 4 1789." *Revue Européenne des Sciences Sociales* 45, 71–94.

(2009). "Urgency." *Inquiry* 53, 399–411.

(2013). *Securities against Misrule*. Cambridge: Cambridge University Press.

(2017). "Emotions and Constitution Making." *Scandinavian Political Studies* 40, 133–56.

(forthcoming). "Enthusiasm and Anger in History." *Inquiry*

Elster, J., and Le Pillouer, A. (2015). "Semi-public Voting at the *Constituante*." In J. Elster (ed.), *Secrecy and Publicity in Votes and Debates*, 52–71. Cambridge: Cambridge University Press.

Holmøyvik, E. (2012). *Maktfordeling og 1814*. Oslo: Fagboksforlaget.

Hommerstad, M. (2015). *Christian Magnus Falsen*. Oslo: Cappelen.

Kuhnle, S. (1972). "Stemmeretten i 1814." *Historisk Tidsskrift* 51, 373–90.

Langslet, L. R. (2014). *Christian Frederik*. Oslo: Cappelen.

Lebègue, E. (1910). *Thouret*. Paris: Alcan.

Lerner, J., and Keltner, D. (2001). "Fear, Anger, and Risk." *Journal of Personality and Social Psychology* 81, 146–59.

Linvald, A., ed. (1943). *Kong Christian VIII.s Dagbøger og Optegnelser*, Copenhagen: Gyldendal.

Olafsen, A. et al., eds. (1914–18), *Riksforsamlingens Forhandlinger*, Vols. 1–4. Oslo: Grøndahl.

Poisson, S.-D. (1837). *Recherches sur la probabilité des jugements en matières criminelles et matière civile*. Paris: Bachelier.

Redvaldsen, D. (2014). "Great Britain and the Norwegian Constitution of 1814." *Parliaments, Estates, and Representation* 34, 182–202.
Rubenfeld, J. (2001). *Freedom and Time*. New Haven, CT: Yale University Press.
Schelling, T. (1960). *The Strategy of Conflict*. Cambridge, MA: Harvard University Press.
Steen, S. (1951). *1814*. Oslo: Cappelen.
Weinberg, J. (12009). "A Model of Overconfidence." *Pacific Economic Review* 14, 502–15.
Wergeland, H. (1857). *Norges Konstitutions Historie*. Christiania: Chr. Tönsbergs Forlag.
Wergeland, N. (1830). *Fortrolige Breve til en Ven, Skrevne fra Eidsvold i Aaret 1814*. Christiania: Malling.

7

Chain of Legitimacy

Constitution Making in Iceland

Thorvaldur Gylfason

In a democracy, what does it take to break the chain of political legitimacy? A common answer suggested by political philosophers is that this question must be answered primarily on the basis of procedural features that shape political institutions and underlie the decisions made as well as on the basis of the substantive outcomes realized.[1] For example, Carlton (1986, 23) defines political legitimacy as follows: "In a democracy, government legitimacy derives from the popular perception that the elected government abides by democratic principles in governing, and thus is legally accountable to its people." Jon Elster stated the case clearly[2] on national television in Iceland May 13, 2012: "If the people approved the constitutional proposal I think Parliament would find it difficult to override the moral authority of the people."

This chapter suggests that the Icelandic parliament, one of the world's oldest (est. 930), is on the verge of violating the normal requirements of political legitimacy, thus jeopardizing Iceland's standing among democratic nations (Gylfason 2016b). Iceland's financial system crashed in 2008, leading the people to demand and the parliament (Althingi) to promise a new constitution to be drawn up by representatives directly elected by the people. The protesters demanding, and the parliamentarians promising, a new constitution did not explicitly blame the old constitution for the crash nor did they suggest that a new constitution was needed to

[1] *Stanford Dictionary of Philosophy*; see http://plato.stanford.edu/entries/legitimacy/. See also Beetham (2013).

[2] See www.youtube.com/watch?v=IthLUGAjsdI. The quoted words commence at 3:59.

Professor of Economics, University of Iceland. Prepared for a conference on "Perspectives on Constituent Assemblies" hosted by the Institute of Religion, Culture and Public Life at Columbia University and the Department of Political Science at the University of Oslo and held at Columbia University in New York April 1–2, 2016. I wish to thank Andrew Arato, David Dyzenhaus, Jon Elster, Roberto Gargarella, Kim Scheppele, Hélène Landemore, Gabriel Negretto, Björn Erik Rasch, and other participants at the conference, and also Sigríður Ólafsdóttir for helpful comments and suggestions. Moreover, I thank the editors for further rounds of helpful suggestions.

prevent future financial crises. Rather, the presumption appeared to be that a society long dominated by its clientelistic political class (Kristinsson 1996) and now suddenly struck by a deep financial crisis for which politicians and their banker friends were widely held responsible – an impression shortly afterward confirmed by the parliament's Special Investigation Commission (2010) – might be well advised to take a hard look at its constitutional foundation, unchanged in essence since 1849. A constituent assembly was elected in 2010 and convened according to law. The assembly drafted a new constitution that was accepted by 67 percent of the voters in a 2012 national referendum called by the parliament. Then, bolstered by signs that the International Monetary Fund (IMF)–orchestrated economic rescue operation financed in part by loans from Danish, Finnish, Norwegian, Polish, and Swedish taxpayers was headed for success, the parliament reverted to its old habits, putting the new constitution on ice almost as if no referendum had taken place (Gylfason 2016a).

Here the story will be recounted in four parts. First, for the reader to understand Iceland's precarious political situation, it is necessary to provide historical background to the postcrash constitutional revision process. Second, drawing on earlier writing, I will offer a brief account of some aspects of the constitution-making process during 2010–13, including the work of the constituent assembly of which I was a member. Third, I will describe the parliament's ongoing attempt to undermine the substance of the constitutional bill accepted by the voters in the 2012 referendum. Fourth, I will briefly compare the process of ratification of constitutional reform in Iceland with the United States in 1787–8 and Germany in 1948–9.

I. BACKGROUND

After the collapse of Iceland's entire banking system in 2008, resulting in the destruction of assets equivalent at the time to seven times the country's annual gross domestic product (GDP), ordinary people from all walks of life took to the streets to confront their visibly shaken politicians. The government resigned, paving the way for a new parliamentary election two months later, in April 2009, an election that produced a majority government including neither the Independence Party nor the Progressive Party which had, one or the other if not both at once, governed Iceland virtually without interruption throughout the history of the Republic, founded in 1944 when Iceland unilaterally declared full independence from Nazi-occupied Denmark. Over the years, those two parties had seen their combined vote in parliamentary elections decrease from 70 percent to less than 50 percent.[3] Simply put,

3 From 1944 to 2016, the Independence Party was in government for 55 years, the Progressives for forty-seven years, the Social Democrats for thirty-six years, and the Left Greens and their predecessors for

their legacy is (1) economic advances that enabled Iceland within two generations to close the gap in living standards as measured by per capita incomes that had separated Iceland from Denmark in 1904 when Iceland was granted home rule by Denmark and (2) a country whose politics is considered corrupt by 67 percent of Gallup's Icelandic respondents compared with 14 percent in Sweden and 15 percent in Denmark (Gallup 2013).[4] Around 1900, Denmark was roughly twice as affluent as Iceland in terms of per capita GDP. In 2007, Iceland shared with Norway first place in the United Nations Human Development Index (UNHDI), sliding to sixteenth place in 2014 six years after the crash.

As O'Toole (2010) has written of Ireland, Iceland is, in economic terms, a first-world country marred with a third-world political culture characterized by patrimonialism, personalization, and politicization (Gylfason 2015a; Kristinsson 1996; Kristjánsson 2011, 2012). The problem was duly acknowledged by the parliament itself in its unanimous 2010 resolution, adopted with 63 votes to 0, no abstentions, that "criticism of its political culture must be taken seriously" (my translation). Some concerned observers have suggested that Iceland may be too small to be sustainable as a sovereign state, aware that small island nations tend to have some political features that differ from those of larger states (Anckar 2006). Others have shown that, even though they do not benefit from scale economies and large pools of talent, small countries with cohesive societies can be successful as long as they are open to the world (Alesina and Spolaore 2003; Gylfason 2009a). Be that as it may, Iceland's political class leaves behind a long record of corrupt, criminogenic behavior, including bank scandals that were swept under the carpet in the 1930s, illegal profiteering around the US military base in the 1940s and 1950s, and Russian-style treatment of natural resources since the 1980s, declared unconstitutional by the Supreme Court

nineteen years. During 2007–9, the Social Democrats were in government with the Independence Party with the Progressives and Left Greens in opposition.

4 Gallup asked random samples of voters about political corruption whereas Transparency International, which also ranks Iceland behind other Nordic countries, asks business people, country experts, and others about corruption, defined as the abuse of entrusted power for private gain. Specifically, in 2015, Denmark, Finland, Sweden, and Norway ranked 1, 2, 3, and 5 in Transparency's international corruption ranking while Iceland ranked 13 out of 168 countries. The World Values Survey (2014) ranked interpersonal trust in Iceland far behind that in other Nordic countries even long before the crash of 2008 (Gylfason 2015b). These surveys were taken before Iceland surfaced at the center of the Panama Papers scandal in early 2016 when it came to light that the names of about 600 Icelanders, including three cabinet ministers and the First Lady, were among those found in the Panama Papers (2012–16), 11.5 million leaked documents that detail financial and attorney–client information for more than 200,000 offshore entities, exposing how wealthy individuals and public officials may have used offshore bank accounts and shell companies to conceal their wealth or avoid taxes. Two of the three ministers in question, the leader and deputy leader of the Independence Party, were still in office as prime minister and Minister of the Interior in early 2017 after having run successfully for reelection in October 2016, as did the former prime minister, who resigned from office under public pressure after the scandal broke.

in 1998 (Gylfason 2009b; Kristjánsson 2011). Under political pressure, the Supreme Court reversed its verdict eighteen months later only to have it reconfirmed in 2007 by the United Nations Human Rights Committee (UNHRC 2007), which, in a binding opinion, instructed Iceland to remove the discriminatory element from its fisheries management system and pay damages to those who had been discriminated against. In 2012, the UNHRC released Iceland from its obligation to mend its ways against the government's promise of a new constitution guaranteeing a nondiscriminatory allocation of fishing rights, a promise that the UNHRC appeared to find credible; even so, the government shows as yet no sign of intending to keep its promise.[5] All this was accompanied by a strong dose of asset stripping à la russe, including a corrupt privatization of the banks that paved their road to the cliff in 2008 and that the parliament has proved unwilling to investigate. It was not until after the crash of 2008 that the IMF openly expressed support for a fee-based and nondiscriminatory – and constitutional – system of fisheries management in Iceland.

To begin with, the new postcrash government listened to the people and their demands. The ex-prime minister turned governor in chief of the failed Central Bank, mired in controversy,[6] was removed from office only to be installed by the oligarchs as editor of what used to be Iceland's largest newspaper. The oligarchs are mostly vessel owners enriched by the parliament's granting them hugely valuable fishing quotas since 1984. The IMF was called to the rescue following a botched attempt by the Central Bank to procure a big loan from Russia to avoid IMF assistance or the "Kiss of Death" as one key Independence Party operative described it (Gunnarsson

[5] In February 2009, a new Minister of Fisheries reaffirmed on behalf of the Icelandic government that it had been decided to strengthen the human rights provisions in Iceland's constitution by adding a clause to the effect that Iceland's fish resources belong to the people. In a letter dated May 29, 2012, the UN Human Rights Office of the High Commissioner informed the government of Iceland that during its 104th session in March 2012 the committee had "decided, in light of the measures taken so far by the State party to give effect to the Committee's Views, not to examine the case further under the follow-up procedure, with a note of a partly satisfactory implementation of its recommendation." Members of the Constitutional Society, an Icelandic nongovernmental organization, have called the attention of the UNHRC to Iceland's noncompliance, including its refusal to award damages to those discriminated against.

[6] Wade (2009) and the Special Investigation Committee (SIC 2010) describe the ill-fated pegging of the króna to the euro when there were hardly any foreign exchange reserves left, a decision made by the Central Bank governors without consultation even with the bank's chief economist, triggering a still unaccounted-for hemorrhage of remaining reserves. The Central Bank has refused to share with the parliament, let alone make public, a recording or transcript of a telephone conversation just before the crash between the governor and the prime minister, who was later, along with two other ministers, the three Central Bank governors, and the director of the Financial Supervisory Authority, declared guilty of negligence in the sense of the law by the SIC (2010). The former prime minister, Geir Haarde, was likewise found guilty of negligence by a special Court of Impeachment convened by the parliament in 2012 and headed by the Chief Justice of the Supreme Court, and was appointed ambassador to the United States in 2014.

2009, 51). No political party distanced itself from the Central Bank's overture to Russia, which came to nothing (Iceland is a founding member of NATO). A Special Prosecutor's Office was set up, and managed to secure a number of convictions of senior bankers and others, but some of those convictions remain on appeal to the Supreme Court. By late 2017, the Supreme Court had sentenced thirty-five bankers and others to a total of eighty-eight man-years in prison for crash-related offences, including breach of trust, market manipulation, false reporting, and fraud. Several further indictments and verdicts are expected to result from the roughly eighty cases referred to the Special Prosecutor by the Financial Supervisory Authority (FME), which, designed as it had been to fail, had slept through the crash alongside the international rating agencies but was now alert under a new postcrash director who, three years and seventy-seven referrals to the Special Prosecutor later, was hounded from office. In 2010, a 2,400-page report by a Special Investigation Commission (SIC) appointed by Parliament described legal violations on top of recklessness, regulatory capture, political capture, media capture, academic capture, and so on, even if the report failed to connect its analysis to the relevant law-and-economics literature on white-collar crime (Akerlof and Romer 1993; Black 2005).[7] The academic capture part of the story is recounted to chilling effect in Ferguson (2012, chapter 8). The parliament discussed the report only cursorily.

A key promise given by the postcrash government in early 2009 concerned the constitution which, drawn up in haste at the time of Iceland's full separation from Denmark in 1944, the parliament had promised to revise ever since without keeping its word, partly perhaps because it was not impelled by crisis to do so (Elster 1995). In his New Year's address to the nation in 1949, Iceland's first president, Sveinn Björnsson, reminded the political parties of their failure to fix the constitution, saying that "… we still have a mended garment, originally made for another country, with other concerns, a hundred years ago" (my translation). The postcrash government concluded that since the politicians had failed to revise the constitution for almost seventy years it was time to bestow the task on a special constituent assembly – that is, to have a new constitution drafted by representatives elected directly by the people rather than by the parliament. This promise constituted a welcome admission of failure as well as an undeclared acknowledgement that a constituent assembly elected in accordance with the principle of "one person, one vote" was better suited to the task than MPs elected on the basis of current electoral laws granting rural voters up to twice as much influence in parliamentary elections as voters in the Reykjavík area, one of the most controversial issues in Icelandic politics

[7] Johnsen (2014) reviews the main findings of the SIC report. For a short version of some of the highlights of the story, see Gylfason (2010). For more on the crash in a historical and political context and its aftermath, see Gylfason et al. (2010, chapter 7), and Gylfason (2015a, 2016a).

since 1849 when the first written proposal of equal voting rights – equal apportionment of seats in Parliament if you prefer[8] – was put forth, but in vain. There was no presumption that the 1944 constitution was directly to blame for the financial crash. It was widely understood, however, that thorough constitutional reform was long overdue, reform that might strengthen Iceland's laws and political culture and thus perhaps reduce the likelihood of a repeat.[9]

So, it is important for the reader to understand that the trouble with Iceland started long ago. We could begin the story in the 1870s, but let us wind fast forward to the 1940s and World War II that saw a unilateral decision by the parliament and the electorate to leave the royal union with Nazi-occupied Denmark, unable to fend for itself. The political parties stood united behind this decision and made an all-out effort to muster the support of 98 percent of the voters for the decision plus a new constitution, essentially a copy of the Danish one from 1849 with a hereditary king replaced by a president.[10] The parties could enlist broad popular support by promising a new constitution. Meanwhile, the main political parties got along miserably with one another owing, among other things, to a deep disagreement about unequal voting rights that culminated in a 1942 constitutional amendment designed to reduce the rural bias of the electoral laws. The Progressive Party, the main beneficiary of unequal voting rights because of its strength in rural areas, fought the amendment tooth and nail, and lost. Even so, the equalization of voting rights was only partial, an example of reluctant progress – too little, too late. The political parties were unable to form a coalition government, inducing the governor, Sveinn Björnsson, elected president in 1944 when the Republic of Iceland was established, to appoint an extraparliamentary government 1942–4, albeit one firmly anchored in the dominant political parties, the Independence Party and the Progressives, virtually not on speaking terms with one another at the time.

The 1950s saw an uneasy truce among the dominant parties, a truce that was broken in a new battle in 1959, as in 1942, about a constitutional amendment to secure more equal voting rights. Once more, the Progressives, still heavily overrepresented in the parliament, fought fiercely against the amendment, and lost again.[11]

[8] The terms "equal voting rights" and "equalization of voting rights" accord with Icelandic terminology, referring to equality among parties in Parliament as well as among voters in different electoral districts. The term "equal apportionment of seats" is commonly taken to refer only to the latter, i.e., to equality among parties in the parliament, hence the usage in the text.

[9] No specific provisions pertaining to the financial sector were included in the constitutional bill of 2011 for reasons laid out in Gylfason (2012a, 2012b).

[10] The Danish constitution of 1849 was replaced (de jure, but de facto only revised) in 1866, 1920, and 1953 so it was the 1920 constitution that the Icelanders copied in 1944.

[11] Again, fierce resistance by the Progressives contributed to the piecemeal nature of the equalization of voting rights. History shows that fierce resistance by a resolute minority can slow down or derail reform. Led by President Johnson, the US Congress was able to secure equal rights for African Americans 100 years after President Lincoln took the first step with the emancipation of slaves in 1865.

As a result, the two main parties were unable to work together again until the mid-1970s. All along, the economy remained heavily regulated with prices, interest rates, and the exchange rate of the króna determined by politicians and their appointees in the banks. An important respite was provided by a major economic liberalization effort in the 1960s when huge fiscal subsidies to the fishing industry were converted to indirect support through devaluation of the króna and privileged access to subsidized bank credits, an arrangement meaning essentially that the króna would be devalued at the whim of the vessel owners to shore up the profitability of fish exports when needed, undermining financial conscientiousness in Iceland's main export industry. In the 1980s and 1990s an attempt to stabilize the króna meant that government support for the fishing industry thereafter took the form of gratis allocations of hugely valuable fishing rights in Icelandic waters, even if the marine resources were shortly thereafter declared a common property resource by law. The system of gratis quota allocations, ruled discriminatory and unconstitutional by the Supreme Court in 1998 and by the UNHRC (2007), turned a dispersed resource (fish) into a concentrated one (like oil), with all the potential for political cartelization that implies (Wenar, 2016). From then on, because the Supreme Court reversed course in 2000 under open political pressure, suddenly seeing no discrimination in an unchanged system of gratis quota allocations, the vessel owners were basically able to dominate Icelandic politics with a brief interlude during the 2000s when exuberant bankers briefly overshadowed the boat owners until the crash of 2008.[12] The editor of one of Iceland's two main newspapers at the time described as "suicidal" attempts by politicians to rise against the quota kings.[13] The SIC (2010) reports huge payments by the failed banks, before their demise, to political parties and individual politicians, information that would not have come to light without the crash.

President Björnsson, as governor in 1944, emboldened by the first scientific public opinion poll conducted in Iceland, managed to have two key novelties inserted into the provisional constitution that was otherwise kept essentially unchanged from 1874, or 1849.[14] The novelties were that the President of the Republic (1) would be elected by the people, not by the parliament as the political parties wanted (this gave Iceland one of the first popularly elected presidents in Europe)[15] and (2) could veto legislation from the parliament and refer it to a national referendum, a provision that

[12] For an account of events in Iceland before and after the crash, see Gylfason et al. (2010), Benediktsdóttir et al. (2011), Johnsen (2014), and Gylfason (2015a).

[13] See Gunnarsson (2009, 206). "Quota kings" and "quota queens" are commonly used terms in public debate in Iceland, like "oligarchs" in Russia. By contrast, oil kings and oil queens are unheard of in Norway because the Norwegian government made sure from the outset that Norway's oil discoveries would not result in the creation of a class of oligarchs.

[14] On the 1,000th anniversary of the settlement of Iceland in 1874 Christian IX, King of Denmark, brought the Icelanders their first constitution, essentially identical to the Danish constitution of 1849.

[15] Precedents include France in 1848 and Germany in 1919.

lay dormant for sixty years until it was activated in 2004 to block the government's plan to regulate media ownership in a way that would have forced Iceland's largest daily newspaper and the sole television station competing with state television to close down.

Constitutions are by their very nature political declarations outlining the rights and obligations of citizens, including the powers of the organized few versus the unorganized masses and, as such, are naturally conducive to deep disagreements about individual provisions. Rights protected in constitutions entail obligations that may understandably meet resistance. Those who claim, as did the president of Iceland 1996–2016, that constitutional amendments must be approved by consensus are fundamentally at odds with the historical evidence as well as with basic logic, but their position serves the special interests of those opposed to constitutional reform, a point I shall return to in the third section dealing with the parliamentary constitutional committee's efforts to water down three provisions of the bill approved by the voters in the 2012 referendum. But first let me offer some remarks on the work of the constituent assembly in Section III.

II. CONSTITUTION MAKING IN ACTION 2010–2013

With the political class up against the wall after the crash of 2008, a new Icelandic constitution was promised once again.[16] As the coalition government of the Social Democratic Alliance and the Independence Party stepped down in early 2009 under public pressure, the Social Democrats went on to form a provisional minority government with the Left Green Party, with the support of the Progressives who made their support conditional on having a new constitution put in place, to be drafted by representatives elected directly by the people rather than by politicians. After the 2009 election, the two parties of the minority coalition were able to form a majority government. An attempt at constitutional overhaul seemed inevitable at this stage, with the Independence Party, a conservative force in Icelandic politics, reluctantly agreeing to a bill regulating the constitutional revision process (Meuwese 2013). The Independence Party proposed the convention of a National Assembly. During 2009–13, the Independence Party and the Progressives found themselves together in opposition to a majority government in parliament for the first time in history.

In June 2010 the parliament passed the Act on a Constitutional Assembly, laying out a process that included preparations for the drafting by a seven-member extraparliamentary Constitutional Committee, appointed by the parliament (Table 7.1). A National Assembly comprising 950 individuals drawn at random from

[16] This section draws on Gylfason and Meuwese (2017).

TABLE 7.1. *Timeline of Events*

October 7–9, 2008: Government takes over Landsbanki, Glitnir, and Kaupthing Bank
January 26, 2009: Government of Independence Party and Social Democratic Alliance resigns
April 25, 2009: Parliamentary election
May 10, 2009: Government of Social Democratic Alliance and Left Greens is formed
June 16, 2010: Constitutional Committee is appointed by the parliament
June 25, 2010: Parliament passes law on the constitutional assembly
November 6, 2010: National Assembly convenes
November 27, 2010: Election of Constitutional Assembly
April 6, 2011: Constitutional Assembly commences its work
July 29, 2011: Constitutional Assembly delivers its bill to the parliament
June 30, 2012: Presidential election
October 20, 2012: National referendum on the constitutional bill
April 27, 2013: Parliamentary election
November 6, 2013: New Constitutional Committee appointed by prime minister
February 19, 2016: New Constitutional Committee presents three bills to Althingi
October 13, 2016: Parliament adjourns without having discussed the three bills
October 29, 2016: Parliamentary election held six months ahead of schedule

the National Register[17] convened for a day in November 2010, declaring at the end of its deliberations that a new constitution was needed and should include certain key provisions on equal voting rights and national ownership of natural resources, among other things. A national Single Transferable Vote (STV) election of 25 constitutional assembly representatives from a roster of 522 candidates was held on November 27, 2010; the STV method is designed to minimize the number of wasted votes (Helgason 2011). The Constitutional Committee produced a 700-page dossier analyzing the 1944 constitution and including suggestions of new constitutional text for the constitutional assembly to consider.

Former prime minister Geir Haarde from the Independence Party was indicted by Parliament in September 2010 in accordance with Article 14 of the 1944 constitution. He was subsequently cleared of all but one offense; he was found guilty of having failed to keep his ministers sufficiently informed during the 2008 financial crisis in violation of the constitution, but he was not punished. An ad hoc parliamentary committee was set up to propose how the parliament should deal with the

[17] Those who declined to serve were replaced by individuals with similar attributes to reduce potential self-selection bias.

Special Investigation Commission's (2010) finding that three cabinet ministers and MPs were among the seven public officials guilty of gross and possibly unlawful dereliction of duty before the crash. The committee decided that not three but four former ministers should be indicted, but the parliament, including current and former ministers who did not recuse themselves from the proceedings, decided to spare all except the former prime minister. This triggered an unforgiving reaction from the Independence Party, now in opposition, thus extinguishing the hope that government and opposition could unite in honoring their promise to the people of a new constitution.

Undeterred by events in the parliament, and with a strong mandate from of the public, the Constitutional Council[18] commenced its work on April 6, 2011. The Council convened for a bit less than four months, until July 28, 2011, unanimously approving the constitutional bill on July 27, using July 28 to polish and approve the Preamble in time for the complete text to be delivered to the Speaker of Parliament July 29, 2011. No other MPs attended the ceremony, a conspicuous absence that some observers viewed at the time as a sign of things to come.

Several factors contributed to the production and unanimous passage of a constitutional bill combining continuity with fairly radical reform in several areas, including equal voting rights, national ownership of natural resources, freedom of information, environmental protection, and more. First, the bill was consistent with the conclusions of the National Assembly (Gylfason, 2016a). Second, public opinion polls reflected a broad consensus on key constitutional issues. Third, the method used to elect the Council members – one person, one vote combined with STV – produced a group of uniformly competent people from different walks of life with a wide range of professional experience, including five professors and three other academics used to soliciting outside expertise. In the first few days of the Council's deliberations, it was decided to draft a new bill from scratch, as was done in Philadelphia in 1787, rather than amend the 1944 constitution. This was done with due respect for constitutional continuity as Elkins et al. (2012) emphasize in their review of the bill. Also, it was decided to invite outsiders to participate through a specially designed interactive website as well as through social media (Gylfason and Meuwese 2017). The Council website was designed around this process to underscore the popular nature of the constitution-making exercise as opposed to constitution making by politicians and their lawyers.

The open invitation to the public had an important additional benefit in that it made it unnecessary if not inappropriate to invite representatives of interest groups

[18] The Constitutional Assembly was so renamed after the Supreme Court intervened to invalidate the Constitutional Assembly election on flimsy technical grounds and the parliament reacted by appointing the elected representatives to a Constitutional Council (Gylfason, 2013, section 6).

to meet with the Council the way that, for example, the South African constitution was put together during 1994–6. This invitation was in the spirit of the opening sentence of the Preamble: "We, the people of Iceland, wish to create a just society with equal opportunities for everyone."

After some exchanges between the parliament and the Council, the parliament called for an extra four-day Council meeting in March 2012 for the Council to answer some questions about its text. At this meeting the twenty-one Council members present (four of the twenty-five could not attend) gave unanimous answers to the parliament's queries, in some cases suggesting alternative formulations without changing the substance of the provisions in question. Not long thereafter, the parliament decided to put the bill to a referendum. The opposition in the parliament – the Independence Party and also the Progressives who had reversed course – now fought fiercely against the reform process, managing to delay the referendum beyond the presidential election June 30, 2012, a date preferred by the government on the grounds that voter turnout is always high in presidential elections, which would thus have secured a high voter turnout in the constitutional referendum. Instead, the referendum was held October 20, 2012.

The bill as a whole as well as its key provisions put on the ballot by Parliament won overwhelming support across the board with only two exceptions: the provision on equal voting rights was not accepted in two of the three rural constituencies and the provision on church and state was not approved. The overall support for the bill was 67 percent, the support for equal voting rights was also 67 percent, and for national ownership of natural resources, 83 percent (Gylfason 2012b). Turnout was 49 percent, a remarkably high figure in view of the fact that the referendum was an orphan as well as having been delayed beyond the presidential election. Even the government coalition parties that called the referendum did almost nothing to promote the bill or to encourage their supporters to vote. Among the parties in Parliament, only the smallest one, The Movement, an opposition party that had entered Parliament in 2009 with three seats out of sixty-three, showed an interest in presenting the bill to the voters. Along with Movement members, ordinary citizens, including former Constitutional Council members whose mandate had expired long ago, traveled around the country at their own expense to present the bill to the voters.

After the referendum, the haggling in the parliament intensified. The majority in the parliament that had shown little interest in its own referendum proved an easy prey for the fierce opponents in the minority which, with the economy gradually recovering under the IMF-supported rescue program, sensed that the shadow of the financial crash grew shorter and shorter. Even if thirty-two MPs out of sixty-three had declared in writing their support for the parliament's ratification of the bill in accordance with the outcome of the referendum, the parliament adjourned in March 2013 without having voted on the bill.

According to the 1944 constitution, it can be amended by a simple majority in two successive parliaments with a general election in between. The strategy of the supporters of the bill was to pass the bill unanimously in the Constitutional Council and go on to win the referendum by a solid majority of the voters, thus making it inevitable for the parliament to ratify the bill before the 2013 election as predicted by Jon Elster on national television in Iceland on May 13, 2012[19] and thus, ultimately, making it difficult for a new parliament after the 2013 election to refuse to provide the second ratification without provoking riots. This strategy failed because Ásta Ragnheiður Jóhannesdóttir, Speaker of Parliament, violating parliamentary procedure, failed to bring the bill to a vote before the Parliament adjourned on March 27, 2013.[20]

III. THE PARLIAMENT'S CONSTITUTIONAL COMMITTEE 2013–2016

Six months into his new government's term, the prime minister appointed a constitutional committee in November 2013, the latest in a long line of such committees since the 1940s.[21] The new committee comprised two members representing each of the two governing parties, the Independence Party and the Progressives, and one each from the four smaller opposition parties plus a chairman appointed by the prime minister. The committee's official mandate was to present to the parliament a constitutional text for the parliament's approval based on the bill approved in the 2012 referendum. The committee's unofficial mandate was to reach consensus by preparing a document that all nine committee members could sign – that is, find the lowest common denominator. The setup was deeply flawed. It amounted to an undertaking to negotiate after the fact with those who had lost the 2012 referendum. The thinking behind this setup recalls President John F. Kennedy's famous dictum: "What's mine is mine, what's yours is negotiable." Everyone knew that the committee was destined, if not designed, to fail, as had all earlier constitutional committees appointed by the parliament for seventy years.

The committee can be said to have been appointed deliberately to look for ways to water down or disregard the results of the 2012 referendum. A clear first sign of things to come was the prime minister's choice of chairman of the committee, a

19 Recall footnote 2.

20 The details of this episode are described in Gylfason (2016a). The Speaker's violation was a simple one. An amendment to a bill should always be brought to a vote before the bill itself. The Speaker brought a related bill to a vote without first bringing an attached amendment – the constitution bill – to a vote.

21 This section draws on my comments to the parliament's constitutional committee, published in *Fréttablaðið*, Iceland's largest newspaper, as well as on the parliament's website. The committee received comments, most of them devastatingly critical, from sixty-three individuals.

retired law professor in his eighties who had repeatedly declared himself opposed to constitutional change both before and after the 2012 referendum. When he retired in 2014 "due to age and other work" the committee chair was transferred to a lawyer in the Prime Minister's Office, an individual who previously as head of a small group of local lawyers had been seen to violate the clear instructions of the Constitutional and Supervisory Committee (CSC) of Parliament during 2012–13 by proposing material changes in the Constitutional Council bill against the express instructions of the CSC that the lawyers' team was authorized solely to propose changes in wording but not in substance. The CSC understood then that the parliament could not permit itself to disregard the will of the voters as expressed in the referendum of 2012 in much the same way as the US Congress did not permit itself to change as much as a word in the bill proposed by the Constitutional Convention in Philadelphia in 1787, neither before nor after the bill was brought to a vote in the states.

It behooves to recall how the chairman of the constitutional committee disobeyed the instructions of the CSC during 2012–13. Along with a few other lawyers chosen by the CSC, the chairman delivered to the CSC a radically revised statement concerning the Constitutional Council's natural resource provision. The revised statement repeatedly maintains with different wording that "The provision does not affect such property rights to resources that may already exist and the entitlements implied by such rights." (My translation, here and below.) Also: "The provision does not affect utilization permits or indirect property rights already in existence." And this: "*in accordance with the intentions of the Constitutional Council* [my italics], that those property rights already in existence, protected by the constitution, will not be affected." None of this is consistent with the original statement of the Constitutional Council. The lawyers, moreover, seemed to suggest that vessel owners had acquired property rights to catch quotas even if both the current law on fisheries management and the Constitutional Council's bill clearly state that this is not the case. Did the lawyers think that the Constitutional Council's natural resource provision had been passed unanimously by twenty-two votes (two abstained, one representative was absent), followed by spontaneous applause, to celebrate unchanged fisheries management? Did they think that 83 percent of the voters had approved the Constitutional Council's natural resource provision in the referendum to nail down an unchanged fisheries policy regime? Former Constitutional Council representatives pointed this out to the CSC at the time as did many others. The reason for these goings-on was clearly not of a legal nature such as, for example, to avoid retroactive legislation. If that had been the case, an argument to that effect would presumably have been put forward in writing. Rather, this was a blatant attempt, disguised in legal language, to protect the *status quo* against the result of the referendum.

This account is needed to shed light on the background of the work of the parliament's constitutional committee at its forty-eight or more meetings since 2013, all held behind closed doors, with only minimal information given sporadically to the public. The committee selected just 4 of the 114 provisions in the Constitutional Council bill for revision and ultimately gave up on reaching agreement on one of the four, the one dealing with the transfer of state powers considered by many crucial to avoid constitutional challenges to, e.g., Iceland's pending application for EU membership, filed by the parliament in 2009 and laid on ice in 2013 by the current government, not by the parliament. What happened here is that opponents of EU membership – that is, the majority of the four government representatives on the committee plus the chairman – do not want the constitution to permit membership. This outcome, if allowed to stand, would make Iceland unique in Europe.[22] Thus, by refusing to accept the Constitutional Council bill's provision on the transfer of state powers, the opponents of reform thereby declare that they do not accept the right of the people to decide by popular referendum whether Iceland should join the EU or stay out even if this is an inalienable right conferred on the people in the bill.

This omission left the committee with three provisions all of which it sought to weaken compared with corresponding provisions in the Constitutional Council bill. The committee seems to have sought the lowest common denominator to cater to those who lost the referendum in 2012 as if election results can subject to negotiation after the fact. The result is three draft bills that are essentially inconsistent with the results of the referendum, leading the representatives of two of the parliamentary parties on the Committee, the Social Democrats, and the Pirate Party, to publicly express dissatisfaction with the draft bill and thus to break ranks with the rest of the committee. The Pirate Party which in opinion polls from 2014 until the 2016 election[23] consistently received support from well over a third of the voters has resolved to respect the results of the 2012 referendum. The Social Democratic member of the parliament's constitutional committee, Ms. Valgerður Bjarnadóttir, who chaired the Parliament's CSC during 2012–13, has written: "The outcome [i.e., the constitutional committee's proposal] is what the reactionaries [i.e., opponents of constitutional reform] can accept."[24] Hence, the parliament's plan to produce unanimity failed.

It can be said that the three bills submitted by the committee constitute an improvement on the 1944 constitution, but they constitute a much smaller improvement than that approved by the voters in the 2012 referendum. Others think that acceptance of anything from the parliament's constitutional committee is tantamount to acquiescence to a coup against democracy.

[22] Denmark introduced a clause on the transfer of state powers into its constitution in 1953 to remove a potential obstacle to foreign relations, including EU membership, and Norway did so in 1962.

[23] In the 2016 election, however, the Pirates won 15 percent of the vote.

[24] See http://herdubreid.is/um-stjornarskrartillogurnar/

Let me now discuss the specific ways in which the constitutional committee bills subtract from the Constitutional Council bill.

A. *Natural Resources*

The constitutional committee's draft bill on natural resources is characterized by retreat. The tone is set right from the start: "Iceland's natural resources belong to the Icelandic people." The Falkland Islands belong to Britain, true, but the British do not own them. The statement accompanying the bill admits the retreat (p. 17): "This wording does not refer to traditional property rights." The implication is that national ownership is inferior to other forms of ownership. (The first chairman of the constitutional committee is known for having stuck to the view that there can be no such thing as national ownership.) The committee reaffirms its retreat by replacing the words "common and perpetual property of the nation" at the very beginning of the provision by a simple reference to "property of the nation" in the middle of the text – i.e., neither common nor perpetual. Further, the stipulation that "government authorities may grant permits for the use or utilization of resources or other limited public goods against full consideration and for a reasonable period of time" is replaced by a formulation where the word "full" is replaced by "normally fair," a double discount to the vessel owners – double because of the twofold qualification from "full" to not just "fair" but "normally fair." In addition, the time limit "for a reasonable period of time" has been removed.

The statement with the draft bill does not mention whether it is "normal" for vessel owners to expropriate 90 percent of the fisheries rent, as has been the case thus far (Thorláksson 2015). A representative in the constitutional committee has said publicly that he prefers "normally fair" consideration to "full" consideration on the grounds that this would facilitate support for socially important projects, etc., through a constitutionally protected discount from full charge. This idea entails that a harmful and outdated method of economic management – hidden indirect subsidies in lieu of transparent direct subsidies through the government budget – be enshrined in the constitution. The words "which are not in private ownership" have been replaced by "which are not subject to private property rights." Here an unambiguous choice of words by the Constitutional Council – everyone knows what "private ownership" means – is let give way to unclear and ambiguous wording that invites legal dispute. Everyone knows that vessel owners eventually do not own the fish in the sea for that is the law, but they could try to claim to have earned property rights to the resource.

The statement with the constitutional committee's bill has indeed no legal force, but, if allowed to stand, it is likely to undermine the advancement of their rights that the voters granted themselves when 83 percent of them expressed their support in 2012 for the national ownership provision proposed in the Constitutional Council bill. The constitutional committee statement declares that its bill "does not, however, automatically lead to change in current utilization permits" and "the provision will not automatically disturb the indirect ownership rights that may be implicit in the utilization or exploitation rights that may already have been established vis-à-vis state rights and resources that according to the bill will be considered in public ownership." The report thus conveys the impression that vessel owners have, in effect, acquired some form of ownership rights to the fisheries. The report also says: "If the fee is not determined in the market it can be expected that the fee be based on the profitability of exploitation ..." The message of the constitutional committee to the vessel owners is clear: Just keep piling up debts as you have in years past without worry and you will be granted a constitutionally guaranteed discount from full charge for the right to fish as a matter of course.

The constitutional committee includes a single academic reference in its statement (Willmann and Kelleher 2009),[25] a World Bank study known for its advocacy of privatization of common-property fisheries, without referring at all to the literature explaining the efficiency gains from regulating access to common property resources in a nondiscriminatory fashion by fee (see, e.g., Matthíasson 2001).

Just as the constitutional committee tries to demote the concept of national ownership, it downplays the concept of sustainable development by removing the sentence, "The utilization of the resources shall be guided by sustainable development ...," replacing it by a weaker formulation as follows: "They [Iceland's natural resources] ought to be utilized in a sustainable way ..." The phrase "sustainable development" is by now deeply anchored in international discourse on environmental protection whereas "utilized in a sustainable way" has no such direct connotation and is, therefore, legally ambiguous.[26]

The statement with the draft bill of the constitutional committee discusses at length various legal texts of limited relevance but fails to mention the seminal 1998 Supreme Court verdict that declared the fisheries management system to be discriminatory and thus in breach of the current constitution. Nor does the statement mention the binding opinion of the UNHRC of 2007 that confirmed the 1998 verdict of the Supreme Court.

The statement also offers a revealing paragraph: "There can hardly be found any examples of economies that are as dependent on natural resource utilization as the Icelandic one." This statement is not only false (the fishing industry accounts at

[25] I owe this observation to the comments submitted to the constitutional committee by Dr. Níels Einarsson, Director of the Vilhjálmur Stefánsson Institute at the University of Akureyri.

[26] I owe this observation to the comments submitted to the constitutional committee by my fellow Constitutional Council member Mr. Ómar Ragnarsson, Iceland's most prominent environmentalist together with Björk.

present for 10 percent of Iceland's GDP and 25 percent of export earnings) but this is a worn piece of propaganda from the National Federation of Icelandic Fishing Vessel Owners (LÍÚ, now SFS). That this rehash of an old untruth should find its way into the constitutional committee statement is worthy of note in view of the well-documented fact that the first quota law was drawn up in the offices of LÍÚ (Jónsson 1990). Nearly half of all countries of the world are more dependent on natural resources than Iceland based on World Bank figures on natural resource rents in proportion to GDP and comparable data for Iceland compiled by Mr. Indriði H. Thorláksson (2015), former Director of Revenue Iceland.

The constitutional committee's statement with its draft bill on natural resources needs to be rewritten and rectified so as to reflect fully the statement of the Constitutional Council with its resource provision which, among other things, offers a precise definition of the concept of national ownership as distinct from state ownership and private ownership, a concept that the constitutional committee has tried to disparage in accordance with its original chairman's view that there is no such thing as national ownership even if practically every Icelander knows exactly what that means. For example, the law from 1928 about the national park at Thingvellir, the venue of Iceland's ancient parliament, declares the park to be the property of the nation.

B. *Environment and Conservation*

The constitutional committee bill on the environment also misses the mark. Telling is the committee's removal of the Constitutional Council's sentence "Previous damage shall be repaired to the extent possible" from the text. This sentence was included in the Constitutional Council bill to acknowledge Iceland's perhaps most serious environmental problem, soil erosion largely due to private grazing on public lands. The constitutional committee seems to have omitted the sentence to defer to those bent on continued degradation of the environment. The sentence "Everyone is under obligation to respect it and protect it [Iceland's nature]" has been omitted apparently for the same purpose. Further, the reference to "protection of sites of natural interest, unpopulated wilderness, vegetation and soil" has been omitted without explanation even though the wording of the omitted text was carefully argued in the statement of the Constitutional Council with its bill with reference to the experience of other countries. Finally, the constitutional committee has deleted without explanation the Constitutional Council's text elaborating the meaning of sustainable development, including the reference to the rights of nature and future generations: "The use of natural resources shall be managed so as to minimize their depletion in the long term with respect for the rights of nature and future generations."

C. Direct Democracy

Like its other two draft bills, the constitutional committee's bill on direct democracy subtracts a great deal from the corresponding provisions in the Constitutional Council bill. This is remarkable in view of the fact that in the 2012 referendum 73 percent of the voters declared themselves in favor of direct democracy with increased reliance on national referenda. The constitutional committee narrows considerably the provision of the bill approved by the voters by (1) increasing the minimum number of signatures by half, from 10 percent to 15 percent of the electorate, without comment on the Constitutional Council's careful justification for the 10 percent mark; (2) reducing the time available for collecting signatures demanding a referendum from three months to four weeks (a bungle, according to a public statement by a member of the committee); (c) introducing a de facto threshold for minimum participation in national referenda that is so high as to make the provision likely to be a dead letter;[27] and (4) by removing altogether the provision on parliamentary business on the initiative of voters, stipulating, in the words of the Constitutional Council, that "two per cent of the electorate may submit an item of business in the Althing [Parliament]." Thus, the revised provision on direct democracy offered by the constitutional committee subtracts a great deal from the corresponding provision on democracy in the constitutional bill.

Following the National Assembly of 2010 and in keeping with a legal process laid out by the parliament, the Constitutional Council bill answered the call of the people for a new constitution, new mores, a new political culture, a new beginning. The bills proposed by the parliament's constitutional committee aim to undermine this appeal, not only by watering down three provisions in the Constitutional Council bill but also by ignoring everything else, including the provision on equal voting rights (equal apportionment of seats), a key provision of the bill, and also the provision on the transfer of state powers. Thus, the 2016 parliamentary election was held under election laws that 67 percent of voters rejected in the 2012 referendum, giving the Independence Party 33 percent of the seats in Parliament even if it won only 29 percent of the vote. Further, without a new provision on the transfer of state powers MPs will continue to face accusations that they deliberately violate the current constitution, which does not contain a clear transfer provision.

[27] Specifically, the provision stipulates that to overturn bills approved by Parliament in a referendum requires not only a majority of the votes but also at least 25 percent of the electorate. Average participation in national referenda in Iceland since 1908 (except 1944, a special case) is 57 percent. If a government supported by 33 percent of the voters (as at present) instructs its supporters to stay at home, bringing voter participation down to 38 percent, it would take a 66 percent majority of the voters (i.e., 25/38) to overturn the legislation.

IV. COMPARISONS WITH THE UNITED STATES AND GERMANY

The upshot of the argument presented in this chapter is that the failure of the Icelandic parliament to ratify the constitutional bill approved in the 2012 national referendum can be attributed primarily to the subservience of the political establishment to special interests in conjunction with the constitutional requirement that the parliament ratify the new constitution – not once, but twice. A detailed account of how other countries have gone about ratifying their constitutions is beyond the scope of this chapter. Even so, it may be useful before concluding to offer a brief comparison of Iceland with the United States and Germany.

The similarities between Iceland in 2011–12 and the United States in 1787–8 are significant. Both constitutional bills took four months to write and both were within a year or so referred to voters for acceptance or rejection (Gylfason 2012c; Maier 2010). In the United States, Congress did not consider it appropriate to take a stand on the bill drafted by the Federal Convention, let alone amend it. Instead, Congress forwarded the bill as received to the thirteen states for acceptance or rejection in keeping with the Federal Convention's resolution that acceptance by nine states would suffice for the bill to take force. The states sent the bill either to their legislatures for acceptance or rejection or, better still, to special assemblies to keep state legislators from acting as judges in their own case. When, nine months later, nine states had approved the bill, it became the law of the land. In view of the fact that the margin of victory was quite narrow in several of the state elections, it appears quite possible that amendments to the text by Congress would have created new controversies and doomed the ratification process. Congress did the right thing by not inserting itself into the reform process.

The ratification of the German constitution of 1949 is also of interest here. In 1948, on the initiative of the allied powers, the prime ministers of the eleven German states in the allied occupation zones appointed a Parliamentary Council comprising sixty-five politicians (plus five nonvoting members from West Berlin) to draft a new constitution. When ready two months later, rather than submitting the bill to a national referendum for ratification as the allied powers wanted (Markovits 2008), the Council sent the bill to the legislatures of the eleven Länder, all of which except Bavaria ratified the bill. After a gestation period of about nine months as in the United States, the Parliamentary Council adopted the constitution (Basic Law, *Grundgesetz*) in 1949 by a vote of 53 to 12. While the allied proposal of ratification by plebiscite aimed to avoid conflicts of interest in the spirit of the American precedent from 1787–8, the German method of ratification involved only politicians in the Länder as well as in Bonn, the latter a mere formality. Consequently, unlike in Iceland, a common sense of ownership was absent: in 1955, six years after ratification, only 30 percent of German voters approved of the constitution while 51 percent admitted to not knowing its content (Markovits 2008, 1337).

The obvious thing for the Icelandic parliament to do after the 2012 referendum was to follow the example set by the US Congress in 1787–8. Instead, MPs decided to take advantage of the provision in the 1944 constitution that requires two successive parliaments to ratify constitutional change with a parliamentary election in between. This provision invites self-dealing by making constitutional reform conditional on the cooperation of those whom the reform aims to restrain and who, therefore, will resist if they think they can get away with it. This is precisely why, after the 2008 financial crash, Iceland's discredited parliament outsourced constitutional reform to a popularly elected assembly, thereby admitting its own inherent inability to revise the constitution and implicitly affirming the superior legitimacy of the people. The parliament then reversed position on this fundamental matter of principle in mid-stream after the 2012 referendum, despite written declarations of support for the ratification of the new constitution by a majority of MPs. These events raise concerns about the need for constitutional reform by extraconstitutional means as was, in fact, done in Iceland when its 1944 constitution entered into force following one parliamentary vote plus a referendum in lieu of two parliamentary votes as prescribed by the preceding constitution, with or without a referendum.

V. CONCLUSION

The bills proposed by the constitutional committee reveal a clear determination by the 2013–16 majority in the parliament to disrespect the will of the people as expressed in the 2012 constitutional referendum, including their will concerning the key provision on equal voting rights, a provision that won 67 percent of the vote in the referendum and that the committee did not even consider. The bills are clearly intended to accommodate special interests, those forces that were mostly responsible for putting Iceland on the rocks in 2008 and again in 2016, inflicting serious damage on the country and its reputation in the eyes of the rest of the world. Every single departure from the Constitutional Council bill seems designed to subtract from the bill and to serve the interests of the political class and connected special interests at the expense of the people. Like the banking sector and the Financial Supervisory Authority, the parliament enjoys limited trust among voters in the public opinion surveys by Capacent (18% trust the parliament) and MMR (14 percent trust the parliament).[28]

[28] These surveys were taken before the prime minister, finance minister, and Minister of the Interior along with several other politicians were exposed as holders of significant amounts of money in international tax havens, including the one that has become virtually synonymous with the goings on before Iceland's financial crash of 2008, Tortola in the British Virgin Islands. In early April 2016, the Panama Papers threw Iceland into political turmoil resulting in the sudden resignation of the prime minister and the formation of a new government, though in name only, as well as in a parliamentary

The seriousness of the parliament's failure to abide by the results of the 2012 national referendum manifests itself in many ways. Here two examples will do.

First, an absurd provision of the 1944 constitution remains in force, an obvious remnant from the mid-nineteenth century where kings reigned supreme: "The President grants, either himself or through other government authorities, exemptions from laws in accordance with rules that have been followed thus far." Yes, you might add, and in accordance with President Richard Nixon's final dictum in this 1977 television interview with David Frost: "If the President does it, that means it's not illegal." While this provision has not been invoked to date, it is out of place and perilous in a modern democracy where business, finance, and politics intermingle to an unprecedented degree and where thirty-five individuals have been awarded prison sentences for crash-related violations of the law and where further guilty verdicts appear likely.

Second, the outmoded 1944 provision on the election of the president remains in force. This provision awards the presidency to the candidate with the largest number of votes without requiring that the victor enjoys the support of the majority of voters. The Constitutional Council anticipated the danger that a large number of candidates might result in the election of a president with a small plurality, perhaps 20 percent of the vote or less. This is why the bill stipulates that "Voters shall rank candidates, one or more, at their own choice in order of preference. The person who best meets the order of preference of voters, as further provided by law, is the rightfully elected President." This ensures that the candidate elected has the majority of votes even without a second round of voting. Further, the bill stipulates that "Presidential candidates shall have the endorsement of a minimum of one per cent and a maximum of two per cent of the electorate." This means that a candidate would need to secure a minimum of 2,400 signatures compared with the current requirement of 1,500 signatures, a much lower threshold. Nine candidates ran for president in June 2016. Had eight of them received 11 percent of the vote each, the ninth would have won with 12 percent support. This did not happen, however. As it turned out, the winner received 39 percent of the vote, followed by three other candidates with 28 percent, 14 percent, and 14 percent. By sheer luck, the danger of a new president with minuscule public backing was thus averted. Even so, like the parliamentary election promised in the wake of the Panama papers scandal to be held ahead of schedule in the fall of 2016 rather than the spring of 2017, the presidential election in June 2016 was held according to laws that the voters have rejected, bearing still further testimony to the parliament's deplorable handling of the constitutional reform process in Iceland.

election held six months ahead of schedule in October 2016, an election in which the three aforementioned ministers won reelection (recall footnote 4).

The chain of political legitimacy in Iceland is on the verge of being broken unless swift corrective action is taken. The argument rests on four main pillars.

First, a politically motivated, substantively wrong, and even illegal Supreme Court decision[29] invalidating the constituent assembly election of 2010 was intended to kill in its infancy, or at least to undermine, what is probably the most democratic constitutional reform process the world has ever seen.

Second, while the national and constituent assemblies delivered on schedule everything expected of them by law, the parliament failed to do its part by refusing to ratify the constitution bill approved by two-thirds of the voters in 2012.

Third, the parliament added insult to injury by reversing its original determination to outsource the drafting process to the constituent assembly and by effectively reclaiming the right to meddle with the substance of the constituent assembly bill even after the bill had been overwhelmingly approved by the voters, ultimately producing nothing of value while the government plunged the country into political crisis in the wake of the Panama papers scandal.

Fourth, the parliament's constitutional committee presented proposals that constitute a gross diminution of the bill that was accepted in the 2012 referendum, proposals that were poorly received by the public and were not even discussed in the parliament before it adjourned in October 2016.

In the October election, the outgoing government parties, the Independence Party and the Progressives, the sole active opponents of the constitutional bill, received 40 percent of the vote, down from 51 percent in 2013. The four outgoing opposition parties, including the Left Greens, the Pirates, and the Social Democrats, promised the voters ratification if they could form a government and received 43 percent of the vote, up from 37 percent in 2013. Thus, the supporters of the bill won more votes than its opponents. A new party, Regeneration, whose platform includes its own version of equal voting rights and national ownership of natural resources, received 10 percent of the vote; the rest (6 percent) were wasted. The four outgoing opposition parties and Regeneration came close to forming a coalition in December 2016, on a platform including a precise plan for ratifying the new constitution during the mandate period starting in 2017, but their negotiations failed for other reasons. Thus, the new constitution remains on the parliament's agenda. Declarations of failed reform are premature.

Even so, Iceland remains saddled with a failed political system, a failed political class that has permitted itself to try to undermine Iceland's age-old democracy. The

[29] For details, see Gylfason (2013, Section 6). An earlier, working paper version of Gylfason (2013), no longer in circulation, led a sitting Supreme Court justice to sue me for libel even though the justice was nowhere mentioned in the text. The justice lost his case in a district court in 2014 and then again before the Supreme Court from which he had by that time resigned well before his term expired.

ongoing constitutional impasse cannot be explained by rational doubts about the substance or method of the constitutional bill that two-thirds of the voters declared their support for in 2012. No, the impasse can be traced first and foremost to Iceland's deficient political culture, providing yet another confirmation that politicians as a rule are not fit for constitution making.

A democratic nation cannot under any circumstances permit the outcome of national elections, let alone a constitutional referendum, to be changed after the fact even if the referendum was advisory. The Brexit vote in the United Kingdom in 2016 was advisory. Even so, few if any British politicians would declare the vote irrelevant because it was advisory. Yet, this is what the Icelandic parliament has tried to do, thus undermining its political and moral legitimacy as well as democracy. It is not too late for the parliament to mend its ways.

REFERENCES

Akerlof, George A., and Paul M. Romer (1993). "Looting: The Economic Underworld of Bankruptcy for Profit." *Brookings Papers on Economic Activity* 2, 1–73.

Alesina, Alberto, and Enrico Spolaore (2003). *The Size of Nations*. Cambridge, MA: MIT Press.

Anckar, Dag (2006). "Islandness or Smallness? A Comparative Look at Political Institutions in Small Island States." *Island Studies Journal* 1(1), May, 43–54.

Beetham, David (2013). *The Legitimation of Power*, 2nd edn. London: Palgrave Macmillan.

Benediktsdóttir, Sigríður, Jón Daníelsson, and Gylfi Zoega (2011). "Lessons from a Collapse of a Financial System." *Economic Policy* 26, 183–235.

Björnsson, Sveinn (1949). "Nýársávarp til þjóðarinnar" (New Year's Address to the Nation). Retrieved from: www.forseti.is/media/files/01.01.49.S.B.nyarsavarp.pdf (accessed November 17, 2014).

Black, William K. (2005). *The Best Way to Rob a Bank Is to Own One: How Corporate Executives and Politicians Looted the S&L Industry*. Austin: University of Texas Press.

Charlton, Roger (1986). *Political Realities: Comparative Government*. London: Longman.

Elkins, Zachary, Tom Ginsburg, and James Melton (2012). "A Review of Iceland's Draft Constitution." Retrieved from: http://comparativeconstitutionsproject.org/wp-content/uploads/CCP-Iceland-Report.pdf (accessed January 26, 2016).

Elster, Jon (1995). "Forces and Mechanisms in the Constitution-Making Process." *Duke Law Journal* 45, 364–96.

Ferguson, Charles H. (2012). *Predator Nation: Corporate Criminals, Political Corruption, and the Hijacking of America*. New York, NY: Random House.

Gallup (2013). "Government Corruption Viewed as Pervasive Worldwide" by Jan Sonnenschein and Julie Ray. Retrieved from: www.gallup.com/poll/165476/government-corruption-viewed-pervasive-worldwide.aspx (accessed April 9, 2016).

Gunnarsson, Styrmir (2009). *Umsátrið (The Siege)*. Reykjavík: Veröld.

Gylfason, Thorvaldur (2009a). "Is Iceland Too Small?" *VoxEU* August 19.

(2009b). "Hvað segja lögin? Sameignarauðlindir eru mannréttindi" (What Does the Law Say? Common Property Resources as Human Rights). In *Ragnarsbók (Festschrift for*

Ragnar Aðalsteinsson). Reykjavík: Icelandic Literary Society and Icelandic Human Rights Center.

(2010). "Iceland's Special Investigation: The Plot Thickens." *VoxEU* April 30.

(2012a). "Finance and Constitutions." *VoxEU* April 11.

(2012b). "Constitution Making in Action: The Case of Iceland." *VoxEU* November 1.

(2012c). "Constitutions: Financial Crisis Can Lead to Change." *Challenge* 56:5, September–October, 106–22.

(2013). "From Collapse to Constitution: The Case of Iceland." In Luigi Paganetto (ed.), *Public Debt, Global Governance and Economic Dynamism*, 379–417. Berlin: Springer.

(2015a). "Iceland: How Could This Happen?" In Torben M. Andersen, Michael Bergman, and Svend E. Hougaard Jensen (eds.), *Reform Capacity and Macroeconomic Performance in the Nordic Countries*, chapter 12. Oxford: Oxford University Press.

(2015b). "Social Capital, Inequality, and Economic Crisis." *Challenge* 58,:4, July–August, 326–42.

(2016a). "Constitution on Ice." In Valur Ingimundarson, Philippe Urlfalino, and Irma Erlingsdóttir (eds.), *Iceland's Financial Crisis: The Politics of Blame, Protest, and Reconstruction*, chapter 10. London: Routledge.

(2016b). "Iceland's New Constitution Is Not Solely a Local Concern." *Challenge* 59:6, 480–90.

Gylfason, Thorvaldur, Bengt Holmström, Sixten Korkman, Hans Tson Söderström, and Vesa Vihriala (2010). *Nordics in Global Crisis*. Taloustieto Oy: Research Institute of the Finnish Economy (ETLA).

Gylfason, Thorvaldur, and Anne Meuwese (2017). "Digital Tools and the Derailment of Iceland's New Constitution." In Corien Prins, Peter Lindseth, Monica Guisse, and Colette Cuijpers (eds.), *Digital Democracy in a Globalized World*. Cheltenham, UK, and Northampton, MA: Edward Elgar.

Helgason, Thorkell (2011). "Greining á úrslitum kosningar til stjórnlagaþings 27. nóvember 2010" (Analysis of the results of the Constitutional Assembly election 27 November 2010). *Icelandic Review of Politics and Administration* 7:1.

Johnsen, Gudrun (2014). *Bringing Down the Banking System: Lessons from Iceland*. London: Palgrave Macmillan.

Jónsson, Halldór (1990). "Ákvarðanataka í sjávarútvegi og stjórnun fiskveiða" (Decision Making in the Fishing Industry and Fisheries Management). *Samfélagstíðindi (Social Science Bulletin)* 10, 99–141.

Kristinsson, Gunnar H. (1996). "Parties, States and Patronage." *West European Politics* 19:3, 433–57.

Kristjánsson, Svanur (2011). "Varð þjóðþingið að þjófþingi? Lýðræðið og kvótakerfið 1983" (Did Parliament Become Kleptocratic? Democracy and the Quota System 1983). *Skírnir* 185, Fall, 261–90.

(2012). "Fragile Democracy – Authority on the Offensive" (Brothætt lýðræði – Valdsmenn í sókn). *Skírnir* 186, Fall, 303–37.

Maier, Pauline (2010). *Ratification: The People Debate the Constitution*, 1787–1788. New York, NY: Simon and Schuster.

Markovits, Inga (2008). "Constitution Making after National Catastrophes: Germany in 1949 and 1990." *William & Mary Law Review* 49:4, 1307–46.

Matthíasson, Thórólfur (2001). "The Icelandic Debate on the Case for a Fishing Fee: A Non-technical Introduction." *Marine Policy* 25, 303–12.

Meuwese, Anne C. M. (2013). "Popular Constitution-Making: The Case of Iceland." In D. Galligan and M. Versteeg (eds.), *The Social and Political Foundations of Constitutions*, chapter 17. New York, NY: Cambridge University Press.

O'Toole, Flintan (2010). *Ship of Fools: How Stupidity and Corruption Sank the Celtic Tiger*. Dublin: PublicAffairs.

Special Investigation Commission (SIC) (2010). "Report of the Special Investigation Commission (SIC)," delivered to Althingi, the Icelandic Parliament, April 12. Retrieved from: http://www.rna.is/eldri-nefndir/addragandi-og-orsakir-falls-islensku-bankanna-2008/skyrsla-nefndarinnar/english/ (accessed August 17, 2014).

Thorláksson, Indridi H. (2015). "Veiðigjöld 2015. Annar hluti" (Fishing Fees 2015. Part Two).

United Nations Human Rights Committee (2007). International Covenant on Civil and Political Rights, CCPR/C/91/D/1306/2004, December 14.

Wade, Robert (2009). "Iceland as Icarus." *Challenge* 52:3, May/June, 5–33.

Wenar, Leif (2016). *Blood Oil: Tyrants, Violence, and the Rules that Run the World*. Oxford: Oxford University Press.

Willmann, Rolf, and Kieran Kelleher (2009). *The Sunken Billions: The Economic Justification for Fisheries Reform*. Washington, DC: World Bank.

World Values Survey (2014). "Interpersonal Trust." Retrieved from: www.jdsurvey.net/jds/jdsurveyMaps.jsp?Idioma=I&SeccionTexto=0404&NOID=104 (accessed September 23, 2014).

8

Constitution Making and Legislative Involvement in Government Formation

Cristina Bucur, José Antonio Cheibub, Shane Martin, and Bjørn Erik Rasch

The majority of democracies in the world today operate a parliamentary constitution, meaning that the government (sometimes referred to as the cabinet or the executive) is politically responsible to the national legislature (Cheibub 2007). A common feature, but not a definitional attribute, of the parliamentary system of government is that the executive is not directly elected but instead somehow emerges from the legislature, typically following a legislative election. Scholars have long been intrigued by which party or parties get to form the executive, particularly when no single party controls a majority of seats in the legislature (Strøm et al. 2003). Yet, relatively little research has been conducted on the formal role of legislatures in government formation in parliamentary regimes (although, see further, Strøm 1990; Strøm et al. 1994; Bergman 1993a, 1993b; Cheibub et al. 2015; Rasch et al. 2015).

This chapter explores the role of national legislatures in government formation. The specific focus is on explaining variation in what we term parliamentary investiture. Parliamentary investiture consists of a vote to demonstrate that an already formed or about to be formed government has the support of a majority in the legislature. While parliamentary investiture votes are a common feature of parliamentary regimes, not all legislatures require them.[1] Where they exist, recent research has identified important variation in investiture rules from one legislature to the next, with significant consequences for how politics operates (Rasch et al. 2015).

Investiture procedures have tended to be shaped at moments of major constitutional design or redesign – of the forty-four European cases since 1834 with some form of constitutionally mandated investiture procedure, thirty-nine (89 percent) originated in the writing of a new constitution or the significant reform of an existing one (Cheibub et al. 2015). Also, after they have been introduced, investiture rules are hardly ever abolished or weakened by constitutional amendments (the French Fifth

[1] In Denmark and Norway, for example, the government comes to office without any vote in the legislature.

Republic is an exception; see Nguyen-Duy 2015). It seems conceivable therefore that the constitution-making process is the mechanism that shapes the investiture process, and through this the formal role of the legislature in government formation.

We take Elster's (1995) concept of "institutional interest" as a starting point for our analysis of the origin of investiture procedures. According to him, an institution that participates in the constitution-making process is likely to write itself an important role into the constitution at the expense of other institutions (Elster 1996, 63). Framers have different motivations to promote the centrality of the institution they belong to in the constitutional structure. Career goals or aspirations to keep the same political office after the constitution-making process ends may act as a strong incentive to reinforce the constitutional role of that institution. A sense of pride and identification with the institution they belong to – "this may be an important institution since I am a member of it" – may also motivate framers to strengthen its constitutional role (Elster 1996, 63–4).

From this perspective, if the legislature (or prospective legislature) is the constituent assembly, then the constitutional framework will be biased in favor of the legislature. As Congleton (2013, 186) suggests, "[T]he procedures chosen and initial assignment of authority tends to align the interests of officeholders and those of the *formateurs*."[2] Elster (1995, 382) also expects institutional interest to act as a strong determinant of the "machinery of government." If true, then we would expect that a constitution-making process dominated by the legislature would lead to a strong formal role for the legislature in government formation. A strong investiture procedure means that the legislature is more intensely involved in government formation. In contrast, executive-dominated constitution making processes should result in a weak or no formal parliamentary investiture procedures. Where neither the legislature nor the executive are involved in framing the constitution (a pure convention), we make no claim as to whether the legislature will have a strong or weak formal role in the formation of new governments.

The constitutional engineering of investiture procedures is particularly important because the cabinet represents the apex of political power in parliamentary systems (Cox 1987; Laver and Shepsle 1994). By defining how access is given to the most important political offices in the state, the rules concerning government formation become a topic of great empirical, theoretical, and normative significance. We need to know not just how investiture rules vary, but why. Elster (1998, 117) warns that "constitutions ought to be written by specially convened assemblies and not by bodies that also serve as ordinary legislatures" in order to reduce the scope for institutional interest. Yet, the link between interests and institutional outcomes is not always robust. For example, Elkins and Ginsburg (2013, 11) argue that "evidence

[2] The *formateur* in this context refers to the constitution makers.

of institutional self-dealing is largely anecdotal" in constitution making and they find no proof that legislatures give themselves more legislative power than do other constitution making entities.[3] By focusing on the origin of investiture rules, we seek to better understand why some legislatures are privileged relatively more in government formation rules and specifically whether any such privileges are the result of institutional interests in the constitution-making process.

The remainder of the chapter is organized as follows. Next, we discuss variation in the design of investiture procedures. To understand better the constitution-making origin of investiture, we then discuss three cases of constitutional design and investiture – France, Ireland, and Romania. We complement these cases with a cross-country analysis of constitutional process and investiture rules. To anticipate, we find evidence that the nature of the constitution-making process impacts the formation rules enshrined in a country's constitution – executive-dominated constitution-making processes tend to result in weaker investiture rules whereas legislative-dominated processes tend to result in stronger investiture processes.

I. WEAK VERSUS STRONG INVESTITURE RULES

Investiture procedures vary along several dimensions.[4] The first one concerns the extent to which the legislature plays a *proactive* role in the selection of a prime minister and cabinet from the beginning of the government formation process. In some constitutions, legislators are entirely responsible for the choice of a head of government but play no further role in the formation of the government. Following the election of a prime minister by a vote of legislators, the government can be removed only if the legislature withdraws its support by passing a censure motion or rejecting a vote of confidence initiated by the government. By contrast, in other constitutions legislatures play no formal role in the selection of the prime minister but must approve the government program and/or composition before a new cabinet takes office. The prime minister designate engages in negotiations with parliamentary parties over the government's program and composition, at the end of which the duly appointed government must be subject to a parliamentary vote. Thus, as opposed to making the first move in the game of government formation, legislators cast a *reactive* vote, which simply confirms or rejects a government that is already

[3] To measure legislative power, Elkins and Ginsburg (2013) employ Fish and Kroenig's (2009) Parliamentary Powers Index. This index has been the subject of criticism from other scholars (see, e.g., Desposato 2012).

[4] It is important to note that we are not discussing whether legislatures matter for government formation. Legislatures obviously influence government formation in all parliamentary systems in the sense that whoever is forming a government must necessarily take into consideration the distribution of seats and other aspects of legislative politics. We are concerned here with the constitutional rules concerning who participates in the government formation process and how.

in office. In other words, the investiture vote is functionally (and often nominally) equivalent to a vote of confidence. Yet, it is not the same as a vote of confidence because the government cannot call it for strategic reasons.

The distinction between proactive and reactive investiture regimes may influence negotiations and the kind of governments that are formed. The latter arrangement provides the *informateur* and/or the *formateur*, an individual in whose selection legislature as an institution tend not to play a direct role (see Bäck and Dumont 2008), with a strong agenda setting position. The *formateur* can exploit the fact that the legislature is effectively faced with an up or down vote on the new government to obtain outcomes closer to her preferences (Romer and Rosenthal 1978). In comparison, the type of investiture in which the legislature plays a *proactive* role is more flexible. The legislature operates as if under an open amendment rule, and more than one coalition alternative might – at least implicitly – be on the table when the investiture vote takes place. Some parliaments even have elaborate procedures to handle the possibility of multiple alternatives; Slovenia, for instance, specifies a complex sequential procedure in the standing orders. Thus, it is plausible to suppose that the difference in the bargaining environment that each of these investiture approaches imply also affects some of the features of the governments that emerge, although not necessarily easily measurable characteristics such as the type (minority or majority) or duration of the governments.

The second dimension along which parliamentary involvement in government formation varies is the number of decision points. This dimension manifests itself in two ways: (1) in terms of the number of chambers involved in the formation process and (2) in terms of the number of times the chamber is called to make a decision about the government.

The majority of bicameral systems in Europe operate under constitutions which specify that government formation is a function reserved exclusively for one chamber, normally the lower chamber (Heller and Branduse 2014; Tsebelis and Money 1997). Yet, some constitutions require the involvement of both chambers (Druckman and Thies 2002; Druckman et al. 2005). For example, in Italy the president appoints the government, and to continue in office the government must win separate confidence votes in the Chamber of Deputies and the Senate within ten days of the presidential appointment.

Legislatures may be involved in multiple decision points even if only one chamber votes to invest a government. In both Ireland and Lithuania the legislature selects a prime minister proposed from within the legislature itself and only subsequently votes on the cabinet. In this sense, the legislature is firmly in control of the entire government formation process: although it empowers an individual to form a cabinet (and possibly negotiate a program), it retains the power to reject that government if it so desires.

A third important dimension of government investiture is the extent to which individual members of the legislature are actively involved in the decision process. This can be captured by the decision rule applied to investiture votes. Although the possibilities are infinite, there are essentially three decision rules employed in practice: negative majority, simple majority, and absolute majority. Absolute majority means that at least 50 percent *of the members* of an assembly need to vote for a government to be invested. Simple majority means that at least 50 percent *of those voting* must explicitly support the government to be invested. Since what counts is only the vote of those casting a Yes or No ballot, abstentions make it easier for a government to be invested as the committed supporters of the government might constitute less than half of the assembly. What we here call *negative majority* is the weakest of the decision rules from the point of view of the legislature. Under this rule, a government is invested as long as an absolute majority does not vote against it. Investitures based on a negative majority rule are even weaker than the situation in which the government remains in place as long as a majority, simple or absolute, does not approve a motion of no confidence. Under a negative majority requirement, a prime minister designate could survive even if a simple majority voted against him or her (i.e., as long as this majority has less than half of the MPs). Sweden has a *proactive* version of this decision rule, and Belgium and Portugal use a *reactive* (or confidence vote) variant of the same rule. Table 8.1 illustrates the great variation in rules governing parliamentary investiture across a number of European parliamentary democracies.

The entries in the table are investiture regimes in Europe since the first one we have been able to identify (the vote on the Monarch's Speech in the UK from the 1830s on). There are forty-four cases in total, including three instances of negative investiture rules. Today, a majority of European countries has some kind of investiture vote specified in their constitutions. All of the post-Communist constitutions have investiture provisions, as is true also for other European countries at the beginning of the third wave of transitions to democracy. The share of parliamentary constitutions with no mention of a vote of investiture has declined sharply over the last few decades. Simple majority investiture is more common as a decision rule than absolute majority. Also, the reactive form of investiture – similar to a confidence vote – is clearly more common than proactive rules where the parliament elects the prime minister.

II. EXPLAINING INVESTITURE PROCEDURES

What explains such variation in the formal role of legislatures in government formation? As noted earlier, recent research has suggested that investiture rules were created during constitutional moments – times when new constitutions were written or old ones fundamentally redesigned. As such, investiture rules could be

TABLE 8.1. *Investiture Regimes in Europe, 1834–2015*

	Absolute Majority		Less than Absolute Majority	
	Proactive	Reactive	Proactive	Reactive
Bicameral, single chamber investiture	Germany (1949–)[c]	France (1946–1953)	Austria (1920–1928)	Belgium (1995–)[b]
	Poland (1989–1991)	Poland (1992–)	Ireland (1922–1936)[a]	Bosnia–Herzegovinia (1995–)
	Slovenia (1991–)		Ireland (1937–)[a]	Czech Republic (1993–)
	Spain (1978–)[c]			France (1954–1957)
				Italy (1906–1922)
				Turkey (1961–1979)
				United Kingdom (1834–)
Bicameral, dual chamber investiture	Romania (1991–)	Yugoslavia (1992–2002)		Belgium (1919–1994)
				Italy (1948–)
Unicameral	Hungary (1990–)	Armenia (1995–)	Albania (1998–)	Albania (1991–1997)
	Ukraine (1996–)	Croatia (1990–)	Bulgaria (1991–)	Greece (1952–1967)
		Georgia (2004–)	Estonia (1992–)	Greece (1975–2016)
		Macedonia (1991–)	Finland (2000–)[c]	Latvia (1991–)
		Moldova (2000–)	Lithuania (1992–)[a]	Moldova (1994–1999)
		Serbia (2006–)	Serbia and Montenegro (2003–2005)	Montenegro (2006–)
		Slovakia (1993–)	Sweden (1974–)[b]	Portugal (1976–)[b] Turkey (1982–)

[a] Double investiture in the same chamber.
[b] The decision rule is negative majority.
[c] The initial decision rule may be lowered if no *formateur* pass the specified hurdle.
Source: Adaption of Table 2 in Cheibub et al. (2015).

considered part of a package of constitutional rules regulating the roles, functions, and powers of the national legislature. In other words, the design of investiture procedures occurred in tandem with the allocation of powers between the legislature and the executive. Cheibub et al. (2015) suggest that legislatures are most involved in selecting the government where the executive is endowed with strong agenda-setting power. They provide circumstantial evidence – both statistical and historical – that constitutional framers explicitly and consciously perceive the need to design strong investiture institutions in reaction to creating a relatively powerful executive in the legislative arena. In what follows, we expand on this perspective by exploring the possibility of a link between investiture rules and the form of the constitution-making process.

A number of different actors can participate in the constitution-making process. Constitutions may be written or rewritten by, among others, a constituent assembly, the sitting legislature, or the sitting executive. Here, we explore whether the dominance of either the executive or the legislature in the constitution-making process impacts the type of parliamentary investiture rules provided for in the constitution. Before exploring the issue with cross-national data, we consider three cases of constitutional reform, covering France, Romania, and Ireland. Our goal is to explore evidence of what Elster terms "institutional interests." If the legislature (or prospective legislature) is the constituent assembly, the constitutional framework should be biased in favor of the legislature. If, on the other hand, the executive dominates the constitution-making process, the legislature will not be given as significant a role in investiture. The three countries we have chosen to focus on are broadly representative of the variation in the role that executive and legislative institutions may play in constitution making. France during the Fourth Republic and Romania at the beginning of the country's transition to democracy illustrate the strong role in government formation that constituent assemblies may play. The Fifth French Republic and Ireland point to the opposite roles granted to legislatures by executives that dominate constitution making: while the former stands for the weakening of legislative involvement in the formation of governments in a constitution written by the Executive, the latter shows that legislatures may also be granted a strong role in government formation even when the executive dominates the writing of the constitution. Thus, the variation across and within our case studies provides a useful illustration of the different ways in which executive and legislative institutions may shape constitutions.

III. CASE STUDIES: FRANCE, ROMANIA, AND IRELAND

A. *France*

Constitution making in France during the 1945–6 period illustrates the self-serving tendency of constituent legislatures (Elster 2006, 195). The investiture procedure constituted a key aspect of executive–legislative relations that the Left aimed to keep under the full control of the legislature. Previously, under the Third Republic, the president named the new prime minister who appointed his cabinet and only afterwards came before the Chamber of Deputies for a vote of approval (Williams 1958, 225). The president's involvement in government formation was seen by many legislators as undemocratic. Consequently, starting with the "Law Draft for the Provisional Organization of the French Government," which was approved by the October 21, 1945 referendum as a temporary organizational framework until the constituent assembly adopted a new constitution, an effectively double investiture procedure was introduced. Under these provisional regulations, a single-chamber legislature elected the President of the Provisional Government in a public vote by an absolute majority. The prime minister was then required to submit his cabinet composition and government program to a new vote of the assembly. This procedure was preserved in the first constitutional project that was narrowly passed by the Socialist-Communist majority of the constituent assembly elected in 1945. However, the pure "regime d'Assemblée" (Gicquel and Gicquel 2015, 495) that characterized the first constitutional proposal was defeated in the popular referendum held in May 1946.

The constitutional project adopted by the second constituent assembly elected in June 1946 modified the investiture procedure. Article 45 reflected the compromise between the Left and the conservative Popular Republican Movement (MRP) by keeping the focus of the investiture vote on the prime minister alone, while allowing the president to propose candidates for the head of government (Williams 1958, 226). Paul Coste-Floret, the rapporteur of the 1946 constitution, argued that from the Constitutional Commission's perspective, the designation of the prime minister by the president ensured the former's independence with regard to the political parties and the legislature, while the investiture vote prevented the president from making arbitrary choices and gave the prime minister the necessary authority to form the government (Coste-Floret 1996, 17).

The French people approved the second constitution in the October 1946 referendum. The constituent assembly dissolved itself and elections for the first regular legislature of the Fourth Republic were held one month later. Nonetheless, as legislators were reluctant to accept a head of government without any knowledge of his cabinet, the double-investiture procedure was informally reactivated from the very beginning of the Fourth Republic, as prime ministers accepted a vote of confidence on the composition of their cabinets or effectively formed their cabinets before investiture (Williams 1958, 226). This practice was blamed for much of the governmental crises that characterized the Fourth Republic, as several prime ministers successful in the first investiture vote were unable to pass the second vote; some would even give up presenting a cabinet altogether (Massot 1996, 53). The 1954 reform, which lowered the majority requirement for the investiture of new cabinets from absolute to simple majority, did not make the double investiture practice any easier to cope with (Massot 1996, 56).

The making of the 1958 constitution points in the opposite direction, that is, to the weakening of legislative involvement in the formation of governments in a constitution written by the executive. When General De Gaulle accepted President Coty's invitation to form a government in May 1958, he demanded special powers to draft a new constitution. Out of respect for the institutions of the Fourth Republic, he went through the regular government formation process and obtained the investiture of the National Assembly on June 1, 1958 by 329 votes to 224. Two days later, the Constitutional Law of June 3, 1958 revised Article 90 of the 1946 constitution delegating the new government full power to draft a new constitution. According to this law, the constitutional project had to respect several principles, including universal suffrage, the separation of executive and legislative powers, the government's responsibility to the legislature, and the independence of the judiciary. Procedurally, the government's project needed to be endorsed by a consultative constitutional committee, made up mainly of sitting legislators, and the Council of State before being adopted in the Council of Ministers and put to referendum for popular approval (Gicquel and Gicquel 2015, 514–5). The constitutional draft was adopted by the government on September 3 and overwhelmingly approved by the people in the referendum of September 28, 1958.

The removal of the investiture vote from the 1958 constitution arguably reflected De Gaulle's belief that there was no (formal) place for the legislature in the formation of the government. His constitutional ideas were clearly expressed in the Bayeux speech of June 16, 1946, when he argued that the government should be formed exclusively by the head of state (Gicquel and Gicquel 2015, 497). Thus, the two French constitutions seem to suggest that assembly written constitutions are more likely to result in strong legislative involvement in government formation while constitutions written by the executive are more likely to result in no or weak investiture rules.

B. *Romania*

Following the violent collapse of Romania's communist regime in December 1989, the executive and legislative power was assumed by the Council of the National Salvation Front (CFSN). The provisional body included dissident communists and demonstrators and was led by Ion Iliescu, a former Communist party official (Birch et al. 2002, 91). Among the main tasks of the Council were the appointment of a commission to design a constitutional project and the adoption of an electoral system for the first free elections (Preda 2012, 284). However, the FSN's decision to transform itself into a political party and stand in elections triggered demonstrations that could be appeased only by the formation of the Provisional Council for National Unity (*Consiliul Provizoriu de Uniune Naţională*), which included representatives from other political parties and minority organizations. Half of the CPUN seats were kept by CFSN, with Ion Iliescu serving as president, while the other half was assigned to representatives of political parties and minority organizations (Birch et al. 2002, 92).The CPUN held meetings between February and May 1990, paving the way for concurrent presidential and legislative elections on May 20. The most important document adopted by this unelected body was the Decree Law no. 92/1990 of March 14, 1990 on the Election of the Legislature, the President of Romania and Local Councils.[5] Proposals for this key law were submitted by the CFSN committee responsible for the draft and the registered political parties to public debate, before the CPUN met for the first time on February 9 (Birch et al. 2002, 91–2).

Apart from setting the rules for the first free elections, the decree law provided a general framework for executive–legislative relations and defined the tasks and duration of the constituent assembly. Thus, the newly elected Chamber of Deputies and Senate were set to form a constituent assembly, which would operate concomitantly with their regular functions. However, the constituent assembly was not allowed to transform itself into a sitting legislature at the conclusion of the constitution-making process, as new elections had to be organized within one year following the adoption of the constitution (Article 80). Moreover, the president could dissolve the constituent assembly with the agreement of the prime minister and the speakers of the Chamber and Senate if a new constitution was not adopted within nine months following elections. Additionally, the constituent assembly was to be dissolved automatically if a new constitution was not adopted within eighteen months following election (Article 82).

Most provisions for the postelectoral executive structure were included in Article 82 of the Decree Law, which set out a relatively extensive range of presidential powers over government formation, foreign affairs, defense, and relations with the legislature, including its convocation and dissolution. Following elections, the president was required to appoint as prime minister the representative of the party or political organization with a majority of seats in the legislature. If no party held the majority, then the president had to select as prime minister one of the sitting deputies or senators after consulting the parties and political organizations represented in the legislature. The composition of the government needed to be approved by the Chamber of Deputies and the Senate but there was no mention of

5 Decret-Lege Nr. 92 din 14 martie 1990 pentru alegerea parlamentului si a Presedintelui Romaniei. Retrieved from: www.cdep.ro/pls/legis/legis_pck.htp_act_text?idt=7528 (accessed August 9, 2016).

the government's responsibility to the legislature. A broader debate surfaced during the CPUN meetings regarding the form of government to be adopted, whether presidential, semipresidential, or parliamentary. As this matter was left for the constituent assembly to decide, so was the question of whether the government should be accountable to the legislature or to the president or to both of them.

The transcripts of the CPUN meetings held during March 9–14 when the draft decree law was debated do not reveal any questioning of the [lack of] legislative involvement in the selection of the government (IRRdD 2009a, 2009b). The only proposal in this regard was that both the Chamber of Deputies and the Senate should participate in the investiture vote (IRRdD 2009b, 173). There were some discussions about the president's leeway in selecting a candidate prime minister when no party obtained a majority and whether he was bound to nominate the leader of a parliamentary party or any other legislator (IRRdD 2009b, 176–9). The issue at stake was how much discretion the president should have in selecting a new prime minister when no clear winner emerges from a general election. By and large, though, the legislature's ability to control the choice of the executive seems to have been taken for granted from very early on in Romania's post-Communist constitution-making process.

The presidential and legislative elections held on May 20, 1990 were overwhelmingly won by Ion Iliescu and the National Salvation Front (FSN). Of the 515 members of the new legislature that met as a constituent assembly on July 11, 355 belonged to the NSF. A twenty-eight-member Constitutional Commission was tasked with the drafting of a constitutional project, which was presented to the constituent assembly on December 12, 1990.[6] Debates on this proposal took place in the assembly between February 12 and June 20, 1991, leading to a draft constitutional proposal being published on July 10. New amendments proposed by legislators were debated during plenary meetings held between September 10 and November 14. The final draft constitution was approved by 414 out of the 510 deputies and senators on November 21 (Stănescu-Stanciu 2012, 129–30). In December 1991 the document was ratified by popular referendum and new elections were scheduled for September 1992.

Although the records of the Constitutional Commission have not been made public, we have full access to the transcripts of the plenary meetings of the constituent assembly dealing with the institutional nature of the new regime (Stănescu-Stanciu and Neacşu 2011, 2015). Similar to the debates held during the plenary

6 Interestingly, among twenty-three sitting deputies and senators (thirteen of whom were FSN members) the Commission included five legal experts who had not been elected to the Constituent Assembly. Antonie Iorgovan, the chair of the Commission, was a formally independent senator, but he was considered close to the FSN (Blokker 2013, 191).

meetings of the CPUN in early 1990, the government's investiture by the legislature was not questioned during the meetings of the constituent assembly. Very few proposals to change the provisions made in the Decree Law no. 92/1990 with regard to government formation were put forward. Among them were several suggestions concerning the identity of the prime minister to be selected by the president and the details of the investiture vote. The government's investiture by both chambers and the absolute majority hurdle were never under serious debate.

The concern regarding the legislature's effective power to control the president's choice of a prime minister stands out during the debates of the constituent assembly. Legislators had extensive discussions about how much leeway the president had in choosing a new prime minister and whether the investiture vote concerned the entire composition of the new government, including the prime minister. In his account of the work of the Constitutional Committee, Iorgovan (1998, 238–9) notes the legislators' insistence on denoting the president's choice as a "prime minister candidate," so as to strengthen the principle that a new prime minister and cabinet can take office only after passing the legislative vote of investiture. The selection pool for the prime minister post was also extended beyond sitting legislators, while previously the president was required to choose the prime minister from among elected deputies and senators (Stănescu-Stanciu and Neacşu 2011, 704). Additionally, where the decree law included a somewhat laconic provision that "the composition of the government must be approved by the Chamber of Deputies and the Senate" (Article 82, Decree Law no. 92/1990), the new constitutional draft clearly specified that

> (2) The candidate to the office of Prime Minister shall, within ten days after his designation, seek the vote of confidence of Legislature upon the program and complete list of the Government. (3) The program and list of the Government shall be debated upon by the Chamber of Deputies and Senate, in joint sitting. Parliament shall grant confidence to the Government by a majority vote of Deputies and Senators. (Article 102, 1991 Constitution)

Antonie Iorgovan, the chair of the Constitutional Commission, noted that the "approval" condition was replaced with the specific requirement to "grant confidence" in June 1991 at the recommendation of Swiss experts led by Professor Jean François Aybert. The main concern was that if the Legislature only "approved" the governing program instead of "grating confidence," then it would not have been able to withdraw its confidence through a censure motion (Stănescu-Stanciu 2011, 68). By and large, the evidence suggests that constitution makers were aware of the importance that the investiture vote played in the design of executive–legislative relations and strived to ensure that the legislature would be in a position to control the executive from the beginning of the formation process.

C. *Ireland*

Today, the Irish Constitution provides for a double-investiture vote in the lower chamber of the national legislature. First, in a proactive form of investiture, the legislature elects a prime minister who is then formally appointed by the head of state. Thereafter, the prime minister nominates the remainder of the cabinet for approval by the legislature in a second, reactive, vote. If approved, members of the cabinet are then formally appointed by the head of state. Any change to the composition of the cabinet requires a fresh investiture vote.

Given the assimilation of the Irish political elite into the Westminster parliamentary tradition, it is of little surprise that the fledgling state borrowed many of the practices and procedures from the British political system. Yet, some notable breaks in institutional design and procedures occurred. A key difference enshrined in the provisional *Dáil* Constitution of 1919 concerned the process by which the government would be selected. Retaining the overall character of a parliamentary system of government, the 1919 constitution granted government selection decisions to the legislature. The key break with the Westminster model occurred in requiring an explicit investiture vote, provided for as follows in the 1919 Provisional Constitution:

> 2. (b) The Ministry shall consist of a President of the Ministry, elected by *Dáil Éireann*, and four Executive Officers, viz.; A Secretary of Finance, A Secretary of Home Affairs, A Secretary of Foreign Affairs, A Secretary of National Defence – each of whom the President shall nominate and have power to dismiss.
>
> (d) At the first meeting of *Dáil Éireann* after their nomination by the President, the names of the Executive Officers shall be separately submitted to *Dáil Éireann* for approval.
>
> (e) The appointment of the President shall date from his election, and the appointment of each Executive Officer from the date of the approval by the *Dáil* of his nomination.

Given the limited historical records covering the drafting of the Provisional Constitution, one can only speculate as to the reason for specifying a vote of investiture, both for the head of government and in requiring a separate vote for each individual minister. Given that Ireland would initially remain part of the British Commonwealth, one reasonable explanation concerns the desire of the rebel legislature to ensure that the British monarch not be permitted a role in determining who would govern Ireland. The rebels wanted political power to be vested within Ireland and the obvious way to do this was to empower the lower chamber with the exclusive right and authority to select the government. Moreover, the 1919 constitution provides evidence in favor of Elster's institutional interest thesis: The legislature adopted a constitution which significantly enhanced its role in government formation – departing on this point from the Westminster model that otherwise served as the sourcebook for how executive-legislative relations were to be organized.

Following a peace treaty between Ireland and the United Kingdom, a new constitution was enacted in 1922. As part of the settlement, this constitution deepened the influence of Britain on the Irish political system, creating for example, a governor general as the representative of the British monarchy in Ireland. Yet, the Free State Constitution followed the earlier constitution in not assigning any role – formal or informal – to the monarchy or governor general in relation to the selection and appointment of the government of the Irish Free State.

The drafting of what would become the 1937 constitution was heavily dominated by the executive. In particular, Éamon de Valera, the head of government played a central role in shaping the constitution, although the draft constitution was formally approved by the legislature and subsequently approved in a popular referendum. Regarding the investiture procedure, the only significant change between the 1922 constitution and the 1937 constitution concerned a role for the newly created office of president. The president would formally appoint the *Taoiseach* and government, on the nomination of the lower chamber. Ireland remained a parliamentary system by most accounts, with a president as symbolic head. Notably, the 1937 constitution did not depart from the right of the lower chamber to select the *Taoiseach* and confirm the *Taoiseach's* choice of ministers. The drafters of the 1937 constitution could have assigned the president a more significant role in selecting the *Taoiseach* akin to that of the Britain's head of state in selecting a prime minister. Indeed, aside from formally appointing those nominated by the *Dáil*, the president plays no role in government formation, neither selecting the persons to hold office nor acting as, or appointing, an *informateur* to facilitate negotiations between parties. Thus, despite dominating the process, the executive, felt unable or unwilling to move away from the earlier constitutional process of parliamentary investiture.

The brief review of constitution making in France, Romania, and Ireland with regard to investiture procedures provides evidence that the constitution-making process shapes the investiture process. Ireland appears a notable outlier, with the last constitutional moment dominated by the executive but nevertheless producing a constitution that requires a double investiture vote.

It should be noted that the 1937 constitution did grant significant agenda-control powers to the executive, suggesting the possibility that the strong investiture procedure constituted a form of compensation for the granting of strong executive rights (Cheibub et al. 2015). After all, self-dealing is constrained by the anticipation of who must approve the constitution. Thus, given a status quo that favored the legislature at the time the 1937 constitution was being written, the executive would be hard pressed to remove the legislature's role in investiture knowing that the "offended" body would have to approve the proposal before being presented to voters in a referendum.

IV. CROSS-NATIONAL EVIDENCE

To investigate further the possibility of a relationship between constitution making and a legislature's role in government formation, we conduct a cross-national statistical analysis using two types of data related to the constitution-making process and investiture regimes. First, building on our earlier discussion, we separate investiture requirements into two broad categories. The first one includes negative formation rules (where there is no investiture at all or where the voting rule applied to investiture votes is negative majority) and positive formation rules that require the support of less than the majority of all legislators. This category includes countries such as Iceland and the Fifth French Republic, where there are no investiture procedures, and countries such as Ireland and Italy, where the investiture requirement is limited to a majority of the legislators present and voting. The second category includes absolute majority investiture rules, which represent the highest hurdle that new governments must pass before taking office. This category includes countries such as Germany and the Fourth French Republic (before 1954), as well as a good number of the East European new democracies, such as Croatia and Romania.

We code different types of constitution-making processes according to the coding scheme presented in Ginsburg et al. (2009) and the replication dataset publicly available. Owing to our limited number of observations we focus on the involvement of three particular actors in the constitution-making process: constituent assemblies/legislatures, sitting legislatures, and executives. We categorize constitution-making processes in our countries as either legislature-centered (if the actors involved are limited to a constituent legislature and/or a sitting legislature), mixed executive–legislative (if the executive was also involved in the constitution-making process along a constituent legislature and/or a sitting legislature), or a mixed constituent assembly–executive (if the only actors involved in constitution making are a constituent assembly and/or the executive).

The results of our analysis are presented in Table 8.2. Unfortunately, we have only thirty-eight cases with information on both the dependent and independent variable. The information on constitution-making processes and type of investiture is presented in the appendix. Given the small size of this sample, we refrain from including in the analysis any other variables except for those of primary interest. A probit estimation of the relationship between absolute majority investiture and different types of constitution-making processes suggests that absolute majority investiture is almost three times more likely to be adopted in a legislature-centered

TABLE 8.2. *Absolute Majority Investiture and Constitution Making*

	Probit Estimates (p-value)		
	(1)	(2)	(3)
Dependent variable: *Absolute majority investiture*			
Independent variable: *Constitution-making process*			
Legislature-centered	0.804 (0.075)		
Mixed legislature–Executive		−0.270 (0.607)	
Mixed constituent assembly–Executive			−0.378 (0.463)
Constant	−1.003 (0.004)	−0.495 (0.042)	−0.464 (0.060)
N	38	38	38
Pseudo R^2	0.072	0.006	0.012
Marginal probabilities			
Legislature-centered process	0.42	0.31	0.32
Mixed process	0.16	0.22	0.20

constitution-making process. According to the results presented in Table 8.2 (model 1), the probability of a more demanding absolute majority investiture decreases from 0.42 to 0.16 as we move from a legislature-centered constitution making to a mixed process that also involves the executive and/or a constituent assembly. These results should be interpreted with two obvious caveats: the small number of observations and the significance of our results at 10 percent level. Notwithstanding these limitations, we interpret these results as evidence in favor of the suggestion that the constitution-making process impacts the strength of the investiture rule that is ultimately endowed in a country's constitution.

V. CONCLUSION

The composition of the national legislature plays a key role in determining "who governs" under the parliamentary system of government. In the absence of a single-party majority, the formal rules that shape the role of the legislature in government formation become particularly important. Recent research has begun to unpack the great variety in parliamentary investiture rules.

This chapter explored the possibility of a relationship between the constitution-making process and the rules of parliamentary investiture. A degree of obscurity surrounds the origins of constitutional design. As Elster (1995) observed, constitution making is a craft not well studied or well understood. By defining the rules of political encounters, constitutions create incentives and rewards for some of the actors involved in the constitution-making process. Modern political science focuses heavily on explaining political outcomes by examining the consequences of the preferences of actors' interacted with institutions and rules. Within this research agenda, the understandable practice has been to treat the rules and structures – particularly constitutional rules and structures – as exogenous. Citing a political institution or rule as having a constitutional basis is a typical way to assure readers that the institution in question is truly exogenous of party and political influence.

In reality, political interests and outcomes are not just shaped by constitutions, but also shape constitutions. Political interests also reshape constitutions (Martin and Rasch 2013). Accepting this proposition may seem obvious, but the consequences and challenges of this are significant for scholars of constitutional law, constitutional change, and for political scientists interested in the impact of institutions. The dominant approach of treating constitutionally prescribed institutions as exogenous to particular models and theories of political behavior and political outcomes requires rethinking. The evidence presented in this chapter points to the potential for actors' interests to influence the design of constitutional investiture procedures.

Our point of departure was Elster's (2006) concept of institutional interest. His discussion was mainly to make a normative "argument for the view that constitutions ought to be written by assemblies called into being exclusively for that purpose and devoting themselves exclusively to that task." Our discussion has been empirical: There is a tendency for legislature-centered constitution-making processes to end up with investiture provisions that make legislatures more involved in government formation.

APPENDIX

TABLE 8.A1. *Investiture Procedures and Constitution-Making Processes*

Country	Type of Investiture				
	Investiture Regime	None	Simple	Absolute	Constitution-Making Process
Albania	1998–2013	0	1	0	Executive + legislature
Armenia	1995–2013	0	1	1	Constituent legislature + executive
Austria	1920–1928	0	1	0	Constituent legislating assembly
Bosnia-Herzegovina	1995–2013	0	1	0	None
Bulgaria	1991–2013	0	1	0	Constituent legislature
Croatia	1991–2013	0	1	1	Constituent legislature
Czech Republic	1993–2013	0	1	0	Constituent legislature
Czechoslovakia	1920–1938	1	0	0	Legislature
Estonia	1920–1934	1	0	0	Constituent assembly
Estonia	1992–2013	0	1	0	Constituent assembly
Finland	1919–1927	1	0	0	Legislature
Finland	2000–2013	0	1	0	Legislature
France	1875–1939	1	0	0	Legislature
France	1946–1953	0	1	1	Constituent legislature
France	1958–2013	1	0	0	Executive
Germany	1919–1933	1	0	0	Constituent legislating assembly
Germany	1949–2013	0	0	1	Constituent assembly
Greece	1952–1967	0	1	0	Executive + legislature
Greece	1975–2000	0	1	0	Executive + legislature
Iceland	1944–2013	1	0	0	Legislature
Ireland	1922–2013	0	1	0	Constituent legislature
Italy	1948–2013	0	1	0	Constituent legislature + executive
Latvia	1922–1934	1	0	0	Constituent assembly
Lithuania	1922–1926	1	0	0	Constituent assembly
Lithuania	1992–2013	0	1	0	Executive
Macedonia	1991–2013	0	1	1	Legislature

(continued)

TABLE 8.A1 (*continued*)

Country	Type of Investiture				
	Investiture Regime	None	Simple	Absolute	Constitution-Making Process
Moldova	1994–1999	0	1	0	Executive + legislature
Portugal	1976–1981	0	1	0	Constituent legislature + executive
Romania	1991–2013	0	1	1	Constituent legislating assembly
Serbia and Montenegro	2003–2005	0	1	0	Legislature
Slovakia	1993–2013	0	1	1	Constituent legislature
Slovenia	1991–2013	0	1	1	Constituent legislature
Spain	1978–2013	0	1	1	Constituent legislature + executive
Sweden	1974–2013	0	1	0	Executive + legislature
Turkey	1961–1979	0	1	0	Constituent assembly
Turkey	1982–2013	0	1	0	Constituent assembly + executive
Ukraine	1996–2013	0	1	1	Constituent legislature
Yugoslavia	1992–2002	0	1	1	Legislature

REFERENCES

Bergman, Torbjörn (1993a). "Constitutional Design and Government Formation: The Expected Consequences of Negative Parliamentarism." *Journal of Scandinavian Studies* 16:4, 285–99.

(1993b). "Formation Rules and Minority Governments." *European Journal of Political Research* 23, 55–66.

Birch, Sarah, Frances Millard, Marina Popescu, and Kieran Williams (2002). *Embodying Democracy: Electoral System Design in Post-Communist Europe*. Basingstoke: Palgrave Macmillan.

Blokker, Paul (2013). "Constitution-Making in Romania: From Reiterative Crises to Constitutional Moment?" *Romanian Journal of Comparative Law* 3:2, 187–204.

Bäck, Hanna, and Patrick Dumont (2008). "Making the First Move: A Two-Stage Analysis of the Role of Formateurs in Parliamentary Government Formation." *Public Choice*, 135, 353–73.

Cheibub, José Antonio (2007). *Presidentialism, Parliamentarism, and Democracy*. Cambridge: Cambridge University Press.

Cheibub, José Antonio, Shane Martin, and Bjørn Erik Rasch (2015). "Government Selection and Executive Powers: Constitutional Design in Parliamentary Democracies." *West European Politics* 38(5): 969–96.

Congleton, Roger D. (2013). "On the Inevitability of Divided Government and Improbability of a Complete Separation of Powers." *Constitutional Political Economy* 24: 177–98.

Coste-Floret, Paul (1996). "Rapport de Paul Coste-Floret sur le projet de Constitution du 5 mai 1946." *Pouvoirs, revue française d'études constitutionnelles et politiques* 76:1, 7–26.

Cox, Gary W. (1987). *The Efficient Secret: The Cabinet and the Development of Political Parties in Victorian England.* Cambridge: Cambridge University Press.

Desposato, Scott (2012). "Book Review: The Handbook of National Legislatures, by M. Steven Fish and Matthew Kroenig." *Legislative Studies Quarterly*, 37(3): 389–96.

Druckman, James N., Lanny W. Martin, and Michael F. Thies (2005). "Influence without Confidence: Upper Chambers and Government Formation." *Legislative Studies Quarterly* 30:4, 529–48.

Druckman, James N., and Michael F. Thies (2002). "The Importance of Concurrence: The Impact of Bicameralism on Government Formation and Duration." *American Journal of Political Science* 46, 760–71.

Elkins, Zachary, and Tom Ginsburg (2013). Can We Trust Legislators to Write Constitutions? Paper presented at the conference The Gap between Parchment and Practice: Ambivalent Effects of Constitutions in Developing Countries, American University, May 28–29.

Elster, Jon (1995). "Forces and Mechanisms in the Constitution-Making Process." *Duke Law Journal* 45:2, 364–96.

(1996). "The Role of Institutional Interest in East European Constitution-Making. Explaining Legislative Dominance." *East European Constitutional Review* 5, 63–5.

(1998). "Deliberation and Constitution-Making." In Jon Elster (ed.), *Deliberative Democracy*, 97–122. Cambridge: Cambridge University Press.

(2006). "Legislatures as Constituent Assemblies." In Richard W. Bauman and Tsvi Kahana (eds.), *The Least Examined Branch: The Role of Legislatures in the Constitutional State*, 594. Cambridge: Cambridge University Press.

(2012). "The Optimal Design of a Constituent Assembly." In Hélène Landemore and Jon Elster (eds.), *Collective Wisdom: Principles and Mechanisms*, 148–172. Cambridge: Cambridge University Press,

Fish, M. Steven, and Matthew Kroenig (2009). *The Handbook of National Legislatures: A Global Survey*. Cambridge: Cambridge University Press.

Gicquel, Jean-Eric, and Jean Gicquel (2015). *Droit constitutionnel et institutions politiques.* 29th edn. Paris: L.G.D.J.-Lextenso éditions.

Ginsburg, Tom, Zachary Elkins, and Justin Blount (2009). "Does the Process of Constitution-Making Matter?" *Annual Review of Law and Social Science* 5, 201–23.

Heller, William B., and Diana Branduse (2014). "The Politics of Bicameralism." In Shane Martin, Thomas Saalfeld, and Kaare W. Strøm (eds.), *The Oxford Handbook of Legislative Studies*, 332–51. Oxford: Oxford University Press.

Iorgovan, Antonie (1998). *Odiseea elaborării Constituţiei.* Târgu-Mureş: Editura Uniunii Vatra Românească.

IRRdD (Institutul Revoluţiei Române din Decembrie 1989) (2009a). *Documente privind Revoluţia Română din Decembrie 1989: Activitatea Consiliului Provizoriu de Uniune Naţională. Stenogramele Şedinţelor (9 februarie – 10 martie 1990).* Cluj-Napoca: Editura MEGA.

(2009b). *Documente privind Revoluţia Română din Decembrie 1989: Activitatea Consiliului Provizoriu de Uniune Naţională. Stenogramele Şedinţelor (13 martie–11 mai 1990).* Cluj-Napoca: Editura MEGA.

Laver, Michael, and Kenneth A. Shepsle, eds. (1994). *Cabinet Ministers and Parliamentary Government*. Cambridge: Cambridge University Press.

Martin, Shane, and Bjørn Erik Rasch (2013) "Political Parties and Constitutional Change." In Wolfgang C. Müller and Hanne Marthe Narud (eds.), *Party Governance and Party Democracy* (Festschrift in Honor of Kaare Strom), 205–29. New York, NY: Springer Science+Business Media.

Massot, Jean (1996). "Le Président du Conseil." *Pouvoirs, revue française d'études constitutionnelles et politiques* 76:1, 45–60.

Nguyen-Duy, Iris (2015). "France: Excluding Parliament from Government Formation." In Bjørn Erik Rasch, Shane Martin, and José Antonio Cheibub (eds.), *Parliaments and Government Formation: Unpacking Investiture Rules*. Oxford: Oxford University Press.

Preda, Cristian (2012). *Rumânii fericiţi. Vot şi putere de la 1831 până în prezent*. Iaşi: Polirom.

Rasch, Bjørn Erik, Shane Martin, and José Antonio Cheibub, eds. (2015). *Parliaments and Government Formation: Unpacking Investiture Rules*. Oxford: Oxford University Press.

Romer, Thomas, and Howard Rosenthal (1978). "Political Resource Allocation, Controlled Agendas, and the Status Quo." *Public Choice*, 33:4, 27–43.

Stănescu-Stanciu, Teodora (2011). "Noua Europă Centrală si de Sud-Est si Noile Sale Structuri Politics: Corpusuri Constituţionale. România." In Teodora Stănescu-Stanciu and Gheorghe Neacşu (eds.), *Prima Constituţie a României Postdecembriste*, Vol. 1, 13–71. Ploieşti: Editura Karta-Graphic.

(2012). "Constituţia din 1991." In Gheorghe Sbârnă (ed.), *Constituţiile României. Studii*. Târgovişte: Editura Cetatea de Scaun, 107–47.

Stănescu-Stanciu, Teodora, and Gheorghe Neacşu (2011). *Prima Constituţie a României Postdecembriste*, Vol. I. Ploieşti: Editura Karta-Graphic.

Stănescu-Stanciu, Teodora, and Gheorghe Neacşu, eds. (2015). *Constitutia Romaniei 1991. Documente*, Vol. IV. Ploieşti: Editura Karta-Graphic.

Strøm, Kaare (1990). *Minority Government and Majority Rule*. Cambridge: Cambridge University Press.

Strøm, Kaare, Ian Budge, and Michael J. Laver (1994). "Constraints on Cabinet Formation in Parliamentary Democracies." *American Journal of Political Science* 38, 303–35.

Strøm, Kaare, Wolfgang C. Muller, and Torbjörn Bergman, eds. (2003). *Delegation and Accountability in Parliamentary Democracies*. Oxford: Oxford University Press.

Tsebelis, George, and Jeannette Money (1997). *Bicameralism*. Cambridge: Cambridge University Press.

Williams, Philip M. (1958). *Crisis and Compromise: Politics in the Fourth Republic*. London: Longmans.

9

The Political Psychology of Constitution Making

Jon Elster

I. INTRODUCTION

The topic of this chapter – the psychology of constitution making – includes all stages of a constituent process: the convening of a constituent assembly, the selection of delegates, or *framers*, the drafting and adoption of a constitution by the assembly, and sometimes the ratification by the people, by an executive, or by an elected body. To explain the outcome of this process – or, more modestly, to identify explanatory variables – is a difficult task. Making a constitution involves more than politics as usual, and the explanation of constitution making differs in many respects from the explanation of ordinary legislation. In constitution making, (almost) everything that happens once the constituent body meets is endogenous. Although upstream actors – conveners and selectors – may try to impose their procedural or substantive preferences, they rarely succeed. Legislators are constrained by the constitution, which is obviously not the case of those who make it. Also, the external circumstances of constitution making tend to be more dramatic, as will be abundantly illustrated in the text that follows.

In this chapter, I focus on the motivations (desires, preferences) of the framers and, more briefly, on their beliefs. To explain individual decisions, the desire–belief model is usually adequate, although many issues remain controversial. The case of collective decision making is vastly more complex. Each framer can be assumed to have fundamental preferences over *ends* and beliefs about the appropriate *means* of realizing them. The ends jointly with the beliefs about the means induce a *policy*

The chapter is based on work in progress, in which I propose a systematic comparison of the proceedings of the Federal Convention in 1787 and of the first French constituent assembly in 1789–91. I am grateful for comments when I presented earlier drafts at the Princeton Institute for Advanced Study, at Columbia Law School, and at the departments of Political Science of the University of Chicago, University of Pennsylvania, University of Georgia, and Columbia University. Special thanks are due to my coeditors of this volume.

preference. The step from the many individual preferences and beliefs to a collective decision is much more complex, however, than the step from an individual's preferences and beliefs to his or her choice. Because of the paradoxes of aggregation discovered by Condorcet in 1785 and by Poisson in 1837, collective preferences and beliefs may not be well defined, and the collective decision may depend more on agenda control than on what framers want and think. More important, perhaps, the aggregation procedure may create an incentive for framers to misrepresent their preferences and beliefs, creating a risk that the decision deviates from the one that would have been taken by framers speaking and voting sincerely.

I shall not pursue these issues, which I have discussed elsewhere.[1] My purpose is to analyze some mechanisms of *individual* preference formation and belief formation in constituent assemblies, without proposing an account of how these individual attitudes mesh to bring about a collective decision. It seems likely that for given rules, processes of aggregation are broadly similar in constituent bodies and in ordinary legislatures. There are some differences, notably that vote trading is harder to enforce and probably occurs less frequently in constituent assemblies, notably in "pure" assemblies which meet only for the purpose of writing a constitution and then disband.[2] At the Federal Convention, one component of the "Great Compromise" broke down when the framers reneged on the exclusive right of the lower house to issue money bills that had been worked out in committee.[3] In the West German assembly of 1948–9, "the Minister President of Bavaria ... persuaded the SPD to vote for [the institution of] a *Bundesrat* in exchange for a momentary advantage and concessions which were subsequently all but abandoned."[4] Yet I believe that the micro-mechanisms of constitution making and legislation differ much more than the corresponding macro-mechanisms. Be this as it may, my focus is on the former.

I shall not dwell on the nature of constitutions, but assume familiarity with their basic features: allocation of apportionment, eligibility, and suffrage; sometimes but not always an electoral law; the separation of powers and mechanisms of checks and balance; a bill of rights or at least an enumeration of rights; and finally rules for amending and partially suspending all the preceding elements. In federal systems, the allocation of powers and rights between the central government and the state governments, as well as the system of transfers among the states, are key issues.

The empirical basis of the chapter is limited to Western countries. I shall mainly refer to the Federal Convention (1787), six French constituent assemblies (1789, 1795, 1814, 1848, 1852, 1946), three German assemblies (1848, 1919, 1949), three Nordic

1 Elster (2013), chapter 1.

2 In mixed constituent–legislative assemblies, where members can expect to cooperate at the postconstitutional stage, tit-for-tat reasoning may sustain vote trading.

3 Elster (2013), 254, note 48.

4 Merkl (1963), 69.

assemblies (Norway 1814, Sweden 1969/1974, Iceland 2010), six post-Communist assemblies (Poland 1989, Hungary 1989–90, Bulgaria 1991, Romania 1991, the Czech Republic 1992, Slovakia 1992), two Canadian constitution-making efforts (1990, 1992), and sundry others (Poland 1921, Spain 1931). In addition, I include proto- or quasi-constituent assemblies, such as the Continental Congress, the Round Table Talks in Eastern Europe,[5] and the Consultative Constitutional Committee that, in spite of its lack of formal powers of decision, had a nonnegligible influence on the 1958 French constitution.[6] Occasionally, I shall also refer to American state constitutional conventions.

Drawing on the French moralists, I propose a trichotomy of *reason*, *interest*, and *passion* as the main motivational types,[7] and provide examples of their causal efficacy in the constitution-making process. In my earliest comments on constitution making, I focused exclusively on reason, conceptualizing constitution making as a calm process of rational argument about the public interest.[8] Later, I adopted a more realistic approach, acknowledging the (obvious) fact that framers tend to engage in interest-based bargaining as well as arguing.[9] Even this framework proved too narrow, however, because it did not offer any role for passions, or emotions.[10] Because passion has been more neglected, I consider this motivation at greater length than the other two. I shall also, more briefly, consider *prejudice* – a motivation that the moralists neglected. Next I consider some aspects of belief formation in the constituent process. A brief conclusion follows.

II. REASON AND CONSTITUTION MAKING

Reason can be understood as the rational pursuit of the long-term public interest. Madison embraced this definition, when he referred to "the mild voice of reason, pleading the cause of an enlarged [i.e., not selfish] and permanent [i.e., not shortsighted] interest" (*The Federalist* No. 42). This statement is too starkly consequentialist, however. It should be supplemented by another statement of Madison's, referring to "the rights of another" and "the good of the whole" as the

5 Elster (1996).

6 Volumes I–III of DPS (1988) offer an unusually rich verbatim source of constitutional debates, at several institutional levels. The debates were not, however, shrouded in the secrecy that makes Madison's notes from the Federal Convention (Farrand 1966, Vols. I and II), published several decades later, so invaluable.

7 Elster (1999), chapters II.2, V.

8 Elster (1984), chapter 8.

9 Elster (1999–2000), in which the only reference to emotions of the framers was to the assembly-generated vanity and pride of the speakers. The reason-interest dichotomy is also at the basis of Rakove (1987) and Jillson (1988).

10 Other emotion-based approaches include Rubenfeld (2001) and Sajó (2011).

two values (*The Federalist* No. 10) that need to be protected from interest, and presumably from passion too.[11] Reason, then, has both a consequentialist and a nonconsequentialist side. In constitution making, the first aspect is paramount in designing the machinery of government, whereas the second is central in elaborating the bill of rights.[12] In its consequentialist form, reason also requires cognitive *rationality*, that is, a well-grounded belief about the *means* by which the long-term public interest can be realized.[13]

Often, agents have very different conceptions of what reason requires – different ends as well as different beliefs about means. Although some differences may be due to some agents holding irrational beliefs, that is by no means always the explanation. Framers may, for instance, attach different weights to liberty, equality, and fraternity, or to justice and efficiency. For some, the constitution should first and foremost be a bulwark against tyranny; for others, against anarchy. Some view the constitution as mainly a constraint on the pursuit of self-interest by future political agents, while others see it as tool for restraining their passions. When writing a constitution for a federally organized country, framers may disagree over the degree of centralization of power. When engineering the electoral system, some may be more concerned with achieving representativeness, others with ensuring governability. These examples mostly involve disagreements over ends. To cite one example of disagreement over means, among those who want the constitution to ensure governability some may argue that proportional elections with a high threshold is preferable, others that a majoritarian system is better. For another, we may consider the debate at the Federal Convention over whether the congressional majority to overturn a presidential veto should be two-thirds or three-fourths. Generally speaking, none of these differences can be ascribed to irrational beliefs. Moreover, these examples show that constitutional bargaining need not be based on private interests or group interests, as framers may also seek to reach a compromise over different conceptions of the public interest.

What *all* conceptions of reason have in common is the striving for *impartiality*. Constitutions should be designed neither to *favor the interests* nor *reflect the prejudices* of any particular group, including the framers themselves.[14] Reflecting a maxim by La Bruyère, "To think only of oneself and of the present time is a source of error in politics," framers should strive for impartiality over time as well as across persons.

[11] For a fuller discussion of the political psychology of Publius, see Elster (forthcoming a).

[12] This is only a rough correlation. The machinery of government is to some extent constrained by civil and political rights. Conversely, since *implementing* rights can be costly (Holmes and Sunstein 2000), they are to some extent constrained by consequentialist considerations.

[13] See Elster (2009a) for the relation between reason and rationality.

[14] They may favor group interests indirectly, by "disparate impact" rather than by "disparate intent." In that case, amending the constitution can be a remedy.

As constitutions are intended to endure for the indefinite future, they should not reflect the interests or values of the framing generation only. This statement obviously implies that the founding generation should not enable itself to deplete the natural resources of the nation. Another implication is less obvious, but more relevant: framers should allow for relatively easy amendment of the constitution.

To what extent is actual constitution making governed by reason thus understood? One answer is that framers are motivated by "ideas" if and only if "interest" has no purchase on the issue at hand.[15] The "if" part of this biconditional would be invalidated by cases in which interest has no purchase, but passion rather than reason dictates the choices of the framers. I offer some examples in the later discussion of the passions. The "if only" part would be invalidated by cases in which interest does have a purchase, but the choices are nevertheless dictated by reason. Framers do, in fact, sometimes disregard their particular interests in favor of the common good or general interest, as the following examples will suggest.

In the debates on the presidency at the Federal Convention, Madison at one point considered the option of direct election of the president by the people, which "with all its imperfections he liked … best," and went on to consider and answer some objections to this idea. Although direct election would be disadvantageous to the South because slaves would not count, he thought that "local considerations must give way to the general interest. As an individual from the [Southern] states he was willing to make the sacrifice."[16] In 1919, the German Social Democrats knowingly disregarded their electoral interests when they wrote female suffrage into the Weimar constitution.[17] In the Constitutional Committee of the Polish parliament after 1989, "some groups expressed [a preference for proportional representation] despite a potential party interest to the contrary."[18] In 1990, Vaclav Havel imposed a similarly counterinterested proportional system, to allow a place for his former Communist enemies in the constituent assembly.[19] One of Havel's close associates told me in 1993 that "this decision will be seen either as the glory or the weakness of the November [1989] revolution: we were winners that accepted a degree of self-limitation."

Two complications arise, however. First, a choice or a position may be *dictated by reason*, yet *correspond to the interest* of the relevant agents. The views of the suffragettes provide an example. In their case, nobody to my knowledge has claimed that their demand for female suffrage could be reduced to interest group politics.

15 This view is explicitly articulated for the Federal Convention by Jillson (1988), 14–17.

16 Farrand (1966), Vol. II, 111.

17 Evans (1980), 550.

18 Rapaczynski (1991), 617. He explains this fact by a general preference for ideology over Realpolitik among the Polish framers.

19 Elster (1995).

Other cases can be more ambiguous. In Norway, there is a consensus that sparsely populated peripheral districts should have a more-than-proportional number of seats in parliament. Although this apportionment is definitely in the interest of these districts (their enhanced log-rolling power enables them to build more roads and bridges than they could otherwise do), the general support for the policy is due to a belief that it is also in the *national* interest, broadly construed. In Iceland, by contrast, the (much greater) overrepresentation of the rural districts in parliament is widely seen as unacceptable and interest driven, as reflected in the fact that in 2013 the parliament tabled the proposal for a new constitution that would have removed this imbalance.

Second, the choice may be *dictated by interest* yet *correspond to (some conception of) reason*.[20] As I have argued, the general idea of reason as impartiality can be spelled out in many different ways. This fact creates an *opportunity* for self-interested framers to present their proposals as motivated by reason. They can also have a *motivation* to misrepresent their real motives, because of the opprobrium that attaches to brute arguments from self-interest. Thus large parties may be motivated to propose a majoritarian electoral system because it's good for large parties, but argue in public that it should be adopted because it promotes governability. Small parties may be motivated to propose a proportional system because it's good for small parties, but argue in public that it should be adopted because it promotes representativeness. Innumerable other examples could be cited to illustrate the basic fact of politics that agents, including framers, tend to present interest-driven proposals as motivated by the public good.

There are four checks on this tendency. First, some agents are genuinely motivated by the common good, as they understand it. Second, even those who are not so motivated cannot adopt disinterested arguments in a completely opportunistic way. Once they have made a principled argument in one context, they are stuck with it on future occasions as well, even when it is contrary to their interest (a "consistency constraint"). Third, principled arguments that fit the agent's interest *too* well may not be credible. Rather than proposing a measure tailor-made to the interest of her group, an agent may substitute a measure that benefits a few members of other groups and most but not all members of her own (an "imperfection constraint"). Finally, for some interest-driven proposals there may not exist *any* public-good argument, not even an imperfect one. Red-haired individuals would be happy if the constitution accorded them special pension rights, but it is hard to imagine a facially impartial argument for this claim.[21]

20 For an elaboration of the ideas in the following paragraphs, see chapter V of Elster (1999), further developed in chapter 4 of Elster (2013) and in chapters 24 and 25 of Elster (2015).

21 Strictly speaking, this obstacle could be overcome by stating a number of facially impartial criteria that, by design, are jointly satisfied by all red-haired individuals and only by them. I cite a famous

Hence the causal efficacy of reason can be direct or indirect, depending on whether it serves as a motivation or as a constraint. The German, Polish, and Czechoslovak examples cited earlier illustrate the direct effect. For an example of the indirect effect, consider the use of literacy as a criterion for the right to vote and to be elected. Many framers on various occasions have wanted to impose economic qualifications on suffrage and eligibility, yet have been reluctant to propose a system that would blatantly be in the interest of the wealthy. Use of the literacy criterion makes the proposal acceptable by diluting it, because, despite an overall correlation, some rich individuals are illiterate and some literate individuals are not rich.

III. INTEREST AND CONSTITUTION MAKING

In the discussion so far I have relied on an intuitive notion of interest. It is time to be slightly more precise. The idea will be understood as the pursuit of advantage at a scale smaller than that of the relevant collectivity as a whole, and further subdivided into personal interest, group interest, and institutional interest. By "advantage" I mean ultimately personal welfare, but also the means to achieve it, notably money and power. Now, strictly speaking, because groups are not actors, they cannot pursue anything. Yet group *members* may for reasons of their own seek to promote the advantage of the larger entity to which they belong. If a framer expects to stand for office in the first ordinary legislature, he has an interest in an electoral system that will work to the benefit of his political party. This indirect effect of personal interest is distinct from direct effects, such as the interest of the same framer in a system of government that favors the legislature at the expense of the executive. He has an interest in the institution to which he aspires to belong being a powerful one, even though the public interest may be better served by a more even-handed arrangement. However, as we shall see later, he may also have a self-aggrandizing tendency to believe that an institution to which he belongs ipso facto serves the public interest.

By and large, *group interest*, notably party interest and the interest of the states in federal systems, is more important than the direct personal interest of the framers. Parties want to win elections, and states to obtain a large share of the national pie. Constitutions can affect their ability to achieve these aims. I have already noted how large and small parties may have different interests in designing the electoral system. The balance of these interests at the constitution making level will often shape the system that is adopted. Similarly, if the constitution of a federal system shapes the system of financial transfers among the states, it will induce different interests in

American case of this kind in Elster (1999), 379. I do not know, however, of any examples from the context of constitution making.

wealthy and poor states. Some federal constitutions (Germany, Canada, and India, among others) impose equalizing transfers, while others do not. I have not been able to verify whether the federal constitutions that lack equalizing clauses were shaped by the stronger bargaining power of the rich states.[22]

Institutional interest, that is, the interests of the members of an institution that participates in the constitution-making process, can also serve as input to the process.[23] I shall give four examples, all related to the institutional interest of an upper house in the legislature. After Napoleon's defeat in 1814, when the allies debated the nature of the successor regime, Talleyrand persuaded Napoleon's senate to express a wish for the return of the Bourbons, as the allies would not accept any solution that could not be presented as desired by the French nation. The senate used the bargaining power conferred on them by this situation to offer, on April 6, a constitutional draft that, among other things, stipulated strong political powers and extravagant economic privileges for the existing senators. It turned out that the senators had overreached themselves. Their self-serving draft created so much public indignation that Louis XVIII was able to defeat their ambitions.[24] Regarding the Consultative Constitutional Committee that debated the drafts of the 1958 French constitution, an observer commented that "it would not be wrong to say that the members of the committee who were also senators thought of themselves as essentially representing the Senate, whereas the members who were also deputies [in the lower house] tended to see themselves as representing their respective parties."[25] In 1992, the Czech senators in the Czechoslovak parliament made a successful bargain. As a condition for stepping down when the federation broke up, they demanded and obtained the creation of an upper house in the newly created Czech Republic, whose seats would be filled by themselves.[26] Finally, institutional interest formed an obstacle, which was eventually overcome, to the abolition in 1969 of the bicameral system in Sweden. Regardless of party affiliation, members of the to-be-abolished upper house tended to be against its abolition.[27]

[22] Neither of two comprehensive comparative works on fiscal federalism (Boadway and Shah 2009; Shah 2007) raises this issue.

[23] For diverging views about the importance of institutional interest in constitution making, see the Chapter 2 by Negretto and 8 by Bucur et al. (this volume).

[24] For details and references, see Elster (2004), 25–7.

[25] François Goguel in DSP, Vol. II, 676. Gicquel (1988), 783, cites the discredit into which the National Assembly had fallen as an explanation of the lack of influence of the deputies. If the convener of a constituent assembly is part of a flawed regime that has to be reformed, why should the assembly respect its instructions?

[26] Pehe (1993).

[27] Stjernquist (1996), 290.

To show how *personal interest* can shape constitution making, I shall first cite two examples from the making of the post-1989 constitutions in Eastern Europe. They spring from the interaction between constitution making and measures of transitional justice, notably punishment of leaders of the earlier regime and confiscation of their ill-gotten gains. During the Round Table Talks in Hungary in 1989, Communist leaders insisted on the creation of a strong Constitutional Court as a backup protection in case they did not win a majority in the first free elections.[28] They predicted, correctly as it turned out, that if they lost the elections, parliament would enact strict retributive legislation, but that the Court would strike it down. Article 41.7 of the Romanian constitution says that "Property is presumed to have been acquired legally," which is an unusual sort of provision. To make sense of it, we may look to a decision by the Czechoslovak government on September 26, 1991, that future bidders for state-owned businesses would have to prove where their money came from. The measure was intended to block the use of "dirty money" that had been illegally accumulated by members of the former nomenklatura. The law created a presumption of guilt: the government did not have to show that the funds had an illegal pedigree. Instead, citizens had to prove that their money was clean. It is likely that the Romanian clause was intended to preempt such measures. In these cases, Communist or ex-Communist framers acted on their direct personal interest in avoiding prosecution or confiscation.

The role of personal financial interest in the making of the American constitution has been the object of much discussion. As holders of state or federal war bonds and speculators in the Western lands, some of the framers had clear interests in specific institutional arrangements, such as the assumption of the war debts by the federal government and the terms on which future states would be admitted to the Union. A substantial number of delegates who held either federal or state debts voted against their interest regarding their assumption, while others voted for proposals tailor-made to their interests.[29] (It may be worth while noting that the interpretation of Charles Beard's "economic interpretation" of the constitution as a claim that the framers were motivated by their economic interest is manifestly false.[30]) Overall, the interests of the states counted much more heavily than the personal interests of the framers. The interests of the slaveholder states were also to some extent promulgated by delegates from non-slaveholding states, who feared that the constitution might fail to be ratified in the required number of states if it were too hostile to slavery. From an impartial point of view, even a constitution flawed by interest may be better than the status quo.

28 Schiemann (2001), 29.
29 McDonald (1992), 106.
30 Ibid., 12–13; Elster (2013), 225–6.

IV. PASSION AND CONSTITUTION MAKING

I shall understand passion as mainly including emotions such as anger, fear, enthusiasm, and pridefulness.[31] Except for the last, these emotions are episodic, usually triggered by events such as war, revolution, or a financial crisis. In this respect they differ from prejudices (racism, xenophobia, misogyny), which are permanent features of an agent.

I shall defend and illustrate six factual and causal propositions about the role of passion in constitution making.

1. Constitutions tend to be made in times of crisis.
2. Crises tend to go together with strong passions.
3. Strong passions tend to undermine rational belief formation.
4. Only strong passions can generate the political will needed for constitution making.
5. Therefore, constitution making tends to be flawed.
6. Therefore, constitutions tend (weakly) to be flawed.

Propositions 1–5 express strong tendencies, or mechanisms.[32] They are not universally true, but exceptions are few. Proposition 6 expresses a weaker tendency.

Proposition 1: Constitutions tend to be made in times of crisis. Let me begin by citing an editorial, "The Fuse under the Fifth Republic," in the *Financial Times* of August 16, 2014:

> France's national crisis expresses itself in multiple ways. It is about poor economic growth, rising public debt and high unemployment. It is about the smouldering anger of France's ex-colonial minorities. It is about discredited political parties: the left trapped in anti-capitalist platitudes that its reformist wing is unable to squash, the right overwhelmed by scandals and factional disputes. More and more, however, France's crisis is about the presidential system of government and the Fifth Republic itself…
>
> The notion of a Sixth Republic, less presidential in nature, was a theme in the 2007 campaign of Ségolène Royal, the Socialist candidate … She lost, but the idea remains alive. True, fundamental constitutional change tends not to occur smoothly in France. Each of the earlier four French republics expired – in 1804, 1851, 1940 and 1958 – in a coup or a war. But the fuses under the Fifth Republic's

[31] Other "hot" states, such as intoxication, may also be at work. It has been claimed, for instance, that the decrees adopted by the French constituent assembly on August 4, 1789 were due, in part, to the fact that many framers were not only "drunk with disinterestedness," but also drunk in a more literal sense, after a good dinner (Kessel 1969, 193).

[32] Elster (1999), chapter 1; Elster (2015), chapter 2.

presidential system are burning. Politicians must waste no more time before giving new life to French democracy.

One can restate these facts from the perspective of the birth rather than the demise of the republics. The First Republic was established in August 1793, in the context of war and internal massacres; the Second in 1848, as the result of revolution; the Third in 1871, in the aftermath of the Franco-Prussian war; the Fourth in 1946, after the defeat of the Vichy regime; and the Fifth in 1958, under the pressure from generals in Algeria.

The French historical record also includes other constitutions that were made in times of crisis. The constitution of 1791 was the outcome of an acute general financial crisis, as well as violence in Paris and in the countryside; that of 1795 marked the end of the Terror; those of 1799, 1802 and 1804 represented successive stages in Napoleon's ascent to absolute power; the Charters of 1814 and 1815 marked the restoration of the monarchy; the Charter of 1830 came about through a revolution; and that of 1852 by a coup d'état. Compared to these epochal moments, today's French crisis does not seem very deep, which is not to exclude that things could get so bad that a movement for radical constitutional change becomes irresistible.

It is not easy to define conceptually what amounts to a crisis. For my purposes, I would emphasize widespread popular beliefs or elite beliefs that the current political system is (i) severely malfunctioning and (ii) unable to reform itself. Causes of such beliefs include a revolution or counter-revolution, a foreign or civil war, widespread terrorism, defeat in war, regime implosion, national bankruptcy, and massive unemployment. These causes do not always lead to constitution making, since dictatorship and anarchy, for instance in the form of warlordism, can also occur. My claim is only that in my universe of cases, successful constitution making occurs mainly in a crisis.

Empirically, the link between crisis and constitution making is shown in Figure 9.1.

The "many others" include virtually all the processes that I listed in the Introduction. The two Canadian failed attempts to write a constitution in the absence of a crisis also support Proposition 1. According to Peter Russell, "the present generation of Canadians will not try again to reach an accord on a broad package of constitutional changes designed to prevent a unity crisis. If in the near future Canada plunges once again into the constitutional maelstrom, it will be because there is *an actual, not an apprehended crisis* of national unity."[33] The Icelandic case is not yet settled, but it seems that the popular outrage that was caused by the 2008 financial crisis and that was strong enough to set the constituent process in motion, lost strength as the

[33] Russell (1993), 190; my italics.

IS THERE SUCCESSFUL CONSTITUTION MAKING?	IS THERE A CRISIS? YES	IS THERE A CRISIS? NO
YES	US 1787 France 1789 Many others	Sweden 1969/1974
NO	Iceland 2010?	Canada 1990, 1992

FIGURE 9.1. Crisis and constitution making.

economy recovered. The Swedish reform of 1969/1974 provides a strong counterexample to Proposition 1. It has in fact been called "institutional change" rather than "constitutional change" because of the routine manner in which was carried out.[34] There may be other such cases of constitution making "à froid," but I do not know of any. Partial *amendments*, to be sure, are often adopted without any preceding crisis, but not wholly new constitutions.[35]

Proposition 2: Crises tend to go together with strong passions. In the crisis-generated constituent processes I have studied, the proposition seems to hold pretty universally. It may not, of course, apply to every single framer. In France in 1789–91, the cautious Breton Thouret tried in vain to stem the tide of enthusiasm on several occasions. In Norway in 1814, the members of the union party kept a cool head and refused to embrace the exalted mood of the independence party. (These were not parties in the modern sense, but fluid groupings.) The independence party got its way.

Fear, a common emotion triggered in constitutional moments, can arise in several ways. In *revolutionary* constitution making, the leaders of the regime may use or threaten to use force against the opposition. In December 1989, the Bulgarian president Mladenov was caught on camera saying "Let the tanks come" when crowds outside the parliament protested against the delay in amending the article in the

34 Immergut (2002), 243. I would be cheating, however, if I refused to acknowledge this counterexample by claiming that it was not "really" a case of constitution making.

35 To see the importance of the word "partial" is important, we may note that the post-Communist constitution in Hungary was adopted by a series of amendments to the existing Communist constitution that, taken together, left little more than the name of the country.

constitution that proclaimed the "leading role" of the Communist party. He had to step down. Two centuries earlier, Louis XVI tried, equally ineptly, to scare the French *constituants* by calling in soldiers from the provinces.[36] He managed only to anger the citizens of Paris, not to scare them.

In *counterrevolutionary* constitution making, rulers or elites fear the people rather than the other way around. In my opinion (a minority one), this fear explains both the decision to convene the Federal Convention and some of the decisions taken by that body.[37] Shays' rebellion in particular scared the Eastern elites. In the famous "Tree of Liberty" letter to William Smith on November 13, 1787, Thomas Jefferson wrote that "Our Convention has been too much impressed by the insurrection of Massachusetts: and in the spur of the moment they are setting up a kite [a hawk] to keep the hen-yard in order. I hope in God this article will be rectified before the new constitution is accepted." I do not know which article he had in mind. Various articles cite "rebellion" (Article I.9), "domestic violence" (Article IV.4), and "insurrection" (Article I.8). It is clear, however, that he thought the framers had adopted the article in question under the influence of a sudden panic, "in the spur of the moment." The pervasive fear among the Southern delegates to the Convention of slave rebellions may also have contributed to the adoption of these clauses.[38]

With important nuances, the Prussian constitution of 1850 and the French constitution of 1852 can be seen in this perspective. Both were imposed after a short period of democracy, marked by the institution of universal suffrage. Both inaugurated regimes that were more autocratic than the predemocratic regimes had been. Measured on the dimension of popular participation in government, they represented two steps backward after the one step forward that both countries had taken in 1848. In one summary, "a decisive element in the success of revolution was ineffective crisis management and a loss of confidence on the part of political leaders. Collapse at the center demobilized both state agencies – bureaucracy and army – and social elites. Recovery [that is, counterrevolution] would be engendered by social fear."[39]

Fear can also originate from other sources. Even though the French framers of 1789 stood up to Louis XVI, they were scared by the antiseigneurial measures – looting of castles, burning of records, and in some cases killing of nobles – that took place in the French countryside over the summer of 1789. Their reaction to these events went from "fight" to "flee" in twenty-four hours. After an initial decision to crush the uprising, they virtually abolished feudalism overnight on August 4.[40]

36 For details and references see Elster (2013), 218.

37 Elster (2012).

38 Klarman 2016, 164.

39 Price (2000).

40 Elster (2007, 2011, 2012); Kessel (1969).

Subsequently, the important decisions by the constituent assembly to give the king a suspensive veto only and to reject bicameralism were caused, in part, by fear that the crowds in Paris might injure or kill those who voted against these popular measures.[41]

As a last example of how fear can trigger a process of constitution making as well as shaping specific clauses in the constitution, we may consider the birth of the Fifth French Republic. Under the pressure of events in Algeria, the parliamentarians of the Fourth Republic granted (virtually) unconstrained constitution-making powers to de Gaulle on June 1, 1958. As he said later, in inimitable telescoping, "I had a problem of conscience. I could just let things take their course: the paratroopers in Paris, the parliamentarians in the Seine, the general strike, the government of the Americans: it was written on the wall. Finally a moment would have arrived when everybody would have come looking for de Gaulle, but at what price? Thus I decided to intervene in time to prevent the drama."[42] It makes sense to assume that some parliamentarians feared for their lives and that their visceral fear affected their decision to abdicate from power. A crucial event that led credibility to the beliefs that triggered their fear, beyond what mere rumors could do, was the landing on May 24 in Corsica of paratroopers from Algeria, who ruled over the island through a Committee of Public Safety. The parliamentarians authorized de Gaulle to create a constitution with a strong executive power, hoping that he would solve the Algerian problem and then, like Cincinnatus, retire to his homestead. Their first expectation was fulfilled, but not the second.

Very importantly, we have to note the semantic ambiguity of "fear."[43] *Prudential fear*, as when we say "He took an umbrella because he feared it might rain," is simply a belief–desire complex. No emotion is involved. *Visceral fear*, as when we say "He ran away from the snake on the path because he feared it would bite him," is a gut feeling that can even arise before explicit cognition. In the political context, it can be difficult to distinguish between visceral panic and rational prudence. Tell-tale signs of viscerality are reactions that are disproportionate to the threat as well as irrational belief formation (see comments on Proposition 3). Moreover, one might want to distinguish visceral fear from visceral *anxiety*, the former being triggered "by an objective and present threat [and the latter] by an uncertain event that may or may not occur in the future."[44] In constitution making, fear may be triggered by the presence of soldiers surrounding an assembly, whereas anxiety can be caused by the belief that rebellions might occur unless the constitution is designed to allow for harsh repressions.

41 Elster and Le Pillouer (2015).

42 Peyrefitte (1994), 262.

43 Gordon (1987), 77.

44 LeDoux (2015), 11. Sajó (2011), 123–4, makes a similar distinction between hot and cold fear.

Enthusiasm, unlike fear, has not occupied the attention of emotion theorists. I shall follow the *Oxford English Dictionary* and define it as "Rapturous intensity of feeling in favor of a person, principle, cause, etc.; passionate eagerness in any pursuit, proceeding from an intense conviction of the worthiness of the object."[45] In the present context, the object will be a *political* principle or cause. We can most easily recognize the emotion by its behavioral effects: supernormal energy, subnormal need for food and sleep, and, crucially, lower risk aversion (or more optimistic risk assessments). It seems somewhat similar to the state of hypomania, "characterized by elation and a feeling of well-being together with quickness of thought" (*Oxford English Dictionary*). According to Marx, in the bourgeois revolutions of the eighteenth century (he probably referred to the French Revolution), "ecstasy [was] the everyday spirit."[46] Another striking example is found in the behavior of the Norwegian framers in 1814. According to one historian, they were characterized by "an incredibly vitality and restless activity" – "enthusiasm was their normal state of mind."[47] Although a more cool-headed member of the assembly dismissed their attitude as sentimental (*Schwärmerei*),[48] their behavior did not fit Oscar Wilde's definition of sentimentality: the desire "to have the luxury of an emotion without paying for it." They were exalted, but they *acted* on their emotion. They knew they might fail, although they underestimated the risks (see later).

In France, the decisions on August 4, 1789, were, as Tocqueville says, "the combined product, in proportions impossible to measure, of fear and enthusiasm."[49] Although the renouncement of feudal privileges may initially have been triggered mainly by fear, a wildfire of enthusiasm then swept the assembly. While their renouncement of their personal feudal privileges may have been due to visceral fear, the abolition of the privileges of towns and provinces was apparently carried on the wave of enthusiasm. On May 16, 1791, enthusiasm also made the framers declare themselves ineligible to the first ordinary legislature. In the words of the biographer of one of them, the framers were "drunk with disinterestedness."[50] In a revealing letter, some of the slave-owning deputies wrote that although the

45 In Elster (forthcoming b) I discuss whether enthusiasm satisfies the conditions that are usually required for something to be an emotion; specifically, the condition of having cognitive causal antecedents. The belief in the worthiness of the cause cannot be sufficient: the agent must also believe that its realization is *feasible*. However, in some cases (America in 1776, Norway in 1814) that belief appears to have been the *effect* of the emotion, not its cause. Be this as it may, the existence of this state of mind and its causal efficacy are undeniable.

46 Marx (1852), 19.

47 Steen (1951), 143–4.

48 Aall (1859), 359, 361, 422; see also my "A Race against Time," Chapter 6, this volume.

49 Tocqueville (2001), 148.

50 Lebègue (1910), 261.

assembly was "drunk with liberty," they counted on time "cooling the spirits."[51] On both occasions, the actual motivational mix was more complex. Vanity, malice, vengeance, self-interest, and a desire to derail the revolution also motivated some of the framers. Yet to deny any role of enthusiasm would be excessive.

Enthusiasm and fear also went together in the making of the 1848 French constitution. The process took place in a context of popular violence, the workers of Paris rising up on three occasions. On February 22, their rebellion brought down the reign of Louis Philippe and led to elections of a constituent assembly; on May 15, they invaded the assembly to protest against the government's lack of solidarity with the oppressed Polish people; on June 23, they took to arms and raised barricades in protest against the closing of the National Workshops. By June 27, the insurrection had been violently crushed. The Committee of the Constitution began its work on May 19 and delivered its first report on June 19 and its final report on August 30. Whereas the first report reflected a visceral fear of offering too little to the workers, the second was inspired by a visceral fear of offering too much. Tocqueville, a member of the Committee, characterized the atmosphere in which it worked as follows:

> [The] nation had a sort of frenzied desire to see the work of constitution making finished and to see authority established ... The Assembly shared this longing and was constantly goading us, though there was hardly any need to do so, for memories of the 15th May and apprehensions of the days of June, combined with the sight of a divided, weak and incapable government in charge of affairs, were enough to drive us on. But the thing that most effectively deprived the Committee of its freedom of mind was ... *fear of outside events and the enthusiasm (entraînement) of the moment.* It is difficult to appreciate how much this pressure of revolutionary ideas affected even those minds least subject to such influence, and how it almost unconsciously drove them farther than they meant to go, and sometimes even in a different direction.[52]

Anger, too, may shape constitution making. This emotion seems, for instance, to have been an important motive behind the Icelandic constitution-making process that began in 2010. As a leading reformer has written, "When countries crash, a natural thing for their inhabitants to do, *inter alia*, is inspect their legal and constitutional foundations to look for latent flaws and to fix them. This was, in fact, one of the demands of the 'Pots-and-pan' revolution' that shook Iceland after the country's spectacular financial crash in October 2008."[53] In the words of another observer, "the public *outrage*, which after the economic collapse was directed at

[51] RFAE, Vol. VIII, Document 10, 9, 12.

[52] Tocqueville (1987), 169; my italics. The word "entraînement" is polysemic, but one of its meanings (at Tocqueville's time of writing) is "enthusiasm."

[53] Gylfason (2012), referring to how Icelanders took to the streets banging pots and pans in protest against the government.

the government, converged on the issue of writing a new constitution."[54] More generally, social uprisings, whether or not they lead to a new constitution, are often fueled by anger, triggered, for instance, by a stolen election or an unkept promise of reform. *Grievances*, by themselves, may not be enough: a government is less likely to be overthrown if it does not hold elections or does not promise reform than if it steals the election or does not keep a promise it has made. Anger, like many other emotions, is triggered by an *event*, not by a standing condition. Until the 1760s, the American colonies patiently endured the long-standing Navigation Acts and other discriminatory measures, but rebelled after the (by comparison) relatively mild attempts by Great Britain to tax them. The taxes then transformed the latent grievances into conscious resentment.[55]

Enthusiasm and anger can go together, as can also be illustrated by the American Revolutionary War. An insightful observer describes its inception as follows:

> The revenues of Britain were immense, and her people were habituated to the payment of large sums in every form which contributions to government have assumed; but the American colonies possessed neither money nor funds, nor were their people accustomed to taxes equal to the exigencies of the war. The contest having begun about taxation, to have raised money by taxes for carrying it on would have been impolitic. The temper of the times precluded the necessity of attempting the dangerous expedient; for such was *the enthusiasm of the day*, that the colonists gave up both their personal services and their property to the public, on the vague promise that they should at a future time be reimbursed ... Though the colonists ... had neither gold nor silver, they possessed a mine in *the enthusiasm of their people*.[56]

Pridefulness, finally, can also motivate framers. Whereas ordinary language and dictionaries do not distinguish sharply between pridefulness and pride, psychologists make a distinction that parallels the one between shame and guilt.[57] Shame and pridefulness are triggered by the agent's belief that she has a bad or a good *character*,

54 Ólafsson (2011); my italics. It is usually assumed that the action tendency of anger is to *punish* the offenders, not to prevent them from doing harm in the future. In Iceland, the demand for a new constitution did in fact go together with a demand for punishment of those who were held responsible for the crisis. As the new constitution could be expected to remove some deputies or officials from public office, the first demand probably also had a punitive component.

55 Ramsay (1789), Vol. 1, 75–76. He cites (118) British politicians who claimed that things were the other way around: "though the duty on tea was the pretence, the restrictions on their commerce, and the hope of throwing them off, were the real motives of their disobedience." I believe Ramsay's Tocquevillian interpretation is more plausible.

56 Ibid, p. 255–6; my italics; see also Ramsay (1789), Vol. 2, 84. It may seem surprising that the colonists were averse to taxing *themselves* merely because their rebellion was triggered by taxation *by the British*, but the claim is confirmed by the foremost historian of the finances of the war (Ferguson 1961, 30). It casts an interesting light on the psychology of the founding generation.

57 Tangney (1990) refers to them as respectively alpha pride and beta pride, and Lewis (1992, 79–80) as hubris and pride.

whereas guilt and pride reflect the belief that she has performed a bad or a good *action*. Pridefulness is close to egocentricity, or amour-propre, the tendency to believe that my possessions are good because they are *mine*, that my choices are good because *I* made them, or that an institution is good because *I* belong to it. In the words of an eighteenth-century English reformer, John Jebb, "[one] maxim, which will be found to predominate, more or less, in the minds of individuals in every corporation, consists, in an overweening opinion and extravagant zeal for the interest of that body, to which, as it is often expressed, they 'have the honor to belong.'"[58] This statement applies with particular force to members of constituent assemblies, who are often extremely conscious of their historical role. This statement is illustrated by Marx's devastating comment on the French framers of 1848: trying to model themselves on the revolutionaries of 1789, they replayed the tragedy as farce.[59] Tocqueville, too, ridiculed the actors of 1848, commenting that "the tepid passions of our day were expressed in the burning language of 1793."[60]

Proposition 3. Strong passions tend to undermine rational belief formation. This proposition, though hardly novel, is sometimes contested. Although emotions can provide knowledge about oneself – I didn't know I could be envious until I felt envy – I do not believe they can enhance our knowledge about the world. This is not the place, however, to defend this controversial claim.

I shall discuss three ways in which emotions can undermine rational belief formation: by motivated belief formation, by urgency, and by a hot–cold empathy gap. Before I proceed, I should point out that emotions can also affect the formation of desires or preferences. The action tendency of an emotion may be seen as a temporary motivational change, such as the desire to retaliate against an offense. The temporary character of the preference change follows from the fact that emotions typically have a "short half-life" (after "counting to ten" the desire may abate). Little if anything is known about the rate of decay or about the shape – convex, concave, or linear – of the decay curve. The fact that these preferences are temporary does not, of course, imply that they are irrational. Indeed, with irrelevant exceptions the very idea of irrational preferences is meaningless.

58 Cited after Langford (1991), 210.

59 I do not think *shame* and *guilt* are prominent emotions in constitution making. Let me mention, however, a possible example. On two occasions in the late 18th century, framers wrote into the constitution a narrower franchise than the one under which they had been elected (Morrison 1917, p. 26; Troper 2006, p. 89). In 1848, however, the awkward character of this procedure seems to have struck the German framers: "An assembly elected at least in considerable part by manhood suffrage was *uneasy* about the exclusion of large portions of the labouring classes … as proposed by the Constitutional Committee" (Eyck 1968, p. 368; my italics). Possibly, cognitive dissonance is a better description of their uneasiness than either anticipated guilt or shame.

60 Tocqueville (1987), 74.

Emotions can also affect risk preferences, an effect that can be hard to distinguish from the impact on beliefs.[61] Thus one study found that fear made people more pessimistic and more risk averse, whereas anger had the opposite effect on both dimensions.[62] I conjecture (and shall assume) that enthusiasm is like anger in both respects.[63] In practice (outside the laboratory), it is probably impossible to determine when the impact of these emotions on behavior is mediated by irrational belief formation and when it is due to changing risk attitudes, or both. I shall refer, therefore, to irrational belief formation even when the real cause could be a change in risk attitudes.

To illustrate how emotions can induce motivated belief formation, I can cite a verse by La Fontaine: "Each believes easily what he fears and what he hopes." The tendency to believe what one hopes – wishful thinking – is well-known, and easily understandable in terms of something like Freud's Pleasure Principle. Counterwishful thinking – believing what one fears, against the preponderance of the evidence *and* against one's desires – is more puzzling.[64] The numerous fear-inspired rumors in recorded history are conclusive proof of the existence of the phenomenon.[65] Panics with no evidential basis, such as the Great Fear of 1789 or rumors of the return of Napoleon I caused great distress and, crucially, were used as the basis for action, e.g., in both cases cutting the grain before it was ripe. Panics based on unfounded rumors in financial markets are also well known. However, a convincing explanation is lacking.

The proto-constitutional actions of the American revolutionaries were largely based on wishful thinking or, perhaps, on motivated ignorance. A contemporary observer wrote that "the [colonists'] ignorance of the military art, *prevented their weighing* the chances of war with that exactness of calculation, which, if indulged in, might have damped their hopes." They were "buoyed above the fear of consequences by an ardent military *enthusiasm*, unabated by calculations."[66] Concerning the use of paper money to fund the war, he wrote that although it inevitably led to "a general wreck of property," a "happy ignorance of future events, combined with the ardor of the times, *prevented many reflections* on this subject, and gave credit and circulation to these bills of credit."[67]

The strong emotions of the night of August 4, 1789 induced a temporary preference change in many deputies. Did they also induce irrational belief formation? One

61 Below, I note that a similar problem arises when trying to distinguish between *time attitudes*.
62 Lerner and Keltner (2001).
63 I am gratified that Jennifer Lerner, an expert in these matters, agrees with my hunch.
64 For a discussion, with explicit reference to La Fontaine, see Thagard and Nussbaum (2014).
65 Elster (2015), chapter 22.
66 Ramsay (1789), Vol. 1, 146; my italics.
67 Ibid., 283.

may argue that the intended effect of calming the peasantry by these concessions was based on wishful thinking. Commenting on the Revolution generally, Tocqueville argued that such concessions can be counterproductive: "The evil that one endures patiently because it seems inevitable becomes unbearable the moment its elimination becomes conceivable. Then, every abuse that is eliminated seems only to reveal the others that remain, and makes their sting that much more painful. The ill has diminished, to be sure, but sensitivity to it has increased."[68] Commenting specifically on the decrees of August 1789, Jean Jaurès wrote that:

> Not only did the nobles think that the abolition of the tithe without compensation would increase their income from land, but they believed above all that this immediate satisfaction obtained at the expense of the clergy would make the peasantry less eager to pursue the abolition of the feudal dues: they hoped to divert the storm towards the goods of the church. *What a poor calculation!* Quite to the contrary, the peasants were all the more unlikely to accept the need for compensation with regard to the feudal dues as they had been dispensed with compensation for the tithe.[69]

The phrase I have italicized may be read as saying that the nobles were wrong, but not necessarily irrationally so, or as affirming that they were indeed irrational. Whatever Jaurès had in mind, I opt for the second idea. When ruling classes ignore the fact that reactive concessions (as distinct from preemptive ones) tend to generate demands for more concessions, they are subject to irrational wishful thinking.

The making of a constitution for an independent Norway was an exercise in wishful thinking that, like the American movement for independence, proved successful.[70] Rational observers of the international situation after the Treaty of Kiel (January 1814), which transferred sovereignty over Norway from Denmark to Sweden, knew that the chances of independence were nil. Deputies belonging to the union party knew it as well. Yet in their enthusiasm, framers affiliated with the independence party refused to test the international waters. On May 17, 1814, while the Swedish crown prince and de facto ruler Bernadotte was busy on the continent in the end-stage of the Napoleonic wars, they blithely proceeded to elect the Danish crown prince as king of an independent Norway and adopted the most liberal constitution in Europe. Remarkably, once the realities of international politics and the return of Bernadotte forced the Norwegians to accept subordination to Sweden, they managed to retain virtually all the clauses of the constitution that did not have a direct link to the issue of sovereignty. Contemporaries and historians

[68] Tocqueville (2011), 157. In addition to their effect on preferences, concessions may also shape beliefs, by supporting an inference that those in power are weak and that further demands will also be granted.

[69] Jaurès (1968), 469.

[70] See my "A Race against Time," Chapter 6, this volume.

all agree that a negotiated constitution based on a sober assessment of the situation would have been much more unfavorable to Norwegian interests. Fortunately for the Norwegians, their enthusiasm did not last long enough to make them wage war against Sweden, which would inevitably have led to defeat and an imposed and much inferior constitution.

The elections to the French constituent assembly of 1848 also illustrate the role of wishful thinking. As Tocqueville notes, in establishing universal suffrage in the elections to the constituent assembly, the revolutionary leaders "gullibly imagined that to summon people to political life was enough to attach them to their cause; and that, if they gave the people rights but no advantages, it was enough to make the Republic popular."[71] As noted, in 1919 the German Social Democrats were more realistic: they did not expect women to vote for them when they established female suffrage in the elections to the Weimar constituent assembly.[72] In France, the *constituants* of 1848 also showed massive wishful thinking, or perhaps amour-propre (fear of appearing to be afraid), when they ignored the fact that the overwhelmingly likely outcome of having the president chosen in direct elections would be the choice of Napoleon Bonaparte, whom most of them detested.[73]

Pridefulness, or amour-propre, can lead framers to make decisions based on an exaggerated belief in their own importance, a form of wishful thinking. The two illustrations I shall offer are mostly speculative and a priori, but with some empirical basis.

First, members of mixed constituent/legislative assemblies may be tempted to write a very important role for the legislature into the constitution, with few checks on its activities. They will, therefore, tend to be opposed to bicameralism, executive veto, and judicial review. These tendencies were realized in the French constitutions of 1848 and 1946, and the Polish constitution of 1921. Pure constituent assemblies, such as the Federal Convention, the Norwegian assembly of 1814, and the German assembly of 1948–9, are less likely to have this legislative-centric bias.[74] The bias may, however, be due to institutional interest (see earlier) rather than to pridefulness.

Second, the belief of the framers in the excellence of their constitution may induce a preference for strict amendment clauses, to prevent lesser mortals in the future from tampering with it. I shall cite at some length, partly for its amusing

[71] Tocqueville (1987), 97.

[72] Evans (1980), 550.

[73] A good summary of the debates is Bastid (1945), Vol. I, 105–22; see also Elster (2018).

[74] Ginsburg, Elkins, and Blount (2009), p. 213, do not find this tendency in their constitutional data set. I question, however, the validity of their classification. They include, for instance thirty-three constitutions of the Dominican Republic, four of them enacted by the dictator Trujillo. See also Chapters 2 by Negretto and 8 by Bucur et al. (this volume).

language, a passage in which Bentham heaps ridicule on the attempt by the writers of the French constitution of 1791 to make revision of their document virtually impossible:

> Twelve hundred infallible persons [the number of deputies to the *Constituante*] deriving their infallibility like the Brahmins from birth, like the popes from election, or like the Grand Lama from something between both, to all this I am ready to subscribe without difficulty. But an assembly of the same number of men brought into the world without a miracle, subject to human infirmities and passions, selected by their fellow citizens it is true, but taken out of the general mass, from the moment of their taking their seats doubting, disputing, changing, struggling, wrangling, sometimes one man's notions prevailing, sometimes another, that all this heterogeneous mass after a ferment of two years and a half, should all of a sudden at a certain hour of a certain day have *worked itself up into infallibility*, each man resolved that the whole nation, that a nation of 25 million, shall instantly become and to the end of time continue satisfied with the whole and very part of a composition with which taken in its totality not a single one of them is so much as satisfied himself, a measure of inconsistency and presumption like this is almost too much to believe.[75]

Although Bentham does not explicitly attribute the presumption of the French framers to their amour-propre, the passage is certainly consistent with this view. The same comment applies to a passage where Tocqueville decries the strict amendment clause of the 1848 constitution, which could be revised only by a new constituent assembly if the national assembly voted to do so with a majority of three quarters. Commenting on this clause (and mistakenly asserting that a four-fifths majority would be needed), Tocqueville wrote that it "made any regular amendment practically impossible … I have long thought that, instead of *trying to make our forms of government eternal*, we should pay attention to making methodical change an easy matter. All things considered, I find that less dangerous than the opposite alternative. I thought one should treat the French people like those lunatics whom one is careful not to bind lest they become infuriated by the constraint."[76]

Fear-induced counterwishful thinking in constitution making can have several sources. Revolutionaries may overestimate the ruthlessness and the capacity of rulers (or would-be rulers), and rulers overestimate the same qualities in the people. The constitutional transitions in Eastern Europe in 1989 may perhaps illustrate the first case. Although it is clear in hindsight that the fears of a Soviet invasion were groundless, the proposition that the oppositional forces were needlessly fearful, given

[75] Bentham (2002), 278–9; my italics.

[76] Tocqueville (1987), 181; my italics. The reason he offers against very tight amendment rules is somewhat eccentric. A more general argument is that if the constitution makes it impossible to adopt measures that are consistently favored by a large majority of the citizens, they may take extraconstitutional, revolutionary action.

what was known at the time, is hard to prove. Perhaps the best evidence comes from Hungary. Here, the older generation, who had experienced the crushing of the 1956 uprising, tended to be more cautious and make less radical demands than younger people.[77] The second case can be illustrated by counterrevolutionary constitutions that are so harsh that that they generate more hatred than fear, thus working against their purpose. I cannot cite, however, any unambiguous historical instances.

Urgency is an important feature of emotions. By this term I understand a preference for immediate over delayed *action*, as distinct, at least analytically, from a preference for immediate over delayed *reward*.[78] Urgency may also be characterized as a form of *inaction–aversion*. In situations that do not require immediate action, urgency can be a source of suboptimal investment in information, as illustrated by the saying, "Marry in haste, repent at leisure." The repentance may be due to the short half-life of the emotion, but also to the agent devoting insufficient time to find out whether the other person might have some undesirable properties. (In some societies, the norm of a long engagement period counteracts both effects.) Also, urgency may prevent the agent from gathering information that might correct her wishful thinking, which is, after all, somewhat constrained by facts.[79] In a constitution-making context, urgency can make an assembly ignore its own rules about proceeding slowly, for instance, by a rule that a motion cannot be adopted on the day it is proposed. In 1814, the Norwegian framers a proposal made on April 16 that was adopted on the same day, although several speakers objected that the rules adopted on April 12 prevented discussion of a subject that had not been announced the previous day.[80] The rules were swept away by the very emotions they were supposed to contain, just as anger may cause one to ignore the rule of counting to ten before acting in anger.

Earlier, the French *constituants* behaved in the same manner. Many of them were familiar with the British system of requiring several readings of a parliamentary bill to prevent impulsive decisions. Following that model, the Règlement that the constituent assembly adopted on July 28, 1789 contained two delay clauses. Article IV.4 says that "No proposal can be discussed on the day of the session in which it has been proposed, except if the matter is urgent and the assembly decides that the proposal should be discussed immediately." As acts of self-binding go, this is not very constraining. An addition to Article IV says that "Any proposal in legislative or constitutional matters must be brought to discussion on three different days." Almost from the beginning, and certainly on August 4, the assembly ignored this rule. In a letter

77 Schiemann (2005), 41–9 emphasizes the risk-averse attitude of the older generation, but, as I noted in the text, their cautious behavior could also be explained by a pessimistic cognitive bias.

78 Elster (2009b).

79 Klein and Kunda (1992).

80 Aaal (1859), 410; see also 413.

to his constituency, the Comte d'Antraigues complains that in order to "engage the … assembly to consent to all the decrees of August 4 one had to … destroy the wisest rules of the assembly itself, which put a brake on hasty deliberations." Having tried to stem the tide on August 4, the Marquis de Foucauld also referred to the violation of the rules in a speech on August 6. In response, those who wanted immediate action said that "an élan of patriotism does not need three days" and "since one cannot vary in such sentiments, the three days would be a pointless waste of time."[81] The first statement reflects urgency, the second the hot–cold empathy gap (see later).

The recent Icelandic constitution making process was shaped in part by anger-induced urgency, or inaction–aversion. It is at least arguable that the urgency led to flawed cognition. The crisis created an enormous impetus to *do something*, and the prospect of making a new constitution provided an outlet for the urge. If the organizers had taken the time to reflect more deeply on the causes of the crisis, it is not clear that constitutional flaws would have been among the most important. The Icelandic banks were victims of the hubristic overstretching that was observed in many other countries, where few if any groups blamed the constitution for the disaster. The Icelandic constitution *was* flawed, and Iceland *did* have a crisis, and in the urgency of the moment the causal link from the first fact to the second may have seemed obvious.

The *hot–cold empathy gap* refers to the fact that "when in a 'hot' state (i.e., craving, angry, jealous, sad, etc.) people have difficulty imagining themselves in a cold state, and thus miscalculate the speed with which such a state will dissipate."[82] This failure to recognize that emotions have a short half-life is a form of irrationality. In the Norwegian and French examples just cited, the framers may have been willing to waive the rules because they were certain that they would never waver about *this* decision, even though a few days earlier they had recognized the abstract possibility of impulsive decision making. Yet although urgency and an empathy gap often go together, they are analytically distinct. Sometimes, people say, "Let's punish now, while we're still angry."

Proposition 4. Only strong passions can generate the political will needed for constitution making. Whereas propositions 2 and 3 imply only a claim that

[81] Kessel (1969), 127, 200.

[82] Loewenstein (2000), 428. He also identifies a "cold–hot" empathy gap: "when in a 'cold' state (i.e., not hungry, angry, in pain, etc.), it is difficult to imagine what it would feel like to be in a 'hot' state or to imagine how one might behave in such a state" (ibid.)). It may also be difficult to imagine how *others* would behave: In 1779, "the British supposing the Americans, to be influenced, by the considerations which bias men in the languid scenes of tranquil life, and not reflecting on the sacrifices which enthusiastic patriotism is willing to make," thought they could bring the colonies to their knees by devastating their possessions (Ramsay 1789, Vol. 2, 68). Americans who should have known better made the same mistake in the Vietnam War (MacMaster 1997, 163).

constitution making and passion tend to go to together, Proposition 4 asserts that constitution making *requires* passion to succeed. As the saying has it, "Never let a good crisis go to waste." As an example, consider the redrawing of the map of France during the Revolution. Although the inefficiencies and pathologies of the old divisions of the country into provinces and other subunits were widely recognized, any reform was blocked by the vested interests of one privileged group or another. On October 19, 1789, when the constituent assembly debated the new division of the country into *départements*, the *constituant* Clermont-Tonnerre said that "Anarchy is a frightening yet necessary passage, and the only moment one can establish a new order of things. It is not in calm times that one can take uniform measures." As a further example, consider a passage from *The Federalist* No. 49:

> All the existing [state] constitutions were formed in the midst of a danger which *repressed the passions most unfriendly to order and concord*; of an *enthusiastic* confidence of the people *in* their patriotic leaders, which *stifled the ordinary diversity of opinions* on great national questions; of a universal ardor for new and opposite forms, produced by a *universal resentment and indignation* against the ancient government; and whilst no spirit of party connected with the changes to be made, or the abuses to be reformed, could mingle its leaven in the operation (my italics).

Quite generally, a major obstacle to a political reform arises when it hurts powerful and concentrated interests, which are usually better organized than the more numerous and more diffuse beneficiaries. To overcome these interests, passion is needed. In a famous maxim, La Bruyère said that "Nothing is easier for passion than to overcome reason; its great triumph is to conquer interest." One might add, as a corollary, that nothing is easier for interest than to overcome reason, except when reason allies itself with passion. Enthusiasm embodies this alliance. Kant asserted that without this emotion, "nothing great in the world has even been done."[83] He added, consistently with Proposition 3, that while enthusiasts may choose the right ends, they are incapable of determining the right means. For them, the best easily becomes the enemy of the good.

Emotions of anger or fear can also overcome entrenched interests. As noted by *The Federalist*, divergent interests of the thirteen American states would have created an insuperable obstacle to collective action in 1774, were it not for the anger against Great Britain that united them. When the war was as good as won, the emotion subsided and private interest regained supremacy. Commenting in 1782 on the failure of a plan to arm the slaves in the fight against the British, George Washington wrote, "I must confess that I am not at all astonished at the failure of your plan. That Spirit of Freedom, which at the commencement of this contest

[83] For references, see Elster (2013), 90, note 267.

would have sacrificed everything to the attainment of its object, has long since subsided and *every selfish Passion* has taken its place."[84] Tocqueville claimed that the only reason why the Paris bourgeoisie managed to crush the worker insurrection of June 1848 was the acute character of the danger: "If the rebellion had been less radical and seemed less fierce, probably most of the bourgeoisie would have stayed at home."[85]

Proposition 5. Constitution making tends to be flawed. If it is true (a) that the adoption of a constitution requires passion and (b) that passion undermines rational belief formation, there will be a tendency for the constitution-making process to be flawed, that is, to be based on irrational cognitions. As this proposition is a logical consequence of two earlier ones, I need not adduce separate evidence for it.

Proposition 6. Constitutions tend (weakly) to be flawed. The idea of a flawed constitution can be understood in several ways. One can understand it as pointing to an intrinsic instability or inefficiency of the political system. Illustrations include the French constitution of 1848, which set an apparently omnipotent executive up against an apparently omnipotent legislature, and the American Articles of Confederation that were unable to prevent free-rider behavior by the member states. One might also understand the idea of a flawed constitution along normative lines, if it creates a narrow suffrage or eligibility, a skewed apportionment, or a regressive tax system. Although the presence of these flaws may also destabilize the constitution, that fact is not the only reason why they are flaws. Whether or not they have a destabilizing effect, such constitutions are flawed because they fail the test of impartiality. On different normative grounds, we may also say that a constitution is flawed if it has a strong status quo bias, either because it is very difficult to amend or because the machinery of government has numerous veto points that make even legislative change difficult. I believe the American constitution suffers from both of the latter flaws.

Whichever conception of flawedness we adopt, a constitution that is flawed because of the process by which it was adopted may be superior to the preceding state of affairs. The American constitution, although shaped by excessive fear of "democracy," is certainly superior, by any criterion, to the Articles of Confederation. The constitution of the Fifth French Republic is flawed, partly because of the urgency with which it was adopted and that left many issues unresolved, but it is arguably superior to that of the Fourth Republic, which invested too much power in the legislature.

Also, that a process is flawed does not imply that the constitution it produces is flawed. In France in 1789, the adoption of a merely suspensive royal veto and the

[84] Cited from Taylor (2016), 233; my italics.

[85] Tocqueville (1987), 144.

rejection of bicameralism were caused, at least in part, by the fear of violence by the crowds in Paris. Although much of the fear was based on groundless rumors, it was causally efficacious in shaping some of the votes. Yet it would be hard to make the case that an absolute veto and a bicameral legislature would have been better. In Norway in 1814, urgency and wishful thinking affected the process, but – apart from the claim to independence – not the substance of the document.

Haste is perhaps the most common reason why constitutions are flawed. Urgency can prevent framers from taking the time to examine whether their document is coherent and whether clauses that appear innocuous in isolation might have undesirable effects when taken together. I shall give some examples from the American constitution, the German constitution of 1919, and the French constitution of 1958.

The American constitution was written in less than four months, and left many gaps. One of the scenarios it allows has been summarized as follows.

> Let us assume that I am elected vice president and am an evil, diabolical man. I behave badly, even criminally, in office. The House of Representatives impeaches me. I solemnly march into the Senate chamber for my trial. My team of lawyers takes its place in the designated spot on the floor. And I pick up the gavel and assume my post as the presiding officer at my own impeachment trial.[86]

This absurd possibility follows logically from the conjunction of Article I, Section 3, Clause 4 of the constitution and Clause 6 of the same Article. The vice presidency also opens for another possibility that the framers never anticipated, that a presidential candidate might deliberately choose a vice president who is so bad that Congress would never dare to impeach the president. Richard Nixon is said to have joked that Spiro Agnew was his insurance against impeachment.[87]

The Weimar constitution offers another example. It was adopted after the assembly had deliberated for six months, serving both as a legislative and a constituent body, in a context of domestic violence and international pressures. If the assembly had been able to deliberate calmly and methodically, it might have detected the anomaly arising from the conjunction of two clauses. Article 48 said that "In case public safety is seriously threatened or disturbed, the Reich President may take the measures necessary to reestablish law and order, if necessary using armed force … The Reich President has to inform Reichstag immediately about all measures undertaken which are based on paragraphs 1 and 2 of this article. The measures have to be suspended immediately if Reichstag demands so." The last clause was presumably intended to provide a check on presidential discretion. It was

86 Paulsen (1998), 75. For a different view, see Goldstein (2000).

87 Kyvig (2008), 118, 144. Strictly speaking, this issue arises only in modern times, when candidates for the presidency and the vice presidency form a ticket.

undermined, however, by Article 25: "The Reich president has the right to dissolve the Reichstag, but only once for the same reason. New elections, at the latest, are held 60 days after the dissolution." Using Article 25, the president could (and did) threaten to dissolve the Reichstag should it vote to annul any measures taken under Article 48. This mechanism opened the way to power for Hitler.

The constitution of the Fifth French Republic also suffers from having been adopted in a hurry, in the wake of a nearly successful coup by the generals in Algeria. Two of its flaws or gaps that appeared with time could have been anticipated by a more deliberate procedure. First, while the constitution states that the prime minister is appointed by the president, it neglected to say that the president can dismiss him. To fill this gap, de Gaulle asked his prime ministers to sign an undated letter of resignation when they were appointed.[88] Second, at the time no one seems to have envisaged the possibility of "cohabitation," with the president and the prime minister belonging to opposite political parties. Had they done so, they would perhaps have inscribed simultaneous elections and equal length of tenure for the president and for the deputies.

One should add, however, that urgency can be rational. We need to distinguish between objective haste, dictated by circumstances, and subjective (needless and harmful) haste, dictated by the urgency of emotion. A country undergoing a crisis may not be able to afford to take the time that a careful legal construction would require, any more than a person seeing a shape on the path that might either be a stick or a snake would be well advised to take the time to find out what it is (LeDoux 1996, 163). To some extent this may have been the situation of the American framers in 1787, the German framers in 1919, and the French framer(s) in 1958. The urgency of the Norwegian framers of 1814 was, paradoxically, both subjectively motivated and objectively justified. They did not know that they were engaged in a race against time which they would not have won but for their emotion-induced urgency. Although the issue is hardly amenable to historical investigation, I conjecture that objective and subjective haste tend to go together. In stylized form, suppose that the abstractly optimal duration of a constituent assembly is one year. Objective haste would dictate a duration of six months, and subjective haste might speed it up to three months. To complicate matters further, the assessment by the framers of the objective haste might also be subject to wishful or counterwishful thinking. It is possible that some of these interactions effects could be studied in the laboratory.

Wishful thinking can induce an illusory sense of security. As noted earlier, the French assembly of 1848 adopted election of the president by direct popular vote. Many framers had misgivings, anticipating that the choice would fall on Napoleon Bonaparte and fearing that he might stage a coup. On the very last day of the debates,

[88] Peyrefitte (2000), 90–1.

they adopted a parchment barrier) against this eventuality: "Any measure by which the president of the Republic dissolves the national Assembly, prorogues it, or creates an obstacle to the exercise of its mandate, constitutes high treason. By this very fact, the president is ousted from his office; the citizens are obliged to refuse to obey him; the executive power passes automatically to the national Assembly" (Article 68). In the words of the foremost historian of the Second Republic, this last-minute change "testifies ... to the fact that the Assembly was haunted by the fear of a coup d'État by the President directed against itself. One is astonished that these precise and manifest worries led to nothing but tragically illusory precautions."[89] By their wishful thinking, the framers opened the way to power for Napoleon Bonaparte.

The American constitution was flawed, I believe, because of its origin in the elites' unfounded and visceral fears of the people.[90] Specifically, the fears of leveling "agrarian laws," paper money, and debtor relief rested on an irrational failure to understand the special character of war and postwar conditions. The unrest and violence that occurred in some states in the 1780s were due not to the democratic nature of their constitutions, but to the blatant injustice of speculators seeking to redeem at full value, and at the expense of the taxpayers, wartime bonds bought at bargain-basement prices. Although Madison justified the profits as a reward to risk, that argument loses its force when we take account of the fact that the original sales of war bonds were often bargains of desperation. In addition to authorizing money and troops for repressing rebellions, the constitution created two veto points on popular representation: the Senate and the presidency. According to some scholars, the third veto point of review by the Supreme Court of federal legislation, although not mentioned in the constitution or in *The Federalist*, was implicit in these documents. These veto points burdened posterity with an excessively counter-majoritarian constitution.[91]

V. PREJUDICE IN CONSTITUTION MAKING

The phenomenon of prejudice defies easy analysis. As I shall understand it, it always involves an unjustified belief by a member of one group about either the inferior cognitive capacities or the dangerous behavioral propensities of the members of another group. Prejudice may be "cold," as in Lord Chesterfield's condescending observations on women in his letters to his son, or "hot," as in alarmist claims about papists, Jews, or gypsies. In the latter form, prejudice may trigger emotions of

89 Bastid (1945), Vol. II, 147–8; Elster (2018).

90 For a fuller (yet still sketchy) presentation of this argument, see Elster (2012).

91 Today, filibustering in the Senate and the Hastert Rule in the House of Representatives constitute two further counter-majoritarian practices. As far as I know, though, these were not motivated by fear of popular demands.

contempt, hatred, and visceral fear.[92] With some exceptions, prejudice is based on ascribed rather than on achieved features. Its object is what the prejudiced person perceives as essential, intrinsic, and permanent features of the target group. Gender, age, race/ethnicity, and membership in a lower caste or estate are prominent examples, and religion an important counterexample. Yet even if religion is in principle an object of choice, in practice it is usually a lifelong commitment of the individual, and perceived as such by others. By contrast, in societies with some degree of social mobility, the exercise of an occupation does not lend itself easily to prejudice against the person who exercises it.

In the context of constitution making, the main tendency of prejudice is to exclude members of the targeted group from participating in politics, as voters or deputies. The effect of prejudice can also extend to the denial of civil rights, such as the right to own property or to exercise certain professions. Historically, the overwhelmingly most important example is the exclusion of women from politics and the denial of their civil rights. The word "exclusion" may be too strong, however, if taken to imply a deliberate decision. For centuries or millennia, the prejudice against women was so deep-seated as not even to be an object of reflection or discussion. For most of the time, it was a paradigmatic cold prejudice, based on a tacit belief about the inferior cognitive capacities of women rather than about any dangerous behavioral propensities. Yet even though misogyny has led to the exclusion of women, it has not been its only cause. Female suffrage was delayed in several countries because radical politicians feared, often with some justification, that women would vote conservatively. This (prudential) fear explains, for instance, why French women got the right to vote only in 1946. It also explains why Spanish women did not get the right to vote in the 1931 elections to the constituent assembly, while the lack of fear may explain why women got the right to be elected to the assembly. There was a risk that women might vote for conservatives, but conservative women were unlikely to stand for office.

As far as I can tell, the very common practice of excluding individuals from the suffrage on economic grounds has not reflected prejudice, but either a belief that only those who contribute to the public funds have a right to dispose of them ("no representation without taxation") or a belief that were the poor given the right to vote they would either dispossess the rich or sell their votes to them. Although some rich have always talked about the poor in contemptuous terms, their feelings have been much less virulent than, say, the contempt that nobles felt for commoners in the French ancien régime.

92 I treat emotions and prejudice separately, however, because I want to focus on episodic rather than on standing or permanent emotions, and because some forms of prejudice, as noted, do not trigger emotions. This is merely a book keeping arrangement, with no substantive implications.

By contrast, exclusion from politics or citizenship on religious and ethnic grounds has very often been based on prejudice. Earlier, I referred to the Norwegian constitution of 1814 as the most liberal of its time. Although I believe the statement is overall correct, one must nevertheless note the following clause in the constitution: "The Jesuits and monastic orders are prohibited. Jews are still not allowed to settle in the state." Remarkably, this seems to have been a cold prejudice.[93] There were no Jews or Jesuits in Norway at the time. The framers based their decision on free-floating European clichés, which did not reflect any personal experience with either group. Their prejudices may have induced an unfounded prudential fear, but no visceral fear. By contrast, the Spanish constitution of 1931, which severely restricted the activities of the church and prohibited religious orders from engaging in education, may have been based on a "hot" Republican prejudice against Catholics. (I know too little about Spanish politics in the period to affirm with confidence that the extreme Republican beliefs were unjustified.) Here, too, Jesuits were a particular target.

Ethnic or racial prejudices can shape constitution making if a majority of framers belong to one ethnic or racial group and use their power to restrict the rights and liberties of other citizens, often but not necessarily a minority. In the nineteenth century, many American state constitutions denied the suffrage to free blacks,[94] a practice that was overdetermined by interest and prejudice. In modern constitution making, majorities have denied minorities the right to vote, to form political parties, to be educated in their own language and to have it recognized as an official medium in the courts and the administration. Some examples from constitutions of former Communist countries may be cited.[95] In several Baltic states, the large Russian-speaking minorities have been deprived of the right to vote or to stand for office. In Bulgaria, the Turkish minority was prohibited from forming its own political party. In Slovakia, the language rights of the Hungarian minority were severely curtailed. In the Bulgarian case, prejudice, as I have characterized it, was certainly at work. I am agnostic about its role in the other cases.

VI. BELIEF FORMATION IN CONSTITUTION MAKING

Motivations, by themselves, do not determine choices. To return to an example from the earlier discussion, risk preferences do not by themselves generate choices: risk assessments, that is, *beliefs* about the magnitude of the risk, are also needed. As we have seen, the constitution making process itself can generate irrational beliefs,

93 Equally remarkably, the clause banning Jesuits was not abolished until 1956. The clause banning Jews was abolished in 1851.

94 Keyssar (2000), 54–9.

95 For details, see Zielonka (2001) and Zielonka and Pravda (2001).

through wishful thinking, counterwishful thinking, urgency, and a hot–cold empathy gap. I shall not discuss these any further. Urgency-generated beliefs can also be rational, however. I give some examples shortly.

I shall distinguish two sets of beliefs.

First, framers form beliefs that concern the process itself, up to the final adoption of the constitution. The rules of order and the division of labor between committee work and plenary debates reflect beliefs about the arrangements most conducive to the (partial or impartial) goals of the framers. Framers need to form beliefs about the motivations and beliefs of other framers and, if need be, those of the ratifiers. When designing the electoral system, framers will often try to form beliefs about voter preferences, to maximize the number of seats of their party in the first ordinary legislature.

Second, framers may try to form beliefs about the postconstitutional politics that the constitution shall regulate. Given that the constitution, unlike ordinary legislation, cannot be easily updated to reflect demographic trends and economic development, framers may need to form some beliefs about these matters. At the Federal Convention, some framers wanted to base the constitution on the premise that America would remain frozen in time. Elbridge Gerry, for instance, said that "[the] people have two great interests, the landed interest, and the commercial including the stockholders."[96] He used this premise to argue for elections to the Senate by the state legislatures, to protect the commercial against the landed interest. This was the class conflict behind Shays' rebellion: bondholders versus taxpayers/farmers. Gouverneur Morris, however, was more farsighted: "We should not confine our attention to the present moment. The time is not distant when this Country will abound with mechanics & manufacturers who will receive their bread from their employers. Will such men be the secure & faithful Guardians of liberty?"[97] Framers may also need to form beliefs about the motivations of future political agents, including the voters, and about how to neutralize motivations that, according to their beliefs, will represent a danger to the (partial or impartial) goals of the framers.

My overall assessment is that these processes of belief formation are quite fragile. The sheer urgency of the situation can make it impossible to gather the information that would be needed. At the proto-constitutional First Continental Congress in 1774, for instance, the state delegations had to decide how they were to decide in the future: should each state have one vote or should votes be proportioned to population and/or wealth? The Congress adopted the first procedure and "Resolved,

[96] Farrand (1966), Vol. I, 152. Paralleling the distinction between risk assessments and risk preferences, one might ask, however, whether Gerry *believed* that the American class structure would remain unchanged or whether he only *cared* about his own generation – that is, whether he was subject to cognitive or to motivational myopia.

[97] Ibid., Vol. II, 202. Madison made the same point (ibid.).

That in determining questions in this Congress, *each Colony or Province shall have one Vote*. The Congress not being possess'd of, or at present able to procure proper materials for ascertaining the importance of each Colony." It would have been irrational, given the urgency of the situation, to try to gather reliable information for a proportional system. In 1814, the urgent need for the Norwegian framers to finish the constitution before the return of Bernadotte prevented them from gathering information about the international situation. As noted, wishful thinking may also have led them to underestimate the need for information.

When a constitution marks the transition from an autocratic to a democratic regime, it can be hard to form rational beliefs about the likely outcome of the first free elections. In the Polish and Hungarian transitions of 1989–90, Communists, members of the opposition, and external observers all overestimated the electoral attraction of the Communist Party. If the Communist leaders in Poland had been able to anticipate the outcome of the first (partly) free elections, they would probably not have agreed to the compromises made in the Round Table Talks. In Hungary, the Communist party accepted, as a compromise, a mixed majoritarian-proportional system, believing that their candidates would be favored by the majoritarian component. As it turned out, their successes came mostly from the proportional component on which their opponents had insisted.

As these examples show, framers do not always have rational expectations. The point is confirmed by the fact that in the 1960s and the 1970s, several American state constitutions were rejected in popular referenda, in some cases by large majorities.[98] It would be imprudent, nevertheless, to generalize on this point. In Bulgaria, the expectation of the Communist leaders that their preferred electoral system would give them a majority in the first constituent assembly was confirmed. In many cases, constitutions subjected to popular ratification have been accepted, or rejected only by a narrow majority. Framers sometimes get it right. Yet the basic fact that constitution making differs from politics as usual implies that anticipations based on ordinary political behavior may be unreliable. The reason why the Canadian Charlottetown accord and some of the American state constitutional proposals were rejected in referenda may have been precisely that the voters objected to the framers behaving in the mode of politics as usual, striking deals in the proverbial smoke-filled back rooms.

Framers may also be unable to anticipate how the constitution will work in practice. In addition to the example from the Weimar constitution already cited, I can mention two examples from the 1958 French constitution. Michel Debré, de Gaulle's main legal advisor, asserted that (what became) Article 49 (3), which allows the government to stake its existence on the adoption of a law, would be used only

[98] Lenowitz (2007).

in exceptional circumstances.[99] In the same debate, Paul Reynaud asserted that the clause would be a "paper wall" with no effect.[100] They were both proven wrong: the Article became a central, routinely employed legislative tool of the government. The constitution asserts that the vote of deputies should be "personal," that is, allowing only limited votes by proxy. In practice, the parliamentarians of the Fifth Republic have managed to work around this encumbering clause. In the words of James Bryce, it is hard "to keep even a written and rigid constitution from bending and warping under the actual forces of politics."[101] This statement applies with particular force to the rights-clauses in the constitution. The members of Congress who adopted the Second Amendment to the American constitution would have been surprised to see it used to justify individuals carrying concealed handguns.

Framers may also form *beliefs about the motivations and beliefs* of future political agents. I shall ignore "beliefs about beliefs," which are probably of marginal importance. By and large, and speaking very generally, there seems to be a divide between framers who believe that future agents will be dominated by their interests and passions (prejudice is rarely mentioned) and seek to reduce that influence through constitutional engineering, and those who put their faith in the reason (virtue) of future voters and elected officials.[102] Virtue, too, in the latter view, may be the subject of engineering, for instance, by limiting suffrage and eligibility to persons who have observable properties believed to be correlated with the unobservable property of virtue. The numerous early constitutions that imposed public voting in national elections may, at least in part, have rested on the assumption that the need to defend one's vote before others would induce a more impartial attitude. John Stuart Mill certainly thought so.[103] The fact that most constitutions leave the choice whether to vote or to abstain up to the individual indicates that their framers had at least a minimal belief in the virtue (or perhaps in the irrationality?) of the citizens.

As these brief remarks suggest, the exact mix of interest, passion, and reason in the motivations of future political agents is an elusive matter, about which it is hard to form robust beliefs. Hume argued, though, that framers do not need to form beliefs, but can rely on maxims. "It is … a just *political* maxim, *that every man must be supposed a knave*: Though at the same time, it appears somewhat strange, that a maxim should be true in *politics*, which is false in *fact*."[104] In other words, framers should act on the worst-case assumption that future political agents will be

[99] DPS (1988), Vol. II, 505–6.

[100] Ibid., 303.

[101] Bryce (1995), 90.

[102] See notably Troper (2006), 78. He makes this observation in the context of the French constitution of 1795, but I believe it has a wide application.

[103] Buchstein (2015).

[104] Hume (1742).

relentlessly self-interested. That argument gives too much weight, however, to the merely possible, and not enough to the probable or the plausible.[105]

In any case, self-interest is *not* the worst case: passions can be far more destructive. When designing political institutions, framers often pay as much attention to the task of neutralizing passion as they do to the task of neutralizing partisan interest. To cite only one example, it is a constitutional cliché that bicameralism will have the dual effect of preventing passions from arising and of giving them time to cool down. By requiring members of the upper house and their electors to satisfy higher age requirements and stricter economic qualifications, and by giving them longer terms in office, one will supposedly create a more reflective and less impulsive body than a lower house with less stringent eligibility requirements. At the same time, the slowing-down of decision making inherent in any bicameral system, even one in which the upper house is a mere carbon copy of the lower, will also lead to a cooling-down of passion. Although these claims have often been made in constitutional debates, there is little evidence that they are valid. The idea that income and wealth are reliable proxies for intellectual and moral qualities is very fragile. There is little evidence that the American Senate is more panic-resistant than the House of Representatives.[106] Yet the belief seems to persist.

Finally, framers will often form beliefs about the main causes of structural regime failure, and design institutions to prevent them. As suggested by the literature on the availability heuristic,[107] their attention will often be focused on recent, salient breakdowns. Constitution making is sometimes *reactive*, in the sense that framers try to address the flaws of the previous regime regardless of whether the problems are likely to recur. The constructive vote of no confidence that the Germans adopted in 1949 was largely a reaction to the coalition of extremes – Nazis and Communists – that had brought down governments of the Weimar Republic. The situation in Germany in 1948–9 did not in itself justify that measure. De Gaulle's obsession with the negative role of political parties during the Third and the Fourth Republics caused him to neglect their essential democratic function. Examples could probably be multiplied.

105 For the dangers of possibilistic reasoning in politics, see Elster (2013), 46–7 and Vermeule (2012).

106 In 1798, the Sedition Acts passed the Senate by a wide margin, but obtained a bare majority of 44 to 41 in the House. In 1964, the Resolution of the Gulf of Tonkin passed the House by 416 votes to 0, and the Senate by 88 votes to 2. In 2001, The Patriot Act passed by 98 votes to 1 in the Senate and 357 to 66 in the House of Representatives. The "Authorization for Use of Military Force against Iraq Resolution of 2002" passed the House by 297 votes to 133 and the Senate by 77 votes to 23. In none of these cases did the Senate show much resistance to the whipped-up atmosphere of hysteria. For similarly skeptical comments, see Mueller (1996), 192–3, who also cites the Gulf of Tonkin episode.

107 Tversky and Kahneman (1974).

VII. CONCLUSION

According to a common conception, to which I have unfortunately contributed,[108] framers are in the role of *Peter when sober legislating for Peter when drunk*. This idea is based on faulty conceptual and empirical assumptions. In fact, the opposite statement, although also inaccurate, would be closer to the truth: framers behave like *Peter when drunk legislating for Peter when sober.*

Conceptually, "soberness" or dispassionateness does not imply a concern with the public interest. If passion and reason were the only motivations of political actors, that implication would hold, but because they may also be motivated by *sober interest*, it does not.

Empirically, as I have tried to show, the Peter-when-sober paradigm does not stand up to the historical record. In the large majority of cases, framers have been "drunk" – under the influence of passion – rather than dispassionate. Moreover, they will often assume that future political actors will act out of interest rather than from passion. To the extent that these statements hold, constitution making is indeed a case of Peter when drunk legislating for Peter when sober.

REFERENCES

Aaal, J. (1859). *Erindringer*. Christiania (Oslo): Cappelen.

Bastid, P. (1945). *Doctrines et institutions politiques de la Seconde République*. Paris: Hachette.

Bentham, J. (2002). *Rights, Representation, and Reform*. Oxford: Oxford University Press.

Boadway, R., and Shah, A. (2009). *Fiscal Federalism*. Cambridge: Cambridge University Press.

Bryce, J. (1995). *The American Commonwealth*. Indianapolis, IN: Liberty Fund.

Buchstein, H. (2015). "Public Voting and Political Modernization." In J. Elster (ed.), *Secrecy and Publicity in Votes and Debates*, 15–51. Cambridge: Cambridge University Press.

DPS (1987, 1988, 1991). *Documents pour servir à l'histoire de l'élaboration de la constitution du 4 octobre* 1958, Vols. I–III, Paris: La Documentation Française.

Elster, J. (1984). *Ulysses and the Sirens*, revised edn. Cambridge: Cambridge University Press.

(1995). "Transition, Constitution-Making, and Separation in Czechoslovakia." *Archives Européennes de Sociologie* 36, 105–34.

(1999). *Alchemies of the Mind*. Cambridge: Cambridge University Press.

(2000). *Ulysses Unbound*. Cambridge: Cambridge University Press.

(2004). *Closing the Books*. Cambridge: Cambridge University Press.

(2007). "The Night of August 4 1789." *Revue Européenne des Sciences Sociales* 45, 71–94.

(2009a). *Reason and Rationality*. Princeton, NJ: Princeton University Press.

(2009b). "Urgency." *Inquiry* 52, 399–411.

(2011). "The Two Great Fears of 1789." *Social Science Information* 50, 317–29.

(2012). "Constitution-Making and Violence." *Journal of Legal Analysis* 4, 7–39.

(2013). *Securities against Misrule*. Cambridge: Cambridge University Press.

[108] Elster (1984), chapter II. 7, corrected in Elster (2000), chapter II.

(2015). *Explaining Social Behavior*, revised edn. Cambridge: Cambridge University Press.
(2018). "The Resistible Rise of Louis Bonaparte." In C. Sunstein (ed.), *Can It Happen Here?* New York, NY: Dey Street Books.
(forthcoming a). "The Political Psychology of Publius." In J. Rakove and C. Sheenan (eds.), *The Cambridge Companion to The Federalist*. Cambridge: Cambridge University Press.
(forthcoming b). "Enthusiasm and Anger in History." *Inquiry*.
Elster, J., ed. (1996). *The Round Table Talks in Eastern Europe*. Chicago, IL: University of Chicago Press
Elster, J., and Le Pillouer, A. (2015). "Semi-public Voting at the *Constituante*." In J. Elster (ed.), *Secrecy and Publicity in Votes and Debates*, 52–71. Cambridge: Cambridge University Press.
Evans, R. (1980). "German Social Democracy and Women's Suffrage 1891–1918." *Journal of Contemporary History* 15, 533–57.
Eyck, F. (1968). *The Frankfurt Parliament 1848–49*. London: Macmillan.
Farrand, M. (1966). *Records of the Federal Convention*. New Haven, CT: Yale University Press.
Ferguson, E. (1961). *The Power of the Purse*. Chapel Hill, NC: University of North Carolina Press.
Gicquel, J. (1988). "Le rôle des ministres d'Etat." In *L'écriture de la Constitution de 1958*, 77–84. Paris: Economica.
Ginsburg, T., Elkin, Z., and Blount, J. (2009). "Does the Process of Constitution-Making Matter?" *Annual Review of Law and Society* 5, 201–23.
Goldstein, K. (2000). "Can the Vice-President Preside over His Own Trial? A Critique of Bare Textualism." *Saint Louis University Law Journal* 44, 849–70.
Gordon, R. (1987). *The Structure of Emotions*. Cambridge: Cambridge University Press.
Gylfason, T. (2012). "From Collapse to Constitution: The Case of Iceland." Munich: CESIFO Working Paper No. 3770.
Holmes, S., and Sunstein, C. (2000). *The Cost of Rights*. New York, NY: W. W. Norton.
Hume, D. (1742). "On the Independency of Parliament." In Hume, *Essays: Moral, Political, and Literary*.
Immergut, E. (2002). "The Swedish Constitution and Social Democratic Power: Measuring the Mechanical Effect of a Political Institution." *Scandinavian Political Studies* 25, 231–57.
Jaurès, J. (1968). *Histoire socialiste de la Révolution Française*, Vol. 1. Paris: Editions Sociales.
Jillson, C. (1988). *Constitution Making*. New York, NY: Agathon.
Kessel, P. (1969). *La nuit du 4 août 1789*. Paris: Arthaud.
Keyssar, A. (2000). *The Right to Vote*. New York, NY: Basic Books.
Klarman, M. (2016). *The Framers' Coup*. Cambridge, MA: Harvard University Press.
Klein, W., and Kunda, Z. (1992). "Motivated Person Perception: Constructing Justifications for Desired Beliefs." *Journal of Experimental Social Psychology* 28, 145–68.
Kyvig, D. (2008). *The Age of Impeachment*. Lawrence, KS: University Press of Kansas.
Langford, P. (1991). *Public Life and the Propertied Englishman, 1698–1798*. Oxford: Oxford University Press.
Lebègue, E. (1910). *Thouret*. Paris: Alcan.
LeDoux, J. (1996). *The Emotional Brain*. New York, NY: Simon and Schuster.
(2015). *Anxious*. New York, NY: Viking Press.
Lenowitz, J. (2007). "*Rejected by the People: Failed U.S. State Constitutional Conventions in the 1960s and 70s*." Department of Political Science, Columbia University.

Lerner, J., and Keltner, D. (2001). "Anger, Fear, and Risk." *Journal of Personality and Social Psychology* 81, 146–59.
Lewis, M. (1992). *Shame*. New York, NY: The Free Press.
Loewenstein, G. (2000). "Emotions in Economic Theory and Economic Behavior." *American Economic Review: Papers and Proceedings* 90, 426–32.
MacMaster, H. (1997). *Dereliction of Duty*. New York, NY: Harper.
Marx, K. (1852). *The 18th Brumaire of Louis Bonaparte*, New York, NY: International Publishers 1988.
McDonald, F. (1992). *We the People*. New Brunswick, NJ: Transaction Books.
Merkl, P. (1963). *The Origins of the West German Republic*. Oxford: Oxford University Press.
Morrison, S. (1917). *A History of the Constitution of Massachusetts*. Boston, MA: Wright and Potter.
Mueller, D. (1995). *Constitutional Democracy*. Oxford: Oxford University Press.
Ólafsson, J. (2011). "An Experiment in Iceland: Crowd-Sourcing a Constitution?" Retrieved from: https://www.uio.no/english/research/interfaculty-research-areas/democracy/news-and-events/events/seminars/2011/papers-yale-2011/Yale-Olafson.pdf
Paulsen, M. (1998). "Someone Should Have Told Spiro Agnew." In W. Eskridge and S. Levinson (eds.), *Constitutional Stupidities, Constitutional Tragedies*, 75–6. New York, NY: New York University Press.
Pehe, J. (1993). "Constitutional Imbroglio in the Czech Republic." *RFE/RL Research Report* 2: 5.
Peyrefitte, A. (1994). *C'était de Gaulle*, Vol. I. Paris: Fayard.
(2000). *C'était de Gaulle*, Vol. III. Paris: Fayard.
Price, R. (2000). "'The Holy Struggle against Anarchy': The Development of Counter-revolution in 1848." In D. Dowe, H.-G. Haupt, D. Langewiesche, and J. Sperber (eds.), *Europe in 1848*, 25–54. New York, NY: Berghahn Books.
Rakove, J. (1987). "The Great Compromise: Ideas, Interests, and the Politics of Constitution Making." *William and Mary Quarterly* 44, 424–57.
Ramsay, D. (1789). *The History of the American Revolution*, cited from the reprint. Indianapolis, IN: Liberty Fund 2011.
Rapaczynski, A. (1991). "Constitutional Politics in Poland." *University of Chicago Law Review* 58, 595–632.
RFAE (1968). *La Révolution Française et l'abolition de l'esclavage: Textes et documents*, Vols. I–XII. Paris: Editions d'Histoire Sociale.
Rubenfeld, J. (2001). *Freedom and Time*. New Haven, CT: Yale University Press.
Russell, P. (1993). *Constitutional Odyssey*, 2nd edn. Toronto: University of Toronto Press.
Sajó, A. (2011). *Constitutional Sentiments*. New Haven, CT: Yale University Press.
Schiemann, J. (2001). "Explaining Hungary's Powerful Constitutional Court." *Archives Européennes de Sociologie* 42, 357–90.
(2005). *The Politics of Pact-Making*. London: Macmillan.
Shah, A., ed. (2007). *The Practice of Fiscal Federalism*. Montreal: McGill-Queens University Press.
Steen, S. (1951). *1814*. Oslo: Cappelen.
Stjernquist, N. (1996). *Tvåkammartiden*. Stockholm: Sveriges Riksdag.
Tangney, J. (1990). "Assessing Individual Differences in Proneness to Shame and Guilt." *Journal of Personality and Social Psychology* 59, 102–11.

Taylor, A. (2016). *American Revolutions*. New York, NY: W. W. Norton.
Thagard, P., and Nussbaum, D. (2014). "Fear-Driven Inference." In L. Magnani (ed.), *Model-Based Reasoning in Science and Technology*, 43–53. Berlin: Springer.
Tocqueville, A. de (1953). *L'ancien régime et la Révolution*, Vol. II. Paris: Gallimard.
(1987). *Recollections*. New Brunswick, NJ: Transaction Books.
(2001). *The Old Regime and the Revolution*, Vol. 2. Chicago: University of Chicago Press.
(2011). *The Ancien Régime and the French Revolution*. Cambridge: Cambridge University Press.
Troper, M. (2006). *Terminer la Révolution: La Constitution de 1795*. Paris: Fayard.
Tversky, A., and Kahneman, D. (1974). "Judgment under uncertainty." *Science* 185, 1124–31.
Vermeule, A. (2012). "Precautionary Principles in Constitutional Law." *Journal of Legal Analysis* 4, 181–222.
White, M. (1987). *Philosophy, The Federalist, and the Constitution*. Oxford: University Press.
Zielonka, J., ed. (2001), *Democratic Consolidation in Eastern Europe*, Vol. 1. Oxford: Oxford University Press.
Zielonka, J., and Pravda, A., eds. (2001). *Democratic Consolidation in Eastern Europe*, Vol. 2. Oxford: Oxford University Press.

Index

Books in the Series (continued from page iii)

Constitutional Courts as Mediators
Julio Ríos-Figueroa

Perils of Judicial Self-Government in Transitional Societies
David Kosa

Making We the People
Chaihark Hahm and Sung Ho Kim

Deprivation on Trial
Cesar Rodríguez-Garavito and Diana Rodríguez-Franco

Unstable Constitutionalism
edited by Mark Tushnet and Madhav Khosla

Magna Carta and Its Modern Legacy
edited by Robert Hazell and James Melton

Constitutions and Religious Freedom
Frank Cross

International Courts and the Performance of International Agreements: A General Theory with Evidence from the European Union
Clifford Carrubba and Matthew Gabel

Reputation and Judicial Tactics: A Theory of National and International Courts
Shai Dothan

Social Difference and Constitutionalism in Pan-Asia
edited by Susan H. Williams

Constitutionalism in Asia in the Early Twenty-First Century
edited by Albert Chen

Constitutions in Authoritarian Regimes
edited by Tom Ginsburg and Alberto Simpser

Presidential Legislation in India: The Law and Practice of Ordinances Shubhankar Dam
Social and Political Foundations of Constitutions
edited by Denis J. Galligan and Mila Versteeg

Consequential Courts: Judicial Roles in Global Perspective
edited by Diana Kapiszewski, Gordon Silverstein and Robert A. Kagan

Comparative Constitutional Design
edited by Tom Ginsburg